Secondary Education in England 1870–1902

In this comprehensive and extensively researched history of secondary education in England from 1870 to 1902 John Roach argues for a reassessment of the relative importance of state regulation and private provision. Although the public schools enjoyed their greatest prestige during this period, in terms of educational reform and progress their importance has been exaggerated. The role of the public schools, he suggests, was social rather than academic, and as such their power and influence is to be interpreted principally in relation to the growth of new social elites, the concept of public service, and to the needs of the empire for a bureaucratic ruling class. Lasting progress was also made in the modern progressive movement, launched by Cecil Reddie, and in the private provision for young women. Even before the 1902 Education Act, however, the State had spent much time and effort in regulating and reforming the old educational endowments, and it is in these initiatives that the foundations for the public provision of secondary education and educational reform are to be found.

John Roach, Emeritus Professor of Education, University of Sheffield, has published numerous articles and books on the history of education, including *A History of Secondary Education in England 1800–1870* (1986).

Secondary Education in England 1870–1902

Public activity and private enterprise

John Roach

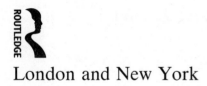

London and New York

First published 1991
by Routledge
11 New Fetter Lane, London EC4P 4EE

Simultaneously published in the USA and Canada
by Routledge
a division of Routledge, Chapman and Hall, Inc.
29 West 35th Street, New York, NY 10001

© 1991 John Roach

Typeset in 10/12pt Times by Input Typesetting Ltd, London
Printed in Great Britain by T J Press (Padstow) Ltd, Padstow, Cornwall

British Library Cataloguing in Publication Data
Roach, John
  Secondary education in England 1870–1902.
  1. Great Britain. Secondary education, history
  I. Title
  373.09

Library of Congress Cataloging in Publication Data
Roach, John
    Secondary education in England, 1870–1902 : public activity and private
  enterprise / by John Roach.
    p. cm.
    Follows the author's: History of secondary education in England, 1800–1870.
  1986.
    Includes bibliographical references and index.
    1. Education, Secondary—England—History—19th century.
  2. Public schools, Endowed (Great Britain— History—19th century.
  3. Private schools— England—History—19th century. 4. Education,
  Secondary—Social aspects—England History— 19th century.
  5. Education and state—England—History—19th century. I. Roach, John,
  1920– History of secondary education in England, 1800–1870.
  II. Title.
  LA631.7.R63 1991
  373.42'09'034—dc20   90-24541

ISBN 0-415-03572-4

To the memory of
Patrick Bury 1908–1987
Scholar   Teacher   Friend

Contents

List of tables

Preface and acknowledgements

This book completes a study of secondary education in the nineteenth century, the first part of which appeared as *A History of Secondary Education in England 1800–1870* (Longmans, 1986). It is natural that many of the same themes should run through both books, though there are substantial differences between the periods before and after 1870. It is not, I think, possible to organize the complex events of the last thirty years of the nineteenth century round any single dominant theme, but one major thread in the story is suggested in the title of the book – the relationship between public activity and private enterprise. Though there was no publicly organized and financed system of secondary education in England before the passing of the Education Act of 1902, the state had spent much time and effort in regulating and reforming the old educational endowments.

The story of how this was done and how effective were the results forms a large part of this book. Part I, on the endowed schools, is based very largely on the Ed. 27 files in the Public Record Office at Kew. Those files contain a great mass of material which is not easy to use and only a small part of which can be tackled by an individual researcher. Enough has been done, I believe, to throw interesting light, both on official attitudes to educational planning and on local reactions to reform in general, to the claims of the middle classes, and to the rights of the poor. Nor, in the general area of public activity, must the interlocking worlds of the Science and Art Department, of the higher grade schools, and of the technical instruction committees be forgotten. The efforts of all these bodies were uncoordinated, much criticized, and sometimes wasteful, but they did lay a foundation for public involvement in secondary education before the 1902 Act, the importance of which has not always been fully appreciated.

If those were the fields of public activity, the most successful examples of private enterprise were the public schools, which grew in this period into their modern form and enjoyed at this time their period of greatest prestige and power. I have argued that their role was social rather than academic or intellectual, and that it is to be interpreted principally in relation to the growth of new social elites, to the concept of public service, and to the expansion of the empire overseas. Within the scope of this book the public schools take only a limited place, and I would argue that their comparative importance has been exaggerated by historians of education. Nevertheless they do form a major part of the story, and one reason for their growth was the fact that, despite the efforts of the educational reformers, there was no effectively organized system of state secondary education to compete with them.

Though the private schools were far less important in the later part of the century than they had been at the beginning, I have tried to show that they played a larger part than has often been recognized. For example, the modern progressive movement, launched by Cecil Reddie at Abbotsholme, which has been a considerable force in twentieth-century education, descends from the tradition of the nineteenth-century private schools.

Those schools, down to 1900 and later, were especially important in the education of girls, and it was there that the most remarkable developments of the period 1870–1902 took place. Though reforms had begun in the 1840s and 1850s, it was really after 1870 that the new girls' high schools grew strong and that women participated in higher education. The opening of new opportunities to girls and women makes a remarkable story, involving some outstanding individuals, much selfless devotion, and a great sense of new freedom – even of excitement – among the participants, both teachers and taught. Though the pioneers faced many difficulties, many of which, at the end of the first generation, had not been overcome, they did a great work. To some extent they had benefited – in the area of public activity – from the old endowments, but without the stimulus of private enterprise, both through local groups and national bodies like the Girls' Public Day School Company (Trust), much less would have been achieved.

In a story dealing with schools of so many types there are some topics which it has not been possible to cover. I should like to have said more about the development of the secondary school curriculum and to have discussed school buildings and their design, since this was the period when a distinctive type of school architecture developed. Though something has been said about the careers of former pupils, I have not discussed the relationships of the secondary schools with the universities and with professional life in a more general sense. The treatment is limited to England. I have discussed two Scottish schools, Loretto and St Leonard's at St Andrews, because of their relationship to developments in England.

I wish to thank the Public Record Office and Her Majesty's Stationery Office for help with reproducing material in the tables; the source is given in each case. Permission to reproduce material has been given by the following: Bradford Libraries and Information Service (Tables 8.1,

9.1); Manchester Public Libraries; Local History Library (Tables 10.5, 10.6); Leicester University Press (Table 10.4, from M. Seaborne's article in B. Simon (ed.), *Education In Leicestershire 1540–1940*). The Girls' Public Day School Trust have permitted the use of material from their archives, and Dr Maurice Whitehead and Dr Felicity Hunt have allowed me to quote from their PhD theses. Mr J. C. Barry has commented on the typescript and Mrs M. E. Bury has read the proofs. I wish to thank them all for their help and advice. My great and general debt to the late Dr Patrick Bury is signified by the dedication.

List of abbreviations

BC	Royal Commission on Secondary Education, Report and Evidence, 1895 (Bryce Commission)
BJES	*British Journal of Educational Studies*
BOE	Board of Education
BSB	Bradford School Board
CC	Charity Commission
CSC	Church Schools Company
DM	*Derby Mercury*
DNB	*Dictionary of National Biography*
DSA	Department of Science and Art
Ed. 27, 21, 49	'Education' classes, Public Record Office, Kew
ESC	Endowed Schools Commission
GPDSC/GPDST	Girls' Public Day School Company (Trust)
Hansard	*Parliamentary Debates* (all references are to the 3rd series)
HE	*History of Education*
HSE	John Roach, *A History of Secondary Education in England 1800–1870* (1986)
ICS	Indian Civil Service
JEAH	*Journal of Educational Administration and History*
MSB	Manchester School Board
NAPTSE	National Association for the Promotion of Technical and Secondary Education
PGS	*Public General Statutes*
PP	*Parliamentary Papers*
PRO	Public Record Office
REC	Returns on Endowed Charities
Record	*(The) Record of Technical and Secondary Education*
SIC	Schools Inquiry Commission
SSB	Sheffield School Board
TSSA	*Transactions of the National Association for the Promotion of Social Science*
VCH	*Victoria History of the Counties of England*
WR	West Riding of Yorkshire

Part I
The endowed schools

1 The work of the Endowed Schools Commission 1869–74

The Liberal victory in the general election of 1868 began a new period in British political history. Among the major reforms of Gladstone's first government (1868–74) was the Education Act of 1870, which created the nucleus of the modern state system of education. It looked for a brief period as if state intervention in secondary education would also achieve major changes. The report of the Schools Inquiry Commission (1868) had shown both the importance of the grammar school endowments and the many abuses which needed reform. The report had made radical recommendations for change: a system of graded schools; a central body with provincial authorities; and a national council for examinations with power to examine teachers.

When W. E. Forster, vice-president of the committee of council on education, introduced the second reading of the Endowed Schools Bill on 15 March 1869, he emphasized many of the same points. Free education should not be given unless it was the reward of merit. The poor should benefit from endowments, not by favour but as the reward of their own achievements. The interests of the middle classes, who needed good education for their children, should be carefully preserved. The ideal of the future should be that no one class should guide the destiny of England, 'but that England for the future is in truth to be self-governed; all her citizens taking their share, not by class distinctions, but by individual worth' (*Hansard* 194: 1382). The task of reform was put into the hands of three Endowed Schools Commissioners, chaired by Lord Lyttelton. They achieved a great deal and set on foot a major process of change, but in so doing they raised massive opposition, and their work was brought to an end, in its original form, by Disraeli's Conservative administration in 1874. Progress continued to be made, though at a slower rate, by the Charity Commissioners, first created in 1853, who inherited important powers under the Endowed Schools Acts. Much was done to improve individual foundations, but the objective of a new national structure disappeared from sight until it was revived under the very different conditions of the early twentieth century.

Forster told the House of Commons that the proposed reorganization would be completed in four to five years. He and those who worked with him seriously underestimated the complexity of the task. Not only was the passage of each scheme a lengthy and often controversial process, but, as the years went on, it proved necessary to alter and amend earlier schemes. Perhaps the greatest problem, which neither the Endowed Schools Commissioners nor the Charity Commissioners ever solved, was the meritocratic issue – that all citizens should take their share, in Forster's words, 'not by class distinctions, but by individual worth'. This was the dominant creed of Victorian Liberalism; it is seen, for example, in its purest form in the struggle to recruit to the civil service by public examination. To many people, well entrenched in school governing bodies and in local pressure groups, the idea was anathema. First of all it broke down traditional relationships of deference and loyalty in the name of a hard logical creed, which made no allowance for local circumstances. Secondly, it was argued that recruitment by merit provided only an illusory advantage for the poor because those who could afford to pay for the best preliminary education would scoop the prizes. Finally, the abandonment of what the reformers saw as indiscriminate free education was opposed by the poor, who had to find the weekly school pence out of an already insufficient family income.

The issue of 'better education as the reward of merit' dominates the story of the reform of the endowed schools after 1870. Successive commissioners and assistant commissioners were sincere in their belief that they were trying to act for the benefit of all classes of society who used the grammar schools. There was no deliberate plan to force out the poor and to deprive them of endowments in the interest of the middle classes who were in a better position to take advantage of the opportunities offered. Yet inevitably it looked as though that was the commissioners' objective, and they did not serve the cause of reform well by the insensitivity which they often showed to the arguments of their opponents.

Opposition to them took two principal forms. The first, strongest in the earlier years, was the resistance put up by the advocates of a traditional concept of English society. Assistant Commissioner J. G. Fitch had written in his report to the Schools Inquiry Commission that 'the will of the departed founders is constantly quoted as a reason for the maintenance of usages, which are acknowledged, even by their defenders, to be pernicious' (Robertson 1971: 11).

To those defenders the wills of the founders had far more sanctity than the opinions of a newly constituted official body in London. In the 1880s the commissioners came under a new form of attack which was radical not conservative in inspiration. Instead of emphasizing the sanctity of founders' wills, critics like Joseph Chamberlain and Jesse Collings pressed the claims of local democracy and of a much more broadly-based form of political control. Originally this was an urban movement, as can be seen in the struggles for control of the great King Edward's foundation in Birmingham (see pp. 50–7). Later it became connected with the pressure for more democratic government in the countryside, for example, in the Reform Act of 1884, which extended the vote to male rural labourers.

Before the Endowed Schools Bill became law, the clauses providing for examination and inspection were dropped (Gordon 1980: 36). The Endowed Schools Act of 1869 restricted itself to the administrative aspects of the problem. This Act, together with later Acts of 1873 and 1874, controlled the way in which new schemes were made and thus determined the development of the endowed schools in the next generation. It is therefore necessary to analyse them in detail. The Act of 1869 (*PGS*, 32 & 33 Vic. 1869: 197–208) provided for the appointment of up to three commissioners and a secretary with power to make new schemes for endowed schools. They were to do this 'in such manner as may render any educational endowments most conducive to the advancement of the education of boys and girls'. They might alter and add to trusts, make new trusts, alter governing bodies, establish, remove them, and dissolve them.

The provisions of this Act can be divided into two parts: the general definition of powers and the ways in which those powers were to be exercised. The commissioners were required (sect. 11), when they modified the privileges or advantages belonging to any class of persons to 'have due regard to the educational interests of such class of persons', a clause frequently cited in the many disputes about the interests of the poor in the endowments. Section 12 required that provision should be made as far as possible for extending the benefits of endowments to girls, an important provision which was the result of an amendment inserted during the passage of the Bill (S. Fletcher 1980: 25–9). No scheme was to be made for an endowment set up less than fifty years before the passing of the Act without the consent of the governing body, and similar protection was extended to endowments of certain specified kinds (sect. 14). A conscience clause covered attendance at lessons on religious education in day schools, and although this did not apply to boarders, it was provided that a scholar who wished to claim exemption should be allowed to attend as a day scholar (sects. 15, 16). Religious opinions were not to affect the appointment of any person as a governor (sect. 17), and in general no one was to be disqualified for appointment as a master by not being in holy orders (sect. 18). However, special provision was made to exempt from these provisions any school which, by the terms of the original foundation and by continuous usage since that time, had been required to be managed 'according to the doctrines or formularies of any particular church, sect, or denomination' (sect. 19). As might be expected, many disputes occurred concerning the interpretation of this section. The Endowed Schools Commissioners considered that it was narrowly drawn, and that it was difficult to make a case that a school should come under its provisions.

One group of clauses governed the relationship between educational and non-educational endowments, an important subject because it was common to find both types under the control of the same trust. Section 24 provided that, in general terms, that division between the two should exist, which had been practised during the three years before the passing of the Act. Section 29 provided that endowments for the payment of apprenticeship fees or for the maintenance or clothing of children were to be deemed educational endowments. The quarrels over the 'hospital schools', which provided maintenance and clothing as well as teaching, were the most bitter that the commissioners had to face because they involved a direct clash between the rival concepts of awards for merit and of charity to the poor and needy. Section 30 dealt with a related point concerning endowments for objects such as loans, money doles, apprenticeship payments, marriage portions, and so on where it was difficult to use the money because the sums available exceeded the demands made upon them. The commissioners were given power to make schemes applying such funds for educational purposes, though they might do this only with the consent of the governing body concerned. Since in many cases these 'non-educational' funds were essential for major developments like new buildings, sect. 30 gave to governing bodies an important lever in their struggles with the commissioners.

Sections 32–41 regulated the making of schemes. The Endowed Schools Commissioners were given powers to prepare draft schemes, with the provision that governors of endowments with an income of over £1,000 per annum might prepare their own (sect. 32). When draft schemes had been made, they were to be printed and circulated (sect. 33), and the commissioners were to receive objections and suggestions within three months of the date of publication (sect. 34). After that time they might hold an enquiry (sect. 35) and then, after considering further objections and suggestions, they were to submit their scheme to the Committee of Council on Education with the proviso that, in cases where a governing body was permitted to submit its own scheme, that scheme should be sent forward together with that emanating from the commissioners if the governing body so desired (sect. 36). The Committee of Council might consider, approve, and publish schemes, but although they had the power to reject, they had no power to amend. In case of rejection the commissioners were required to frame a new scheme (sect. 37).

When a governing body felt aggrieved by a scheme (certain specific grounds being defined), they might petition the Queen in Council, who could refer the petition to five privy councillors (sect. 39). The scheme could then be referred back to the commissioners or laid before Parliament, where it lay on the table for forty days. If within that period no address was presented in either house for consent to be withheld, Her

Majesty in Council might give approval (sects. 40, 41). The procedure was lengthy, cumbrous, and if it be remembered that at every stage there were many clashing interests to conciliate, there was certainly no danger of over-speedy decision-making. Finally, by sect. 59 of the Act the power of making schemes was to extend to 31 December 1872 or, if so appointed by Her Majesty in Council, 31 December 1873. If that timespan be set against the complexity of the procedures, Forster's estimate of four to five years for completion looks, as it proved to be, wildly over-optimistic.

Though the Act of 1869 was subsequently amended, it remained the principal piece of legislation governing the reform of the schools. The Act of 1873 (*PGS*, 36 & 37 Vict. 1873: 315–20) continued the powers of the commissioners until 31 December 1874 in the case of unopposed schemes and until 15 August of that year in the case of schemes against which a petition had been presented (sect. 17). It also legislated over matters that had caused difficulties in interpreting the 1869 Act. Much time and trouble had been devoted to small endowments for elementary schools. By sect. 3 of the 1873 Act such endowments of a value of less than £100 a year were taken out of the control of the commissioners and made subject to the provisions of the Elementary Education Act of 1870. There had been problems too about the position of *ex officio* governors in newly-made schemes because such governors were often parish clergy-men, and Nonconformists objected to what they saw as a privileged status for such persons. Section 6 permitted such *ex officio* governors where they had been provided for by the terms of the original foundation. Changes were also made in the mechanism for approving schemes. The first period for receiving suggestions after the original publication was reduced from three to two months (sect. 12). The Committee of Council were to allow one month for receiving suggestions or objections after they had published a scheme, and after they had approved it, it might be approved by Her Majesty in Council without being laid before Parliament if no objections were laid against it (sect. 13).

The amending Act of 1873 had been passed by the same Liberal government that had promoted the original legislation. The Conservatives, who came to power in 1874, represented clerical and traditional forces. Their Act of 1874 transferred the powers of the Endowed Schools Commissioners to the Charity Commissioners, established under the Acts of 1853 and 1860, after 31 December 1874, and provided that the existing commissioners and their secretary should cease to hold office from that date (*PP* 1874 II: 79–86; *PGS* 37 & 38 Vict. 1874: 288–90). Two additional charity commissioners and a secretary might be appointed to replace them, and the power of making schemes under the Acts was continued for five years from 31 December 1874. For the remainder of the period control lay in the hands of the Endowed Schools Department of the Charity Commission, their powers being continued as necessary from time to time.

The three commissioners appointed to administer the Act of 1869 were Lord Lyttelton, Arthur Hobhouse, and H. G. Robinson. H. J. Roby was appointed secretary, and he succeeded Hobhouse as commissioner in 1872 when Hobhouse went to India as legal member of the Governor-General's council. Their staff of assistant commissioners had in many cases done similar work for the Schools Inquiry Commission, and some of them were to continue under the Charity Commissioners. The three commissioners of 1869 and Roby were all strong reformers (S. Fletcher 1980: 30–41). Robinson, a clergyman, who had been principal of York Training College, was the most moderate and the only one who was appointed a charity commissioner after the changes of 1874. Lyttelton and Hobhouse were far more doctrinaire, and it may be doubted whether they had the tact and negotiating skills necessary to give them the best chance of success. Lyttelton indeed had been unwilling to accept appointment; he had given way when strongly pressed by Gladstone, who was his brother-in-law. He acted as chief commissioner, and the active part he took in the work can be seen by his many comments, scrawled in a very illegible hand, on the papers that came before him.

If Lyttelton had little idea of the soft answer that turneth away wrath, Arthur Hobhouse had even less. A lawyer who had given up active work at the Bar through ill health, he had become a charity commissioner in 1866. In 1868 and 1869 he gave three lectures strongly critical of what he saw as the excessive deference paid by society to the wills of founders (Hobhouse 1880). He was not hostile, as some Liberals were, to endowments in themselves, but he was convinced that they must be managed according to the needs of his own day. The public must be able, he argued, to regulate the use of endowments through a public tribunal with authority to make whatever changes were necessary. Nor was the matter only one of constitutional and legal theory. Many endowments did much more harm than good because they pauperized and degraded those that came into contact with them. They tended to promote sloth and ignorance, and to deprive men of that personal independence which was the only guarantee of individual and social success.

Hobhouse's was a bracing creed, but not likely to commend itself either to the local notabilities who administered the ancient foundations or to those who benefited from them. Roby, his colleague and successor, wrote much later that, as a commissioner, Hobhouse was too much the lawyer and too little the administrator. His task, as he saw it, was to expound the letter of the law, not to accommodate the law to the demands and prejudices of the traditional order. Indeed, Roby thought, he found it very difficult to appreciate 'the ignorant complacency and blind adherence' of his opponents to founders' wishes (Hobhouse and Hammond 1905: 48–50). From the point of view of a school governing body, the opinion of William Mathews, who had been bailiff (chairman of governors) of King Edward's foundation at Birmingham, is probably typical. He told the select committee of 1873: 'I should say that the feeling of the country is that the action of the Commission is much too revolutionary' (*PP* 1873 VIII: 558: 3518).

Hobhouse himself wrote in 1873, after he had ceased to be a commissioner, that in his view the commission had been much more successful than he had expected when he had reluctantly agreed to serve (Hobhouse and Hammond 1905: 46). The commission's history is really the story of the schemes they had made or attempted to make. Their achievement was also examined in their own reports of 1872 and 1875, and in the report of the select committee of 1873. Their 1875 report gave the statistics of what had been done: 235 schemes had passed with a total endowment income of £93,635, while schemes covering an income of another £85,000 had reached the Education Department. Progress had been slowed during 1874 and 1875 by the select committee inquiry and by new legislation (*PP* 1875 XXVIII: 5). Robinson told the select committee of 1873 that little opposition had been encountered in Yorkshire (*PP* 1873 VIII: 445: 1592). Of the two assistant commissioners who gave evidence, C. H. Stanton said that he had found trustees in Warwickshire and Staffordshire co-operative, and Patrick Cumin pointed out that the only schemes that had met major objections were those for the Westminster hospital schools (ibid.: 493–5: 519: 2814–5). Roby was less optimistic. He told the select committee that opposition had arisen not only because the country was unprepared for the changes, but as the result of 'deliberate efforts to obstruct the putting into force of the plain meaning of the Endowed Schools Act' (ibid.: 373: 659). The commissioners had claimed in their 1872 report that the country had not been prepared for the Act and that there was a general feeling that its powers should not be widely exercised. That was not their view; there were great evils to be fought and it was their duty to use the powers entrusted to them to the full (*PP* 1872 XXIV: 38–9).

The Endowed Schools Commissioners, following the conclusions of the Taunton report of 1868, wished to organize the secondary schools into three grades. The first would be basically classical and would take boys up to the age of 18 to 19. The second grade would take boys up to the age of 16 and would prepare them for business and for many of the professions. The third grade would educate up to about the age of 14. This concept of grading also involved the grouping of schools into areas – a city or large country district – in which schools of different grades might be provided with access from one school to another for boys of ability (*HSE*: 283–4). As an example of such a project the comprehensive plans drawn up for the city of Bristol will be discussed later (see pp. 43–50). In most cases this kind of large-scale planning proved impossible to carry out. Each foundation claimed separate treatment, and trustees were unwilling to co-operate. Moreover, since in the railway age travel had become much easier, it was not found necessary to provide a first-

or second-grade school 'within immediate range of others' (*PP* 1873 VIII: 340–1: 224; 344: 259; 381: 792).

The most difficult and the most long-lasting of all the issues which both the commissions had to face was that of the right of the poor to enjoy the endowments. The conflict was seen at its sharpest in the hospital schools, which provided children with clothing as well as with education. The traditionalists wanted to preserve the rights of the poor to enjoy these benefits. The commissioners saw the clothing and mainten-ance provisions as a means of pauperizing the working class. They wanted to spend the available money on giving the best education possible to the largest number of children, chosen by merit not by patronage. Roby argued that selection by patronage did no good to poor people:

> I think that it is the very worst possible way of trying to help people of that class, by saying that they shall get that help by declaring their poverty and by begging for patronage, instead of by working hard in whatever way they can to improve their position.
>
> (*PP* 1873 VIII: 353: 363)

The reorganization of the hospital schools involved both more publicity and more obloquy for the Endowed Schools Commissioners than any of their other plans. The most famous of these cases, that of Emanuel Hospital, Westminster, brought upon them the powerful hostility of the Lord Mayor and aldermen of London, and the national agitation stirred up by the City did much to slow down the process of reform. Westminster contained several endowments which were partly schools, in which boys and girls were boarded and clothed as well as educated, and partly almshouses. The commissioners' plan was that Emanuel Hospital, which was educating 30 boys and 30 girls, should, together with some smaller foundations, be reserved for boys. The Grey Coat Hospital, which in 1851 had contained 67 boys and 33 girls, should provide for girls exclus-ively (Scott-Giles 1935: 111–12). The Grey Coat governors, who had petitioned against the Endowed Schools Bill, put up a stiff resistance, but their scheme was finally agreed in the summer of 1872. The Emanuel case was much more obstinately fought because it involved the interests and prestige of the City, since the Lord Mayor and aldermen were governors of the hospital.

In March 1870 Roby reported that the 60 boys and girls at Emanuel were taken from Westminster and the City of London, from Chelsea and Hayes in Middlesex, and from Brandesburton in the East Riding of Yorkshire where the trust estate was situated (PRO, Ed. 27: 3363). The parents were of a class rather above that which sent its children to elementary schools. At the time of Roby's visit 6 boys and 12 girls were orphans. In September 1869 the City Solicitor had informed the commissioners that the governors intended to submit their own scheme. They proposed to build a school on a new site, to sell the old school, and to cease to house the almspeople. There would in future be an upper and a lower school. Not less than 70 poor children were to be boarded, fed, and educated free. They were to leave at the age of 15 unless they had been removed to the upper school. Girls might receive only an elementary education. Children who were not on the foundation were to pay fees and the masters might receive boarders.

The governors' scheme was sealed on 28 January 1870. In their reply (15 February) the commissioners expressed themselves unwilling to leave the management of the trust exclusively in the hands of the Lord Mayor and aldermen. They criticized the use of endowment funds to provide lodging and maintenance and also the failure to provide more advanced education for the abler children, especially the girls. The commissioners' scheme, which was sent to the Committee of Council on 21 February 1871, was a development from the ideas expressed in this letter. Emanuel and some smaller foundations were to be united to form the United Westminster Schools. The governing body was to consist of *ex officio*, representative, and co-opted members with only three representing the Lord Mayor and aldermen. There was to be a boarding school within 20 miles of London and two day schools in Westminster. No boy was to remain over the age of 15. Fees were to be charged, but exhibitions were to be awarded to boys from elementary schools, with some specifically reserved for orphans.

The commissioners' plan was in line with their general policy. They wanted to increase the number of children to be educated by reducing the money spent on lodging and maintenance. They claimed that a system of competition would bring forward children who were industrious and of good character. The Lord Mayor and aldermen, on the other hand, wanted to retain their ancient powers undisturbed. They claimed that the school was to be taken away from the poor for the benefit of the middle classes. They denied that schools like Emanuel Hospital had been founded for the benefit of children of brilliant abilities; in the past the boys had earned their livings in industrial occupations and the girls had been trained for domestic service. The two sides seemed to be firing shots across one another's bows rather than trying to resolve their differences by discussion. It is remarkable, particularly since all the actors in the drama were located within the same city, that there appear to have been no meetings between the two sides. Nor had the commissioners made any detailed enquiry, as they did in many other cases before they produced their scheme. Neither side was likely to give way; the battle would be fought to a finish.

A great meeting at the Mansion House condemned the commissioners' plans, and the City tried to win support from other governing bodies. There was much discussion in the press, though the City did not gain universal support; for example, *The Times* strongly supported the commissioners. One Westminster working man wrote to wish them success:

'Our children have such great difficulty in securing patronage from Guild-hall that we wish a *local government* for the Hospital. None of the present Governors take any *real* interest in it except for the Patronage' (Ed. 27: 3363, 1 May 1871). The scheme came before the House of Lords on 24 April and 30 June 1871, with Lord Salisbury as the principal critic of the commissioners. On 30 June he moved a humble address against the scheme on the grounds that it would divert a large proportion of the endowment from the education of the poor and take control away from the Lord Mayor and aldermen 'against whose management no charge has been established' (*Hansard* 205: 1549–75, 24 April 1871; 207: 862–92, 30 June 1871). In the debate the defenders of the scheme had the better of the argument, but Salisbury's motion was carried by 64 votes to 56. The traditionalists had triumphed.

The commissioners then produced a revised scheme which made some concessions to the City. The almshouses were left under the control of the Lord Mayor and aldermen. There was to be a governing body of twenty-one, eleven representing the City and the other ten eventually to be chosen by the London School Board. There was still to be a boarding school and two day schools with a large number of exhibitions for elementary school pupils and for orphans (Ed. 27: 3364). The second scheme was approved by the Committee of Council on 1 May 1872, but the City would have none of it. They appealed to the Privy Council, which finally decided that the scheme should be laid before Parliament (Ed. 27: 3364; *PP* 1873 VIII: 337: 178).

A motion for the rejection of the second scheme was moved before a crowded House of Commons on 13 May 1873. The most interesting speeches in a lengthy debate were those of the Prime Minister, W. E. Gladstone, of Henry Fawcett, and of the Scottish scientist, Lyon Playfair. Gladstone was highly critical of the City and of its attempts to monopolize the foundation. Fawcett attacked the subserviency built into the existing system. He quoted a Westminster working man who had said to him: 'I am not going to crouch and cringe through Temple Bar for this favour; if I ask for it I shall have to give something in return.' Playfair was also critical of the atmosphere of subservience, but he concentrated on the argument that the governors had done nothing to provide a higher level of education for the children (*Hansard* 215: 1875–960). In the division the motion was defeated by 286 to 236, so the second scheme went through; it was finally approved by the Queen in Council on 26 June 1873.

The commissioners had won their case, but at a cost which probably damaged their future effectiveness. In fact their plans were sensible, and there is evidence that they enjoyed support among Westminster working men. They were on strong ground too in their objective of offering an education of a higher standard to more children. John Hymers, Rector of Brandesburton, one of the parishes that benefited from the charity, had commented in a letter to Roby that 'the education given at Emanuel Hospital has been of a very ordinary sort'. When children came back to the village, he thought they showed no superiority 'either in attainment or morals' over those brought up in the local school. Nor in his view did the rich endowment provide any substantial benefit to the poor of Westminster (Ed. 27: 3371, 25 April 1871). In political terms the commissioners were unwise to take on such a formidable opponent as the City of London at such an early stage in their work, and they might have handled the early negotiations more tactfully. However, there were no circumstances in which the City was likely to give way easily when it felt that its interests and prestige were affected. Early Victorian London had been radical/liberal. Hobhouse wrote later that this interference with their 'property' turned the City Tory (Hobhouse and Hammond 1905: 44–5).

2 Poverty, merit, and social differentiation

The argument that the commissioners' plans deprived the poor of rights they had previously enjoyed extended far beyond the controversies over the hospital schools, though it was seen there in its most extreme form. The issue became important again in the 1880s when national figures like Joseph Chamberlain and Jesse Collings took the matter up as part of their campaign to achieve a more egalitarian society (see pp. 63–8). A book on secondary education, published in 1892, commented: 'nothing has caused more local opposition than the proposal to apply to secondary education funds derived from charities originally intended for the poor' (Acland and Llewellyn Smith 1892: 79). 'Poor' is of course a very imprecise word. The master of Emanuel Hospital stated that the children came from 'the reduced middle class' (Ed. 27: 3363, 27 April 1871), and Roby gave a similar picture. At Gloucester the Charity Commissioners' plans for Sir Thomas Rich's charity (1878) were opposed by the tradesmen and skilled artisans who had traditionally benefited from it, but who would not gain any advantage from the scholarships to be provided from elementary schools under the new system because they did not use those schools for their children (Balls 1968: 223–5). In some cases it seems to have been such artisans and tradespeople who opposed the changes which the commissioners wished to make, though at Westminster the 'working men' who supported the Endowed Schools Commission probably belonged to this group. Perhaps in London political Radicalism, linked with a greater awareness of the advantages of educational reform for the children of working men, was a more active force than in the provinces.

The question whether schools should or should not be free was closely linked with debates over the policy to be adopted towards elementary education. Many of the endowed schools had over the centuries become purely elementary, and the position for them was radically changed when the Education Act of 1870 required that education should be provided everywhere as a national service. Since many endowments had mixed objectives, there was also the difficult problem of the shares to be devoted to schools and to more directly charitable objectives like apprenticeship payments for the young and almshouses and dole money for the old. The policy of both sets of commissioners, reflecting the provisions of sect. 30 of the Act of 1869, was to devote as much money as possible to education and to diminish the directly eleemosynary, or charitable, payments. This was part of their fear of patronage and pauperization, though they often met with local opposition, particularly from those who thought that too little attention was being paid to the claims of the old.

A good example of an endowment which, at the time of the Act of 1869, spent a large part of its funds on eleemosynary purposes was the Harpur Trust at Bedford, one of the eight wealthy foundations which had been selected by the School Inquiry Commission for special notice. Their judgement had not been favourable, since they found that the charity 'exhibits the almost unrestrained application of the principle of local exclusion and indiscriminate lavishness' (SIC I (Report): 529; Godber 1973). The new scheme for Bedford was finally ratified in 1873, and the story of its making is of considerable interest. The trustees, many of them directly elected by the townspeople, began by making proposals which were very much in line with the commissioners' policy. Then there was a sharp reaction, caused at least in part by the example of the Emanuel Hospital case. Finally, a scheme was adopted which followed the general lines of commission policy and sharply reduced the amount of directly charitable expenditure.

In April 1870, when the trustees put forward their proposals, they explained that in the previous year their educational expenditure had been £8,952 1s 3d as compared with £1,561 7s 5d spent on apprenticeship fees and on the hospital (which was a children's home) and £2,291 spent on alms. Thus the eleemosynary expenditure amounted to about one-third of the whole. In future they proposed that no part of the endowment was to be used in this way, except for £1,000 a year set aside for the almshouses. They were proposing in fact to exercise their right under sect. 30 of the Act of 1869 to surrender all the remaining non-educational part of the charity for educational purposes. They agreed further to abolish the privileges of Bedford-born children and to open the endowment equally to all. All free education was to be abolished except as the reward of merit, though they were anxious that fees should remain low. The concession of abolishing local privileges 'has not', they noted, 'been made without great difficulty' (PRO Ed. 27: 8A, 1 July 1870).

Unfortunately, it was another year before the commissioners were ready to act, and by that time opinion in the town had hardened against change. In May 1871 a memorial signed by the mayor and 2,079 other persons demanded, among other things, that the elementary schools of the foundation should be free, that no boarders should be allowed, and that apprenticeship fees should be retained, together with both sets of almshouses (one of which had been scheduled to close) (Ed. 27: 8A). The great Mansion House meeting against the Emanuel scheme had been held on 21 April (see p. 11), and the connection between events in

London and Bedford is quite clear. For example, by August 1871 the Bedford trustees were employing the firm of solicitors, Lowless, Nelson, and Jones, which had acted for the City of London, and Mr Nelson came and spoke at one of their meetings (Ed. 27: 9; *Bedford Times*, 26 August 1871). When the commissioners finally produced a scheme in May 1871, which was not very different from the trustees' proposals of the previous year, the trustees rejected it as contrary to the founder's will (8 June 1871). At the end of August they agreed to send a formal notice withdrawing their earlier proposals and refusing to agree to the diversion of any of the charitable funds to educational purposes.

During the remaining months of 1871 and through most of 1872, there is little sign in the files of activity on either side. By Christmas 1872, however, it looks as though Samuel Whitbread, one of the borough MPs, was working behind the scenes to achieve a settlement. Negotiations in the early months of 1873 finally produced a scheme acceptable to both sides. Fees were to be charged in all the schools, though at a low level, and some education was to be offered as the reward of merit. Boarders were allowed, though their numbers were limited. The income of the trust was to be divided into eleven parts, ten of them devoted to the schools and only one reserved for eleemosynary purposes – largely for the almshouses. The trustees accepted the scheme and formally agreed to the apportionment of the educational and eleemosynary funds in March 1873 (Ed. 27: 9, 4, 28 March 1873). Under the scheme, ratified by the Queen in Council on 4 August 1873, the schools of the Harpur Trust prospered mightily. In 1869 the eleemosynary expenditure had been about a third of the whole. After 1873 it was to be one-eleventh. Two-elevenths of the total income was reserved for the elementary schools. Fees were to be charged in them, though exemptions were allowed in cases of poverty.

The problems of free and subsidized education were seen in their most acute form in the many elementary schools which came under the jurisdiction of the commissioners. The surveys of the Schools Inquiry Commission had found that many of the endowed schools were simple primary schools, often less efficient and less well-equipped than the National schools of more recent foundation. Of the schools they examined 340, or 43 per cent of the total number, did not teach Latin and Greek (*HSE*: 282). Nevertheless, in the 1860s, these schools in villages and small towns still performed an important function by providing a basic education to children who might otherwise have received nothing. The situation was drastically changed by the Act of 1870, which made provision for elementary education on national lines, either in voluntary or in board schools. The commissioners argued strongly that, once the Act had become law, there was no case for spending endowment funds on basic elementary education, which would henceforward be supplied by the state and for which parents would have to pay fees. On the other hand, the inhabitants of a parish that had long enjoyed a free school felt that they were being robbed by the diversion of money to other purposes, most commonly, as they saw it, for the higher education of the middle class.

The Forster Act of 1870 influenced the work of the Endowed Schools Commissioners in two ways. The endowed elementary schools wished to take advantage of Education Department grants. In order to qualify it was necessary that the site or building should be assigned to elementary education by scheme, and the commissioners therefore found themselves engaged in making large numbers of schemes for elementary schools. This meant the expenditure of a great deal of time on matters which for them were of only marginal interest (Owen 1965: 257; *PP* 1872 XXIV: 27–8). It was for this reason that the Act of 1873 took elementary school endowments of less than £100 a year out of their jurisdiction. Even after that the commissioners still had difficulties. Scarning in Norfolk, which will be discussed later (see pp. 60–3), was an elementary school maintained under sect. 7 of the 1870 Act.

In the 1870s the general policy of the commissioners was that, since basic elementary schooling was now provided through the public purse, the endowments should be used only for additional objects like the award of prizes and free places, exhibitions to higher schools, libraries, and extra equipment (*PP* 1872 XXIV: 72–5). Roby illustrated the point that small sums of money, which could be obtained just as well from other sources, should not be given to elementary schools by citing the case of Betton's trust, which gave grants of about £5 each to 1,200 schools. 'I know', he argued, 'the consequences of exciting the fears of the managers of 1,200 schools; but notwithstanding that I desire to say very clearly and plainly that I regard that money at present as for all practical educational purposes wasted' (*PP* 1873 VIII: 378: 742; 387: 861).

Where it was possible to do so, the commissioners tried to upgrade endowed elementary schools into schools of the third grade (for children up to the ages of 14 to 15), an area in which, as the Schools Inquiry Commission had pointed out, provision was very deficient. Several of the London foundations were successfully reformed in this way, and something will be said about two of them – the Roan schools at Greenwich (scheme, 1873) and Dame Alice Owen's at Islington (scheme, 1878). In both cases the governing bodies worked closely with the commissioners, and there were no serious disagreements. Girls' schools were established as well as boys', and all were very successful.

At Greenwich there was a considerable endowment – £1,000 a year – which was likely to double within a few years. When the feoffees of the charity submitted their scheme early in 1870 the commissioners suggested that the whole standard of the education provided should be raised. More should be done for girls, and leaving exhibitions established for the abler pupils. Nothing more happened for about two years until

William Latham, an assistant commissioner, wrote to the clerks to the trust (Ed. 27: 3023, 17 January 1872). Since the draft scheme of 1870, he argued, the original educational function of Roan's charity had been superseded by the 1870 Act. Some of the money should be spent on providing additional facilities for elementary school pupils, such as prizes, the award of free education for merit and regular attendance, and help with entry into working life. In addition, schools of a higher type should be set up, charging fees of £3–6 per annum, with free exhibitions from elementary schools and leaving exhibitions to schools of a higher grade. There was a need for a new governing body, including some members nominated by the London School Board. In Latham's view the existing elementary schools should be handed over to a body of managers 'to be conducted as public elementary schools by the usual means'.

The final scheme closely reflected Latham's suggestions. The commissioners' draft had been fairly well received by the feoffees and by local opinion generally, though there was opposition from the vestry of the parish, which claimed that the interests of the poor would be sacrificed. They asked the Committee of Council to withhold approval from the scheme, but they clearly did not expect much support from their MPs. It was agreed that a petition should be sent to Parliament, but nothing seems to have happened (Ed. 27: 3023; *Greenwich and Deptford Chronicle*, 26 April, 3 May 1873). Similar arguments to those used by the vestry were put forward by the Greenwich Advanced Liberal Association which wanted to spend all the money on scholarships and exhibitions for children in elementary schools without establishing any higher schools at all. The problem was, as the commissioners pointed out in their reply to the association, the urgent need for new schools to take pupils up to the age of about 15. Latham commented that there was only one existing publicly supported school in the area where the suggested awards could be held.

The Roan School scheme has many features of interest. It shows the commissioners working in general harmony with local interests to convert an old elementary school endowment into third-grade schools. There was local opposition, but it was not influential; it did not, for example, seem to enjoy the support of the local newspaper. In a place like Greenwich there were likely to be many middle-class people and better paid artisans who wanted what the new schools could offer, particularly since pupils from elementary schools were admitted at half fees. Effective provision had been made for the higher education of girls, and the new governing bodies had a strong representative element with some members elected by the ratepayers and others nominated by the London School Board. What had been achieved in Greenwich realized many of the hopes of the educational reformers.

The changes at Owen's foundation at Islington ran on very similar lines. The governors of Owen's were the Brewers Company. The endowment was large – about £8,000 net, though at the time when the new scheme was instituted 60 per cent of this was spent on the almshouses and only 40 per cent on the school. The company's original proposals suggested a redistribution very much in favour of education, and this was carried out in the final scheme. Again there were to be both boys' and girls' schools with fees of £3–6. There were to be scholarships from elementary schools and a normal leaving age of 15. There was some local opposition to the ending of free education, to the limited amount of the endowment to be devoted to the almspeople, and, from some quarters, to the proposed girls' school. However, as at Greenwich, the opposition was not very keenly pressed, and the scheme went through without major difficulty. In both places the new schools must have met a need, because they established themselves very quickly (Ed. 27: 3117, 3119, 3120 on Owen's foundation).

In both these examples the new third-grade schools were independent foundations. A rather different case, where a third-grade school was created by the reallocation of older charities in order to complement an existing first-grade school, is that of Sherborne. The King's School, as it was called in the nineteenth century, had risen steadily in numbers and prestige under H. D. Harper, who became headmaster in 1850 (Gourlay 1951). By 1870 it had a good claim to rank as one of the much enlarged group of public schools which had grown up around the nine schools investigated by the Clarendon Commission of 1861–4. Like other success-ful grammar school heads, Harper was critical of the Endowed Schools Act, though in fact the commissioners' dealings with Sherborne School were harmonious and speedily completed. A new scheme for a first-grade boarding school was approved on 16 May 1871 (Ed. 27: 907; *PP* 1872 XXIV: Appendices, 86–96).

It is clear from the files that, in the early stages of the negotiations, there was concern about a possible clash between the boarders and the rights of local foundation boys, particularly if it were suggested that the fees should be raised. Harper himself had been anxious to set up a 'middle school' for local boys as early as 1858 (Gourlay 1951: 120). The problem was a common one. Local boys tended to leave early and to want a commercial education. Boarders were of a higher social class, stayed at school longer, were more financially profitable to the masters, and wanted a different curriculum. At two of the major schools, Rugby and Harrow, the clash of interests had been solved by the creation of a separate lower school giving a semi-classical and commercial education (*HSE*: 225).

At Sherborne the claims of the town were met by tapping other charity funds rather than by dividing the endowments of the King's School. J. G. Fitch, the assistant commissioner in charge of the case, wrote to Roby in June 1870 to say that it was important to create a third-grade school as quickly as possible and that he had arranged to meet the trustees of

Foster's and of Woodman's charities (Ed. 27: 906). This policy was supported by a public meeting held at the end of September which discussed questions of free education and of the proposed lower school (Ed. 27: 906; *Sherborne Journal*, 29 September 1870). The meeting adopted a resolution which, after reviewing the history of free education for local boys, recommended that the King's School scheme should be supplemented by another 'for the foundation of a lower school out of other charities', and that £100 per annum should be devoted out of the King's School revenues for 'deserving boys of lower schools'.

Effectively, the town consented to the King's School scheme on condition that a lower school was established out of the other Sherborne charities (Ed. 27: 886, 28 November 1870; McKay 1975). It was common enough, when endowments were reorganized, to divide them in order to provide both upper and lower schools. What is unusual about the Sherborne story is that the resources for the third-grade school were found from independent funds. As a result the King's School was left free to pursue its path as a public school of the first grade without any major commitment to meet the needs of the town of Sherborne. Harper was a strong supporter of the scheme for Foster's School. From his point of view it must have solved many of the difficult problems which beset the heads of rising schools.

At the end of June 1870 Fitch had written to the trustees of Foster's and of Woodman's charities about the possibility of a day school for 70–100 children of each sex (Ed. 27: 886). The idea of a new girls' school was not pursued further, though it was suggested that, when the existing charities were reallocated, the Digby girls' schools should be maintained (Ed. 27: 886, 21 October, 4 November 1870). Though the charities that were to be tapped were numerous, the sums available were not large. Fitch wrote to the commissioners at the end of November 1870 that a capital sum of £1,575 would be available for the new school, plus an annual income of £115. This would provide a third-grade school for about 100 boys at a fee of 4–7 guineas.

The plan was supported by a public meeting, and the various charities, twelve in number, gave their consent as required by sect. 30 of the Act of 1869. It was a considerable achievement to bring so many interests into a common plan. The final scheme followed the lines suggested in the early negotiations. One-half of the income of Foster's charity was to be applied to the education of girls, and a supplementary scheme was to be made for this purpose. The remainder of the endowment was to be applied to 'Foster's Schools'. Buildings were to be erected for 100 day scholars, though the scheme was later modified to include boarders. No boy was to remain over the age of 15. Physical science, French, and Latin were to be taught, but Greek was excluded. A quarter of the exhibitions were to be reserved for boys from elementary schools within a 10-mile radius of Sherborne, and the governors were given power to create further exhibitions to other places of education. The scheme was finally approved on 9 August 1872. Foster's School opened at Easter 1875; it slowly made its way, though in the early days it had a hard struggle to establish itself.

The commissioners' policy in establishing third-grade schools like Owen's and Foster's shows their anxiety to offer educational opportunities to those children who needed rather more than a basic elementary training. Since no endowment, however rich, could meet all the demands made upon it, there had to be some principles of selection and differentiation. The race was to be to the swift and the battle to the strong, which helps to explain why the traditional forces in town and country opposed the changes so vehemently. To those forces the social order was immutable, a proposition that carried with it the requirement that it was the duty of the strong to assist the weak. The reformers would not have accepted the claim that their policies drove the weak to the wall, but they would have gloried in the statement that they offered every opportunity for the strong to advance. To them it was more conducive to the general good to spend money on able boys and girls rather than on the client-families of local notables or on elderly almspeople who, they might have argued, could have provided for themselves had they been more provident.

Since ability was bound to vary between individuals, there was a need for graded structures to provide for differing needs in the most efficient way possible. The concept of schools of three grades related closely to this ideal of personal advancement, based on differentiation of abilities and needs, which lay behind so much of the work of both sets of commissioners. Their attitude helps to explain why in their planning they were so much more favourable to the middle classes than to the mass of working people. The middle classes were ambitious for their children and socially mobile. Their requirements fitted in very well with the meritocratic attitudes which all too easily saw working men as idle, shiftless, and supinely dependent on their superiors. For able working-class children the path would be kept open by the scholarships and exhibitions, which were provided in the new schemes (see pp. 75–83).

This creed of self-help had to operate under the conditions of a very class-conscious age. In nineteenth-century England the growth of industrial and commercial wealth had led to the erosion of many traditional barriers. It may be that, just because these shifts had occurred, men found it necessary to fight especially hard to preserve those distinctions that had survived. The able young people who had climbed the ladder of rigorous open competition were likely to be indoctrinated with the ideals of the group they aspired to join. Neither in numbers nor in ideology were they likely to offer a threat to their social superiors. Their advance could be delimited, contained; it involved none of the waste and muddle which the reformers condemned in the traditional system.

In general, apart from this small minority, the lines of social demarcation remained sharp, and both richer and poorer were highly conscious of them. One of the opponents of the scheme for Owen's School, who wanted free education restricted to children of the parishes of Islington and Clerkenwell, objected to mixing foundation and pay scholars: 'The different castes from which they will be drawn will to my mind give rise to antagonistic feelings' (Ed. 27: 3119, 20 February 1878). The head-master of Repton had told the Schools Inquiry Commission that he had succeeded in gaining fair play in school for the village boys, but that he had had to separate them out of school from the boarders for fear of ill treatment: 'It is not', he said, 'the fault of the boys, it is the fault of society, I think . . . I never saw a man yet who would send his boy to a school in order to associate with those lower than himself' (*Fleming Report* 1944: 23).

This sense of class and group antagonism helps to explain why there was frequent opposition from local residents to the admission of boarders into the grammar schools. It was thought that the masters tended to favour boarders because they brought in more money, and the school curriculum was often adjusted to meet their needs rather than those of local boys, who generally left school younger. Some of the issues raised, both for local people and for headmasters, can be seen in the case of Brentwood School in Essex.

The school had had a troubled history in the early part of the century and had experienced a lengthy law suit (*HSE*: 49; R. R. Lewis 1981). W. D. West, who had been appointed headmaster in 1851, had built up a successful boarding school with a classical curriculum. This was unpopu-lar with many of the townspeople who wanted a commercial education and who wished to get rid of the boarders. From West's point of view the boarders were essential if the school was to be profitable. When the wardens (the school governors) submitted a draft scheme in January 1870, it was accompanied by a letter from the headmaster in which he claimed that the school taught both classical and modern languages. All the boys were treated alike, and there was no basis for claims of 'exagger-ated social pride'. Boarders were allowed under the Act of 1851, which regulated the school. They had always been admitted and he had spent £3,000 out of his own pocket on the boarding accommodation. If the school became commercial in type, all that investment would be lost (Ed. 27: 1060). Clearly the need to protect West's position affected the early negotiations, but in the summer of 1870 he resigned on accepting another headship. Later he asked for compensation for the improvements that he had made to the property, claiming that he would never have moved from Brentwood but for the consequences of the Endowed Schools Act. The commissioners told him that they had no power to grant him anything (Ed. 27: 1060, 19, 20 October 1870). His losses illustrate the vulnerable position of headmasters, who were forced to act as private entrepreneurs in order to attract boarders and make an adequate income.

When plans were being prepared for a new scheme at Brentwood suggestions were made not only by the Wardens but by a more radical committee of townspeople, who suggested that the headmaster should not be allowed to take boarders, that no boy should be allowed to remain over the age of 16, that education should be free in the proposed lower school and at a low fee of only £4 a year in the upper school. The commissioners were not likely to favour plans of the kind put forward by the committee, and when they produced their own scheme, the committee condemned it entirely. Its secretary complained that 'this Endowment would be handed over to the well to do and upper classes of society to the total exclusion of the lower middle and working classes' (Ed. 27: 1060, 19 November 1871). In the final scheme boarders were allowed, and the fees were much higher than the committee of townspeople had suggested.

Dr West was not the only headmaster to face problems of a similar kind. Heads, and to some extent governors, of schools were strongly affected by the increasing tendency to grade and differentiate since, the more sharply lines were drawn, the more important it was to be placed on the right side of them. During the middle decades of the century a much larger community of public schools was emerging. Some of the old grammar schools, like Sherborne and Repton, found their way into it, and as a result severed, to a greater or lesser extent, their links with their own localities. In so doing they attained a higher status, and other schools feared the competition. At Bristol, for example, J. W. Caldicott, the headmaster of the grammar school, showed intense fear and suspicion of Clifton College, one of the most successful of the newly-founded public schools (see pp. 43–7).

By the 1890s the lines of demarcation had to some degree broken down or had at least shifted their position. Schools have always tended, by what seems an inevitable process, to move towards higher status. Bedford Modern School, wrote A. F. Leach in 1908, 'instead of a different type of school, is a mere echo of the grammar school, to which parents whose families are elastic and their purses light, send their boys to save a few guineas at the grammar school. It has been seen as a first-grade school with a low second-grade tuition fee' (*VCH Bedfordshire* II (1908): 177). Schools which had been established in the third grade moved up to the second. At the Roan Schools a revision of the scheme in 1883 allowed boys to stay at school until they were 17, and two years later a girl, Florence Tate, who was under 17 years of age, won an open scholarship at Somerville College, Oxford (Ed. 27: 3025; Kirby 1929: 164). Such changes had their disadvantages because they sometimes left serious gaps in areas of work which the schools had originally been intended to fill, but they did offer increased opportunities at modest cost for boys and girls for whom no such channels would have been open a generation earlier.

For individuals, too, class barriers were getting lower, as material collected for the Bryce Commission of 1894–5 suggests, though such changes had affected boys more than girls. Opportunities for artisans and working people generally were much extended in the large towns by the higher-grade schools set up by school boards to extend the range of education given in their elementary schools. The technical instruction committees of the new county councils offered grants for better facilities and for scholarships. Such grants were not only of value to individual students. They also threw out a life-line to many grammar schools, where poor facilities and defective teaching limited the opportunities open to young people in the districts that they served. The last two decades of the century proved a difficult time for many schools. Resources were often lacking, and the very successes of the reformers emphasized how much remained to be done. It was clear that only state intervention could supply the financial support and the administrative structures, which were essential if England were to enjoy an adequate system of secondary education.

3 Political, administrative, and religious issues

The general work of the commissioners may be examined under three aspects: political, religious, and academic. Effective management was crucial to the success of the new schemes, and what was achieved formed only a fragment of the original plans of the Schools Inquiry Commission. They had proposed a central educational council together with provincial councils, each employing a district commissioner who would act as a local inspector. They also recommended a central council of examinations with power to examine schoolmasters and to register private schools. None of this machinery passed into law. The commissioners in London did provide a central body of a kind, though it acted solely in relation to individual endowments and had no general powers of policy-making or planning. The absence of the provincial councils proved a serious loss, because there was nothing between the central administrative body and the governing bodies of individual schools. The gap could be bridged occasionally by a visit from an assistant commissioner, but it soon became clear that the absence of any forum of local opinion made co-operation between the centre and the provinces far more difficult to achieve. The burdens on the centre did not diminish as time went on because schemes, after they had been made, needed regular revision. In the 1880s the Charity Commissioners were asking for powers to carry out inspections of schools, and they were permitted in 1887 to appoint assistant commissioners as inspectors (CC 27th Rep., *PP* 1880 XVIII: 94; Bishop 1971: 246–7). This work was useful and it helped to bridge the wide gap between the central administration and the schools, but it was only a partial substitute for the provincial organization which had originally been planned.

School governing bodies had been constituted in many different ways before 1869. Some schools were administered by London city companies. Many others, which had originally been controlled by town councils, were managed by municipal charity trustees set up under the Municipal Corporations Act of 1835. Sometimes the appointment of the master lay in different hands from that of the general government of the school. At Bedford, for example, the headmaster and staff of the grammar school, though not the staffs of the other schools, were appointed by New College, Oxford. That right disappeared under the new scheme, though the college was given the right to appoint members to the new governing body. The commonest type was the self-perpetuating group which filled its vacancies by co-optation.

Such co-opted governing bodies were often Tory and Anglican because those groups were the traditional holders of power. In many towns Tory/Anglican governors were opposed by the Liberals and Nonconformists, who often controlled the town councils and who wished to replace the co-opted boards by new bodies, chosen either by direct election or by the town councils themselves. The classic example of rivalry between Tory/Anglican trustees and Liberal/Nonconformist townspeople occurred in Birmingham. The old guard fought a long battle and in the end achieved a good deal of success, aided by the change from a Liberal to a Conservative government in 1874, though some concessions had still to be made (see pp. 50–7).

The pressure for elected governing bodies was a Radical demand going back to the 1830s (*HSE*: 87). To those who supported it, it seemed right that the people should control their own institutions. Schools of public foundation belonged, it was argued, to the public patrimony and not to small and unrepresentative cliques who had gained control over their destinies. To members of the upper and professional classes the men who were likely to be produced by direct election or town council nomination were quite unfitted to manage the schools. Where such a system already existed the omens were not favourable. At Bedford many of the members of the Harpur Trust had long been directly elected. The commissioners were told that these elections had led to the choice of 'objectionable' persons by the dominant political party. This had caused 'the appointment of butchers, bakers, two hairdressers, a horse doctor as well as other individuals of that class and who were wonderfully jealous both of the Masters and of "New College" ' (Ed. 27: 8A, 6 November 1869). The final scheme of August 1873 retained a large number of elected governors, and some of the residents of the town, the grammar school masters and New College all feared that the local elected element was too strong.

Both the composition and the management of governing bodies were closely linked with the struggles of local politics. There was no uniform pattern in such matters. Many boards were Tory and Anglican. The elected members of the Harpur Trust at Bedford were likely to be Liberal and Nonconformist. At High Wycombe local opinion was anxious that all the members of the new governing body should be appointed from the borough and not from the county (Ed. 27: 130, 16 February 1878). Sometimes political control was divided. According to the headmaster of Bristol Grammar School, one party controlled both the Corporation and the Society of Merchant Venturers and the other the Charity Trustees (Ed. 27: 1289, 22 January 1870).

Town councils were often consulted by the assistant commissioners when they were working on schemes, and additional pressures were brought to bear by large public meetings which were Radical in temper and anxious to protect the rights of working men. Such interference, whether municipal or popular, was unwelcome to heads and trustees. The headmaster of Warrington Grammar School wrote to Assistant Commissioner Fearon about a town meeting which in his view had been dominated by a small group of Radicals: 'they passed all the resolutions by acclamation; which they would have done had the proposal been to capitalize the property and invest it in gin to be drunk within the week to the success of the *Warrington Examiner*' [the Liberal newspaper] (Ed. 27: 2304, 10 October 1878). Occasionally, national politics entered the debate. An opponent of the Macclesfield scheme explained that the Liberal candidate had been only forty votes ahead at the last election. If a Conservative government persisted in a policy that violated the intentions of the founder, 'it will be a long time before a Conservative gets in for Macclesfield' (Ed. 27: 270, 21 July 1876).

The commissioners' policy in making new schemes was to take account of all these pressures by setting up governing bodies made up of several elements. They disliked boards chosen entirely by co-optation, though they accepted the need for a co-opted element, which often consisted of members from the old body. In addition, there were to be *ex officio* members, the holders of offices of local importance, as well as representative members chosen by town councils, school boards, and sometimes by direct election. This tripartite pattern – *ex officio*, representative, co-opted – was the norm, though the commissioners were prepared to move towards it gradually. For example, they often allowed the old governing body to retain more co-opted members on the new one than it was strictly allowed to have, with the proviso that numbers should be allowed to fall by natural wastage. They were also anxious to achieve a proper division of function between the governors and the headmaster. The rule was to be that the former should control the general character of the school and the latter its internal management. Heads were to be paid by a fixed stipend plus a capitation fee based on the numbers in the school (Ed. 27: 266, 7 February 1870 (letter from ESC)).

Governing bodies sometimes attempted to reduce the powers of the headmaster to an extent the commissioners thought unreasonable. A more serious issue was the dislike shown by many governing bodies for the idea of representative governors and the fear of interference, through their agency, by the town councils. They could not entirely avoid the representative principle, but many of them fought long delaying actions and tried to reduce the numbers of representative governors as much as they could.

The keenly fought battle at Birmingham will be reviewed later, but that was concluded within seven or eight years (see pp. 50–7). The powers of obstruction and delay deployed by the governors of Leeds Grammar School delayed a new scheme for almost a generation – from 1870 to 1898 – and so far as girls' education is concerned, until 1901 (Ed. 27: 5976, 5978, 5981, 5982, 5983, 5984; REC, West Riding, *PP* 1899 LXXII). The story at Leeds began with abortive negotiations in 1870–1. As usual, the commissioners expressed their desire to introduce *ex officio* and representative governors. The existing board was anxious not to have town council nominees, and they wanted the co-opted governors chosen exclusively by the ancient trustees of Pious Uses and not by the whole board. If this concession were not granted, they argued, they would have to reconsider their offer of a further endowment from the dole fund, which they also controlled. Like many such boards they were prepared to use their powers to transfer money from non-educational to educational purposes under the 1869 Act to get what they wanted in other ways. The headmaster, W. G. Henderson, explained their position in a letter to Arthur Hobhouse (Ed. 27: 5976, 3 February 1871). He defended the existing composition of the governing body. He was certain that in future they would be prepared to choose Nonconformist members, which they had not done in the past because they believed that decisions of the Court of Chancery prevented it (*VCH Somerset* II (1911): 453 – *Baker* v. *Lee* 8 HL 485). It was not unreasonable that co-opted governors should be chosen only by the Pious Use trustees, and he feared that nominees of the town council would take a highly political stance.

Nothing more seems to have happened between the spring of 1871 and 1878 when the Pious Use trustees decided to give a large sum of money to education from their non-educational funds. The subject of a new scheme was raised again in 1884 when Dr Henderson was made Dean of Carlisle. His opposition to the original scheme, minuted Sir George Young, one of the commissioners, had been one reason for its abandonment, together with the decision of the Pious Use trustees to give money for education from their other funds. When the scheme was taken up again, the commissioners would not in Young's view be likely to acquiesce in 'the dread exhibited by the trustees of admitting the Town Council and other popular element to a share of representation on the Governing Body' (Ed. 27: 5981, 7 February 1884).

The negotiations of 1884–8 were no more successful than those of 1870–1. They went over very similar ground, with the addition of a sharp clash about girls' education which will be discussed elsewhere (see pp. 204–6). At first the trustees seemed likely to accept members nominated by the town council and the school board. Later they announced their readiness to make £1,000 available from their other funds for scholarships, 'the offer conditional on the Cons^tn of the Board of Trustees remaining unaltered' (Ed. 27: 5981, 15 July, 6 August 1884). Henderson later claimed that the transfer of £700 a year for scholarships from the Poors Estate under the scheme of 1878 had been made on the understanding that the plan for a new scheme had been given up and that no change in the composition of the board was intended (Ed. 27: 5981, 25 July 1884). No advantage would arise, he argued, from adding representative members to the trustees. In fact, they were prepared to practise a little blackmail in their anxiety to keep out the town council nominees.

Neither side showed any signs of giving way. The commissioners would not agree that the constitution of the board should remain unchanged. When in August 1885 they produced a draft scheme, some of the trustees' objections were on religious grounds. They disliked the fact that the vicar of Leeds could not remain an *ex officio* governor, and they claimed that the changes were 'more likely to be adverse to the continuance of the present religious teachings of the school than the proposal of 1871 would be' (Ed. 27: 5981, 2 December 1885). The new scheme did not reach the Education Department until June 1887. In their comments the commissioners pointed out that the comparatively small numbers in the school suggested that the present system was not satisfactory to Leeds parents. They claimed that the representative governors would provide a new stimulus, and they denied any 'suggested compact' about the use of the Poors Estate money (Ed. 27: 5981, 15 November 1887).

The final sticking point came not over the governing body but over the amount of money to be spent on girls' education. The commissioners were not prepared to accept what the governors were ready to offer. In June 1888 Stanton wrote to Sir George Young to say that he had seen Patrick Cumin of the Education Department. If an agreement could not be reached between the two parties, the three Leeds MPs would all oppose the scheme in the House of Commons, and the government had no chance of getting it through (Ed. 27: 5981, 14 June 1888). The obstinacy of the trustees had defeated a second attempt to make a new scheme.

Nothing more happened until June 1894 when the Leeds School Board took the initiative in restarting negotiations. After their chairman, G. W. Cockburn, who was also a member of the Bryce Commission, had asked to see the vice-president, A. H. D. Acland, the Committee of Council wrote to the governors to say that they proposed to have the scheme approved (Ed. 27: 5982, 30 June 1894). By the middle of the 1890s numbers in the school had fallen a great deal – 161 in 1897 as opposed to 248 in 1884 – and George Young argued that there was need for a new scheme to restore confidence (Ed. 27: 5984, 8 May 1897). The governors, attacked by the Liberal *Leeds Mercury* as a group of Tories and Churchmen (Ed. 27: 5984, 30 November 1895), had not altered their basic position. By this time the question of the money to be made available for girls' education had become the most important issue, but the composition of the governing body was not far behind. The governors were still claiming that the £700 dole money had been handed over in 1878 on condition that their board was not radically changed. From their point of view the situation had become even more difficult because the town council and the school board had become dangerous rivals. The town council controlled the technical instruction grants. The school board ran the very successful higher grade school, which was likely to attract many boys who would otherwise have been in the lower forms of the grammar school. When the governors saw the vice-president in May 1895, they claimed that 'managers of rival schools' should not have a preponderating influence on their board (Ed. 27: 5982).

By 1896–7, however, the omens for a settlement looked more favourable. In June 1896 T. R. Leuty, one of the city's MPs, argued that it was a good moment to go forward because the national government, the town council, and the school board were all in the hands of one party, the Conservatives. Under such circumstances the danger of a group of dissentients playing off one political party against another was much reduced. G. W. Kekewich, secretary of the Education Department, told the commissioners that with some modifications the governors were now prepared to accept the scheme (Ed. 27: 5984, 8 April 1897). Clearly, they were not going to get rid of the representative members, but they still tried very hard to increase the number of the co-optees. The commissioners were prepared to allow this as a temporary measure to ease the transition, but they were adamant in refusing to increase the final number of six co-opted members in the draft scheme. They obviously feared that too many co-opted members would perpetuate the influence of the old order. The scheme was finally approved in May 1898 (Ed. 27: 5983). There were in the first instance to be eleven co-opted members, but these were eventually to be reduced to six as the commissioners had planned.

There was still to be one more set of negotiations before a scheme for the girls' high school was approved in May 1901 (see p. 206). The whole series of events at Leeds is an extraordinary saga of delay, obstruction, and rivalries between local groups, fearful of losing, or anxious to gain, power. Though this surfaces only occasionally, it seems likely that one principal objective of the governors was to preserve the position of the Church of England in Leeds. The growth of the higher-grade school shows the vulnerability of the grammar schools to the competition of new institutions supported by public funds. The long delaying action over girls' education, for which the governors had little sympathy, will be discussed elsewhere. The Leeds negotiations are unique, both in the length of time they lasted and in the obstinacy with which they were contested. The commissioners got their scheme in the end, but only after long delays imposed by a powerful local group, ready to fight a determined rearguard action to preserve its traditional ways.

Such long-drawn-out battles were not universal. Some schemes were completed quickly and without friction. Those who resist always leave more trace in the records than those who agree. Sometimes the most vocal groups were small and not representative. These caveats having been expressed, it cannot be doubted that the resistance was widespread, and as active in the 1880s as it had been in the early 1870s. Jesse Collings, who was an active opponent of the commissioners, told the select committee of 1886–7 that trustees were frightened to apply to the commissioners because they did not want trusts to fall into their hands (*PP* 1887 IX: 348: 7633).

Two commissioners, Sir George Young and D. C. Richmond, gave evidence to the same select committee about the opposition they had experienced. In Young's view the principal objections were made to defend the interests of the poor. Local claims and the demands that endowments should be confined to one parish or to a small area were as strong as ever (ibid.: 50: 529; 80: 746–7). Richmond concentrated on the issues raised by the proposed reorganization of the boys' and girls' hospitals in Norwich. The trustees were anxious to devote almost all the revenues of the boys' hospital to maintain an orphans' home. This was a policy which the commissioners could not accept. 'I do not consider', Richmond told a questioner, 'that it is our business under the Endowed Schools Acts to make provision in relief of the poor law.' The commissioners wished to establish scholarships, a plan which held no attractions for the people of Norwich. 'I am afraid that we have had extremely little indication of any desire to promote the advanced education of the working classes there' (ibid.: 159–60: 1640–2; 178: 1877; 373–5: 5468–9).

Resistance often came from powerful local elites, as at Norwich and Leeds. Sometimes they were supported by large numbers of working men, prepared to go to protest meetings and to sign petitions. Their collective presence can be felt in many instances, though individual working-class leaders cannot often be identified. Sometimes organized groups, made up of working men and members of the lower middle class, tried to influence policy on their own account. At Coventry, for example, the large group of freemen failed in their opposition to a new scheme, but when this was made, their sons were allowed to pay lower fees than other boys, a considerable recognition of their traditional rights (Ed. 27: 5009, 5010).

Sometimes, and particularly over religious questions, the commissioners found themselves perched rather uneasily between the rivalries of local groups. The religious character and teaching of a school were controlled by sect. 19 of the Act of 1869 and the Endowed Schools Commissioners found the rule difficult to apply. Both Lyttelton and Roby would have liked to remove the restrictions altogether on the grounds that founders' intentions could not be respected for ever, and that there was no reason why they should be preserved in religious matters and not in others (*PP* 1873 VIII: 341: 233; 388: 936; 411: 1263). Roby argued that endowments given to the Church of England were endowments given to all Englishmen and could not be restricted by rules made 300 years earlier under quite different circumstances (ibid.: 376: 706–7; 377: 713).

In the early years the commissioners had no easy task in finding their way between the different viewpoints. In later years such difficulties grew much less pressing. It is noteworthy that there is little reference to religious matters in the extensive evidence given to the select committee of 1886–7, and what evidence there is suggests much easier relationships. Sir George Young testified that any difficulties about the operation of the conscience clause had been overcome. D. R. Fearon thought it an advantage that the denominational battle had died down as compared with the position in the early 1870s (*PP* 1886 IX: 84: 788; 414: 5887). Much of the older bitterness had disappeared and religion no longer held the central position in public debate which it had enjoyed in the early part of the century.

4 Academic policies and the curriculum

Much of the commissioners' work was dominated by the administrative, political, and religious issues which were examined in the last chapter. But schools are primarily teaching institutions, and the Endowed Schools Commissioners had very clear views about the curriculum and the ways in which it should be developed. Basic to all their thinking was the concept of the three grades, each with a programme appropriate to the ages at which the pupil was to leave school. In the later decades of the century the Charity Commissioners tended to think in terms of two grades rather than of three – a first grade up to the age of 18 or 19, a second grade to 15 or 16 (*PP* 1886 IX: 112: 1118 (J. G. Fitch)). The third-grade work had in many cases been taken over by the higher-grade schools managed by the school boards. Traditionally, the curriculum of the first-grade schools had been classical, because both Latin and Greek were essential for university entrance. In second- and third-grade schools Latin formed an important element in the curriculum because it was regarded both as a valuable discipline in itself and as a basic introduction to the study of language. Greek was much less prominent or even disappeared entirely, and more time was given to mathematics and English subjects. By the 1860s more attention was being paid to the claims of the natural sciences, though, as yet, they had not been incorporated into the curriculum of the endowed or the public schools (*HSE*: 275–6).

One reform which the commissioners strongly supported was the provision of more schools for girls, a major topic, which will be discussed in detail later (see pp. 201–14). For all young people there was strong pressure towards expanding the range of subjects taught. More attention was to be given to modern languages, to history and, above all, to natural sciences. It was not only a question of finding more time. Much thought was also given to new methods of teaching so that the new subjects might offer an intellectual training comparable in rigour with their older rivals. The royal commission on scientific instruction (1870–5) sought information from 202 endowed schools. Of the 128 schools that replied, only 63 taught science. Of 87 schools giving definite information only 18 devoted as much as four hours a week to the subject. The commission recommended that in all public and endowed schools not less than six hours a week on an average should be devoted to science teaching, and that in all school examinations not less than one sixth of the marks should be devoted to the subject (*PP* 1875 XXVIII: 15, 24). A decade later the royal commission on technical instruction recommended that the Charity Commissioners should establish secondary schools 'in which the study of natural science, drawing, mathematics, and modern languages, shall take the place of Latin and Greek', and that local authorities should be empowered to establish secondary and technical schools and colleges (*PP* 1884 XXIX: 610).

The introduction of curriculum change into the schools was slow and uneven. It was difficult to find teachers for the new subjects and to pay for the expensive equipment necessary for science teaching. The Endowed Schools Commissioners were very conscious of the need for innovation and anxious to incorporate science and the other new subjects into their schemes. Obviously they faced many difficulties from traditionally-minded heads and governing bodies. To expand the teaching of modern subjects in the second- and third-grade schools, where they already had a base, was not too acute a problem. But if they were to win equal status for science and modern languages in relation to classics they needed to create first-grade schools with a modern curriculum, and here they were entering uncharted waters because such schools did not exist.

In their view a first-grade modern school meant a school without Greek, because only by abandoning Greek could time be found for the newer studies. Nor did they favour schools divided into two or more streams – what they called 'bifurcation' – because they believed that, if classical and modern studies were combined in the same institution, the modern studies would prove the weaker and would go to the wall. They feared that headmasters, who had normally received a classical training, would favour the subjects that they knew at the expense of those of which they were ignorant. The commissioners therefore aimed at creating some first-grade modern schools, but, if these were to be a success, one major obstacle had to be overcome. Since a knowledge of Greek was a necessary qualification for entry to the universities, the path to further academic study would be closed to students of the new modern schools unless the rules were changed.

The commissioners' views about Greek and about the curriculum in general were set out in two letters, the first sent in June 1870 to the universities of Oxford, Cambridge, and London, the second in March 1871 to the Duke of Devonshire, Chairman of the Royal Commission on Scientific Instruction (*PP* 1872 XXIV: 60–2, 66–8; *PP* 1875 XXVIII: 27–8). In the first letter they argued that university studies had a profound effect on the work of the higher schools, though only a small proportion of their pupils went on to take degrees. The result had been to establish the dominance of Greek and Latin, though a large number of parents were very suspicious of those subjects and many competent judges thought their educational value overrated. The commissioners then made a case for the educational value of modern languages and of natural science, and for the need to set up schools which would concentrate on those subjects and give up Greek in order to do this. Under the existing system the pupils of such schools would not be able to go on to the universities. Though they had no detailed proposals to make for changing the system, 'we venture to suggest to the Universities to modify those arrangements, so that, for instance, a first-rate man of science who knows no Greek shall not (at least in theory and intent) be at any greater disadvantage than a first-rate Greek scholar who knows no science'.

The letter of March 1871 enlarged in more detail on their plans for science teaching. They proposed that all schools giving higher instruction should teach at least one branch of physical science and that a few schools, devoted to modern subjects, should teach several branches. Under certain circumstances they would be prepared to set up schools with a directly scientific/technical basis. In order to help with their planning they asked the commission for information about the value of the different sciences for education, about the teaching time to be made available for them, about methods and apparatus, about the supply of teachers, and about the best means for encouraging scientific studies after school.

The approach to the universities was a failure. At Oxford the Hebdomadal Council refused to consider any change in the regulations, even in the case of students in physical and mathematical subjects (28 November 1870). London too declined to take any action. At Cambridge the omens at first seemed better. A syndicate was set up, which recommended that a knowledge of French and German might be accepted in lieu of a knowledge of Greek in the Previous Examination, but the Senate rejected their report by a very narrow majority (27 April 1871) (*PP* 1872 XXIV: 63–5). At both Oxford and Cambridge the Greek requirement lasted until after the First World War, which made the original concept of a first-grade modern school very difficult to achieve. The commissioners' anxiety to promote natural science may have had some effect in modifying the secondary school curriculum, but it took a long time for the sciences to reach a position of equality with the traditional subjects.

This review of the Endowed School Commissioners' approach to the curriculum explains the hostility which they displayed in many cases towards the teaching of Greek. Though they claimed that the subject was unpopular with many parents, there were others who defended it strongly. In some instances, as at Brentwood in Essex, the commissioners carried through their policy against local opposition. In the case of Bradford they suffered a resounding defeat. The inclusion or exclusion of Greek was the shibboleth which determined the type and, as local people saw it, the prestige of a school. There is a note in the Bradford file, initialled by H. G. Robinson, which says:

> This is the third Bradford cock that has come to crow over the defeat of the Commrs. The pith of the communication (made in very polite & friendly terms) was 'The Commrs. were <u>well beaten</u> and
> true
>
> <u>well deserved</u> it'.
> false

(Ed. 27: 5721, 24 March 1871)

This at least suggests that Canon Robinson had a sense of humour.

Bradford Grammar School lacked any distinguished record of scholarship before 1869, and the draft scheme provided that the master and usher should retire on pension. In a rapidly expanding industrial town there appeared to be little need for the classics and a great need for modern and scientific subjects. Moreover there was a first-grade classical school only nine miles away at Leeds. Fearon, the assistant commissioner, did not think, after meeting the Bradford trustees, that the arguments in favour of a classical school were likely to be very strong, and he suggested to Robinson that there should be a boys' school with two departments – one for ages 10–16 (second-grade) and one for ages 8–14 (third-grade). Greek should be taught at an additional fee in the upper school (Ed. 27: 5721, 29 March 1870).

When Robinson reported to the full board of commissioners he raised the question whether Greek should be allowed in the upper school at all because, if it were taught, the master would concentrate on a small group of picked boys destined for the university. A draft scheme followed quickly (Ed. 27: 5721, 4 June 1870), which followed the lines suggested by Fearon. Money was set aside for a girls' school and for pensions to the master and usher. The boys' school was to educate pupils only up to 16 years. There were to be two departments with fees of £10–20 and £5–10. Greek was not to be taught except to boys already on the school rolls.

The draft schemes raised two separate but related questions: Was the school to be first- or second-grade? Was it to teach Greek? It is surprising that Robinson, who knew the West Riding well, should have supported proposals which appeared to put Bradford in such an inferior position to Leeds with its first-grade classical school. Local feeling was quickly aroused. The governors argued that the school should be first-grade and that Greek should be taught (30 July), and in September a group of gentlemen in the town sent in a memorial making the same points.

In November 1870 the commissioners explained their point of view in two letters to the clerk to the governing body (Ed. 27: 5721, 12, 26

November 1870). They were prepared to give way on the first-grade question and to allow boys to stay to the age of 19. However, in their view, Bradford needed a school of a modern type because of the needs of industry and commerce, and therefore the grammar school should not aim at distinction in classics. Schools, they argued, could not teach everything; courses of study should be restricted, and schools should have a particular 'line' of their own. If Greek were introduced, other subjects would be sacrificed. They thought that the demand for it would be very small, and they cited the example of Bradford High School, a private school which had found that very few boys wanted to learn the language. As a concession they proposed an arrangement similar to that adopted in other schemes. If twenty boys wanted to learn Greek, it might be taught by a master other than the headmaster at an additional fee of at least £1 per quarter. On more general grounds they dismissed the argument that Bradford Grammar School had in former times attracted the sons of prominent local families and might do so again, because since those days the growth of the new public schools had taken boys away from the local grammar schools.

The governors were not convinced. They claimed that there was a large middle and professional class in the town which needed a first-grade school. They did not consider the High School large or important enough to provide a valid example. They denied that they wished to put modern and scientific instruction in an inferior position and they accused the commissioners of imposing 'detailed and restrictive regulations'. Finally, they asked for an inquiry, a request to which the commissioners assented on 16 December 1870 (Ed. 27: 5721, 9 November, 6, 16 December 1870).

The inquiry was held from 10 to 12 January 1871 (report in Ed. 27: 5722). Twenty-three witnesses were examined: four clergymen, two gentlemen of independent means, three physicians, four merchants, one manufacturer, one Town Clerk, two solicitors, one surgeon, one Dissenting minister, one surveyor, one chemist, one master printer, one warehouseman in receipt of weekly wages. At the end of the inquiry more than twice as many others were waiting to give evidence. The testimony showed that between 20 and 70 boys would learn Greek, and 12 witnesses were prepared to have it taught to their own sons. Dr Taylor, surgeon, for example, testified that he had three sons, the youngest at the grammar school and the two elder at boarding schools in Harrogate. He preferred a home education for his boys, and he would send them to the grammar school if it were conducted in a satisfactory manner:

> His eldest son is intended for the medical profession, and Greek is essential for his examinations. . . . In the London University Greek is compulsory but it is not compulsory in the examinations of the Royal College of Surgeons or the Apothecaries Compy but he con-

sidered that it would give advantage in those examinations if known. His second son is intended for the legal profession where Greek is not absolutely required but is extremely valuable. He is very doubtful if he wd send sons to the Grammar School if Greek were not taught. If it were made a first grade school with instruction in that language he should send them there.

(Ed. 27: 5722)

There were probably many middle-class parents in Bradford who held views similar to Dr Taylor's. Greek had not been a success at the High School, witnesses explained, because there were too few boys and they left school too young. Objections were made to the plan to teach the language on a limited basis, and Fearon himself did not recommend this. The evidence given about the number of boys who would leave school over the age of 17 or who would go to university was less complete than on the Greek issue, but the opinion was clearly expressed that a reorganized school would command more confidence and that boys would stay longer.

Fearon was convinced by the governors' arguments. Local opinion was in support of the new governing body and it was important to give it as much freedom as possible. He examined the means by which the teaching of Greek might be organized and suggested that it might be taught only in the senior department which a boy might enter on passing an examination appropriate to a pupil of 12 or 13. This plan would, he thought, prove acceptable to the governors and memorialists.

And so it was done. According to the revised scheme, approved by the Queen in Council on 19 August 1871, Greek might be taught in the senior school (ages 13–19) if the governors thought fit (Ed. 27: 5721). On the principle of 'by their fruits ye shall know them', the Bradford people were thoroughly justified in their stand. The school, under a new headmaster W. H. Keeling, achieved high distinction both in classics and on the modern side. In 1893 there were 428 boys, over 100 of them the sons of clerks, small tradesmen, and artisans, and about 10 boys a year were going on to university. The Return on Endowed Charities of 1897 commented that the school 'now holds its own against the best schools in the country in respect of open scholarships gained at the universities and subsequent university distinctions' (REC West Riding, *PP* 1897 LXVII Pt 5: 115).

The making of the Bradford scheme has been examined in some detail because it illustrates both the commissioners' ideas about the curriculum and some local reactions to them. They had badly misread local feeling, though they were prepared to withdraw once they appreciated the strength of the resistance. At Brentwood in Essex, on the other hand, they persisted in their plans to make a radical change in the position of Greek. As we have seen, there were differences of opinion between the

existing governing body, the Wardens, and a more radical local committee (see pp. 22–3). Initially both groups wanted to establish separate
upper and lower schools, and they agreed that Greek should be taught
in the upper, though not in the lower school. The correspondence
between the commissioners and the assistant commissioners suggests that
from the beginning they were thinking of a definitely 'modern' orientation
for the curriculum. For example, in December 1869, the Wardens were
told that what was needed was 'a thoroughly good middle-class education', including physical science, modern languages, and drawing. Two
assistant commissioners visited the town. When Patrick Cumin came in
May 1870 the Wardens and Dr West the headmaster spoke strongly in
favour of teaching Greek because there was a demand for 'a Classical
Education such as will fit boys for the University', and their arguments
were reinforced by a number of supporting letters from parents (Ed. 27:
1060).

The commissioners seem to have ignored all these expressions of opinion. In August 1870 they produced a draft scheme in which Greek was
not to be taught, though they explained that they would review this if
the universities did not accept their application that Greek should cease
to be necessary for entry. The second assistant commissioner, William
Latham, came in February 1871. He recommended the establishment of
a first-grade modern school and a third-grade commercial school. A
second draft scheme, published in June 1871, again provided that Greek
should not be taught, though by that time both Oxford and Cambridge
had refused to give up the Greek requirement. In March 1871 Roby had
minuted: 'the attempt at least must be made to exclude Greek from
Modern 1st Grade Schools' (Ed. 27: 1060, 11 March 1871). Roby's
minute, it is true, pre-dated the final decision of the Cambridge Senate
at the end of April, but it seems that, even before that event, the
commissioners had decided to adhere to the policy they had chosen,
almost regardless of the difficulties in the way of implementing it.

Their plans received no support in Brentwood, where both the head
and the Wardens objected to the exclusion of Greek and to the proposal
to raise the fees (Ed. 27: 1060, 2 June, 3 August 1871, 20 February, 7
March 1872). Yet the commissioners, though they made some concessions, were not deflected from their general course. The scheme,
because it came before Parliament too late for approval in the 1872
session, was not finally approved until 3 March 1873 (Ed. 27: 1061). It
was substantially the same as the draft, though a partial concession was
made over the teaching of Greek. This was not in future to form part
of the regular course, but it might be taught by someone other than the
headmaster to day boys whose parents expressly desired it at an extra
fee of not less than £4 a year. This was an awkward compromise,
particularly since Greek might not in future be taught to boarders. Thus

the explicit provision in the scheme that boarders might be admitted to the school was of much less value than it might otherwise have been.

The commissioners, in their determination to create a school of a new and untried kind, had satisfied neither the traditional grammar school lobby represented by the headmaster and the Wardens nor the supporters of commercial education like the committee of townspeople. Both in 1874 and in 1877 the governors' clerk requested that Greek might be taught without extra charge (Ed. 27: 1062, 25 September 1874; Ed. 27: 1063, 2 October 1877). The endowment fell in value as a result of agricultural depression, the governors were forced to raise the fees, which in turn reduced the numbers. In 1871 William Latham had found 81 boys (57 day boys and 24 boarders). At Michaelmas 1890 there were 37 day boys and 15 boarders (Ed. 27: 1063). When in the same year Assistant Commissioner Durnford visited the school he found that Greek was taught to any boy who required it, without extra fee. No natural science was taught and there was no laboratory. No commercial school had been established and there was no possibility of maintaining anything beyond the existing grammar school (Ed. 27: 1063, 14 June 1890). After 1891 a happier period began with a new headmaster and a new scheme. The closing decades of the nineteenth century proved to be a difficult period for many grammar schools, not least because of the effects of agricultural depression on endowment revenues. It would not be fair to attribute all Brentwood's troubles after 1873 to the commissioners, but they certainly contributed by their imposition of a scheme based on theory rather than on experience, which was acceptable to no school of thought in the town. The Brentwood story offers a good example of the strong doctrinaire streak in the commissioners' policy-making and their ability to disregard informed local opinion. We shall meet these characteristics again.

Part of the Brentwood plan was to establish a commercial or modern school alongside the old grammar school. There was nothing novel in this, since similar measures had been taken long before, for example, at Bedford, Birmingham, and Macclesfield (*HSE*: 73–4). The commissioners' policy probably related to their dislike of 'bifurcation' and to their desire to set up separate schools for different age-groups and types of curriculum. In a number of cases the proposed second school did not come into existence at all or after a few years the two schools were united (*VCH Lincolnshire* II (1906): 447–8 (Lincoln); *VCH Staffordshire* VI (1979): 176 (Walsall)). Sometimes the two schools harmed one another by competing in the same market or making rival claims on limited endowments (*VCH Suffolk* II (1907): 336 (Ipswich); *VCH Surrey* II (1905): 219 (Battersea)).

Some successes were achieved in creating schools with a more modern/ scientific curriculum, though there could be serious gaps between expressing intentions on paper and putting them into effect. The project of a first-grade modern school, which had been unsuccessful at Brentwood, had been successful at Giggleswick. After a plan to set up a new school incorporating both Giggleswick and Sedbergh had failed, Giggleswick became a first-grade modern school and Sedbergh a first-grade classical school. By a scheme of 1872 Greek was not to form part of the normal course at Giggleswick, but the governors might permit it if they wished. By the 1890s Giggleswick had some 200 boys, all but 20–25 of them boarders. Awards were generally won in mathematics and science, and the school had gained successes at the universities, in London matriculation, army cadetships, medical schools, and the Indian Civil Service (REC West Riding, *PP* 1897 LXVII, Pt 5: 358–73; *BC* VII: 249–52).

Both sets of commissioners supported schools with a scientific/technical bias. An early example is the Bristol Trade School, which was incorporated into Colston's foundation. The Devonshire Commission reported in 1872 that there was an elementary department of a hundred boys, aged 10–12, and a science department of sixty boys aged 12–15 in which mathematics, geometry, chemistry, and physics were taught (*PP* 1872 XXV: 38–9; see also pp. 50, 90). At Keighley the endowments of Drake's and Tonson's charities had been handed over, by a scheme of 1871, partly to found a girls' school and partly to maintain the trade school founded by the mechanics institute, with particular emphasis on scholarships from the elementary schools. There are several later references to the excellence of the teaching in the Trade and Grammar School which attracted both the sons of local manufacturers and boys of the artisan class who won scholarships (*PP* 1872 XXIV: 108–16; *PP* 1884 XXIX: 543–4; *PP* 1887 IX: 242; REC West Riding *PP* 1897 LXVII, Pt 5: 468–72).

Schools of this kind did not always succeed in achieving their objectives. Parmiter's School, Bethnal Green in London, a school for boys aged 7–16, was described in an examiner's report of 1893 as 'essentially a *modern* school in which special attention is given to science, art, and modern languages, that is to say there is efficient technical teaching of the best kind' (REC London, *PP* 1897 LXVI, Pt 2: 21, 26). A similar school, the Roan boys' school at Greenwich, had a provision in its scheme of 1873 that special attention should be given to industrial and technical training (Ed. 27: 3023; REC London *PP* 1899 LXIX: 288). A Charity Commission inspector's report of 1894 found that the school had a normal second-grade curriculum, but the governors had not been able to adjust it to industrial and technical teaching. Natural science teaching could not be carried very far because the school had no laboratory (Ed. 27: 3026, 26 July 1894). In many such schools the money for effective science teaching did not become available until the Technical Instruction Committees began to make grants in the 1890s. In that decade the Charity Commissioners approved some schemes with a definitely technical emphasis. At Mansfield, for example, the scheme of 1891 for Brunt's Technical School was designed to offer to both boys and girls from elementary schools a course of instruction related to the needs of the trades and manufactures of the district (CC 39th Rep. *PP* 1892 XXVII: 48; *VCH Nottinghamshire* II (1910): 250).

By that time technical education in London had been greatly stimulated by grants from the funds of the city parochial charities (Owen 1965: 283–4, 292–4), and the report and evidence of the Bryce Commission reflect a keen interest in new developments in school curricula. Both the Endowed Schools and the Charity Commissioners had done something over the previous quarter-century to help the new subjects like natural science and modern languages to establish themselves. In their early days the Endowed School Commission had made some bad mistakes. Their policies were too rigid; they paid too little attention to local opinion. The Charity Commissioners, though they shared some of the same characteristics, were generally more moderate. Yet change was very slow. There was a good deal of in-built resistance. There was never enough money. It was difficult to find competent teachers. Yet the pressures applied by the commissioners to broaden and liberalize the curriculum had made some contribution to innovation and to helping the endowed schools to meet more fully the needs of the new age.

5 Conflict in the provinces – Bristol, Birmingham

The work of the commissioners has now been discussed from three aspects: the respective claims of poverty and merit; politics, administration, and religion; and the curriculum. Before saying more about the endowed schools in the 1880s and 1890s, it will be convenient to look in more detail at some endowments. To do this for many cases would be tedious and repetitive, yet so much of the debate was highly localized and related to the concerns of particular groups that it is desirable to provide some specific examples. The general treatment so far has been topical, yet in any situation a whole mass of topics was confused together. The case-study method reminds us that any actual debate was much more disorderly and confused than is suggested by the neatness of thematic treatment. For examples I have chosen Bristol and Birmingham. Both had local groups with strong and contrasting views on political and religious issues, and the two cities are very different from one another.

BRISTOL

Bristol was a place of ancient wealth and strong local traditions, which was not likely to take kindly to what Bristolians would regard as interference from London. It possessed wealthy hospital endowments which presented the same problems as those already studied in the case of Emanuel Hospital. Its grammar school, after a period of decline in the early part of the century, was flourishing under an able head, J. W. Caldicott, appointed in 1860 (Hill 1951). He was very sensitive about the status of his school and very suspicious about what he thought was the tendency of the commissioners to favour Clifton College, founded in 1862, which had quickly established itself as one of the most successful of the new public schools under an able headmaster, John Percival.

The grammar school, together with Queen Elizabeth's Hospital for boys and the Red Maids' School for girls, was administered by the municipal charity trustees set up under the Municipal Corporations Act of 1835. Colston's Hospital for boys was another wealthy foundation, independently administered by the Society of Merchant Venturers. It was always clear that Colston's would need to preserve its separate governing body. It had a strongly denominational character, falling under sect. 19 of the 1869 Act, as the other schools did not. The cathedral grammar school had been merely an elementary school in the 1860s and will not be discussed further here (*VCH Gloucestershire* II (1907): 381–2).

The negotiations over the charity trustees' schools revolved round three major issues: the future status and development of the grammar school; the provision for boarding and maintenance at Queen Elizabeth's and the Red Maids'; and the proposal to establish a girls' high school. In January 1870 Caldicott wrote a long memorandum about the position and prospects of the grammar school (Ed. 27: 1289, 22 January 1870). The school, he explained, had been very successful at the universities and was full to overflowing with 240 boys. The fees varied from £6 to £10 a year according to age. Caldicott thought that they might be slightly increased, though Bristol parents had come to expect very low fees. There was a need for scholarships to enable boys of limited means to come to the school, and for a proper entrance examination.

Despite its status and university connections the grammar school was much the poorest of the major Bristol foundations. According to Caldicott the net endowments were as follows:

	£
Grammar School	705
Queen Elizabeth's Hospital	5,400 (approx.)
Colston's Hospital	3,399
Red Maids' School	2,500 (approx.)

The city was also rich in charities and doles of many other kinds. Caldicott pointed out that the grammar school had to work under many difficulties. The buildings were badly situated and in poor condition, and it would be desirable to move the school to a new site near the residential districts of Clifton and Redland where most of the boys lived. The head and the other masters were seriously underpaid, and there was need for a larger staff, including a master to teach science. The trustees were strongly influenced by political pressures, and they were much more concerned with their other interests than with the grammar school.

Most of the discussions in Bristol in 1870 were concentrated rather on the hospital endowments than on the grammar school. *The Times and Mirror*, the local newspaper most hostile to the commissioners, explained that in future no board, lodging, or clothing were to be given, and all the schools were to become day schools. There would be no free education 'so that the charities left entirely for the instruction of poor children will be made to subsidize an education machinery for the upper and middle classes, which was certainly not what the founders intended' (Ed. 27: 1289, 9 March 1870). The commissioners wrote to J. G. Fitch, their assistant commissioner, in March 1870, pointing out that the three hospital schools (Queen Elizabeth's, Colston's, Red Maids') had a gross income of £14,000 a year and educated 436 children with no arrangements at all for higher training for the more able (Ed. 27: 1289, 15 March 1870). When Fitch himself addressed the town council in July he took up the same line of argument. At that time, he claimed, 80 per cent of the endowments were spent on charity rather than on education. In the wealth of its hospital endowments Bristol came after London and Edinburgh, and there was money enough for a co-ordinated plan of secondary schools of different types so that able children could advance to higher educational levels (Ed. 27: 1289; *Western Daily Press* 7 July 1870).

What Fitch was thinking of can be seen in the extremely ambitious. and far-reaching scheme which he sent to the secretary of the charity trustees in December 1870 (Ed. 27: 1289; *Bristol Endowed Schools*). There would be two governing bodies, one of them for Colston's because of the requirements of sect. 19 of the Act. Fees would be charged in all the schools, but free places, many of them for pupils from public elementary schools, would be reserved as well. Colston's would educate 300 boarders and there would be two day schools in addition. The 'undenominational' schools would fall into four groups. The grammar school would educate 300 boys. The City school (Queen Elizabeth's) would educate both boarders and day boys. The old Red Maids' would become a girls' boarding school (Whitson's School) plus a boys' and a girls' day school. Finally a new school, the Queen's School, would be established as a higher school for 200 girls with the same fees (10–15 guineas) as those charged at the grammar school. The new arrangements would provide accommodation for 1,600 boys and 850 girls.

Detailed recommendations were also made about the sites of the schools and the grades into which they were to fall. The grammar school should be rehoused near Tyndalls Park on the borders of Clifton and Redland. It was hoped to add to its endowments, under sect. 30 of the Act of 1869, the income of the Peloquin trust, an eighteenth-century endowment for poor men and women, which was largely unused. The Queen's School should not be placed too near the city centre. The boarding school on the Red Maids' foundation should be located in the country but not too far from Bristol. There was no proposal to rehouse Colston's, which had moved to Stapleton in 1861. The grammar school, Fitch argued, should develop on lines 'essentially different from that of the great Public Boarding Schools for the richer classes, of which Clifton College is so successful an example'. It seems likely that the commissioners had earlier thought of incorporating Clifton College in some way into the reorganization. Fitch's differentiation between the role and status of the two schools, with Clifton College placed in the superior position, was unfortunate and unwise, and it caused much later trouble with Caldicott and his staff.

The City School was to be second-grade. The boys on the foundation would come at about 13 and 60 per cent of them would be boarded as well as taught. The Queen's School would be of the same type as Cheltenham Ladies' College. Some boarders might be taken and some of the exhibitions reserved for children from the lower schools. The other schools in the plan were to be third-grade. Colston's (boys) and Whitson's (girls) would be for boarders, many of them foundationers (orphans and elementary school children). The remainder would probably be the children of farmers and country tradesmen, and all were to remain only to the age of 15.

Fitch's plan was a remarkably complete exposition of the philosophy of the Taunton and Lyttelton commissioners, so complete indeed that it was not likely to overcome the objections of the many local interests which saw themselves threatened by it. There was no shortage of comment. The Trades Delegates and Working Men's Conservative Association complained that the plan took the benefits away from the class which the founders had intended to benefit (Ed. 27: 1289; *Western Daily Press*, 13 January 1871). The *Western Daily Press* thought that more attention had been paid to founders' intentions than might have been expected, but still found many faults, for example, the high level of the proposed fees for the grammar school (Ed. 27: 1289, 2 February 1871). The grammar school masters concentrated on what they saw as the tendency to favour Clifton College, a proprietary school founded on the basis of class exclusion, at the expense of their own school, which must be allowed to develop on the lines appropriate for a first-class school for the benefit of all the citizens of Bristol (Ed. 27: 1289; *Observations on the Scheme*, March 1871).

The charity trustees, whose views were the most important of all, were critical. They reaffirmed their anxiety to maintain the provisions for clothing and maintenance at Queen Elizabeth's and the Red Maids', and they expressed their confidence in the existing system of education in those schools. They were ready, they claimed, to consider 'judicious modifications', and Fitch accepted that they had gone some way to meet the commissioners' viewpoint, though he noted after a meeting in June 1871 that they were still anxious to educate and maintain the children free of charge, that they had not accepted paying boarders, and that they had made no provision either for a second-grade school for boys or for a higher school for girls.

In August 1871 the commissioners wrote to the trustees expressing their views. They mentioned the Peloquin endowment which would appropriately be used to enable boys from elementary schools to go to the grammar school. They were prepared to allow a slightly lower fee for the school than Fitch had suggested. They accepted the 160 boarders at Queen Elizabeth's which the trustees had suggested, though they were anxious to admit paying boarders as well. The trustees had proposed a leaving age of 14 at the school. The commissioners wanted to raise this to 15, though that would still make the school third-grade rather than second-grade, as Fitch had suggested. So far as the girls' schools were concerned, they wished to admit paying boarders to the Red Maids' and to make one of the proposed day schools more expensive than the other. They regretted the abandonment of the high school for girls, and thought that a clause should appear in the scheme allowing the governing body to spend money on this when funds allowed.

After this detailed description of the positions taken up by the two sides the commissioners' draft scheme, which was forwarded to the trustees in December 1871, can be dealt with briefly (Ed. 27: 1289). All the foundations were to be incorporated as the Bristol United Schools. The charity trustees had a strong representation on the new governing body, which also contained nominees of the town council and of the school board. Queen Elizabeth's was ultimately to contain both boarders and day scholars, and no boy was to remain over the age of 15, or of 16 if special permission was given. The arrangements for the Red Maids' were similar. There were in addition to be day schools for both boys and girls, and a girls' higher school was to be established after the other provisions of the scheme had been carried out. All the exhibitions were to be awarded on merit. At both the boarding schools limits were placed on the number of foundation scholars who were to be maintained wholly without charge.

There were to be lengthy negotiations before the schemes were finally approved by the Queen in Council in May 1875. The principal points of controversy were these. There was strong opposition in Bristol, both from the charity trustees and from Caldicott and the grammar school masters to the incorporation of all the schools into a single foundation, and this plan was abandoned in the revised scheme of February 1873 which made separate arrangements for the grammar school and for Queen Elizabeth's and the Red Maids' (Ed. 27: 1291, 28 February 1873). The change was clearly favourable to Caldicott's plans to maintain the status of his own school, but his fear and suspicion of the commissioners were not allayed. He continued to argue that they favoured the interests of Clifton College against those of the grammar school. For example, he told Lyttelton in a letter that the commissioners' veto over the choice of a new site might be used to destroy his school as a first-grade school. The site suggested by the assistant commissioner was one in which no first-grade institution could succeed. The original site near Tyndalls Park was unacceptable to him because it was too near to Clifton College and would therefore be harmful to its interests (Ed. 27: 1291, 7 October 1873). As a result of this letter, Fitch wrote to Lyttelton denying that he had ever used language or taken measures of the kind about which Caldicott complained (Ed. 27: 1291, 11 October 1873).

The commissioners tried very hard to get money set aside for the higher education of girls, both from the existing endowments and from the non-educational funds like the Peloquin trust. They stressed their responsibilities under sect. 12 of the Act of 1869. 'Looking at the very large endowments already devoted to boys' education in Bristol', Roby wrote to Caldicott, 'it does seem to me very questionable to convert a large amount of non-educational charities to educational purposes in connection with the [boys'] Grammar School only. Girls' education ought to have some more endowment than they have now' (Ed. 27: 1291, 6 August 1873). In May 1873 the charity trustees refused to agree to appropriate endowments either from the grammar school or from the Red Maids' to the girls' high school (Ed. 27: 1291, 26 May 1873). Caldicott argued with some justice that, if the grammar school endowment were to be charged to support the girls' high school, it would be impossible to carry on his school effectively since the funds were already in deficit (Ed. 27: 1291, 19 May 1873). It must be remembered that the grammar school was much the poorest of the major Bristol institutions. Finally, at a conference with the trustees in October 1873, the proposal for the high school was withdrawn. In July the trustees had argued: 'the Girls' Sch is not wanted, would not be used by children of all classes, & is not a proper application of funds left for the poor' (Ed. 27: 1291, 16 July 1873). A proposal that women should be on the grammar-school governing body was also cut out, though they were retained for the Red Maids' and the proposed girls' day schools (Ed. 27: 1291, ESC Board, 5 January 1874).

There was a similar tug-of-war about the disposal of the non-educational funds. The commissioners wanted not less than half the money to be used for the education of girls. The trustees argued that the grammar school needed all the money available. Finally, £5,000 from the Peloquin charity was transferred to the grammar school and £5,000 to the Red Maids', while the grammar school received about £4,500 from other charities. In return for the Peloquin money the school was required to establish exhibitions for poor boys who had attended an elementary school in the borough or Queen Elizabeth's Hospital. The question of how much money would be available to the grammar school also affected the move to the new site. Here the problems were successfully overcome and the new buildings at Tyndalls Park in the area which Caldicott had originally suggested were opened in 1879.

The debate about the reorganization of Queen Elizabeth's and the Red Maids' went over familiar ground – selection by merit and the role of competitive examination, the payment of clothing allowances, the interpretation to be given to 'poverty'. One interesting feature is the strong localism of the Bristolians. There were strong objections to a proposal that some places should be set aside for children from surrounding counties. The trustees would have none of that, speaking in one of their letters of 'their efforts to preserve the endowment left by Bristol worthies, for Bristol orphans, and Bristol poor' (Ed. 27: 1291, 2 February 1872). The governors of Colston's took a similar line. 'They do not wish [the hospital]', commented an office paper of 1871, 'to be a great central institution for the district, but desire to confine 4/5 of its advantages to the children of their own city' (Ed. 27: 1274, 15 June 1871).

The final scheme represented a compromise, which was in many ways favourable to the trustees. There were to be 160 boys as foundation boarders at Queen Elizabeth's and 80 girls at the Red Maids'. All awards were to be made as 'the reward of merit'. For the awards to orphans and poor children:

> candidates to the number of not more than twice the number of vacancies shall be selected on the ground of merit only, to be ascertained as aforesaid, and the admissions shall be awarded to such of the candidates so selected as the Governors in their discretion shall judge most fitting to be objects of bounty.
>
> (Ed. 27: 1293, Scheme, clause 47)

The commissioners had been anxious to admit fee-paying boarders in addition, but that provision did not appear in the final scheme. Since no boy was to remain over the age of 15, and foundation boarders normally not over the age of 14, the level of education was not likely to be very high. Provision was made for the establishment of day schools for boys and for girls, but in fact these were not set up.

The fight was fought to the bitter end since two of the trustees sent in objections after the schemes had reached the Committee of Council in August 1874 (Ed. 27: 1312, 18 September 1874). In the end there was not much left of Fitch's ambitious planning. The grammar school, after initial difficulties, could feel that it had done well. It had gained a new building on a good site and a share in the Peloquin endowment. The girls' high school had been abandoned, and there was no boys' second-grade school to bridge the gap between the grammar school and Queen Elizabeth's. The two hospital schools had been modified but not transformed. The power to provide clothing had been retained by the governors. There were no paying boarders to modify the eleemosynary atmosphere, and the leaving age was kept very low. The proposed day schools were never set up. Perhaps the commissioners, as in other cases, had initially been too ambitious. Perhaps the advent of the school board made the provision of such schools unnecessary. Clearly the need for a girls' high school was quickly felt in the city despite the discouraging tone of the charity trustees. Clifton High School was opened by one body of shareholders in 1877 and Redland High School by another in 1882 (see p. 222; *VCH Gloucestershire* II: 387–8; MacInnes and Whittard 1955: 317–18).

While these protracted negotiations went on with the charity trustees, parallel talks were going on with the Society of Merchant Venturers, who were governors of Colston's Hospital. These too were prolonged; Fitch first met the standing committee of the society in March 1870 and the scheme was finally approved in February 1875 (Ed. 27: 1274). The points of debate were much the same as those already examined, though they were complicated by denominational issues, since Colston's fell under sect. 19 of the Act, and by the existence of Mr Colston's Nominees, a body of patrons and visitors who exercised considerable influence over the management of the trust. The final scheme for Colston's Hospital has three points of special interest. It allowed the admission of boys to the hospital as fee-payers. It incorporated into the foundation the Bristol trade school which had been established by Canon Henry Moseley in 1857 on the basis of an old diocesan school, and out of which later developed the Merchant Venturers Technical College (Ed. 27: 1274; *VCH Gloucestershire* II: 385; *HSE*: 199). It made provision of not less than £200 a year for a girls' school. This was not opened until 1891, when it 'rapidly developed into a secondary school of the highest type' (*VCH Gloucestershire* II: 385). So, by the end of the century, the reorganized Colston's endowment had promoted important new initiatives in the city of Bristol.

BIRMINGHAM

At Birmingham negotiations were even more protracted than at Bristol since the scheme was not settled until March 1878. Though the battle was just as keenly fought, the issues were very different. There was no hospital school and therefore none of the debates which had centred on Queen Elizabeth's or Emanuel at Westminster. The central question was political. The existing governing body, which renewed itself by co-optation, was Tory and Anglican. The town council, which was Liberal and Nonconformist, wanted the endowment controlled by the representatives of the people, who would inevitably have been of their own political and religious colour. One of the governors wrote to Lyttelton in February 1871:

> The political dissenters predominate [in the town council]; they are bent on disestablishing the Church: a perfectly fair intention. But moved by passion they make even the promotion of Education subordinate to their political scheme, and they will not, if they can help it, return a single churchman to the Grammar School Board.
>
> (Ed. 27: 4891, 10 February 1871)

King Edward's foundation was wealthy and with the steady growth of the town getting wealthier. It consisted of the grammar school, which had a high reputation for scholarship, and of four elementary schools for boys and girls, re-established under an Act of Parliament of 1831. Though these schools had been set up for the children of poorer inhabitants, they were in fact recruited from the families of artisans, tradesmen, and small manufacturers (*VCH Warwickshire* VII (1964): 549–55; *PP* 1873 VIII, App. 5, no. 3: 711–12). The report of the Schools Inquiry Commission had pointed out the feeling caused by the exclusion of Liberals and Nonconformists from the governing body, and had suggested a reorganization which would set up second- and third-grade schools alongside a central grammar school, divided into classical, scientific, and mercantile departments (SIC I: 516). The cause of reform was supported in Birmingham by the Free Grammar School Association, set up in 1865, which advocated a revised curriculum and a more open system of management (Allsobrook 1986: 198; Smith 1982: 177).

The attitudes of the two parties were set out in evidence a little later to the select committee of 1873. William Mathews, who had been bailiff (chairman of the governing body) argued that the democratic electorate which chose the town council was not likely to be able to make sound judgements about the work of the schools. There had in practice never been any religious difficulties and the school system had 'always shown the most careful regard for the opinions of Nonconformists' (*PP* 1873 VIII: 540. 3165; 566: 3688). Frank Schnadhorst and the Rev. John Jenkin Brown, both speaking for the Birmingham-based Central Nonconformist Committee, claimed that popularly elected representatives should have a majority on governing bodies and that all restrictions should be removed which gave an advantage to one section of the community over another. On the King Edward's governing body, Schnadhorst claimed, churchmen had 'what may fairly be called an unjust monopoly' (ibid.: 646–76, 693–6). In his view it would be better if no religious instruction were given in schools at all.

The governors put forward their own draft scheme in July 1870 (Ed. 27: 4891). They suggested a reformed governing body with some members elected by the town council, but on which they retained a majority. The governors were to have the power to charge fees and to decide on the proportions of free and fee-paying scholars. The head and second masters should be members of the Church of England, and religious instruction, unless exemption was claimed, should be provided in conformity with its doctrine. An upper school for girls should be established, a requirement which appears in the plans of all the different groups. On this subject there was a major difference of opinion between Bristol and Birmingham. When Assistant Commissioner Hammond was given instructions in December 1870 before a visit to the town, they included the following note on the girls' school: 'this of course is assumed as indispensable, and the only question is of the time' (Ed. 27: 4891, 17 December 1870).

The opinions of the town council and of the Free Grammar School Association were similar to those of the governors, except on the crucial issue of the governing body. A committee of the association argued that there should be no free places except on the result of competitive examination, and that scholarships should be provided for the children of poor parents. They wanted a greater place to be given to modern subjects in the curriculum, and they told Assistant Commissioner Hammond that they regarded the girls' school as the most pressing addition to be made. The governing body, they thought, should have three-quarters of its members chosen by the town council and school board, and the remaining quarter elected by 'combined representatives' (Ed. 27: 4891, 'Suggestions', October 1870).

The town council also supported the upper school for girls and agreed that there should be only a limited number of free places, but they objected to any co-opted members of the governing body (Ed. 27: 4891, 7 February 1871). The mayor was asked to call a public meeting, which was held on 1 March 1871 and which resolved that the governing body of the future 'shall be absolutely responsible to the burgesses, such responsibility being based upon the principle of representation'. *Aris' Birmingham Gazette* claimed that the meeting was a failure because only about 300 people attended (Ed. 27: 4891, 4 March 1871), but among them were many of the leading Liberals. Jesse Collings, later to be an active agricultural reformer, claimed that the school should be managed by the people because it was their property. He, like other speakers, was careful to say that management by the town council would not mean that the endowment would be taken over for the support of elementary education in order to reduce the rates. It was strongly argued by several speakers that what was needed was a system of graded schools which would bring forward the able children of the working class, a system of which the grammar school would be the apex (Ed. 27: 4891; *Birmingham Morning News*, 19 January, 2 March 1871).

In April and May 1871 Hammond wrote a very lengthy report on his Birmingham consultations. On the religious question he thought that most of those who were likely to use the schools would be opposed to any religious teaching of a distinctly denominational kind, and he suggested that the scheme should actually require undenominational teaching. Though he did not make the specific reference, this would presumably have involved something like the Cowper-Temple clause of the 1870 Education Act. He had found general support for the idea of giving free admission only on a competitive basis, though there were differences of opinion about the proportion of free places to be given. Though the governors were in favour of admitting boarders, local opinion was strongly against them (Ed. 27: 4893). Hammond also raised the question of sites. The existing grammar school in New Street was very centrally situated, but the site was otherwise inconvenient and very noisy. The governors thought that in the future the grammar school might be moved, though they did not think that the time had yet come to do this.

The commissioners' draft scheme was sent in confidence to the governors in November 1871, and it was finally submitted to the Committee of Council on 24 December 1872 (Ed. 27: 4893). In the later version there were to be twenty-one governors – twelve representative (eight chosen by the town council, four by the school board), eight co-optative, and one chosen by the staffs of the upper, middle and trade schools. For boys there were to be upper, middle, trade, and lower schools, for girls upper and lower schools, and the girls' upper school was to be the first priority among new developments. All the schools were to be day schools. The governors were to make provision for religious education, and no requirement was made that the head and second masters should be members of the Church of England. The proportion of foundationers in all the schools was laid down. In the original draft it was laid down that the governors should make provision to remove the grammar school from the New Street site. In the December 1872 scheme this was modified so that the governors might make the removal when opportunity offered and with the sanction of the Charity Commissioners.

As was to be expected, the draft scheme of November 1871 produced lengthy comments from all the interested parties, though by that stage there was not much new to be added to the debate. There was general dislike for the proposal to remove the grammar school from New Street. The governors found the provisions for religious education vague, ambiguous, and 'likely to lead to rancorous differences' (Ed. 27: 4893, 7 December 1871). The Central Nonconformist Committee objected to the provision of religious education in the schools (Ed. 27: 4891, 27 April 1872), and the Free Grammar School Association thought that it should not be made compulsory. However the association's tone was conciliatory and they acknowledged that attempts had been made to meet their views (Ed. 27: 4891, 3 June 1872). When the town council discussed their reply, Jesse Collings moved an amendment that the schools should be completely free. The amendment was lost, but it represented a change of view which will come up again later (Ed. 27: 4893; *Birmingham Weekly Post*, 25 May 1872). While these debates were going on, there was a change in the headship of the grammar school. In June 1872, A. R. Vardy was appointed to succeed Charles Evans; he was to reign until 1900.

The scheme was approved by the Committee of Council on 8 February 1873; the only remaining hope for its opponents was that it might be rejected by Parliament. Since the governors were unappeased, the town council and the Central Nonconformist Committee took up the defence of a scheme which in fact gave them a great deal. The town council sent a circular to MPs and a petition to the House of Lords. They regretted that the governing body was not to be chosen entirely by popular election, but they claimed that 'its partial recognition will give increased strength and efficiency to the School' (Ed. 27: 4893). The rejection of the scheme would, they argued, be detrimental to the interests of both the school and the town. The Central Nonconformist Committee thought that it would be most satisfactory to the inhabitants to leave the question of religious education to the governing body (Ed. 27: 4893). Though neither group made the point explicitly, they must have felt that a majority of representative governors – twelve out of twenty-one – would quickly be able to give the affairs of the foundation a direction acceptable to Liberals and Nonconformists.

From the other side the governors prayed that Parliament would address the Queen to withhold her consent. They objected to the new governing body, to the control which would be given to the Charity Commissioners over its decisions, and to the limitations on its administrative powers. They objected to the provisions for religious instruction, the nature of which should be fixed in the scheme itself, to the clause making it obligatory to move the school from New Street, to the numbers fixed for the upper and middle schools, and to the high fees. They objected to the clause that no boy could hold a scholarship in the upper school unless he had previously attended another school of the foundation or an elementary school, and in general they claimed that the scheme would damage the upper school and first-grade education in the town (Ed. 27: 4893, Governors' *Case*). The same point about the harm that would be done to the upper school was made in a printed letter to Lyttelton from the headmaster, A. R. Vardy, to which were added supporting letters from distinguished old boys like B. F. Westcott, J. B. Lightfoot, and E. W. Benson, the former headmasters E. H. Gifford and Charles Evans, and Edwin Abbott, headmaster of the City of London School, who had been an assistant master (Ed. 27: 4893). Privately, the bishop of the diocese, Philpot of Worcester, expressed his support to Lyttelton for the governors' case.

Powerful opposition had therefore been raised to the scheme when Lord Salisbury rose in the House of Lords on 19 May 1873 to move an address that consent to it might be withheld (*Hansard* 216: 74–95). In his speech Salisbury concentrated on the religious issue rather than on the question of political control. The school, Salisbury claimed, had had a religious base for 300 years and this was now being removed. The scheme would hand over control to the town council which was opposed to religious instruction. The school had been well managed under the old scheme and Nonconformists had been liberally treated. From the government benches several speakers emphasized the unrepresentative nature of the old trust; what was proposed was moderate and fair to all parties. Lyttelton himself spoke, arguing that no case could be made for treating the school as a distinctively Church of England foundation under the terms of the Act of 1869. He dealt with various specific points like the control of the headmaster over the lower schools, and in general denied that under the new constitution any one element would be able to dominate the others. Town councils and school boards might be criticized, he said, but they 'were the best representative bodies that the Commissioners could find' (col. 92). The Bishop of Bath and Wells, Lord Arthur Hervey, urged both that the scheme would inflict a heavy blow on the legitimate interests of the Church of England in Birmingham and that if it were approved, other similar schemes would pass. If the scheme failed, 'it would give a breathing time to all parties' (col. 94). Perhaps the bishop's fears summed up the fears of many Tory Anglicans about the future, and their apprehensions were expressed in the vote. Salisbury had a majority of forty-six and so the Birmingham scheme was rejected. He had repeated his success in the Emanuel Hospital Scheme of two years earlier (see p. 12).

After this major rebuff the Endowed Schools Commissioners did no more. In reply to an enquiry in January 1874 from the Central Noncon-formist Committee, they wrote that the House of Lords vote had placed them in a position of considerable difficulty, and they had little hope that they could renew the scheme with any hope of success (Ed. 27: 4893, 28 January 1874). The next initiative was taken by the governors themselves in May 1875. By that time a Conservative government, likely to be sympathetic to their views, was in power and the Charity Com-missioners were in office. In the governors' new proposals (Ed. 27: 4899) the co-opted governors were to have a majority over the representative, and the existing governors were to hold office until their numbers were reduced to the new total. The governors were to provide religious worship and instruction 'except in so far as such practice includes the teaching or learning of any Catechism', which was very similar to Ham-mond's plan of 1871 for undenominational teaching. Fees and free schol-arships were to be settled at the governors' discretion, and they might restrict a proportion of the scholarships to candidates from elementary schools or from other schools of the foundation. The headmaster of the boys' high school was to be a member of the Church of England.

The Charity Commissioners wrote back on 15 June to say that in general terms the governors' plans were acceptable, though there was some debate about the appropriate wording of the clauses covering religious education. Such rapidity of movement suggests collusion between the two sides, though there is no evidence of this in the files. The commissioners' draft scheme was published towards the end of July 1875. It accepted the proposed structure of the governing body. It laid down that the governors should provide for suitable prayers and for instruction 'according to the principles of the Christian faith'. It enabled the governors to remove any of the schools to 'other convenient sites,' and it settled the very low figure of 10 per cent as the proportion of free scholarships in any school.

Charles Evans, who had remained in the district as rector of Solihull, warned at once that serious opposition was likely (Ed. 27: 4899, 22 July 1875). Such opposition came very quickly and from all the expected sources. Naturally the composition of the governing body was a major grievance. During this second set of negotiations the religious question was not raised, but there was a strong demand for free education, whereas it had been generally accepted earlier that fees should be charged. The change was clearly the result of the development of the board schools and of a national system of elementary education since 1870. The board schools themselves were not free, but Radicals hoped that they would become so. Since so many more children were now being educated, there was likely to be a much greater demand for secondary education for many of them, and the charging of fees would cut off opportunities for many children. The governors, on the other hand, argued that to charge fees made it possible to extend the advantages of the foundation to those who could not pay. Both they and A. R. Vardy objected to the very small proportion of free scholarships allowed in the commissioners' scheme (Ed. 27: 4899, 21 September 1875 (Vardy); 22 September 1875, 27 May 1876 (governors)). Vardy explained that about 30 per cent of the boys in the grammar school had at one time or another been in an elementary school. Very few boys were the sons of rich parents, and he feared that a high fee would result in a serious loss of boys (Ed. 27: 4899, 16 October 1876).

Proceedings were suspended at the end of 1875 as the result of the death of the chief charity commissioner, and the scheme was not finally submitted to the Committee of Council until 28 February 1877. In July 1876 the commissioners had informed the governors of some substantial changes to the original scheme. Three of the co-opted members were to be replaced by representatives of the universities of Oxford, Cambridge, and London. The view was reiterated that free education should be ended, but the proposal was made to raise the proportion of free scholars to 33 per cent from the 10 per cent originally suggested (Ed. 27: 4899, 10 July 1876).

The proposed 'university' governors were yet another rock of offence to the town council and their allies, who urged that the people of Birmingham were fully competent to manage their own institutions without outside help (Ed. 27: 4899, 20 February 1877). When the scheme was before the Committee of Council the Mayor with Alderman Collings and the three borough MPs, John Bright, P. H. Muntz, and Joseph Chamberlain, went to see the Lord President and the Vice-President to protest (Ed. 27: 4899; *Birmingham Daily Post*, 12 April 1877), and after the Lord President had approved the scheme, John Bright brought it before the House of Commons. Bright's motion for an address that the scheme should be rejected came up on 5 March 1878. All three MPs spoke in the debate, Chamberlain laying particular stress on the case for free education. Among speakers on the other side there was a strong sense that local elected bodies were not the best people to manage education. Sir Thomas Acland, a man of wide experience in these matters, warned against 'a principle which would compel them to give way to every petty local influence in the boroughs' (*Hansard* 238: 777–95). Bright's motion was lost by 129 votes to 70, so the scheme of 1878 was finally approved. Five years later it was modified when the lower middle schools of 1878 were transformed into grammar schools taking boys and girls up to the age of 16. In their original form these schools had been replaced by the higher-grade schools set up by the school board, and it was appropriate for them to become second-grade schools (Hutton 1952: 52–3). At the end of the century King Edward's foundation comprised a high school for boys, a high school for girls, four boys' grammar schools, and four girls' grammar schools. In the 1890s there were 450 boys and 250 girls in the high schools, 950–1,000 boys and 800+ girls in the grammar schools (*BC* II: 177 (Vardy)). With its great resources the foundation contributed towards giving Birmingham one of the best educational systems of any city in England.

6   The Charity Commissioners after 1875

The Endowed Schools Commissioners had defined their principal objectives in their report of 1872 (*PP* 1872 XXIV: 10). They had endeavoured to put the governing bodies on a more popular basis, to grade or classify the schools, to ensure that substantial fees were charged (with free places for able children), to secure some independence for the head teacher, and to introduce modern subjects into the curriculum. The same threads of policy run through the work of the Charity Commissioners after 1874, though there were substantial differences between the two bodies. H. J. Roby told the Bryce Commission that the Charity Commissioners were much more independent of the government of the day than the Endowed Schools Commissioners had been. The Charity Commissioners had, he thought, 'a certain judicial character, and from long tradition their own method of working', whereas the Endowed Schools Commissioners had been set up as a government agency to carry out a specific task. On the other hand, that close connection with government strengthened the hand of Lyttelton and his colleagues (*BC* IV; 433: 16543).

Perhaps in the end the very independence of the Charity Commission and of its endowed schools department, which Roby noted, was a factor of weakness rather than of strength. They lacked any effective link with Parliament, with the Cabinet or with other government departments. The faults of the Endowed Schools Commission stand out clearly enough and have not been glossed over here. At least Lyttelton and his associates were men of ideas who saw problems against a wide perspective and were prepared to fight on large issues. Their successors often give the impression of competent and hard-worked officials, narrow in their sympathies and insensitive to the ideas and suggestions of people outside their own rather small circle of lawyers and administrators. Their policies were more moderate than those of their predecessors. The reverse side of that moderation was a tendency to be blinkered and over-cautious. They acted like bureaucrats; their predecessors had acted more like entrepreneurs, and perhaps it was entrepreneurs that the endowed schools needed (Bishop 1971: ch. 12).

In terms of work done the Bryce Commission report of 1895 recorded that since 1869 five-sevenths of the total income covered by the Endowed Schools Act had been dealt with. In England 851 schemes and 127 amending schemes had been made (*BC* I: 24–5). This was a substantial achievement, but the work, which Forster had thought could be completed in four to five years, was still unfinished. When the commissioners were examined by the select committee of 1886–7 they claimed that they had acted in the moderate spirit of Canon Robinson rather than in the style of Lord Lyttelton and Mr Roby (*PP* 1886 IX: 93: 910). They had paid more careful attention to points of law than their predecessors, they had been more careful to consider local feeling, and they had kept in their minds the 'due regard' clause (sect. 11) of the 1869 Act, which was thought to safeguard the interests of the poor (ibid.: 168: 1711–12). It was, they thought, an advantage that they, unlike the Endowed Schools Commissioners, could act either under the Charitable Trusts Acts or the Endowed Schools Acts (CC 29th Rep. *PP* 1882 XX: 37). D. R. Fearon, secretary of the endowed schools department, explained that there were advantages in having a single body responsible for both legal and educational work. Relationships generally had improved because the commissioners were in regular contact with the schools over many matters that were not contentious. Having had experience of both sets of commissioners, Fearon thought that after 1874 there were fewer cases not proceeded with or schemes which had not worked in practical terms than had been so before that date (*PP* 1886 IX: 413–14: 5884–6; 421: 5959–61).

Thus the Charity Commissioners made a favourable judgement of their own record. For the first six or seven years after 1875 they worked quietly and without much opposition. Criticism became more vocal in the mid–1880s, culminating in the select committee inquiry of 1886–7. The critics and supporters of official policy were sharply divided in their opinions. James Bryce told the select committee that what had been done under the Endowed Schools Acts had generally benefited the poor (ibid.: 379: 5508–9). A. P. Laurie, reporting on the West Riding for the Bryce Commission, considered that the opportunities of the working classes had diminished when the grammar schools in the towns had become fee-paying (*BC* VII: 201). When fees had been introduced, there had been strong pressure to keep them as low as possible. A prominent head, R. P. Scott of Parmiter's, Bethnal Green, complained that in consequence they had been set much too low so that as a result many schemes had never worked properly (R. D. Roberts 1901: 67–8). The Social Science Association at its 1884 meeting held a general discussion about the secondary schools. Some speakers complained that the commissioners had overridden local wishes. Another speaker cited the case of Worcester where their intervention had brought about major improvements. Those who resisted interference, said another, did so 'because they did not wish to be stirred up to proper action'. Others pointed out the need for a minister of education with powers to control and modify endowments (*TSSA* 1884: 379–86).

Since contemporary opinion about the Charity Commissioners varied so much it is no easy task to form a balanced judgement of their work. They thought that they had done well. They paid little regard to the arguments of their opponents, though the difficulties which they faced must not be underestimated. Once again the best method is to study some actual cases. The select committee of 1886–7 was set up to examine the administration of the Endowed Schools Acts after an earlier committee of 1884 had looked at the Charitable Trusts Acts (*PP* 1884 IX: 3–11). The 1886–7 committee heard evidence in particular on six endowments. Of these Kendal, Sutton Coldfield, and Norwich, which was a hospital endowment, raised matters which have already been fully discussed. The fourth case, the removal of the grammar school from Hemsworth to Barnsley in the West Riding, had been a keenly fought battle, and is the only major example of the transfer of an endowment from one place to another (*PP* 1886 IX: 90: 856–9 (Sir George Young)). The other two cases, Scarning in Norfolk and West Lavington, deserve fuller study. They were both villages, and thus far the impact of educational change on rural communities has not been studied. They attracted the attention of Radicals like Jesse Collings and Joseph Chamberlain, who were campaigning to raise the status of the rural labourer. They throw some interesting light on the ideas of the commissioners and on the ways in which they sought to carry them out.

The commissioners became involved with both Scarning and West Lavington in the 1870s. Scarning Free School was an elementary school which had remained under the jurisdiction of the commissioners because its endowment was above the limit set by the act of 1873 (Ed. 21: 12996, 14 December 1872, 'land let for £210'). A scheme for the school was finally confirmed in May 1882, though it had met with strong opposition from all sections of local opinion (Ed. 21: 12996; Simon 1960: 329–31). The scheme provided that the school was to be maintained as a public elementary school under the Act of 1870 for children of both sexes. Fees 'suitable for an elementary school' were to be fixed by the governors. Small scholarships were to be held in the school, covering the payment of fees and the provision of clothing, and there were to be three 'Secker' exhibitions of not less than £25 a year, each 'tenable for three years at any place of higher education or professional or technical training or study approved by the Governors'. These were to be open both to boys and to girls with a first preference to those educated in the school, followed by children from six neighbouring parishes. The scheme bore all the hallmarks of commissioners' orthodoxy. Fees were to be charged, whereas the school had previously been free. A large part of the endowment was to be spent on scholarships and exhibitions for further education. These awards, the trustees had been told, represented the appropriate charge on the foundation for purposes of higher education (Ed. 49: 5526, 31 May 1880).

The scheme had been opposed by the trustees, by the vestry, by the rector, and by a meeting of the inhabitants. The trustees claimed that, by tradition and in the memory of those who had been educated there, Scarning Free School 'was originally an elementary school and that far beyond the memory of man charges were made for teaching Latin and Greek while Reading, Writing and Arithmetic were taught free of charge'. Because there was an urgent need to spend money on the school building and on the farm which formed the endowment, money was not available for the exhibitions which might be provided when there was a surplus (Ed. 49: 5526, trustees' memorial 5 July 1880). A petition, signed by 276 inhabitants, both men and women, concentrated on the fact that under the new arrangements free education would be abolished. The exhibitions, which had been made the first charge on the endowment, would be useless to the village children, who would not be able to compete for them successfully (Ed. 49: 5526, 9 July 1880). The rector, Augustus Jessopp, who had been headmaster of Norwich School and had therefore considerable experience of education, took a moderate but critical line. He argued that from the trustees' point of view the scheme was acceptable in principle, but that in practice it would be impossible both to fund the exhibitions and to improve the building. The exhibitions ought to be deferred until the property had been improved and its value allowed to increase (Ed. 49: 5526, 12 August 1880).

Both the trustees and the ratepayers petitioned Parliament that the scheme should be laid before Parliament. It duly 'lay on the table' for two months, but no member was found to take the matter up and it became law. Subsequent events were described by Jessopp and by an inhabitant, William Taylor, a ganger on the railway (Ed. 49: 5526, 20 January 1883; *PP* 1887 IX: 275–91 (Jessopp); 292–4 (Taylor)). When the governors introduced a fee of 1d a week in January 1883, a large number of children, accompanied by many adults including some substantial farmers, presented themselves at the school without their fee money and were not allowed to attend. 'The men', Jessopp wrote, 'have since then formed themselves into a *League* or *Union* to resist the payment of the Fee & to intimidate parents & children who still persist in attending the School & paying the Fee.' William Taylor described to the select committee how the villagers had started their own school and maintained it for 12–15 months.

When Jessopp gave evidence to the select committee in February 1887 he was examined by Jesse Collings. Jessopp did not think that the penny fee was regarded as a great grievance, but in William Taylor's view feelings still ran very strongly over the matter (*PP* 1887 IX: 284: 6612; 292: 6764; 294: 6840). Jessopp's general assessment was highly unfavourable to what the commissioners had done. He had advised the parishioners not to adopt a plan of out-and-out resistance, but he had seen the crucial difficulty as being the priority claim on the endowment given to the Secker exhibitions. In fact these had never been awarded, and there was no school within walking distance of the village at which they could be held. The real objection to the commissioners' plans was, Jessopp thought, that they had kept to their rules and had not made any exceptions for Scarning. When he was asked whether the commissioners would listen to requests for change, he replied: 'Judging from the tenacity of purpose which the Commissioners have exhibited in their intercourse with me in the past, I should be very sorry indeed to trust to their willingness to listen to reason' (*PP* 1887 IX: 289: 6710).

It is difficult to understand why the commissioners should have acted as they did in the Scarning case. When Richmond was examined on the subject by the select committee, he used the familiar argument that, if resources were not devoted to purposes like the exhibitions, the money spent on the school would simply save the ratepayers from the education rate, which they would otherwise have to pay (ibid.: 301: 6095; 302: 6913). The commissioners seem to have been obsessed by the argument that the income of an endowed school should benefit people of all classes, and not simply those who needed an elementary education. The priority given to the exhibitions reflects the very reasonable view that able children should have the opportunity to advance to higher studies. Yet they do not seem to have considered what was practicable under the circumstances of a Norfolk village. Jessopp had said that there was no suitable higher school near at hand. Richmond himself admitted that an exhibition of £25 on its own was not 'enough to take the child of a working man to a boarding school' (ibid.: 300: 6888). So even if the money for the exhibitions could have been found, there were not likely to be any candidates who wanted or could afford higher education.

In an earlier age Scarning School, like many others, had attracted pupils to read classics. By 1880 it was simply a village elementary school. The commissioners seem to have devoted their main effort to providing what these children did not want or were not able to take advantage of. Even if there had been a local demand for the exhibitions, was it possible to find the money for them? Informed local opinion thought that, at the time when the scheme was made, this was not possible. No more attention seems to have been paid to that point than to any of the others made by the inhabitants. Well might Jessopp say that he would be sorry to trust to the commissioners' willingness to listen to reason.

The end of the story is pure anti-climax. In 1888–9 the commissioners considered revising the arrangements, and in March 1889 a new scheme was made, which made some money available to pay the fees of poor children with the best attendance records, set aside funds for scholarships, and provided for the instruction of boys in practical mechanics and agricultural chemistry and of girls in cookery (cl. 35). Eight years later a note in the file written to Sir George Young explained that the scholarships were not awarded, that the exhibitions 'seem to have been swept away', that the school was now free, and that nothing appeared in the accounts under cl. 35 for technical education. 'The ratepayers seem to have got the whole, now, for maintenance' (Ed. 49: 5526, 22 December 1897). Such were the practical results of the commissioners' efforts to impose a scheme that no one in the locality had wanted.

The story of Dauntsey's School at West Lavington in Wiltshire brings up some similar problems of rural life. It shows much more determined and long-continued resistance by local people, which achieved a large measure of success, largely because their cause was taken up by Jesse Collings and Joseph Chamberlain. The position of the school was a strange one. There was no independent endowment. Under the will of Alderman Dauntsey, who died in 1553, the Mercers Company of London as beneficiaries had an obligation to make certain payments to the schoolmaster and to the almspeople and to keep the school in repair. They were neither trustees nor visitors, and they did not appoint the master, who was chosen by a local landowner, Lord Churchill (Ed. 27: 5291, 21 June 1878 (from the clerk to the company)). The Mercers claimed that they had always spent more money on the school and almshouses than they were legally obliged to do, but the value of the Dauntsey property had greatly increased, and most of that increment went into their coffers. All through the lengthy negotiations one central point was the amount of money which the company could be persuaded to pay out of the Dauntsey funds.

In March 1878 a group of twenty inhabitants wrote to the Mercers, asking that the schoolmaster, who was also vicar of the parish and so had little time to attend to the school, should be replaced, and that in future the master should be resident in the schoolhouse. Of the twenty signatories to this memorial two described themselves as gentlemen; the others were farmers, millers, bakers, coopers – what might be called the middle ranks of village society (Ed. 27: 5291, 22 March 1878). People of this kind, though they were sometimes divided among themselves about the proper policies to pursue, formed the core of local opposition to any efforts to deprive the village of the benefits of the endowment. They were supported from time to time by some of the local gentry, and more steadily by the labourers who were keenly concerned about the fate of the school.

This move by the local group seems to have led to action by the Charity Commissioners, who sent Assistant Commissioner Stanton to hold a local enquiry in March 1879. The school at that time was purely elementary, and the idea rapidly surfaced in the discussions that the endowment should be divided. West Lavington would get a more efficiently organized elementary school, with a second- or third-grade school in a more central situation, accessible by rail to a wider catchment area. There was, it was argued, no demand for such a school in West Lavington, which lay off the main lines of communication. Several towns in Wiltshire were mentioned as possible sites for the higher school. The most favoured, which was ultimately the one chosen, was Devizes, 5 or 6 miles from West Lavington, with railway connections to other parts of the county.

When Stanton reported in November 1879 (Ed. 27: 5292) he expressed the view that it was very unlikely that anything more advanced than an elementary school could be conducted in West Lavington. An upper department might be added to it, but even then fees would be a problem. No further action could be taken until it was known what financial arrangements would be made by the Mercers. The plan quickly emerged that their obligations should be discharged by the payment of a capital sum, and in June 1882 the company agreed to pay the £30,000 which the commissioners had demanded, on condition that the Dauntsey's property be freed from all liabilities and that a satisfactory scheme be settled (Ed. 27: 5292, 30 June 1882 (from clerk to the company)).

The commissioners then proceeded quickly to what was to be the first of several draft schemes (25 July 1882), which provided for a boys' grammar school for both day pupils and boarders and for an elementary school. The Mercers took a very long time to consider this draft, and it was not until a year later (7 July 1883) that the full board of commissioners adopted 'heads of scheme' for providing a middle-class school 'in the county of Wilts elsewhere than at West Lavington'. This was quickly followed by a printed circular, which was widely distributed in the county, raising the question of a possible county school 'adapted to the wants of farmers and tradesmen'. Devizes was suggested as the possible site, though other towns were not excluded. Wherever the school was to be located, money would have to be subscribed for a site and buildings (Ed. 27: 5292; *Alderman Dauntsey's Charity*, August 1883).

Among the recipients of the circular, many of whom seemed to have little connection with West Lavington, was not included the committee of village people which had existed since 1879, and which seems to have been of similar composition to the original body of memorialists. Among the most active members were the miller, James Webb, and the brothers, William and Samuel Saunders (*PP* 1886 IX: 217: 2728). William was a former MP; Samuel was a fruit-grower who made and sold jam, and who proved to be one of the most active campaigners for the rights of the villagers. The commissioners knew of the committee's existence, and it was surely short-sighted on their part not to bring the committee into discussions, which had now been opened out to the whole county.

Samuel Saunders, as later events made clear, had some interesting and original ideas about the best uses to be made of the Dauntsey money. Some years later Assistant Commissioner W. N. Bruce described him as 'a man of remarkable ingenuity, earnestness and benevolence, but so carried away by enthusiasm and so incapable of adjusting ends to means as to be a positive hindrance to the cause he advocates' (Ed. 27: 5295, 1 April 1889). Perhaps that judgement illustrates not only Saunders' failings, but a certain lack of sympathy and understanding on Bruce's part. At West Lavington, as at Scarning, the commissioners and their staff found it very difficult to move out of the narrow confines of their own planning or to appreciate the views of those who did not belong to their own circle.

Reaction from the village was swift after the commissioners' circular had been published in August 1883. In September Samuel Saunders, who had read about the initiative in the press, pointed out that Dauntsey's will had laid down that the school was to be built in West Lavington, which had the first claim on the endowment (Ed. 27: 5292, 15 September 1883). A month later a memorial from the village followed, pointing out that the commissioners had not communicated with them and claiming that very few parishioners would be able to use the proposed middle-class school. The memorialists asked that information be provided about the property held by the Mercers, that the payments made to the almspeople be not diminished, and that 'the full elementary and higher educational requirements for the children of West Lavington and the surrounding villages, may be provided for before any of the funds are diverted to any other purpose' (Ed. 27: 5292, received 31 October 1883). If the villagers maintained their position a serious clash could not be avoided. In November 1883 the full board of commissioners decided to go ahead with the scheme for a county school at Devizes, 'if the county will furnish a freehold site and a sufficient sum for building' (Ed. 27: 5292, 2 November 1883). In a period of serious agricultural depression this proved impossible to achieve. The commissioners thought that £10,000 would be needed. In June 1884 E. P. Bouverie, a prominent local landowner who had been trying to raise the money, reported total failure – 'his promises do not reach £500'.

By that time the affairs of West Lavington were beginning to attract national attention. In February 1884 Jesse Collings had written an article in the *Pall Mall Gazette* in which he argued that the poor of West Lavington were being deprived of rights they had enjoyed for 300 years. The whole scheme formed part of a plan to take charities away from the poor for the benefit of the middle classes. Only if the management of such charities were put into the hands of elected bodies would the rights of the common people be secured (Ed. 27: 5292; *Pall Mall Gazette* 5 February 1884). Collings' intervention was important. After a successful career in Birmingham he had entered Parliament in 1880, and had become well known as an advocate of free education and land reform. In 1882 he had succeeded in passing the Allotments Extension Act, and he had found the Charity Commission indifferent or hostile to efforts to acquire land for the benefit of the labourers (Collings and Green 1920:

221–4). He was also extremely critical of their educational policies. He was later supported by Joseph Chamberlain, the most influential radical politician of the day, and their joint pressure had a crucial influence on the result of the West Lavington struggle.

Meanwhile the commissioners held on their way unmoved by criticism. Another scheme was prepared which, in its final form (July 1885), set aside £16,000 of the capital available for a proposed county school. The existing school at West Lavington was to continue as an elementary school, charging fees, with an upper department for more advanced work. This scheme was sent to the Committee of Council on 24 December 1885, and was approved by the Lord President on 20 August 1886.

Meanwhile the villagers had not been idle (Ed. 27: 5293). The committee sent in its own proposals for a middle-class school and an elementary school, both to be free to the boys of the village. Samuel Saunders put forward a proposal for a 'technical agricultural education department . . . a new departure in rural economy and popular education', an idea that was to be adopted in the final settlement. When the scheme of 1885 had been approved by the Committee of Council, several petitions were presented against it, signed by people from every class of village society. The largest petition had 165 signatures. They included E. P. Bouverie, the landowner who had tried to raise money for the school at Devizes, Lord Churchill's agent, the vicar, Charles Hitchcock MD, the chairman of the village committee, and humbler folk as well – farmers, labourers, gardeners, a miller, a carpenter, a police constable, an inn-keeper. Just as at Scarning it was clear that people from many social groups were hostile to the commissioners' plans.

The matter had now reached the point where Parliament would have to decide. On 1 February 1887 the schemes were laid before Parliament, and on 29 March an address was moved and agreed in the House of Lords that assent to them be withheld. On 9 May the House was told that the Queen had received the address and would comply with the advice. The first scheme had collapsed when there was no money for the school at Devizes. The second had suffered the rare fate of rejection in Parliament.

The third set of negotiations was ultimately successful, though its path was not smooth. Joseph Chamberlain took a leading part, persuading the Mercers to raise their capital offer from £30,000 to £60,000, and suggesting that a large part of this be spent on an agricultural school (Ed. 27: 5293; *Standard*, 24 October 1887; *The Times*, 28 October 1887). The Mercers were prepared to accept the idea, but the commissioners' attitude was very cautious, and they decided that they could not comply. They were doubtful about concentrating such a large endowment in a country village. They disliked a 'parochial' government (the proposal was that half the governors were to be elected by the parish). They disliked the combination of an elementary school with 'intermediate agricultural education' (Ed. 27: 5295, 27 July 1888 (to the clerk to the company)).

No wonder they were concerned; what was being suggested overturned the fundamental tenets of their orthodoxy. The correspondence in the file suggests that at this point both sides drew back somewhat, and in February 1889 Assistant Commissioner Bruce was sent to West Lavington to hold an inquiry. He found serious doubts about the agricultural scheme, especially among the farmers who did not wish to take advantage of it for their own children, and who did not think that it would be useful for the labourers. It was, however, strongly pressed in London both by Collings and by William Saunders, and after reviewing all the arguments, Bruce concluded that the prospects for an agricultural school for boys aged 12 to 17 were not unfavourable (Ed. 27: 5295, report 1 April 1889).

The commissioners published a draft scheme on 21 December 1889 (Ed. 27: 5295). This provided for elementary schools and for an agricultural school with a curriculum including agricultural chemistry, veterinary medicine, land surveying, and practical instruction in farm work and surveying. There were to be both day boys and boarders. Some boarding places were set aside at a reduced fee for Wiltshire boys, and there were to be day-boy scholarships for boys from elementary schools. Exhibitions were also to be awarded to the Royal Agricultural College, Cirencester.

Some of the West Lavington people were prepared to accept what was offered, but Samuel Saunders and his friends and Jesse Collings in London were not. They all argued that the proposals were a middle-class scheme, putting what was offered 'beyond the reach of the Workingmen Tradespeople and Farmers of the neighbourhood', and they particularly objected to the Cirencester exhibitions (Ed. 27: 5295, 28 May 1890). When the scheme was approved by the Committee of Council in December 1890 there was yet another round of petitions, not only from West Lavington, but from Devizes and from six other nearby villages as well, with a total of 428 signatures (Ed. 27: 5296).

By New Year 1891 the affair had reached the highest levels of government, which clearly feared serious political embarrassment. In February W. H. Smith, First Lord of the Treasury, who had been approached by Collings, wrote to the commissioners, asking that the Cirencester exhibition money should be added to the funds already available to boys from elementary schools, since that change would be advantageous to the poorer inhabitants (Ed. 27: 5295, 24 February 1891; Collings and Green 1920: 226). This the commissioners agreed to do, and in place of the Cirencester exhibitions a sum of up to £200 a year in addition to the original allocation was made available for elementary school pupils (Ed. 27: 5295, 28 February 1891). The original scheme finally passed in March 1891 and the amending scheme incorporating the change in February 1892 (Ed. 27: 5296, 20 March 1891; Ed. 27: 5297, 6 February 1892).

The Dauntsey Agricultural School was opened by Joseph Chamberlain in 1895. By 1904 it had 44 boarders and 15 day boys, who received a general education and were later allowed to specialize in agricultural subjects. Foundation boarders were admitted at a reduced fee, and there were four boys in the school holding Dauntsey scholarships (REC Wiltshire I, *PP* 1908 LXXX: 719–21). Such a small number of scholarship-holders seems a meagre return for the doggedness and persistence of Samuel Saunders, Jesse Collings, and their friends. But they had succeeded in launching a secondary school of a completely new type against the resolute opposition of the commissioners to any deviation from their general policy. Local resistance and parliamentary pressure had won a victory which neither could have won alone.

By the time the West Lavington scheme had finally been approved the commissioners had moved into smoother waters. The tourney of attack and defence set going by the witnesses to the select committee of 1886–7 had finally resulted in a report which was favourable to the commissioners, concluding that they had done much to bring better education within the reach of the poorer classes. Once again the call was made for a better system of local government and for a ministry of education, through which the commissioners' responsibility to Parliament would be better defined (*PP* 1887 IX: 237–47; CC 35th Rep. *PP* 1888 XXXIV: 32). After 1889 the commissioners' work moved into new areas. They were closely associated with the development of a system of secondary education in Wales under the Welsh Intermediate Education Act. They worked closely with the county councils whose technical instruction committees provided both new ideas and new money, particularly for scientific education. In 1894–5 a major inquiry was carried out by the Bryce Commission, and from the subsequent debate emerged the Education Act of 1902.

7   The endowed schools about 1890

The endowed grammar schools had certainly made progress since 1869. Fearon told the select committee of 1886–7 that between 1868 and 1883 the numbers of boys and girls in schools for which schemes had been made had more than doubled – from about 13,000 to about 27,000 (*PP* 1886 IX: 65: 627; 66: 629). A similar impression is conveyed in the local surveys conducted for the Bryce Commission, where improvements were noted in counties as different as Surrey and the West Riding (*BC* VII: 8 (Surrey); 265 (West Riding)). In the latter county Fitch, in his report to the Taunton Commission, had counted twenty-nine schools with 1,836 pupils giving some secondary education. At the time of the Bryce survey there were thirty-six schools with 3,597 pupils. Yet it is easy to over-estimate the success of the reforms. Some schools had certainly made major advances – Bradford Grammar School, the Harpur Trust schools at Bedford, Dulwich College in London. A few like Tonbridge or Sedbergh had moved into the ranks of the public boarding schools. Yet the successes were comparatively few, and most of them were schools which had been fairly successful before 1869, or had a large endowment, or both. Many – perhaps the majority – of the grammar schools were in a weak position in the last decade of the century. Numbers fluctuated rapidly; success could be followed by failure within only a few years.

The situation differed a good deal between the large towns and the country districts. In the major cities there was often competition between the grammar school, the higher-grade schools of the school boards, and the technical college. The French observer, Max Leclerc, praised Birmingham for its well-organized system, though he thought Manchester deficient in secondary schools and criticized the standards attained (Leclerc 1894a: 132, 163). Even at Birmingham the criticism was made that the King Edward's schools were inadequate to meet the demand (Acland and Llewellyn Smith 1892: 258, 275). At Manchester the grammar school, which had a fine academic record, suffered from the competition of the higher-grade schools and of the Hulme Grammar School, which opened in 1887. Manchester was a pioneer, however, in trying to harmonize the work of the various institutions. In 1894–6 the 'Manchester

Concordat' was drawn up between the grammar school, the school board, the technical education committee, and the university (Mumford 1919: 416).

A. P. Laurie, who reported on the West Riding schools for the Bryce Commission, commented on the lack of such co-ordination at both Leeds and Sheffield. At Bradford, however, the higher-grade schools enabled boys to carry their education forward either to the technical school or to the grammar school so that they could progress according to their interests and levels of ability (*BC* VII: 164, 177, 186–7). Laurie's report showed great weaknesses in other West Riding towns. At Halifax the Heath Grammar School had been rebuilt in 1879. In 1882 there were only thirteen boys and it had been closed from 1883–7. With accommodation for 175 it had only 97 boys, though the higher-grade school was successful (*BC* VII: 193–7; REC West Riding *PP* 1899 LXXI: 274–5). At Huddersfield there were no educational endowments, and the proprietary school had recently closed. Nothing was likely to be done until it was the duty of the town council to do it (*BC* VII: 188, 192).

Conditions were particularly difficult for grammar schools in small towns and country areas, and many examples of schools with few pupils, poor buildings, and little money are to be found in the Bryce Commission surveys and the *Returns on Endowed Charities* (*PP* 1899 LXXII: 519–20 (Wortley, near Leeds)). Some interesting evidence about rural schools in Gloucestershire was given to the select committee of 1886–7 by H. L. Thompson, Rector of Iron Acton, who had visited the schools on behalf of a county committee (*PP* 1886 IX: 289: 4082–298: 4296). The smaller schools were not flourishing, though those in the larger towns were more successful. Excluding Gloucester and Cheltenham there were ten schools with endowments of £2,280 educating 280 scholars, who were paying fees very similar to what parents would have paid in private schools. The great problem was the shortage of pupils. At one end of the scale boys had been drawn off to public and proprietary schools; at the other the elementary schools had greatly improved, so that the pool on which grammar schools could draw had become much smaller. The master had to teach too many subjects, there was little emulation among the boys, and very little competition for scholarships. The private schools provided an alternative education which middle-class parents could better appreciate: 'There is a strong impression that a master whose success depends on his own exertions entirely is more likely to do his best, and therefore they like the private adventure schoolmaster better than the endowed schoolmaster' (ibid.: 294: 4203).

Many of the problems came down in the end to shortage of money. Often the endowment was not sufficient to provide a solid backing for the school, and in many cases agricultural rents had fallen badly as the result of agricultural depression. D. C. Richmond told the select committee of 1894 on the Charity Commission that it had been common for school incomes to fall by half, especially in the midland and eastern counties (*PP* 1894 XI: 115–16: 1325, 1330–1). Nor could the deficiencies be made good by higher fees because it was difficult for parents to afford the fees which were really required if the schools were to pay their way (*PP* 1886 IX: 166: 1682; Acland and Llewellyn Smith 1892: 171).

In the rural districts the farmers had little interest in education for their own children and disliked any changes which might make their labourers more independent (*BC* VI: 390 (Norfolk)). In the smaller towns of the West Riding there were schools like Batley which worked effectively with a good provision of scholarships and a commercial/scientific curriculum (*BC* VII: 222). For the comparable towns of south Lancashire, F. E. Kitchener painted a very gloomy picture. In some cases there had been no progress since the days of the Taunton Commission. Sometimes the scheme, which provided that the headmaster should receive a fixed salary plus capitation payments, was ignored. The school was 'farmed' to the head who received a small allowance from the endowment in return for which he had to educate the free boys. After that he undertook to pay the expenses of the school and received the fees. The heads themselves, Kitchener thought, were conscientious men doing sound work, but their position was impossible:

> [The headmaster] lives in a fever of anxiety as to whether the school will go up or down next term, his buildings are often old-fashioned, with sanitary arrangements of the rudest periods, his very blackboards are often got at his own expense, and if he has any staff at all, he has either to sacrifice his own salary to get a decent colleague, or he has to put up with an inferior kind of student teacher.
>
> (*BC* VI: 189)

Once again a case-study from a different part of the country illustrates the general argument. A scheme was made for St Bartholomew's Grammar School at Newbury in Berkshire in 1883 (Ed. 27: 70, 71, 73). The school was not short of pupils, but it had a very inadequate building, and the main problem was to find the capital necessary for a new one. Additional funds were made available through the appropriation of money from Kendrick's charities, in recognition of which scholarships were created, the junior awards to be held at elementary schools and the senior at the grammar school. The sum of £50 a year was set aside for apprenticeship fees as the result of local pressure that boys should be able to learn trades. There was some opposition of the usual kind to the scheme, but it was not particularly serious and the scheme was not delayed by it. The new buildings were good, but they were not filled. With room in them for 100 boys, there were 66 in 1896 (17 of them boarders), and there was not much likelihood of any increase.

It soon became clear that the scheme was not working well. Though the junior Kendrick scholarships were popular, it was difficult to fill the senior awards in the grammar school. Schoolmasters did not send in their best boys, and there was no great readiness to compete. Parents removed their boys from the elementary schools after they had passed standard V, and the payment of £12 a year was not sufficient inducement to keep them on at the grammar school. In January 1896 the commissioners were informed by the governors that they were doubtful whether they could maintain the school under the existing scheme. A few months later the commissioners noted that the scheme was not being observed and the head was 'farming' the school.

In 1891 and 1896 the school was visited by assistant commissioners (Ed. 27: 73). By 1896 the apprenticeship payments, which had been falling for some years, had ceased. The school did not enjoy much support in the town and was under strong competition from a private school 'to which the better class of inhabitants send their sons'. The head, John Atkins, was regarded as a poor teacher and organizer, and dissatisfaction with him meant that no aid was received from the county council until 1897, when £100 a year was granted towards the salary of a science master. In 1896 Atkins had only two regular assistants, one aged 24, the other aged 19, who was described as 'little more than a boy'.

A new scheme of 1899 reorganized the scholarships and abolished both the apprenticeship payments and the junior awards which had been held at elementary schools. By that time fees in elementary schools had generally disappeared, but it may be doubted whether the withdrawal of money from those schools was really in accordance with Kendrick's original gift, or the promises implicit in the scheme of 1883. The story of Newbury Grammar School is very mundane; there were no scandals, no dramas, but it is very characteristic of the fate of many of the smaller schools. Academically the school's record seems to have been satisfactory. A few boys went up to university, examination results were good, and examiners' reports favourable. Perhaps Mr Atkins was not such a poor teacher and organizer after all, though circumstances were certainly against him.

It was frequently said throughout the period that parents of higher social rank had ceased to use the local grammar schools and were sending their boys to public boarding schools. A Nonconformist minister in Huddersfield told the Bryce Commission that 'the provincial dialect in the neighbourhood of Huddersfield does not quite please the ear of the wealthy parents, and therefore they prefer to send their children away to Harrow, Rugby, Harrogate, Scarborough, Clifton and other places out of town' (*BC* III: 66: 6662 (Rev. Robert Bruce)). The complaint that access to the grammar schools had been made more difficult for the poor has been one of the main themes of this study. The clientele that remained were the substantial groups in the middle of society – commercial, mercantile, manufacturing, with some boys from professional backgrounds – and with variations from place to place according to the local social and economic background.

Examples from schools in different parts of the country and of somewhat differing kinds exhibit a broadly common pattern. Macclesfield in Cheshire had both a grammar school and a modern school on the same foundation. The town was a major centre of the silk industry. The occupations of the parents of the ten highest and ten lowest day scholars in the two schools and of boarders in the grammar school are shown in Table 7.1.

Table 7.1 Occupations of parents, Macclesfield, 1869

Grammar School		Modern Free School			
Army officer	1	Author	1	Policeman	1
Clergyman	4	Bank manager	1	Silk dyer	1
Coroner	1	Boot- and shoe-maker	1	Silk finisher	1
Gentleman	4	Grocer	1	Silk manager	1
Manufacturer	7	Joiner	1	Silk manufacturer	3
Solicitor	1	Land steward	1	Silk staffman	1
Tradesman	2	Leather merchant	1	Silk throwster	1
		Plumber and glazier	1	Spirit merchant	1
				Widow	1
				Orphan	1

The parents of eleven boarders in the grammar school were:

Banker	1	Manufacturer	3
Gentleman	2	Solicitor	2
Ironmaster	2	Surgeon	1

Source: PRO, Ed. 27: 266 (letter from the school governors, 27 April 1870).

A very large sample is provided by a list of the parents of boys in the grammar and English schools of King Edward's, Birmingham in 1877 (Ed. 27: 4910). Most of the parents of the 585 boys belonged to the commercial and manufacturing classes of a city with a very varied industrial base. Some of the larger groups were independent gentlemen (16), Church of England clergymen (29), Nonconformist ministers (11), surgeons (29), and solicitors (12). There were 32 merchants of various kinds, 22 manufacturers, 16 jewellers, 14 managers, 13 agents, and 24 commercial travellers. Schoolmasters numbered 14 and there were 9 'teachers' (of languages, music, etc.), plus 24 clerks. Occupational descriptions are difficult to interpret accurately, but there were probably about 20 workmen at weekly wages, as well as 27 widows and 2 orphans.

Statistics of some London schools, of a rural school in the south of England and of three West Riding schools illustrate the position in different parts of England in the 1890s. The three West Riding schools are Bradford, a highly successful first-grade school in a large town, Batley, a school in a small industrial town, and Ripon, a small school

in a cathedral city with a rural hinterland and made up of two thirds
day boys and one third boarders. The occupational breakdowns are
shown in Table 7.2.

Table 7.2 Occupations of parents at three Yorkshire schools, 1897–9

	Total	Bradford	Batley	Ripon
Professional men	177	120	21	36
Manufacturers, large merchants and tradesmen	233	183	45	5
Small tradesmen, clerks	159	91	45	23
Farmers	9	–	–	9
Artisans	52	13	35	4
No occupation	32	22	9	1
Totals	662	429	155	78

Source: REC, West Riding. *PP* 1897 LXVII, Pt 5: 125–6 (Bradford); 1899 LXXI: 92
(Batley); 1899 LXXII: 636 (Ripon).

The variations between the schools are much what might have been
expected. A large town like Bradford would naturally have a considerable
number of professional men and of large merchants and manufacturers.
Ripon was likely to be the only one of the three to have some parents
who were farmers. Batley had a comparatively large total both of small
tradesmen and of artisans. Many of those entered as of 'no occupation'
were probably widows.

The rural school in southern England is Newbury, about which a good
deal has already been said. In 1891 there were 81 boys, including 20
boarders. If the parental occupations are classified in the same way as
in the case of the West Riding schools already cited, the breakdown is
as shown in Table 7.3.

Table 7.3 Occupations of parents, St Bartholomew's Grammar School,
Newbury, *c.* 1890

Professional men (including four 'gentlemen')	17
Manufacturers, etc.	9
Small tradesmen, etc.	29
Farmers	12
Artisans	1
Deceased	11
Retired	1
No occupation	1

Source: PRO, Ed. 27: 73 (from a list of boys in the school).

Again, the resemblances and differences with other lists are much what
might have been expected. The list is really dominated by the farmers
and small tradesmen of a rural neighbourhood. The last group includes
one clerk and one commercial traveller. The 'artisan' is a grocer's assist-

ant. The small group of manufacturers and larger tradesmen consists of an auctioneer (1), bank manager (1), boot manufacturer (1), brewer (2), iron manufacturer (1), maltster (1), and miller (2).

The London figures all relate to second- or third-grade schools. In 1898 Owen's School, Islington, had 420 boys. The 'class in life' of their parents is shown in Table 7.4.

Table 7.4 Occupations of parents, Owen's School (boys'), Islington, 1898

Manufacturers on own account and managers of important works	18
Tradesmen and shopkeepers	115
Officials (minor, as tax collectors, etc.)	26
Schoolmasters	17
Professions (doctor, solicitor, minister)	29
Clerks, agents, warehousemen, civil servants	129
Artisans (principally junior county scholars)	66
Widows and others with no specified employment	20

Source: PRO, Ed. 27: 3120 (Dame Alice Owen's Foundation).

The social composition of the Roan School, Greenwich (1894) was similar. There were 361 boys, a majority of them under 14. Of the parents, 34 were professional men, 41 artisans, and the remainder belonged to the lower middle class (Ed. 27: 3026, 26 July 1894).

The small number of professional men and the large number of clerks and tradesmen are noteworthy in both schools. It is also true of three schools in the eastern district of London cited by Llewellyn Smith: professional 10 per cent, middle class 74 per cent, working class 16 per cent. The eastern district was not a favoured residential area, and it was easy in London to send a boy to a first-grade school in another part of the metropolis, so that parents were not dependent on schools in their immediate neighbourhood. Llewellyn Smith also gave some interesting details about working-class parents of boys in two unnamed East London schools. At Bethnal Green a total of 47 boys was divided as follows: building trades 6; clothing trades 15; other skilled trades 23; street-sellers and labourers 3. At Poplar there were 27 such boys: 18 had fathers who were skilled tradesmen, 8 worked on crafts associated with the river, and one was the son of a labourer (Acland and Llewellyn Smith 1892: 161–2). The very small number of unskilled workmen should be noted; such parents needed to send their children to work as soon as they could.

From working-class boys it is natural to move on to the subject of scholarships since most of them probably entered the schools by that route. First of all the words 'scholarship' and 'exhibition', as they are used in the sources, must be defined. Sir George Young's definition to the select committee of 1886 was as follows. A scholarship was an award, the money for which was provided by the endowment of the school in which it was held. An exhibition was an award held in some other place of education from that which provided the money (*PP* 1886 IX: 57: 578). Thus we speak here of scholarships to grammar schools awarded either at entrance or to boys already in the school, and of exhibitions to places of higher education, or of exhibitions where the endowments of schools which had been closed were devoted to awards held at other schools. It was common for schemes to provide a number of entrance scholarships up to 10 per cent of the total number of pupils in the school and for half of these to be reserved for candidates from public elementary schools. The Charity Commissioners' reports make it clear that these provisions were not always carried into effect. Sometimes the governors used the money in other ways, or claimed that the funds were insufficient to do what the scheme required (CC 30th Rep. *PP* 1883 XXI: 349; 31st Rep. *PP* 1884 XXII: 351–2).

There were two major returns in the 1880s which give valuable information about scholarships and exhibitions: the so-called 'Fortescue' return of 1884 which gives statistics of schemes approved up to 31 December 1880, and a return from 101 schools drawn up for the select committee of 1886 and covering the three years ending 31 December 1884. Both returns include schools in England and Wales and both give figures for boys and for girls (House of Lords paper no. 29 1884 (*Return of Schemes etc.*: 41–85; *PP* 1886 IX: 539–76). According to a return of 1882 from the Charity Commissioners, the scholarships could be divided as shown in Table 7.5.

It is difficult to draw any firm conclusions from these figures because none of the schemes was more than ten years old, and it is clear from the Fortescue return that many of them were only just getting under way. Yet, if these limitations are borne in mind, some features of interest can be picked out. The preponderance of all awards was held by boys, though the proportion of girls from the public elementary school group was higher. Most of the awards given to elementary scholars were held in second- and third-grade schools, and the average number of such awards per school was small: first-grade, 1.76; second-grade, 2.6; third-grade, 4.54. By the early 1880s the elementary school scholars had entered the system to only a small extent. The detailed comments given in the Fortescue return reinforce this conclusion even further. In many schools no awards had been made or fewer had been given than the scheme directed, usually on the ground that funds were not available. In many cases there were few candidates or none at all, and the comment made about one third-grade school – that elementary schoolmasters were unwilling to send in their best boys – probably had a wider application. Among second-grade schools with a good record for giving scholarships were Wyggeston's at Leicester, Rivington in Lancashire, and Skipton in the West Riding. Among third-grade schools were Hele's at Exeter, Tiffin's at Kingston-on-Thames, and Warwick Middle School.

The return prepared for the select committee of 1886 is rather different

Table 7.5 Scholarships at secondary schools, 1882

	Secondary schools under scheme making returns	Secondary schools in which scholarships were held, 1882	Number of scholarships			Number of scholarships held by children from public elementary schools		
			Boys	Girls	Total	Boys	Girls	Total
First-grade	59	45	771	28	799	66	13	79
Second-grade	124	95	575	40	615	233	18	251
Third-grade	113	79	1,019	228	1,247	574	90	664
Total	296	219	2,365	296	2,661	873	121	994
Miscellaneous awards					227			151
Totals					2,989			1,145

Source: Charity Commissioners, 31st Report, PP 1884 XXII: 350–1.

in nature from the Fortescue return. Its purpose was to discover how many children awarded scholarships in the three years up to 31 December 1884 were the children of parents employed in manual labour, how successful these children were in their school work, and how they were received by their schoolfellows. This return was more selective than the Fortescue return, covering 101 schools in all (88 boys' and 13 girls'). The schools were described by type and geographical location, but they were not named. Information was also given about leaving exhibitions and about the subsequent careers of award-holders and some interesting comments and value judgements were added.

In general the 1886 return suggests a higher level of success for scholarship schemes and more keenness to take up places than in the case of the Fortescue return. It is difficult to believe that the four years' gap between the two returns can have made much real difference, but the impression remains. The average number of scholars per school in the second- and third-grade schools had risen too, though the sample is small, and there is no means of knowing how it was selected. The figures given in Table 7.6 relate to boys' schools only.

Table 7.6 Scholarships and occupations of parents, 1884

	Schools with scholarships awarded to sons of manual workers or to fatherless boys	None or no return	Total of scholars	Average per school
Second-grade	32	10	241	7.5
Third-grade	24	3	364	15.2

Of the 19 first-grade schools in the return only 7 had scholars in this category (30 boys in all). The occupations of their parents were (the number is that given to the school in the return):

87 Boot-maker
    railway pointsman
89 plumber
    joiner
91 cabinet-maker
    painter
    printer
    tin-plate worker
94 in furniture shop
    clicker[a]
    engineer
    clicker (deceased)
    quartermaster

96 very small working tenant farmers (4)
    railway porter
97 gardener
    carpenter
    plumber
    working farmer (2)
98 widows (3)
    painter
    wire-drawer
    tailor
    joiner

Source: Calculated from figures in return from 101 secondary endowed schools, *PP* 1886 IX: 539–76.
[a] Foreman shoemaker.

The number of scholarships awarded was related not only to the funds available and to the supply of candidates, but to the general sentiment of society about levels of ability and the opportunities likely to be open to boys who had received a good education. Here the common estimate was rather restrictive. It was argued that the really able should have the chance to progress, but it was not expected that there would be very many of them, and there was anxiety about creating an educated class that would not be able to find suitable work. H. J. Roby told the Bryce Commission:

> I should be most sorry that any boy who really had the capacity and industry should not obtain a very high education, but I do not think that such boys are very numerous. May I add that I do not think it desirable that boys who have not got capacity and industry should be forced up into a totally different stratum to which they are not used, and where they will not move with ease.
>
> (*BC* IV: 457: 16752)

The sole exponent of the broader view that what was important was not a ladder for the clever few but a better education for the mass of the people was Jesse Collings. He argued that scholarships served only to take boys away from their own class and the places where they had been brought up (*PP* 1887 IX: 355–61: 7705–77). His views were similar to those expressed in the 1920s by R. H. Tawney. They elicited no support in the 1880s.

Once the elementary school boys had won their scholarships, they faced two sets of difficulties, one intellectual, one social. Could they do the work? And how readily would they be accepted by their schoolfellows? The 1886 inquiry asked the heads of the selected schools questions on both these issues. On the intellectual side there was widespread agreement that, after initial problems over new subjects like French and Latin, they quickly settled down and did well academically. This view is supported by the evidence given to the Bryce Commission by A. R. Vardy of King Edward's, Birmingham, that, of his highest block of 72 boys, 13 had at one time or another been in elementary schools (*BC* II: 195: 1932), though not all of these will have been elementary school scholars.

On the social side most of the heads thought that the elementary scholars settled down well and were happy and well accepted by their fellows, though here opinions were more divided. When difficulties had occurred, they appear to have stemmed from the parents of the fee-payers. One head remarked: 'the difference between them [the scholarship boys] and the ordinary scholars seems to be felt. The parents strongly object to admission of boys from elementary schools.'

In some parts of the country, on the other hand, the elementary schools were used quite widely as preparatory to grammar schools by boys, many of whom entered as fee-payers. Once again the Bryce papers provide information. E. F. M. MacCarthy, head of King Edward's, Five

Ways, Birmingham, one of the second-grade grammar schools of the foundation, explained that in those schools one-third were foundation scholars, of whom a half must be pupils from elementary schools. In his own school over the years 1887–92, 58 per çent of the admissions had been pupils from elementary schools and, in the boys' school of King Edward's, Camp Hill, the figure was as high as 73 per cent (*BC* III: 44–5: 6387). A. R. Vardy's evidence was similar (*BC* II: 181–2), and the same comments were made about the middle and commercial schools of Liverpool College and Bury Grammar School in Lancashire (*BC* VI: 140, 157). In London, D. R. Fearon had noted in 1886 that there was a tendency for the middle class to make more use of elementary schools so that their children might be able to compete for scholarships given by the school board (*PP* 1886 IX: 85: 803).

The keenness of competition for awards varied from place to place. Often there were not many candidates and sometimes the situation got worse as the higher grade schools provided an alternative route to a better education (*BC* VI: 116 (Manchester); VII: 193–4 (Halifax)). There were occasional complaints that elementary schoolmasters were unwilling to put forward their best boys (REC West Riding *PP* 1897 LXVII, Pt 5: 752 (Skipton)). Often the pupils who had won awards stayed at school for only a short time. At Manchester almost the whole of the grammar school endowment went into providing 160 free places. These were awarded for three years; of the scholars elected between 1877 and 1894 only 56.8 per cent completed their tenure (*BC* IV: 456: 16740; 458: 16758). In London elementary scholars entered grammar schools between the ages of 11 and 13 and did not as rule stay much beyond the age of 14 (Acland and Llewellyn Smith 1892: 185). In such a brief time they could gain little benefit from the teaching of the secondary school.

Frequently, this very short school life was the result of the poverty of the parents. One head recorded in the 1886 return that the quality of his scholarship boys was high and that, when parents could afford to keep them at school, they had won prizes. 'Owing however to the poverty of their parents, their school life is very short, few remaining longer than 18 months' (*PP* 1886 IX: 545). For poor parents free education was not enough unless a maintenance allowance was given as well, and these were uncommon. Sidney Webb, discussing the arrangements made by the technical education board, thought that, if scholarships were really to become available to children in the poorer districts of London, an allowance of not less than £10 a year must be given in addition to free schooling. 'You must practically provide the whole maintenance of the boy or girl from the age of 13 if you are to succeed in enabling the parents to withdraw that boy or girl from the labour market at 13' (*BC* II: 259: 2591).

The problem was not entirely one of money. For many parents who were not necessarily very poor the secondary grammar schools seemed to offer nothing directly related to their work or interests. Particularly in the industrial districts there was plenty of work for boys, and the expectation was that they would earn their own livings as soon as they could. For them a higher education had no cash value. The Roman Catholic parish priest of the West Riding port town of Goole explained the shortage of candidates like this:

> even if larger sums were given, they would not avail to prevent the parents in a trading town like Goole withdrawing their children from school at the earliest possible moment, in order to place them in a trade or business. In his own school he had never been able to persuade a child even to present himself for examination.
>
> (*PP* 1899 LXXIII: 531)

There is plenty of evidence from different parts of the country to show that elementary scholarships benefited not the children of the poor but those of the rather better off who could afford to keep their boys at school. Canon Evans, who had been headmaster of King Edward's, Birmingham, 1862–72, told the select committee of 1886 that awards were taken by 'the children of rather well-to-do parents of the upper artisan class or of the lower middle class' (*PP* 1886 IX: 282: 3942). J. G. Fitch said much the same about both London and Bristol (ibid.: 138: 1496). At Leeds the Poor's Estate scheme of 1878 had created scholarships at the grammar school, some of them reserved to boys from elementary schools. The parentage of the sixteen boys holding such scholarships in March 1896 was as follows: shopkeeper's widow, farmer, printer, clerk, foreman of works, timber merchant, copper-plate engraver, Nonconformist minister, grocer's widow, sanitary inspector, commercial traveller, tradesmen's widows (2), hairdresser, cashier, under-manager (REC West Riding *PP* 1899 LXXII: 366). Like many similar lists which could be quoted, it has a distinctly lower middle-class flavour.

On the whole the same flavour characterizes the future careers of elementary scholars, so far as these can be traced. A book published in 1892 commented that:

> the great majority of boys holding scholarships from elementary schools finish their education early and remain in a condition of life not far removed from that of their parents. . . . And in the schools of which there are many scholars of this kind it is constantly reported that boys from them are much sought after by employers, not only as clerks or shop-assistants, but for many other positions.
>
> (Acland and Llewellyn Smith 1892: 86)

The return of 1886 gave a great deal of detailed information, most of it relating to second- and third-grade schools. Clerks of all kinds were very numerous – solicitors', telegraph, post office, factory, warehouse, bank. There were many pupil teachers and schoolmasters, including a few boys who had become assistants in their own schools. Many were working in skilled trades – harness-maker, draftsman, engraver, die-sinker, pattern-maker, carpenter. Work in retail trades was popular. There were a few reporters and sailors and a civil servant. Only a few were earning their living by manual labour. A similar pattern to that recorded in the 1886 return can be traced in the careers of elementary scholars from some of the smaller West Riding schools which are given in the Return on Endowed Charities (*PP* 1899 LXXI: 146, 538, 696, 851, 893).

For a few of the boys mentioned in the 1886 return the ladder of opportunity had stretched considerably further. Among second-grade schools one technical school in Yorkshire had sent several boys to study science in London. One boy who had been a half-timer had gone to the Royal College of Science. In another school in the north-west a free scholar had risen to the top of the school and was likely to go to university. One boy from a first-grade school had gone to Cambridge to read medicine. In some cases the lack of leaving exhibitions had made such progress impossible (Gordon 1980: 113), but where these existed elementary school scholars did win them. At King Edward's, Birmingham three such scholars had gone to Oxford and Cambridge between 1878 and 1886. One of these had graduated in mathematics and the other two were both scholars of their colleges. Two more boys had held exhibitions at Mason College, Birmingham, and six more had been able to stay at school long enough to pass London Matriculation (*PP* 1886 IX: 283: 3954). A. R. Vardy told the Bryce Commission of one boy who had gone to university, who was the 'son of an artisan, a man in receipt of a weekly wage which I should think probably never exceeded 40 shillings, even if it has been as much as that' (*BC* II: 196: 1935).

The information about Manchester Grammar School is similar. Between 1887 and 1893 358 entrance scholars were elected from Manchester elementary schools. Of these 35 had reached the sixth form and 19 had gone to university. There were 52 boys still in the school. The comparable figures for Salford elementary schools were 96, 13, 5, 19 (*BC* VI: 123). Of the 196 Salford scholars 37 had come from one voluntary fee-paying church school:

> At present [1894–5] four of these scholars are at Oxford, one a mathematical scholar of Corpus and junior mathematical scholar of the university; a second a classical exhibitioner of Balliol and Craven scholar; and the third holding a science post-mastership at Merton.
>
> (*BC* VI: 132)

Most of these boys are mere statistics in a list, but one of the Manchester scholars can be identified. Ernest Barker was the son of a general handyman and former miner in a Cheshire village and grandson of a small farmer. He won a scholarship to Manchester Grammar School at New

Year 1886/7, won the top classical scholarship at Balliol, and eventually became Principal of King's College, London, and Professor of Political Science at Cambridge (Barker 1953).

There were not many Manchesters or Birminghams but, in the very different environment of some of the London second-grade schools which possessed leaving exhibitions, there were successes too. In these London examples elementary school scholars were not always identified, but from the details already given about parental occupations, it is clear that the majority of boys in these schools came from modest family backgrounds. At Parmiter's, Bethnal Green, six exhibitions had been awarded – two in 1890, two in 1892, two in 1893. The parents of the successful candidates were: clerk (2), cabinet-maker, boot-maker, master mariner, grocer (mother a widow). One boy had become a naval engineer, training at Portsmouth dockyard; another had won a science scholarship at Christ Church, Oxford (REC London *PP* 1897 LXVI, Pt 2: 27). At the Roan School, Greenwich, a report of 1894 showed that, of the twelve boys who had won the school exhibition since 1882, seven had attended elementary schools and three had held scholarships. Awards had been held at Balliol, at Edinburgh, at University and King's Colleges, London, and (a majority) at the London medical hospitals. The two most distinguished boys had been elementary school scholars (Ed. 27: 3026, 26 July 1894). At Owen's, Islington, the school exhibitioners for 1891–3 had become schoolmasters, barristers, an engineer, and a cashier at Portsmouth dockyard, though nothing is recorded about their parentage or previous schooling (Ed. 27: 3120).

The ladder of opportunity was still both narrow and steep, and the children of labourers and unskilled workers rarely reached it at all. However, some of the plans and hopes of the reformers had come to fruition, and perhaps they had achieved more success in opening the way for the poor but able boy than their modern critics have recognized.

Part II

Public activity in secondary education

8   'Our new Secondary Education . . .'

The phrase at the head of this chapter was used in the report of the Bryce Commission to describe the scientific and technical education which had grown up under the aegis of the Science and Art Department (DSA), founded in 1853 (*BC* I: 102–3). The Charity Commissioners had, as we have seen, supported such studies in a number of endowed schools, though the old endowments could make only a minor contribution to solving what had become a major national problem. The sense that Britain was falling badly behind its European neighbours and commercial rivals was first clearly expressed in the 1860s, for example, by a parliamentary select committee in 1868 under the chairmanship of the Cleveland ironmaster, Bernhard Samuelson.

Two royal commissions – on scientific instruction (Devonshire, 1870–5) and on technical instruction (Samuelson, 1881–4) – had recommended more science teaching in schools (see pp. 33–4), and by the early 1880s there was growing interest throughout the country in technical education. In 1887 the National Association for the Promotion of Technical (and Secondary) Education (NAPTSE) was founded. Its secretaries were the chemist Henry Roscoe, who had been a member of the Samuelson Commission, and the Liberal MP, A. H. D. Acland, who was to be Vice-President of the Committee of Council in the Liberal governments of 1892–5. The National Association was an important pressure group, and its journal, the *Record*, is a mine of information on new developments. Only a year after its creation came the establishment of the county and county borough councils (1888), which, through their technical instruction committees, were to play such an important part in the progress of education during the 1890s.

In the discussions of the time 'technical' education was interpreted in very wide terms. One major area was that of the further education of working adults, usually in evening classes. A major landmark here was the foundation of the City and Guilds of London Institute for the Advancement of Technical Education, incorporated in 1880, the technological examinations of which set new standards for technical and trade training. The London Polytechnics, beginning with Quintin Hogg's

Regent Street Institution, formed an another important group. Their work was greatly extended through funds made available under the City Parochial Charities Act of 1883 (Owen 1965: 276–98).

It is difficult, particularly in the case of the Science and Art Department, to disentangle the scientific and technical education of adults from that of boys who were still at school. Our concern here is with the schoolboys, and to a lesser extent the schoolgirls, though the parallel involvement of adults must also be remembered because it frequently affected what the boys and girls had to do. Since this overlap between adults and school pupils existed, it is often difficult to differentiate between 'technical' and 'secondary' education. Bernhard Samuelson told the Social Science Association in 1874 (*TSSA* 1874: 356–62) that technical instruction included not only the teaching of industrial manipulation and the application of science to industrial purposes, but also 'drawing, mathematics, the physical sciences, which are the basis of the industrial arts'. He wanted a thorough scientific training for scholars between the ages of 8 and 17. He did not think it would be desirable to teach them applied science, but he thought that work in the laboratory was a necessity. The report of the Bryce Commission, though it accepted that there were differences between the two aspects, argued that any satisfactory definition of secondary education must include technical instruction within it (*BC* I: 135–6; Musgrave 1964: 105–11).

After 1902 the policy of the Board of Education imposed a much sharper separation between these two areas, but that was not characteristic of the period before 1900. The real problem in the earlier years was not the division between scientific and technical but rather that between secondary and elementary education. The Elementary Education Act of 1870 and its successors had never defined the term 'elementary education'. The larger school boards, once they had met the basic requirements of their areas for instruction in the three 'Rs', had quickly moved on to provide a more advanced education for their pupils which overlapped with secondary work in science and languages, and which was taken up by families much wealthier than those for whom the elementary schools had originally been planned. In many large towns there was a great lack of junior secondary schools taking children up to the ages of 14 or 15, and the boards, in trying to fill this gap, were meeting a real need.

The Cross Commission on elementary education in its final report (1888) recognized that the higher elementary schools were doing very useful work which was not being done by other agencies, but they stressed the need for a much clearer definition of the respective spheres of elementary and secondary education (*PP* 1888 XXXV: 177–8, 201). The problem was discussed by several of the witnesses to the Bryce Commission. G. W. Kekewich, Secretary of the Education Department, thought that it was impossible to make a clear division between the two sectors because they dovetailed into one another. This view was shared by an experienced local administrator, C. H. Bothamley, director of technical instruction for Somerset. In Kekewich's view the higher grade elementary schools worked very well (*BC* II: 114: 1024 (Kekewich); 291–2: 2879–80 (Bothamley)). On the other hand, his colleague, Sir John Donnelly, secretary of the Science and Art Department, argued that primary education for the boy who left school at 13 should be quite separate from that provided for a boy who was to stay until he was 16 or 17; 'a properly-formulated secondary education should have a primary education of its own, different from that of the ordinary primary school' (*BC* II: 131: 1183).

The provision of higher elementary/junior secondary/technical education – for what was offered can be defined under any of these three heads – was the the work of three public agencies – the Science and Art Department, the school boards, and the technical instruction committees. By the 1890s a ramshackle structure had developed which did valuable work, spent a lot of money, and produced a certain amount of overlap and waste. The Bryce Report spoke of 'dispersed and unconnected forces, needless competition between the different agencies, and a frequent overlapping of effort' (*BC* I: 18). The historians, like the Commission, have tended to concentrate on the mistakes that had been made. Yet there is a positive side too, for much had been done to create new schools, to enlarge their curriculum, and to provide wider opportunities through scholarships.

In 1856–7 the Department of Science and Art had become part of the new Education Department, though the elementary and scientific branches were administered quite separately. The DSA had, as its name suggests, dual responsibilities for science and for art, though in its early years the work of promoting a wider knowledge of science had got off to a very slow start (Argles 1964: 15–44). Expansion began only with the adoption of a system of payment for examination successes which had earlier been used in the art division and which was to be applied to elementary education generally by the Revised Code of 1862.

A minute of 2 June 1859 set up a system of examinations for both teachers and students (DSA 7th Rep. *PP* 1860 XXIV: 84; 8th Rep. *PP* 1861 XXXII: 7). Originally teachers took a qualifying examination to enable them to teach under the scheme, but after November 1866 they qualified on the basis of an approved performance in the ordinary examinations. Students who were successful earned payments for their 'schools' according to the grade of success which they gained. Provision was also made for prizes and medals, and later scholarships and exhibitions were established. The grants were originally limited to adult artisans or to the children of parents with incomes of less than £100 a year, though these limits were later considerably extended (Balfour 1898: 177). The examinations were always taken by students who fell outside the income limits, but who found them valuable; they earned no grants for their successes. For example, the City of London School and two London private schools sent in candidates as early as 1860 (DSA 8th Rep. *PP* 1861 XXXII: 27–8). The original subjects for examination were practical and descriptive geometry, physics, chemistry, geology, mineralogy, and natural history, though the list was soon enlarged; in 1862 it included fifteen subjects (DSA 10th Rep. *PP* 1863 XVI: 46).

The expansion of the science examinations was rapid. The first general examination in May 1861 was held at thirty-five centres: 1,000 papers were distributed to about 650 students (DSA 9th Rep. *PP* 1862 XXI: 328). In 1870 there were 799 'schools', which in DSA parlance meant subject examination groups: 34,283 persons were under instruction and 16,515 were examined, plus another 1,207 who had not been taught by certificated teachers (DSA 18th Rep. *PP* 1871 XXIV: 88). The DSA annual reports do not give details of the ages and status of those examined, but most of them were clearly adults. The 16th report observed that there was as yet no demand to support science colleges or 'superior schools' in the towns at which children of better paid artisans and small shopkeepers might be educated up to the ages of 14 or 15. One of the very rare examples of such a school was the Bristol Trade School, which had a fine record of success in the examinations (DSA 13th Rep. *PP* 1866 XXV: 398; 15th Rep. *PP* 1869 XXIII: 214, 226–7; see also p. 41).

By the early 1870s day pupils in elementary schools were sitting and passing the examinations at elementary level. A diagram of the ages and success rates of students in 1873 and 1874 shows that some candidates were sitting as early as their eleventh year. During those years 9,850 students in their thirteenth year came up in the elementary stage of the science subjects and 44 per cent of them were successful (DSA 22nd Rep. *PP* 1875 XXVII: 155). In 1874 no pupil might be presented who had not passed standard V of the elementary code (generally 11 to 12 years old) (ibid.: 143), and in 1876 the restriction was raised to standard VI (12 to 13 years) (DSA 24th Rep. *PP* 1877 XXIII: 37). These measures suggest that the numbers of young candidates from school were becoming a problem, particularly because it was believed that they were easy to 'cram' for success.

By the mid-1870s the DSA examinations in science, which had been intended for working adults, had become a major target for many children at school. The change reflects the fact that levels of achievement in elementary schools were rising. It also shows that schoolmasters and school managers had quickly appreciated that the DSA grants might form an additional source of income to be added to the basic elementary grants. In fact, the examinations were not well adapted for school use. The mathematical and scientific curriculum had been divided up for DSA purposes into a large number of separate subjects. In 1877 there were twenty-four of them (DSA 25th Rep. *PP* 1878 XXXVI: 27) and many of them bore little relationship to the kind of basic science course suitable to boys of 12 or 13.

Teachers entered their pupils for individual subjects with more regard for the likely success rate than for the educational suitability of what was offered. The subjects were not interrelated, and in the earlier years at least no practical work was required. What a clever boy could do is seen by the performance of William Garnett, later secretary of the London Technical Education Board, when he was a boy of 16 at the City of London School. In 1867, when he took the examinations, twenty-four subjects were offered. Because of a time-table clash it was possible to take only twenty-three, which Garnett did. He passed in all of them with one gold, one silver, and three bronze medals, 'much to the surprise of the invigilator who foretold a collapse' (Allen 1933: 12). It was a remarkable achievement by a clever boy, but it bore little relationship to a course of progressive study in science suitable for a wider constituency of more ordinary boys.

As time went on scientific instruction under the department grew less desultory, though change was slow. More students entered for several subjects so that the single course taught by a solitary teacher declined in importance. Building grants were given. Exhibitions to institutions of higher education and school scholarships were created, partly financed by DSA and partly by local effort, in which the school boards became closely involved. Practical examinations were introduced in some subjects, and stress was laid on the provision of laboratory accommodation.

A minute of 24 November 1871 introduced a three-year course of instruction for 'Organized Science Schools', which might be either day schools or evening classes (DSA 19th Rep. *PP* 1872 XXIV: 293–5). These three-year courses were regarded as a very important innovation, but they developed very slowly, and the three-year evening courses hardly at all because they formed too heavy a burden of work for part-time working students. By 1883 there were still only six such schools (Butterworth 1968: 211). A few years later one of the inspectors commented that these schools had not developed because it was easier to earn grants in other ways (DSA 38th Rep. *PP* 1890–1 XXXI: 34). A basic course of study was laid down for the first two years. In the third year specialization was allowed in one of five groups: physics, chemistry, metallurgy; mechanics (steam and machine construction); mechanics (building construction); biology; physiography, geology, mineralogy, mining (DSA 34th Rep. *PP* 1887 XXXIV: 422–5). Additional payments were offered for students who attended a full course of instruction, though there were always difficulties about the large numbers who did not complete the course.

At the local level the progress of scientific and technical education was profoundly influenced by the work of the school boards and later by that of the technical instruction committees. The codes of 1871 and later years permitted pupils in the higher standards to be examined in, and to earn grants for, advanced or 'specific' subjects, which included mathematical subjects, languages, physical geography, botany, physiology, and domestic economy. The code of 1882 created a seventh standard in addition to the six already in existence (Adamson 1930 (1964): 372).

Most children still left school at the earliest possible age, and attendance long remained a problem, but there was a growing tendency for more children to stay on and to take the more advanced subjects. Such children were not numerous in any one school, even in large cities, but there were enough of them to create serious problems of classification and management within an area. It was an obvious solution to collect such children together into a single school. To do this would be more efficient and economical, for example, in the employment of teachers. As a result larger grants might be earned. Better opportunities could be created for the able, and efforts were soon being made to found scholarships so that boys who had gained a good post-primary education might progress to grammar or technical schools. Girls were not excluded from these calculations, particularly since they provided most of the pupil teachers, but the boys received most of the attention since they could expect to command most of the jobs.

The result of all these pressures was the foundation by many school boards of higher grade schools to meet the needs which have been outlined (Vlaeminke 1987). The name provides no exact definition. Titles and patterns of organization varied from place to place, but, if these points are remembered, 'higher grade school' will serve well enough as a descriptive term. One major reason for the vagueness was that these schools in themselves could have no legal existence since they had to be set up within the general limits of a school board's powers to provide elementary education. Consequently, most of the children within these schools were being taught and examined within the standards, though more advanced DSA work was gradually developed. The boards could charge only the fees permitted for elementary schools which, according to section 3 of the 1870 Act, were not to exceed 9d a week.

The Education Department permitted and even encouraged the higher grade schools to develop, but long before the Cockerton Judgment of 1900–1 (see pp. 250–1), there was an undercurrent of unease about the legal position. In 1879–80, for example, the Sheffield School Board was planning its Central Higher School. Though the Department concurred with the general policy of collecting pupils together for more advanced teaching, it commented:

My Lords direct me, however, to add that they may at some future day find it necessary to place some restrictions upon higher grade

schools, in order that no departure may be made from the terms on which the Parliamentary grant is made for Primary Education.
(SSB *Minutes and Reports*, Board, 4 March, 1 April, 14 July 1880)

There was also local opposition to plans which extended the range and thus the cost of elementary education. At Bradford it was argued that the pupils in higher-grade schools would probably be the children of more prosperous working-class families for whom the school board had no responsibility. Such families should educate their children in private schools (A. J. Evans 1947: 58–9). In London the opponents prevented the creation of higher-grade schools until after 1890. It was claimed that the schools would accelerate the trend away from manual work towards overcrowded clerical occupations (Rubinstein 1969: 32). At least one important school board – Liverpool – preferred to develop its existing schools rather than create a central institution (Acland and Llewellyn Smith 1892: 245).

Despite these difficulties the movement to create higher-grade schools took a definite hold, especially in the manufacturing districts of the north of England. The Bryce Commission report said that there were 60 such schools in England, excluding Monmouthshire and London, 35 of them in the counties of Durham, Lancaster, and York. They had, the report commented, helped to meet the major need pointed out by the Schools Inquiry Commission for third-grade schools taking boys up to the age of 14 (*BC* I: 10, 53). Precise definitions were, as has already been suggested, difficult to provide. E. F. M. MacCarthy of King Edward's, Five Ways, Birmingham, concurred with the suggestion of one of the Bryce commissioners that a higher-grade school was 'a secondary school for boys of average ability who have gone through the elementary course entirely and whose parents are able to keep them for a year or two longer under education' (*BC* III: 55: 6526). A modern writer suggests three principal characteristics: the division between an elementary and more advanced course; the existence of work beyond the standards, financed by DSA grants; and, in the latter part of the period, the organization of part of the advanced classes as an 'organized science school' (in the DSA terminology already defined) (Murphy 1985: 210–12).

One major distinction was between those boards like Sheffield which admitted pupils on a competitive basis after an examination and those like Bradford which offered a course designed for children of the upper working/lower middle classes whose parents wanted an education of a type higher than that provided in the ordinary schools. Though all the schools admitted children in the standards because of the need to earn grants, there was a good deal of variation in the ages of entry. In 1894 the Bradford School Board collected information as part of an enquiry into fees. Table 8.1 gives information about the standards offered in the schools of twenty-six boards.

Table 8.1 Standards taught in higher-grade schools, 1894

All standards taught	8 (including one school which admitted infants)
Standard III and upwards	3
Standard IV and upwards	9
Standard V and upwards	8
Standard VI and upwards	2
Standard VII and upwards	1

Source: Bradford School Board, *Return relating to Higher-grade Board Schools with special reference to the payment of a fee* (March 1894).

The grand total (31) is about half the Bryce total of 60 schools. It is slightly greater than the number of boards replying because in a few cases more than one school is listed or separate figures are given for boys and girls. Slightly over half the 31 schools admitted pupils in standards IV or V, that is at 10–12 years old.

9   Higher-grade schools: Bradford, Sheffield, Manchester

Three northern cities – Bradford, Sheffield, and Manchester – were pioneers in the higher-grade school movement, and were very proud of what they had achieved. Bradford's first such school, Feversham Street, had been opened as an ordinary board school in 1874. Shortly afterwards an HMI report recommended that the fairly small number of older children in all the board's schools should be concentrated into a few schools in order to provide them with a better education. As the Feversham Street building was not fully used, it was decided to adapt it for that purpose (*Bradford Education in 1970*: 19). Other schools were opened during the following years. The most important of them, catering for both boys and for girls, were Belle Vue, opened in 1879, and Hanson, opened in 1897 and named after James Hanson, a former chairman of the board.

The Bradford schools were not planned as central schools, but rather as schools for children of a superior class whose parents could afford an education better than the average. Hanson himself told the Cross Commission that all the standards were taken, though there were not many children in the lower standards. Pupils usually began in the ordinary elementary schools, and then entered in standard III or upwards. Those who attended the higher-grade schools were, Hanson said, 'children of the thoughtful and better-to-do working people, the children of clerks, managers, foremen, and artisans, and some of what you would call small tradesmen – the lower middle class'. The fees were 9d a week. The girls' schools were nearly self-supporting. The boys' schools cost about the same as ordinary board schools, though the cost of building was a charge on the rates. In his view the children who attended these schools had as much right to their share of the rate money as anyone else (*PP* 1888 XXXVII: 739: 35252; 739–40: 35255; 751: 35540; 740: 35267–8; 747–8: 35407; 746: 35405; and compare *PP* 1881 XXXIII, App. no. 7: 113–14). The school board, in the information they provided for the Bryce Commission, gave an account of the social background very similar to Hanson's (BSB *Report 1891–4*: 115).

The more advanced teaching in the schools was closely linked with the specific subjects offered under the elementary code. In its 1879 report the board cited Latin, French, mathematics, animal physiology, domestic economy, physical geography, botany, and English literature, though not all of these subjects were taught in all the schools (BSB *Report 1876–9*: 23). Work for the DSA examinations was taken up more slowly than in other towns. Boys from Belle Vue and Feversham Street first sat the DSA examinations in May 1888 and achieved good results in them (BSB, *Report 1885–8*: 99). The subjects taught in 1894 are shown in Table 9.1.

Table 9.1 Subjects taught in Bradford higher-grade schools, 1894

Specific subjects	– boys	heat, chemistry, algebra, light
	– girls	domestic economy, animal physiology
DSA subjects	– boys	mathematics, sound, light and heat, practical, plane and solid geometry, magnetism and electricity, 2nd grade art
	– girls	human physiology, hygiene, mathematics, 2nd grade art

Source: Bradford School Board, *Report 1891–4*: 116.

French was taken in both the boys' schools, and work was also done for the Cambridge junior local and commercial certificates (BSB *Report 1891–4*: 116). As Hanson had told the Cross Commission, science rather squeezed literature out in the curriculum (*PP* 1888 XXXVII: 751: 35544–8). The reason is simple: it paid better.

Organized Science Schools (Schools of Science) with a three-year course were set up comparatively late in Bradford – at Belle Vue in 1896 and at Hanson when it opened in 1897 (*Bradford Education in 1870*: 21). In October 1900 there were 362 pupils (214 boys and 148 girls) in the school of science at Belle Vue and 210 (93 boys and 117 girls) at Hanson. Of these 91 were aged 15–16, 15 aged 16–17, and 6 aged 17–18. In 1894, that is before the schools of science were organized, there had been 1,791 children in all the higher-grade schools, 1,505 of them in standard IV and above. Of these (boys and girls) 332 were aged 13–14, 142 aged 14–15, 37 aged 15–16, and 2 aged 16 (BSB *Report 1891–4*: 116–17). The proportion of the total number of children who were of full secondary age was therefore fairly small. HMI reports of 1902 on both Belle Vue and Hanson paid tribute to the excellent work of the schools, but also commented on the large number of pupils who did not complete their courses (BSB *Report 1900–3*: 366, 368).

Nevertheless the school board had good reason for expressing their satisfaction, in their submission to the Bryce Commission, on what had been achieved. Boys won scholarships to the grammar school and in a few cases had taken university awards. Girls had won scholarships at the girls' grammar school. Other pupils had moved on to the technical college, some of whom had gone to university, to the Royal College of Science, or had become chemists or engineers (BSB *Report 1888–91*: 92; *Report 1891–4*: 77–9). A scholarship scheme for entry to the higher grade schools had been inaugurated in 1877, partly financed by the board and partly by individual donors. In 1898 the number of scholarships was massively increased to 500 and arrangements made that all pupils in the second or later years of the science schools should be regarded as free scholars (BSB *Report 1900–3*: 371–80). The Bryce assistant commissioner commented that Bradford, through its higher-grade schools, technical school, and grammar school, possessed the nucleus of an organized structure of secondary education (*BC* VII: 186–7).

However, the opposition voiced to the original proposal for the Feversham Street school was never entirely silenced (see p. 93). When an organized science school was set up at Belle Vue, both the grammar school and the technical school petitioned the Science and Art Department against it, though the department refused to intervene (A. J. Evans 1947: 168–9; A. Elliott 1981: 18–23).

Like all the major school boards, the Bradford board suffered from the policy initiated by the new Board of Education (see p. 251). In 1899 the Board of Education had queried the accounts submitted for Belle Vue school, urging that items relating to the school of science should be deleted from them. The school board refused to do this since the accounts had already been approved by the auditor, and the dispute rumbled on for some time. It looks indeed as if both sides were stalling until the forthcoming Education Act should pass into law (BSB *Report 1897–1900*: 160–8; *Report 1900–3*: 266–9; *Bradford Education in 1970*: 24). In 1900 the school board applied for the recognition of the new Carlton Street school as a commercial school under the Higher Elementary School Minute of 1900. The request was refused since it was not a school of science of an elementary character as the minute required, nor was the Board of Education satisfied that it was needed. A deputation from Bradford went to see Sir John Gorst, who showed no signs of yielding to their application (BSB *Report 1897–1900*: 170–6; *Report 1900–3*: 269–72). By that time the problems of individual schools had become engulfed in the national controversies over education, which raged as keenly in Bradford as everywhere else and out of which was to emerge the Education Act of 1902 (see pp. 248–52).

The Sheffield board proceeded on rather different lines from its Bradford counterpart. A site for a projected central school was approved as early as 1873, though it was some years before operations could begin (SSB *Report to 25 November 1875*: 1). The formal opening of the school on 15 July 1880 was attended by the Archbishop of York and by both the lord president, Earl Spencer, and the vice-president, A. J. Mundella, who was a Sheffield MP (SSB *Report 1879–80*: 2–3). The objectives of the board were explained in their reports and in a statement by their chairman (SSB *Report 1870–6*: 4; S. Cole 1882: 16–18). Scholars from all the elementary schools, irrespective of class, were to be eligible, and it was hoped to provide scholarships for children of ability. Great advantages would ensue if the abler children could be collected from the elementary schools and given a more advanced education. There was a need to create a link between those schools and the higher training provided in Firth College, the nucleus of the later university. A few with exceptional ability and perseverence would be able to take advantage of such opportunities. Many more would be able to use their scientific and technical knowledge in local industry. Others would become pupil-teachers and would thus help to raise the standard of teaching in the board's schools.

The Central Schools consisted of an infant school, a junior mixed school (standards I-IV), a mixed school (standards V-VI), and a higher school (Bingham 1949: 175). Admission to the higher school was by examination. At the initial examination 587 candidates presented themselves, of whom 305 were admitted. The subjects taken in the first year were geography, history, grammar, literature, domestic economy (girls), mechanics, chemistry, mathematics, Latin, French, and physical geography. For the board the new school was an expensive venture. The total cost per pupil was £51 11s 2d, which was twice the comparable cost of the most expensive elementary school (£23 13s 10d). Much of this must have been due to the choice of an expensive central site, since such a school had to be accessible to all parts of the town (SSB *Report 1879–80*: 9).

The first HMI report on the higher department commented that the school had made an excellent start under an able head and a hard-working and efficient staff. Favourable remarks were made about both the elementary and the specific subjects. Mechanics, mathematics, and chemistry were all taught (SSB *Minutes*, Board 21 July 1881). The DSA examinations were taken from the beginning and successful results achieved. The first subjects offered were mathematics, inorganic chemistry, and animal physiology (SSB *Minutes*, School Management Committee, 14 July 1881). A laboratory with accommodation for thirty-two students was fitted up, and much attention was given to workshop practice. The equipment was given by local manufacturers since the board had no legal power to provide it.

The Samuelson Commission on technical instruction visited the school and commented favourably on the practical work, which comprised:

the production of simple but perfect solids and surfaces in iron and wood . . . the construction of models in wood, suitable for use in schools . . . and various kinds of wood joints, model doors etc.; likewise the construction of simple apparatus to illustrate by actual experiment the principles of lever, pulleys, wheel and axle, the crane, strains on beams with different positions of load, and the mechanics of the roof, arch and bridge.

(*PP* 1884 XXIX: 539)

Some scholarships were provided with funds from the sale of the old Lancasterian school, and some of the scholarship holders went on to win awards at the Royal School of Mines and Normal School of Science at South Kensington and at the Royal School of Science in Dublin. Other scholars won awards at Firth College and Queen's scholarships for teachers. The clerk to the school board, J. F. Moss, described the school to the Social Science Association meeting at Huddersfield in 1883. There were 500 scholars, standard IV being the minimum level for admission. The age of the scholars ranged from 10 years to 16, though most left at 14 or 15. Good results had been obtained in the DSA examinations and in workshop practice. Every industrial centre, Moss urged, should have such a school 'at which pupils, who can remain sufficiently long, may receive special courses of instruction in science, more advanced teaching in art, and some practical experience in the use of tools' (*TSSA* 1883: 301–11).

During the late 1880s and the 1890s the Central School grew much larger. An extension containing 'chemical and physical laboratories, machine drawing room, lecture and demonstration rooms, workshops for wood and iron, laundry &c' was opened in 1895 (SSB *Report 1894–5*: 14). During that decade numbers were generally about 1,200–300. After the entrance examination in March 1898, for example, there were 1,309 pupils, of whom 367 were standard ex-VII, that is, above the level at which they could earn Education Department grants, and 148 were in the school of science (SSB *Minutes*, School Management Committee 6 April 1898). An organized science school had been set up in 1887 (SSB *Report 1886–7*: 7), and in 1894 the DSA rules were modified so as to allow a better balance between the scientific and the non-scientific subjects (SSB *Minutes* Board, 21 February 1895; see p. 106). It is clear from the school board minutes and reports that initial numbers at the beginning of the year were not maintained and that many pupils did not complete their courses or even finish the school year.

J. F. Moss explained the financial position of the school to the Bryce Commission of 1894–5. In the previous year the grant from the education rate amounted to £1,526 5s 9d. The DSA grant was £785 11s 4d, and the Education Department grant, paid on those children who were qualified to earn it, was £691 14s 0d. He explained that no objection had been raised by ratepayers to the expenditure of rate money on pupils beyond the seventh standard (for whom no Education Department grants could be claimed), though he was not himself satisfied about the board's legal powers to do this (*BC* III: 86: 6928–30). By that time the school was free. When the Elementary Education Act of 1891 was passed it was originally planned to reduce the original fee, but, after considering a memorial that to abolish fees would give all classes an equal chance to use the school, the board decided that after 2 November 1891 no further charges should be made (SSB *Minutes*, Board, 20 August, 17 September, 15 October 1891).

Reports on the school, both from HMI and the DSA inspectors, were usually good. So far as the school of science was concerned, a rather critical report in 1897 was followed by something much more favourable in 1898. Praise was given to the practical physics and chemistry and theoretical physics was well taught. Mathematics was good and metalwork was selected for special praise. The arts subjects were not neglected. French had improved and good work was being done in English literature and geography, though history was only fair (SSB *Minutes*, Board 19 August 1897; 21 July 1898). Moss had told the Bryce Commission that the literary subjects were well taught and that the school gave 'a pretty full Secondary Education' (*BC* III: 85: 6911). Despite the new buildings opened in 1895 there was a serious problem of space. The HMI report of 1898 judged both the accommodation and the playground to be inadequate, and the board was advised to build a new school for girls on another site (SSB *Minutes*, Board, 21 July 1898). The buildings still exist. When one looks at them now, it is astonishing that they could have housed 1,200–1,300 boys and girls.

In one sense the overcrowded condition of the school was a tribute to its success. In 1892–3, as the result of an initiative from the Sheffield Chamber of Commerce, it was decided to give more time to modern languages and commercial arithmetic. German, shorthand, and bookkeeping were added to the subjects taught, along with commercial geography (SSB *Reports 1891–2*: 8–9; *1892–3*: 9). In 1899 a further reorganization under a new headmaster involved yet more development on the commercial side and the provision of better facilities for girls who wished to take science. At that time the number of boys and girls in the school was almost exactly the same (SSB *Report 1898–9*: 8). The school received some assistance from the technical education funds of the city council, but the aid was small and much of it earmarked to be spent on evening classes. The city council did not, they explained, favour 'practical illustrations of the application of electricity' or commercial education, an attitude that was perhaps surprising in the leaders of a great industrial city (SSB *Minutes*, School Management Committee, 11 May 1893). However, the technical education fund did finance a scholarship to the technical school (1897), which was to be open to scholars over the age of 15 (SSB *Minutes*, School Management Committee, 24 June 1897; Bingham 1949: 192).

Like the Bradford board the Sheffield board was deeply involved in the controversies that preceded the 1902 Act. There were legal problems about financing evening classes from the school fund, and short-term help was received for this purpose from the city council. In May 1900 the Sheffield board applied to the Board of Education for the recognition of the Central Higher School as a higher elementary school under the minute of 1900. They requested that the rigid exclusion of children at the end of the school year in which they reached the age of 15 might not be insisted upon, but the Board of Education replied that they had no power to make any exceptions to the regulations (SSB *Minutes*, School Management Committee, 31 May, 21 June 1900). After the school board had submitted very detailed curricula, the necessary recognition was given, but only for the science branch. Just as at Bradford the 'commercial and literary branch' was excluded on the ground that Parliament had never authorized the application of exchequer grants to 'the teaching in Day Schools, either Elementary or Secondary, of advanced technical or literary instruction' (SSB *Minutes*, School Management Committee, 25 October 1900). The Board of Education was arguing that it had no legal power to do what the Sheffield board had requested. Logically, the Whitehall case seems weak. The connection between 'technical' and 'literary' is strained, and in fact the technical instruction committees had for a decade been spending money on very similar purposes. Of course, the school boards had not benefited substantially from those grants (see p. 251).

The school board had now to reorganize the curricula and time-tables to meet the new circumstances, and they encouraged boys and girls to enter at 10 or 11 years old in order that they might complete a full course. The Board of Education refused to relax the age limit of 15 years (SSB *Minutes*, Board, 21 March 1901), and they cut the numbers drastically. In August 1901 there were 1,146 children in the school (SSB *Minutes*, School Management Committee, 25 July 1901). In December, Whitehall agreed to accept only 640 places, though in their reply the school board argued that there was room for 940 and that the accommodation had earlier been recognized for many more than that. Finally, 910 places were accepted, which Whitehall claimed was the largest number possible if there was to be a proper balance between the pupils in each of the four years of the course (SSB *Minutes*, School Management Committee, 12 December 1901, 23 January 1902). There was a case for reducing the numbers because the school was probably overcrowded, but in general it had done excellent work in the preceding twenty years, and it seems that Whitehall was cutting back ruthlessly on developments which had been very promising. The last HMI report in the school board minutes, dated 6 October 1902, says of the school's science work: 'there is still a tendency to cover too much ground, and to undertake work of too advanced a character' (SSB *Minutes*, Board, 16 October 1902). Perhaps the teachers were trying to cram the children. It may be, on the other hand, that the children had the ability to do work of a higher level than the new order thought appropriate for them.

The first of the Manchester higher-grade schools dated from 1877 (*BC* III: 332: 9912). The Central Board School in Deansgate with accommodation for 1,027 children was opened in August 1884. It had been planned to include a chemical laboratory, a room for drawing classes, and a gymnasium (MSB, *4th Report 1879–82*: 4; *5th Report 1882–5*: 4). Ten years later it was admitting boys in standard V and girls in standard VI (MSB *8th Report 1891–4*: 64). By that time (1894) there were five Organized Science Schools in the city with 728 pupils in standard VII and beyond. They studied mathematics, geometry, chemistry, physics, and machine construction, while some pupils took such subjects as human physiology and physiography. The great majority took art and all studied French, book-keeping, and shorthand. Most took English and French literature and many geography and history. There were fifty science and art scholarships available, partly financed by DSA and partly by local subscriptions, and a few Lancasterian scholarships, financed as at Sheffield from an old school endowment (MSB, ibid.: 63, 68, 70).

The Deansgate site was later sold to a railway company and a new Central School opened in Whitworth Street in 1900. This was built for 1,450 children, including 500 in the organized science school and 250 in the pupil teachers' centre. The accommodation included dining rooms, rooms for teaching cookery and laundry work, gymnasium, manual instruction room, chemical and physical laboratories, and a machine drawing room (MSB *9th Report 1894–7*: 65–7; *10th Report 1897–1900*: 55–6). Some statistics of the new school for the year ended 31 May 1897 fill out the picture. The highest number of pupils during the year was 1,040 (775 boys and 265 girls), and the numbers in the school of science were 343. The number of older children, from 13–14 years upwards was 707, almost all of them aged between 13 and 16. The great majority of those admitted during the year came between the ages of 11 and 14 (481 out of 574). Just as at Bradford and Sheffield many of them did not stay for very long: 202 left after less than one year, 207 between one and two years, and 143 between two and three years (MSB *9th Report*: 145–6). It is not surprising that the Manchester board had required parents to give an undertaking to keep children at school for twelve months or to pay a sum equal to the amount of the grant lost if they did not (MSB *8th Report*: 65).

The Manchester higher grade schools had certainly been a success. By 1900 there were 1,035 pupils in the five schools of science (MSB *10th Report 1897–1900*: 71), and there is evidence that the schools contained boys who might otherwise have competed for scholarships at the grammar school (Mumford 1919: 375, 380). The Cross Commission heard some evidence on this point. The chairman of the school board, the Rev. Joseph Nunn, argued that the system was abused. Because of their low fees the higher grade schools withdrew children from the grammar schools and other schools whose fees were much higher. Parents who could afford to pay a higher fee were using the cheaper schools and their children were qualifying for the science and art exhibitions. Pupils were even coming into the city by train to attend the higher grade schools who were not the children of Manchester ratepayers at all. On the other hand, the fee of 9d a week was sufficiently high to exclude the children of labouring men to whom the schools ought to have been open (*PP* 1887 XXIX: 775: 36281–3; 776: 36322; 776–7: 36228; 796: 37042, 37052, 37056).

The other side of the case was put by the headmaster of the Central School, James Scotson, who argued that, since the more well-to-do parents paid large rates and taxes, it was entirely proper that their children should attend the school (ibid.: 273: 23000–1). H. E. Oakeley, HMI, after describing Mr Scotson's school, accepted that the schools encroached into the field of secondary education, but they met a great need. There was, Oakeley claimed, a large population of foremen and skilled workmen who wanted an education for their children up to the age of 14 years or so, but who did not want a secondary education up to the age of 15 or 16 (ibid.; 675: 59307). Manchester people certainly seemed interested in these schools. When Cheetham higher-grade school held its first 'at home' on the afternoon of 26 June 1900, about 1,000 visitors came (Cheetham School, log book 1894–1924).

10 The 1890s: the technical instruction committees

The 1890s was a decade of major developments in which the Department of Science and Art, the Charity Commissioners, and the new county and county borough councils all played an active part. The annual DSA reports of the later 1880s had already referred to the effort to create organized science schools, to the growing involvement of school boards in DSA work, to improved laboratory provision and better standards of teaching, and to the increased number of science and art scholarships awarded. For some boys these provided important career openings. The higher-grade school at Cambridge, for example, had several successes of this kind, like the scholar of 1879 who had gone to the Perse Grammar School, then to St John's, and had become senior wrangler and a college fellow (DSA 38th Report *PP* 1890–1 XXXI: 22–3). After 1890 the reports make frequent reference to the provision of facilities by the new local authorities with the local taxation grants at their disposal. The county boroughs tended to limit themselves to the purely technical field, but many of the counties gave money to endowed schools to provide better laboratory accommodation and to pay science teachers (*BC* I: 32–9). These new activities made some of the more elementary DSA work unnecessary. After 1892 the payments for second class examinations, elementary stage, were discontinued, and the grants for advanced work and for honours raised (DSA 39th Report *PP* 1892 XXXII: 57–8).

One of the major changes during the 1890s was the steady increase in the number of organized science schools, which had grown so slowly during the 1880s. In 1893 there were 70 day schools with 8,469 pupils and 9 evening schools with 1,061 (DSA 41st Report *PP* 1894 XXXII: 8–9). By 1897 there were 143 Schools of Science (the name was changed by new regulations of that year) in England and Wales. Of these 62 were held in higher-grade schools, 55 in endowed schools, and 38 in technical and other schools (DSA 43rd Report, *PP* 1898 XXIX: 251, 254). It is noteworthy that the number of host endowed and technical schools (partly financed by the counties and county boroughs) exceeds that of the higher-grade schools (which were the responsibility of the school boards). This disparity, which reflects the activity of the technical instruction committees, is even more marked in a parliamentary return of 1902 which gives the statistics of Schools of Science on 1 May 1901 (see Table 10.1). This return shows that, although the school board examples had the larger average size, their numbers, unlike that of the other main group, were not growing very much.

Table 10.1 Schools of Science, 1901

	Schools	Pupils
Not attached to or connected with a public elementary school		
established prior to 1897	78	8,200
established 1897 or subsequently	75	4,395
Attached to public elementary schools not conducted by school boards		
established prior to 1897	4	395
established 1897 or subsequently	4	226
Conducted by school boards and attached to public elementary schools		
established prior to 1897	44	8,173
established 1897 or subsequently	8	793
Totals	213	22,182

Source: Return of the Statistics of Schools of Science conducted under the Regulations of the Board of Education, 24 March 1902, *PP* 1902 LXXX: 863–77.

The Science and Art Department has always been much criticized on the ground that its system promoted cramming and enforced a rigid curriculum which favoured the sciences at the expense of other subjects. H. G. Wells, himself a product of the world of DSA examining, thought that many of these defects resulted from the adaptation to the school system of plans originally made for adults (Wells 1894: 526; Butterworth 1968: 227). One of the department's own inspectors wrote:

> The curriculum is often of a doubtful and uncertain character. . . . I am informed that successes in the May Examinations are often earned by devoting the whole of March and April to cramming, the literary and other subjects being almost entirely neglected.
>
> (DSA 45th Report, *PP* 1898 XXIX: 326)

The Department certainly made serious attempts to improve the situation. There was a movement away from making grants on examination results towards a system which gave weight to good attendance and to good reports from inspectors (DSA 43rd Report, *PP* 1896 XXX: 11, 74–5; 45th Report, *PP* 1898 XXIX: 253–4, 254–5).

In order to make the new system possible and to ensure better supervision of practical work thirteen inspectors had been appointed in 1893 (DSA 41st Report, *PP* 1894 XXXII: 65). Their reports give a clear picture of the work done in the schools during the latter years of the decade. In 1895 there was a major revision of the course in organized science schools. The minimum of instruction in science and art was reduced from 15 to 13 hours per week. In addition, not less than 10 hours was to be given to literary or commercial subjects. The course was to include at least one modern language and two hours were to be given to manual instruction. The course was to occupy either three or four years, and the grant might be discontinued if the numbers attending fell below a certain level (DSA 42nd Report, *PP* 1895 XXXI: 72; Balfour 1898: 173).

The inspectors' reports were generally positive and encouraging, though clearly all the difficulties had not been sorted out. The organized science schools varied greatly in standard. Efforts were being made to improve the practical work, though one inspector commented that many of the teachers had no experience of it themselves (DSA 44th Report, *PP* 1897 XXX: 58). The criticism was made that the subjects studied were not properly co-ordinated, and the complaint, already noted, was repeated that pupils tended to leave much too early in their course. However, there were many good reports too. One inspector noted that the demand among employers for boys who had passed through the organized science school course was greater than the supply (DSA 45th Report, *PP* 1898 XXIX: 321). It was thought that standards of science teaching were rising and that the broadening of the curriculum and the extended time given to literary studies had had a good effect. The number of Schools of Science in Lancashire and the West Riding is shown in Table 10.2.

Table 10.2 Schools of Science in Lancashire and Yorkshire (West Riding) 1901

	Lancashire	Yorkshire (West Riding)
Not attached to elementary schools	10	15
Attached to elementary schools		
not conducted by school boards	4	—
Conducted by school boards	11	8

Source: Return of the Statistics of Schools of Science, *PP* 1902 LXXX: 863–77.

The inspector for the Manchester division had reported in 1896 that there were sixteen Organized Science Schools in his district:

> In the majority the instruction is distinctly good, and I consider that there has been a marked improvement in the work during the present session owing to the inauguration of the new scheme. The methods employed are more scientific and practical, and the greater freedom allowed will, I feel sure, be beneficial in many ways.
>
> (DSA 43rd Report, *PP* 1896 XXX: 92)

General interest in technical education had been quickening during the 1880s. In 1889 the government introduced a Bill which became the Technical Instruction Act 1889. County and county borough councils and urban sanitary authorities were permitted to raise up to a penny rate for technical education, and they might set up a technical instruction committee, to which co-opted members might be added. The council might delegate its powers over education to this committee, except for the powers to raise a rate and to borrow money (Roscoe 1906: 209; Sharp 1968: 14–22). The new legislation made little immediate impact. Though some technical instruction committees were set up, for example, in the West Riding, few councils took powers to raise a rate. The major change occurred with the passage of the Local Taxation (Customs and Excise) Act 1890. The original Bill had proposed to raise a duty on spirits and beer, one purpose of which was to compensate the owners of superfluous public houses. The plan raised keen opposition from the temperance interest, and the government found itself in the position of having a residue of money, after the other purposes of the legislation had been met, for which there was no obvious purpose in view.

On 10 June 1890 A. H. D. Acland proposed in the House of Commons that £350,000 of this money should be applied 'for the purpose of agricultural, commercial, and technical instruction', citing the example of powers already given by the Welsh Intermediate Education Act (see pp. 247–8). The parliamentary manoeuvres that ensued need not be recounted in detail. Finally, after the Chancellor of the Exchequer, G. J. Goschen, had refused to accept the idea of any commitment of funds for secondary education in general, it was decided that the county and county borough councils might, if they wished, contribute the whole or part of the residue under the proposed Act to technical education within the meaning of the Act of 1889, and that this contribution should be independent of any sum raised under that Act (53 & 54 Vic. c. 60, sect. 1: 2).

The sums of money involved were large. In the first year £709,000 was available, and by the end of the century the grants amounted to almost £1,000,000 (Sharp 1968: 19; 1971: 31–6). Though the councils were not required to spend the money on technical education, almost all of them did spend all or a large part of it in this way. Their technical instruction committees became a major force in educational development, not least because the term 'technical' was interpreted on very broad lines to include provision of almost every type above that provided under the Elementary Education Acts (*BC* I: 13). In 1898–9 £770,000 out of the £827,000 available in England was being spent on education and only £57,000 on general county purposes (*Record* VIII (1899): 166–7). Nor was progress limited to manufacturing areas and big cities. The DSA annual reports sometimes named counties where they thought that the work deserved special praise. Among those selected were the West Riding, Cheshire, Surrey, Hampshire, and Somerset, counties with a wide spread of economic interests and occupations (*PP* 1895 XXXI: 110;

1898 XXIX: 333; 1897 XXX: 53; 1898 XXIX: 323; 1899 XXVII: 342, 356).

The technical instruction committees made a major contribution to the development of English education (Gosden 1970). Their administrative structures provided the model for local education authorities after 1902. *The Record of Technical and Secondary Education*, the journal of NAPTSE, wrote of their work for secondary education in enthusiastic terms:

> In several localities, e.g. Durham, Hampshire, Surrey and Wiltshire, the attendance of pupils at the public secondary schools has been almost, or more than, doubled through the scholarships and grants offered by the County Councils; many new schools organized on modern lines have been established; facilities for giving practical technical instruction, where none existed previously, have been provided on a scale suitable to the needs of the whole area; while the curricula and the teaching staffs of the schools have, in many cases, been entirely re-modelled. It is thus quite evident that Local Authorities have not fallen into the error of subordinating the very important claims of secondary education to those many imperative duties committed to their care under the Technical Instruction Acts.
>
> (*Record* XII (1903): 167)

These words supply no mean epitaph, and the actual sums expended reinforce the points made even further. A return of 1896–7 on expenditure by counties and county boroughs on secondary schools covers capitation payments, teaching staff, maintenance, apparatus and equipment, buildings and scholarships. Forty-two counties made grants totalling £124,664 15s 0d and twenty-one county boroughs grants of £20,206 7s 2d. Of the grand total of £144,871 2s 2d, £65,597 4s 10d, or about 45 per cent, was spent on scholarships (*Record* VI (1897): 424–6). In 1900 24 of the 61 county boroughs subsidized secondary schools (*Record* IX (1900): 85), though the boroughs tended to be more committed to grants for technical education. In 1891–2, for example, Manchester had £10,425 to spend. Of this £3,600 went to the school board, £1,000 to Owens College, £4,000 to the technical school and £750 to the school of art. The remaining £1,075 was spent on a number of smaller grants, including £250 to Manchester Grammar School (*BC* II: 323: 3337).

The most complete system of secondary and technical education was that developed by the London Technical Education Board with Sidney Webb as chairman and William Garnett as secretary (Allen 1933; Brennan 1959: 85–96; 1960: 27–43; 1961: 146–71; Maclure 1970: 68–76). Though London had a highly efficient school board, it had been a slow starter in promoting more advanced work. The county council took no action to develop technical instruction until a special committee was set up in 1892, which commissioned Hubert Llewellyn Smith, who had been associated with A. H. D. Acland, to make a report on technical education in the metropolis. Llewellyn Smith recommended both grants in aid for secondary and technical schools and a system of scholarships, and his suggestions were adopted by the technical education board set up in 1893. In its first year the board made grants of £12,215 for maintenance and equipment to thirty-nine secondary schools, which in return were required to observe a code of regulations and to grant free places to London County Council scholars. Webb told the Bryce Commission that his board was aiding almost all the public secondary schools in London except those with high fees (*BC* II; 276–7: 2736; 278: 2745; *Record* (IV) 1895: 169). In its report the commission described the London board as 'the only example at present existing in England of a systematic local organization for the control of Technical and Secondary Education' (*BC* I: 37).

The counties varied in their performance as promoters of secondary education. One of the leaders was the West Riding, the first county to spend rate funds under the Technical Instruction Act of 1889, though county boroughs had done so earlier (Gosden and Sharp 1978: 7). The West Riding witnesses told the Bryce Commission that their income for 1891–2 had been £30,698 3s 5d. The whole grant was made available for educational purposes by the county council. The council retained control over the whole sum rather than subdividing it between smaller areas. The money, which aided classes, schools, and other institutions, comprised a capitation grant, grants for approved subjects, for new buildings and apparatus, for extension work and travelling lectures. Fixed payments were made to institutions under special conditions like admitting a certain number of students without fee. Subventions were made to the Yorkshire College at Leeds and to Firth College at Sheffield. There was also an extensive scholarship scheme (*BC* IV: 197–200). The DSA inspector for the area spoke of 'an elaborate and far-reaching scheme by which aid is given to students and teachers in all parts of the county within its administrative area' (DSA 42nd Report, *PP* 1895 XXXI: 110).

Though London and the West Riding were the leaders, they did not stand alone in the movement to aid the secondary schools. In Devonshire the technical instruction grants had revolutionized the teaching of science in secondary schools (*BC* VI: 61), and nearby Somerset had also been active (*BC* II: 290–322). Surrey had accomplished more than most. H. Macan, organizing secretary of the technical instruction committee, told the Bryce Commission that, when they began, no one in the county was 'accustomed to education at all above the elementary stage' (*BC* II: 437: 4530). They had spent money both in aiding secondary schools and on scholarships and exhibitions, and were planning to set up new schools. The Bryce assistant commissioner commented that the use made by Surrey of its funds went a long way towards justifying its claim to become the local authority for secondary education. The county's achievement had destroyed his own prejudices against the educational work of the county councils (*BC* VII: 42–3).

The new local authorities also founded some schools and re-established others. At Richmond-on-Thames, Surrey County Council decided to build a secondary school/technical institute, and the town council also made a grant towards the cost of the building. The Richmond County School, opened in 1896, had 170 boys by 1901. The upper four forms constituted a School of Science, and German and Latin were also taught. The average leaving age was 16 and rather over one-third of the pupils had been at elementary schools. The fees for Surrey boys were £6 a year plus 10 shillings a term for books, and other boys paid £10. The county council made an annual grant of £450 and provided a modern languages master for the upper forms. The actual cost of the education given was about £12 per head. There were fifteen minor scholarships providing free education and books for three years, and some additional senior scholarships (*Record* X (1901): 363–8 (A. E. Buckhurst); Gosden 1970: 38).

Some schools were the product of efforts by several local bodies. At Swindon in Wiltshire the Mechanics' Institution had applied in 1891 to Wiltshire County Council for a grant towards the cost of erecting a technical school. A committee representing several local bodies was formed and the school opened in 1896. A School of Science was established, which had been transferred from a higher-grade school under the school board. Girls were admitted in 1898, evening classes were conducted, and at the turn of the century more laboratory accommodation was being built (*Record* XI (1902): 463–8).

The boys' and girls' high schools at Middlesbrough provide an example of existing schools being taken over by a local authority. The boys' school, founded in 1870, and the girls' school (1874) were conducted under a trust deed of 1877. In 1887 the upper part of the boys' school was enrolled as a School of Science. Ten years later, when there were 83 boys in the School of Science, 52 younger boys, 117 girls, and about 50 in the preparatory school, the financial situation had become very difficult. DSA grants had become more difficult to earn, the fees had been reduced, and middle-class parents disliked the introduction of scholarship holders from elementary schools. After negotiations had taken place, the schools were handed over in 1900 to the town council, which had already been contributing an annual subsidy. The normal age range of pupils was to be from 8 to 17, and one place in ten was to be given to a scholarship holder, one-half the total number of scholarships being awarded to pupils from elementary schools (PRO Ed. 27: 5587, 5588; Butterworth 1960: 27–34).

These examples of new and re-established schools illustrate how deeply the counties and county boroughs had become involved in the management of secondary education before the 1902 Act. They also made a major contribution through their scholarships schemes. Initially there had been uncertainty whether the new authorities had the power to make such awards, but this was cleared up by an Act of 1891 which enabled authorities to finance education outside their own districts and to provide scholarships either within or outside those districts (54 & 55 Vic. c. 4). Scholarships fell into one of three groups: junior, awarded at ages 11–13, which formed the majority; intermediate for the 16–19 age-group, and senior for higher education. Provision varied a good deal from authority to authority. In London, which had one of the most complete schemes, the technical education board report for 1896–7 explained that there were 2,139 scholarships and exhibitions, of which 1,294 were junior. For the 600 junior scholarships awarded there had been 3,725 entries. Of the total number of junior scholars, 1,000 were attending secondary schools and the remainder the upper standard departments of elementary schools. 136 junior scholars had had the tenure of their scholarships extended (*Record* VI (1897): 389). Unlike some of the scholarships financed by the old endowments which have already been considered, there was no shortage of candidates. One reason for this was probably that London gave maintenance awards as well as free education (see p. 80).

The *Record* gave very detailed information about scholarships. Figures for the years 1894–5 and 1899–1900 show both the extent of the provision and the way in which it grew. In 1894–5 seventy councils awarded 8,708 scholarships of all kinds to a yearly value of £56,470. In addition, 2,961 scholarships had been renewed to the value of £37,745. The total annual value of all scholarships was therefore £94,215, of which £45,208 had been spent on scholarships at secondary schools, or about 48 per cent of the total sum. In 1899–1900 ninety councils awarded 19,971 scholarships of all kinds to an annual value of £156,793. Of this total £77,349 was spent on awards at secondary schools, or about 49 per cent of a much larger total (*Record* V (1896): 151; X (1901): 287; Sharp 1974: 36–50). The increase in the number of scholarships awarded had contributed in many areas to an increase in the total number of pupils in the secondary schools (*Record* IX (1900): 66–7). The management of such a large number of awards involved quite complex problems of publicity and administration. The Incorporated Association of Headmasters, founded in 1890, had inaugurated a scheme for the award of minor scholarships, and by 1900 twenty councils used the examinations of the joint board set up by the county councils and the association (*BC* III: 27: 6176–8; IV: 157: 13,991; *Record* X (1901): 351; Gordon 1980: 152–3).

The social backgrounds and future careers of scholarship holders in the grammar schools have already been discussed, and the boys who entered these schools with county council scholarships came from similar backgrounds (see pp. 75–83). The *Record* set out the principal occupations of parents of county scholars from an official return covering the years 1896–9 (see Table 10.3).

Table 10.3 Occupations of parents of county scholars, 1896–9

	Junior scholars	Intermediate scholars
Professional and general	544	93
Clerks, agents, warehousemen	495	60
Building trades	477	42
Retail dealers and salesmen	385	55
Engineering and metal trades	304	23
Railway and transport service	287	14
Widows, 'No occupation'	256	41
Official	242	33
General labour	234	11
Domestic and personal service	204	18
Other miscellaneous trades (including agriculture and mining)	1,168	122

Source: *Record of Technical and Secondary Education* X (1901): 23, 360, from 'Return showing the occupation of the parents of the winners of county council scholarships during the past three years (1896–9)' (*PP* 1900 LXIII: 59–224).

A very few of these scholars rose right to the top. E. Cunningham of St John's College, Cambridge, senior wrangler in 1902, had gone from an elementary school to Owen's School, Islington, with a governors' scholarship. He was later awarded an LCC intermediate scholarship and, when he gained a college award, a senior county scholarship which was extended for a fourth year to enable him to take Part II of the Mathematical Tripos, in which he gained a first class in 1903 (*Record* XI (1902): 259; Tanner 1917: 581, 584). Most county scholars went into clerical occupations or posts in industry and commerce. The occupations of former junior scholarship holders in Leicestershire, a county of mixed farming and industry (1893–9), are given in Table 10.4.

Table 10.4 Occupations of former county scholarship holders, Leicestershire, 1893–9

Clerical posts	22
Pupil-teachers	14
To universities	6
Surveyors' offices	5
Engineering offices	2
Apprentice to chemist	2
Wesleyan ministry	2
Other professions	5
Other posts	4
Total	62

Source: M. Seaborne, 'Education in the nineties. The work of the Technical Instruction Committees', in B. Simon (ed.) *Education in Leicestershire 1540–1940. A regional study* (1968: 190).

The social fabric was changing, though rather slowly, as wider opportunities became available through better education. The Science and Art Department was one major agent in the change. The two friends, the novelist H. G. Wells and the editor of *Nature*, Richard Gregory, provide good examples of careers based in the first instance on DSA qualifications. Wells, after an early life in retail trade and private school teaching, gained his DSA certificates and won a place at the Normal School of Science at South Kensington. Gregory won his place at South Kensington after being an apprentice in a boot and shoe factory and a laboratory assistant. In later years Gregory wrote to Wells about his novel, *Love and Mr Lewisham* (1900), which describes the world of the DSA student: 'Mr Lewisham impresses me very much because I have lived the life which you describe' (Armytage 1957: 48; Wells 1934). William Ripper, professor of mechanical engineering at Sheffield 1889–1923 and vice-chancellor of the university 1917–19, is another example of a man whose career developed through the new educational institutions. Starting life as an engineering apprentice, he trained as a teacher and became the first science master at the Sheffield Central Higher School. Later he moved to the technical school, which was later to form part of the university. His scientific work there won the praise of H. E. Roscoe, no mean judge (Roscoe 1906: 206).

The DSA qualifications were unique because they could be gained through adult classes, in many grammar schools, and in the higher-grade schools. In the places where they existed the higher-grade schools gave a training which, to many artisan and lower middle-class parents, seemed more appropriate for their children's future than anything the traditional grammar schools could offer. It is not possible to draw a precise line between the social classes catered for by the two groups of school since there was considerable overlap between them. In broad terms the higher-grade-school group came from a lower social stratum; the pupils, for example, left at an earlier age, which provides a sound test.

More detailed information about some of the higher-grade schools can be given. The Bryce assistant commissioner for the West Riding divided the parents of children in the science school of the Halifax Higher Grade School into the following groups: 26 managers and foremen, 30 artisans and labourers, 38 tradesmen, 22 manufacturers (presumably men owning their own works), 20 professional men, 63 miscellaneous. Of that final group 14 were clerks and book-keepers, 12 widows with small means, and 8 commercial travellers (*BC* VII: 273). The composition of a much larger group, the 925 parents of pupils of the Manchester Central School for the year ending 31 May 1897, which is shown in Table 10.5, is not dissimilar.

In both schools tradesmen, clerks, skilled workmen, and foremen were well represented. There were not many professional parents. Nor at the other end of the scale were there many labourers and unskilled workmen. A witness to the Cross Commission had indeed reported that almost all

Table 10.5 Parents of pupils, Manchester Central School, 1896–7

Independent	9
Professional	18
Teachers	19
Manufacturers	31
Manufacturers (managers)	35
Farmers	11
Retail tradesmen	139
Commercial travellers	53
Salesmen	69
Clerks	173
Subordinate public positions (postmasters, etc.)	25
Foremen	20
Workmen (skilled)	225
Workmen (unskilled)	27
Others	71

Source: Manchester School Board, *9th General Report 1894–7*: 146.

the pupils of the Birmingham Seventh Standard School belonged to 'the real working classes' (*PP* 1887 XXIX: 553: 30890), but, since Birmingham was very much a town of skilled artisans and small masters, it is a reasonable guess that 'working class' in this case means skilled rather than unskilled men.

Where their own careers can be traced, the pupils of the higher-grade schools seem to have followed occupations very similar to those of their fathers, though a few did achieve higher social and economic levels. Some detailed figures for Sheffield, Leeds, and Manchester are given in Table 10.6. I have not recorded each individual case, but have concentrated on the main groups; in some instances no information was avail-

Table 10.6 Occupations of former pupils of higher grade schools, Manchester, Sheffield, Leeds, 1894, 1897

	Manchester		Sheffield		Leeds
	boys	*girls*	*boys*	*girls*	*boys*
Clerks	350	45	47	1	26
Other office and semi-professional work (laboratory assistants, draughtsmen, accountants)	17	—	16	—	19
Teachers	2	26	12	45	5
Artisans/industrial workers	3	—	39	—	20
Shops, retail trade	(no entry)		23	—	12
At home, small shops	—	65	—	72	—
University, technical college	14	—	—	—	6

Source: The figures for the Sheffield and Leeds higher-grade schools are for 1894 (Bryce Commission Evidence VII, *PP* 1895 XLVIII: 274–5). Total numbers recorded: Sheffield 161 boys and 148 girls; Leeds, 135 boys. The Manchester figures are for 1897 (Manchester School Board, *9th Report*: 146). Total numbers recorded: 488 boys and 165 girls.

able. The Sheffield and Manchester figures include girls; the Leeds figures are for boys only.

In these three cities the hopes of the pioneers that the higher-grade schools would provide valuable skills for local industry had hardly been realized. Even in Sheffield, with its strong artisan and craft culture, the number of artisans and industrial workers was smaller than the number of clerks; and in Manchester, which was a great commercial centre, the clerks formed a massive majority. Indeed the large number of clerks in all the samples is the predominant feature of the returns. In Manchester a few girls had begun to enter office work, though this was hardly the case in Sheffield. Otherwise the girls became teachers or stayed at home and helped in shops; the two duties dovetailed into one another when home was above the shop premises. The number of other occupations recorded for girls is minute. A few of the Leeds and Manchester boys had gone to university or technical college, and perhaps some of those in the 'semi-professional' group were on their way to higher status and rewards. In the return just quoted no Sheffield boys were recorded as university entrants. However J. F. Moss, clerk to the school board, gave the Bryce Commission details about the careers of 65 Lancasterian scholars of the Sheffield school. They were likely to have been both more able and more committed to their studies than the average pupil. Of them (again quoting only the larger groups) 36 had become teachers of one kind or another, 5 worked in chemical laboratories, 8 were clerks, and 5 university or college students (*BC* III: 108: 7249).

Though in social composition as in other ways there was overlap between the secondary grammar and the higher-grade schools, there was considerable rivalry between them, as the evidence to the Bryce Commission makes clear. Dr Forsyth, head of the Leeds higher-grade school, argued that there was no essential difference between elementary and secondary education and that there was room for secondary education of several types. The grammar school was good for some students, but not for all: 'We ask that all systems should be encouraged, but we do object to education which goes in one groove being called Secondary Education' (*BC* III: 208: 8492). Another well-known head, R. P. Scott of Parmiter's, Bethnal Green, argued on the other side that secondary schools should not be continuation schools from elementary schools; they should contain their own primary departments (*BC* IV: 177: 14198). The experienced HMI, J. G. Fitch, thought that there were two different types of secondary school, one giving a liberal education and leading to the universities, the other simply completing the education of the elementary school (*BC* III: 275: 9228).

By the mid–1890s the Science and Art Department, the school boards, the technical instruction committees had done much to broaden the range of both elementary and secondary education, to increase the quantity of scientific and technical subjects taught, and to enlarge the opportunities open to children of poorer parents. What was needed, as the report of the Bryce Commission made clear, was a new national structure for secondary education as a whole. The key question was whether this should be closely related to and arising out of the elementary schools, or whether the two systems should be independent of each other, with only narrow bridges across a great divide. The resolution of this issue in the Education Act of 1902 was crucial for the development of English education in the twentieth century.

Part III
The public schools

11 The public school image

In 1870 the public schools, after twenty years of steady progress, stood at the beginning of their greatest era of prestige and success. The Clarendon Commission (1861–4) had examined the nine great schools – Eton, Winchester, Westminster, Harrow, Rugby, Shrewsbury, Charterhouse, plus the two London day schools, St Paul's and Merchant Taylors – though only the first seven were covered by the Public Schools Act of 1868. In addition to the Clarendon schools a number of old grammar schools, like Tonbridge, Repton, and Sherborne, had been moving, under able headmasters, towards public school status, which was also rapidly acquired by many of the Victorian foundations like Cheltenham (1840), Marlborough (1843), and Wellington (1859). By the end of the century the public school community consisted of about 100 schools, made up from the same three groups, though these differed widely in status and importance among themselves.

It is extremely difficult to define a public school. A. F. Leach (Leach 1899: 6–7) argued that it was a school with high fees attracting the richer classes, that it was entirely or almost entirely a boarding school, that it was under the control of a public body, and that it drew its pupils from all parts of the country. Leach and everyone of that time assumed that it was a school for boys. The control by a board of governors, as opposed to ownership by a private individual, and the recruitment from a group of comparatively well-to-do parents can be accepted as general characteristics of the type. However, schools varied very much in the fees they charged and therefore in the social groups they attracted. Although the best-known schools were entirely or predominantly boarding and therefore non-local, there were day schools that had a better claim to the title 'public school' than many boarding schools. The outstanding examples here were the great London day schools like St Paul's, Merchant Taylors, City of London, and Dulwich, though there were similar schools in the provinces like Bedford, and it would be difficult to exclude some of the great city grammar schools like Manchester.

A satisfactory definition should look not only, as Leach did, to the preconditions but also to the product. A public school could be judged in terms of how long it retained its pupils, how many of them went on to university and won university awards, how many of them entered the prestigious professions like the army, the law, and government service, and how many old boys attained distinction in their chosen careers. Most of the schools that established themselves by these criteria during the 1870s and 1880s retained their positions, but some fell out and others, through the work of a distinguished head like Sanderson of Oundle (1892–1922), entered the group. The borderlines were indeterminate and they changed from decade to decade. In the last resort a school ranked as a public school because the public opinion of the day considered it to be such. The judgement itself was made in terms of the factors which have been considered, though it is impossible to lay down any hard-and-fast rules by which they were made. In practical terms the late Victorians and Edwardians knew what they were talking about, though they might have been hard-pressed to substantiate what they said.

The Clarendon Commission had passed rather contradictory judgements on the nine great schools. They were critical of the intellectual attainments of most of the boys when they left school, and they wanted more time to be given to the study of subjects like science and mathematics. On the other hand, they were full of praise for the moral and religious atmosphere of the schools and for their success in producing boys of sound character, ready to take responsibility in the great world. The fruit of the system, it was believed, was personal self-reliance, based on high moral character, on manliness, and on the ability to work as a member of a team (*HSE*: 264). Among all the schools the commission treated Rugby with almost exaggerated respect. The Rugby tradition, shaped under Thomas Arnold (1828–42) and reborn under Frederick Temple (1858–69), offered a prominent example of the qualities which they so greatly valued. Rugby was not, of course, the only source of the new public school ethos, but more than any other school it was a great colonizer, and its alumni and former assistant masters took its gospel all over the country. Two Rugby masters in turn, G. E. L. Cotton and G. G. Bradley, established the fame of Marlborough. Another pair, A. G. Butler and E. H. Bradby, created Haileybury. E. W. Benson shaped Wellington and John Percival Clifton, while J. S. Phillpotts developed and enlarged Bedford. One Old Rugbeian, Henry Hart, built up the reputation of Sedbergh in the northern fells. Another, F. W. Walker, was head of two great urban schools, St Paul's and Manchester.

Temple, who had been a member of the Schools Inquiry Commission and had written part of its report, left Rugby in 1869 on his appointment to the see of Exeter, where he continued to enjoy considerable influence in educational matters. Rugby and the other Clarendon schools were given new constitutions by the Public Schools Act of 1868, and although there were problems in particular cases in working out the new system, they were free from any danger of government interference and began a period of untrammelled freedom and development which lasted at least until the First World War. However, both the old grammar schools and the new foundations felt very apprehensive about their position under the Endowed Schools Act of 1869, fearing that their work would be damaged by outside interference. Particular fears were expressed about the initial proposals for inspection and examination, though these were dropped before the Act was passed.

The fear of interference was removed from the new foundations since the Act of 1869 provided that no scheme was to be made for an endowment set up less than fifty years before the passing of the Act without the consent of the governing body (see p. 5). Those grammar schools that aimed to attain public school status enjoyed no such protection. They were subject to the radical policies and doctrinaire view of the Endowed Schools Commissioners in the same way as any decayed village grammar school. The commissioners wished to regulate all the grammar schools on a common plan. The leading schools claimed that, though they depended to some extent on their ancient endowments, they had transformed themselves through their own efforts. Since they had made themselves schools of a new kind, they ought to be entitled to the independence enjoyed by Harrow, Rugby, or Shrewsbury, all of them local grammar schools in their day but now secure behind the provisions of the Public Schools Act of 1868.

What the heads of the leading endowed schools wanted was expressed by the headmaster of Repton, S. A. Pears, discussing the constitution of his governing body:

> The whole thing will be settled by the Commissioners, whether Repton is to be regarded as a Public School or a Village School. If a Village School, let the Vestry manage it, but if a Public School, then the Board of Governors must be of much wider constitution. . . . One thing I stand out for, to keep its character as a Public School.
>
> (B. Thomas 1957: 56)

The headmasters of these schools were able men who had increased numbers, attracted more boarders, and extended buildings and facilities. One of the most senior of them was J. I. Welldon of Tonbridge (1843–75), who had been second master at Shrewsbury. Later came H. D. Harper of Sherborne (1850–77), who had previously been head of Cowbridge Grammar School in South Wales, Pears of Repton (1854–74), already mentioned, who had been a master at Harrow under C. J. Vaughan, John Mitchinson of King's School, Canterbury (1859–73), who had been a master at Merchant Taylors, and Edward Thring of Uppingham (1853–87), a former Eton colleger, personally the most outstanding of the group but not the most typical, for in many ways he stood apart from his colleagues and contemporaries.

'All we ask for', Harper argued,

is fair play . . . do not make it now a misfortune to us that we spent the best part of our lives and earnings upon our Schools; do not let us be so burdened, so unfairly handicapped, that . . . a fixed impassable barrier shall be placed between us and not only the 'Public Schools' . . . but also between us and the higher Proprietary Schools.

(Lester 1896: 76)

In fact, the negotiations for a new scheme for Sherborne went very smoothly. One point of difficulty was removed since the school was recognized as falling under sect. 19 of the Act, and the scheme was approved as early as 16 May 1871 (see p. 19). Thring at Uppingham had a far more difficult passage. He resented what he regarded as the interference of outsiders with matters of professional skill and judgement, like the examination of masters before appointment. He claimed that if, as seemed likely, the school was not covered by sect. 19, faith would have been broken with himself and his colleagues who had invested large sums of money in what they regarded as a distinctively Church of England foundation. Indeed he threatened that, if their interpretation were not accepted, they would have no alternative but to withdraw the investments which they had made in the school and start again. The tension still crackles in Thring's account of the meeting with the commissioners in May 1873. Lyttelton and Thring were both obstinate and strong-willed men. Lyttelton told Thring that he was running his head against a brick wall. 'I answered that that was exactly what we meant to do; we were going to run our heads against a wall if necessary' (Parkin 1898: i, 192). Thring was supported by his masters and by an influential group of parents, and eventually he won his case. The church character of Uppingham was maintained, and the internal management of the school was left in the hands of the headmaster and his staff.

The major importance of these local struggles was that the headmasters saw that, if they co-operated with one another, they might exercise more influence over the course of events than if they stood alone. The first initiative came from Mitchinson of Canterbury who wrote to the other heads, suggesting that they should meet either in London or in Oxford to confer about the proposed Bill. His letter was followed by a letter from Harper suggesting a deputation to W. E. Forster. Thring was at first very unwilling to attend the London meeting, but, pressed by Mitchinson, he finally decided to go. He went to two London meetings, found them valuable, and in March 1869 suggested an annual meeting of headmasters, the first of them to be held at Uppingham at Christmastide 1869. Between sixty and seventy invitations were sent out, but in the end only twelve came (Parkin 1898: i, 198–207). Clearly those who came were those who felt themselves threatened. Eleven of them were heads of endowed schools, and there were only two heads of the new foundations, George Butler of Liverpool and R. E. Sanderson of Lancing.

In addition to Thring, who was the host, all the prominent heads of endowed schools who have been mentioned were there. There were no representatives of the Clarendon schools nor of the leading Victorian foundations. Thring and Mitchinson agreed that the great schools must come in only on the basis of common work and not because of their prestige. Thring, an Etonian himself, was no admirer of the great schools which he thought inefficient and lacking in educational purpose.

Thus, as a measure of defence against outside attack, was born the Headmasters' Conference (Lester 1896: 131–61; Baron 1954–5: 223–34; Percival 1969; Roche 1972). The second meeting at Sherborne in December 1870 was attended by thirty-four heads, including Moss of Shrewsbury and Ridding of Winchester, who was appointed chairman of the standing committee. At Highgate in 1871 fifty heads were present and the major schools attended in force. In later years both conference and committee were dominated by the larger schools, not always to the liking of the smaller ones. By the mid–1870s the threat of government intervention had faded after the supersession of the Endowed Schools Commission. The endowed schools had acquired their new schemes and found the arrangements tolerable. What had begun as an association for defence among schools of the second rank had developed into a forum for discussion with the major schools in the lead, though they had not been the pioneers in the venture.

In 1879 eighty-nine heads were invited, a total that had grown to 101 by 1899. Like the term 'public school' itself, membership of conference lent itself to no exact definition. In 1877 it was decided to make membership dependent not on any defined rule but on a decision by the committee after 'consideration of the general character of each individual school and of the status of its headmaster' (Baron 1954–5: 224). In the 1880s and early 1890s little of moment was going on, and between 1882 and 1895 the conference met only biennially. Later, external affairs broke in once again. When the Incorporated Association of Headmasters was set up in 1890, the conference forbade its members to belong to both bodies, but this exclusive policy was soon abandoned and the two bodies worked harmoniously together. Conference refused to submit evidence to the Bryce Commission though they submitted a memorandum. Subsequently they discussed the report, and later they passed resolutions that, in any reform of secondary education, the first requisite was a strong central authority. Despite the educational and social prestige of the public schools the conference played very little part in the great debate about national education, which produced the Education Act of 1902. The public schools had few points of contact with those who were demanding a more effective national system. Indeed they drew much of their strength from the absence of such a system.

By the end of the nineteenth century the schools had developed into a distinctive group, large enough to set its own standards, powerful enough to maintain its own independence and to have considerable influence on those outside its pale. John Honey has developed the idea of a public school community, based on the interaction of schools with one another in athletics, rifle shooting and the cadet corps, though he admits that there are limitations to his arguments (Honey 1977: ch. 4). On the basis of this model he suggests a Class A list of about fifty schools and a Class B list of another fifty-four. The HMC list of about 100 schools he regards as a long list of eligible schools, though inclusion on this list was becoming increasingly important as evidence of public school status. Though there are discrepancies between the various methods of reckoning, a grouping of about 100 schools, varying a good deal in status between themselves, seems to be a generally acceptable statement of the position in 1900.

Though university success was certainly a criterion of high status, it should be noted that Honey's measures are based on interaction in non-academic activities, especially games. More will be said later about athleticism in the schools and in society generally, but Honey is developing a point which had been made in the report of the Clarendon Commission. The commission was critical of academic standards but laudatory of the moral and religious tone and the social atmosphere. The schools had been, the report said, 'the chief nurseries of our statesmen'. Their pupils had learned habits of social equality, had made enduring friendships, and formed lasting habits; 'they have had perhaps the largest share in moulding the character of an English gentleman' (*PP* 1864 XX: 56). This concept of public school education, already established by the 1860s, did not vary very much before the First World War.

At this point it is convenient to return to Honey's model. His Class A schools shared some common characteristics (Honey 1977: 284–7). They were predominantly Anglican. The only Nonconformist school included was the Methodist Leys School, Cambridge, with Mill Hill in Class B. Class A included no Roman Catholic school, though Jesuit Stonyhurst appeared in Class B. The rise of the Nonconformist and Roman Catholic schools was to be a feature of the twentieth century. The Class A schools were not exclusively boarding, and included St Paul's, Dulwich, Merchant Taylors, and the two Bedford schools (Grammar and Modern). Fees varied very much and the day schools were comparatively cheap. Almost all the Class A schools were in England (as opposed to other parts of the United Kingdom), and a large proportion of them in the south of England.

In the early part of the nineteenth century boys had often entered public schools very young, but the growth of the preparatory schools after the 1860s limited the age-range in public schools to a 5–6 year period from 13 years upwards. Important landmarks here were the foundation of the Association of Headmasters of Preparatory Schools in 1892 and of the Common Entrance examination to public schools in 1904

(Leinster-Mackay 1984). After 1870 the list of public schools was not much extended. The great period of growth from 1850 to 1870 had largely coincided with the years of great prosperity for the middle classes which also stretched from 1850 to 1870. After 1870, in the period of the so-called 'Great Depression', though middle-class incomes did not decline, they did not advance very much. It also seems likely that education became a greater burden on family budgets than it had been earlier, partly because more of it was demanded in an increasingly competitive society. There must in any case have been a limit to the number of schools which the upper and middle classes could support, but the closing of the lists after 1870 may well have been related to the slowing-down in middle-class fortunes, just as the expansion in numbers in the earlier decades had been related to their growth (Banks 1954).

An important part of the impact of the schools on English society was the image which they presented, both to their old boys and to the world at large. Inclusion within the privileged group had to be won, and when won retained when circumstances proved difficult. It is surprising how quickly schools like Clifton and Haileybury, both opened in 1862, established themselves. It seems almost as though, at a certain point of time in the 1860s and 1870s, English society was waiting to enthrone new members of the public school pantheon. It was always important to maintain the status of a school, and unsuccessful headmasters were sometimes jettisoned (see pp. 142–3). The dangers of losing rank can be exemplified from the case of Lancing College, the most prominent of the group of Anglo-Catholic schools founded by Nathaniel Woodard (*HSE*: 167–9). Its position as a public school had been established in the long and successful reign of R. E. Sanderson (1862–89) (Handford 1933). Academic results were good and the school built up a strong reputation in association football. In 1886 there was an outbreak of enteric fever in which two boys died, and numbers fell steadily until the end of the century. As numbers fell, the financial position worsened. Sanderson's successors had difficulties with the chapter of the Woodard foundation (the governing body), and there was friction because the chaplain held a position independent of the headmaster. In 1897 the Lancing old boys protested to the chapter. They complained about the difficulties in the head's position, about the poor salaries of the staff, about the fact, as they saw it, that too much attention was given to the other schools of the foundation whose status was lower than that of Lancing. They were anxious, they said, that Lancing should take its proper place among the public schools. As a result of their complaints a Lancing school committee was set up which continued under a new head, appointed in 1901 with enlarged powers, who doubled the numbers in the school in less than ten years.

The new head, B. H. Tower, was himself an old boy who had been put under considerable pressure to come. The Lancing old boys had intervened to preserve the status of their school. The strength of such old boy feeling is shown by the appearance at this time of old boys' associations, serving both as a general focus of loyalty and as a convenient way of collecting money for school purposes. The following list was compiled almost at random from the respective school histories. Cheltenham (1868) and St Paul's (1872) were very early examples; Marlborough (1884); Shrewsbury and Tonbridge (1886); Radley (1889); Malvern (1894). This kind of structured affection, which maintained the loyalties of schooldays into later life and carried them all over the world as old boys met in Madras or Melbourne, was something new in English society.

J. H. Skrine, who had been one of Thring's lieutenants at Uppingham and who was warden of Glenalmond from 1888 to 1902, published an article, 'The romance of school' (Skrine 1898: 430–8). This element of romance, Skrine said, was something new because fifty years earlier school had been regarded as 'a bleak land of exile'. The training given by the school resembled that given in the days of chivalry to the page and the squire. The life of chivalry was not all good. On the one hand, it placed a high value on brotherhood, hardiness, and courage; on the other, it subordinated the convictions of the Christian to the class feelings of the gentleman. It had, however, the great merit of setting higher standards and more gracious manners before the sons of 'burgess homes' who now filled the schools. In them, in Skrine's phrase, industrialism and militarism had met and exchanged gifts. If this chivalry was to be genuine, the public schools must not surrender to greed and materialism. They must ask themselves the question: 'are we rearing there a knight errantry fit to keep the marches of the empire and to purge the land nearer home of wrong, violence, lust?' Skrine's brief article expresses many of the master ideas of the late nineteenth-century public school – the appeal to the knightly ideal, the emphasis on service rather than material values as the goal of life, the glorification of empire. He was conscious that one major task of the schools was to gentle and civilize the children of new money. He placed on the schools a heavy task of social responsibility, and he emphasized that this was a duty only recently assumed.

One of the main agents in publicizing the public school image to the late Victorian/Edwardian world was the school story (Quigly 1982; Musgrave 1985). The two great exemplars, *Tom Brown's Schooldays* (1857) and *Eric, or Little by Little* (1858), belonged to an earlier generation, but they went on being republished and they were read by many people outside the public school circle, as well as by those within it. By the early twentieth century many of the well-known schools had become the subject of at least one such tale. An important landmark was the launching in 1879 of the *Boys' Own Paper* which serialized the stories of Talbot Baines Reed, the best known of which was *The Fifth Form at*

St Dominic's, published as a book in 1885. In Reed's books the public school appears as a highly structured institution with a strong corporate spirit and an organized system of team games. Reed was not himself the product of a boarding school – he was at City of London – but the schools which he imagined reflected the change which had taken place between the spontaneous and sometimes disorderly world of Arnold's Rugby, as depicted in *Tom Brown*, and the much more regulated world of the late nineteenth-century school.

In 1899 Rudyard Kipling published *Stalky and Co.* The United Services College, Westward Ho!, at which Kipling himself was a pupil from 1878 to 1882 and on which the story is based, was hardly a public school in the sense in which the term has been used here, nor were Kipling's characters the conventional heroes and villains of schoolboy fiction. Yet behind their rule-breaking and high spirits Kipling is preaching a message of hierarchy and order, though he also wished to preserve the personal initiative which boys would need in order to do their work in the world. It has been claimed that *Stalky* is the only school story in which a direct parallel is drawn between life at school and life in the Empire. The connection was natural because so many of Kipling's schoolfellows were destined for India and the service of the Crown. 'India's full of Stalkies – Cheltenham and Haileybury and Marlborough chaps – that we don't know anything about!' (Kipling 1913: 271). Though they were not school stories, the numerous novels of the Old Westminster, G. A. Henty, should not be forgotten. In whatever historical period the story was set, the hero was generally a public school boy with the air of command which his school had given him (Carleton 1965: 78).

Many attempts were made to analyse the results of a public school education. At the beginning of our period S. A. Pears of Repton compared the systems of England and of Switzerland. The average intellectual attainment was, he thought, higher in Switzerland. In every other respect the English system was preferable. 'The English school is better adapted to provide men able to teach, to lead and to govern' (B. Thomas 1957: 60). Such men enjoyed the rank of gentlemen though, like most English social groupings, the boundaries of gentility were not very precise. The French observer Max Leclerc argued that the men of new wealth had been incorporated into the ruling class through their education in public schools and universities. In this way a new breed of gentlemen had grown up which the ruling democracy had accepted as its leaders (Leclerc 1894b: 239–40). J. H. Simpson, himself a Rugbeian, claimed that in 1900 the public schools stood for the rule of the gentleman class, which consisted, in addition to the aristocracy, of the officers in the armed services, of the professions, of the county families, and of the second and third generations of those who had made money in business. They enjoyed incomes of at least £1,200-£1,500 a year, and were prepared to spend not less than £120 a year for seven or eight years to educate a son at preparatory and public school (Simpson 1954: 48–9).

The products of this seven or eight years of expensive education won praise for their courage, modesty, and unselfishness, sometimes for their Christian principles, but some commentators also sounded a note of caution. The schools tended to produce types rather than individuals. Some boys were certainly very able. G. G. Coulton thought that those who went to university from the Rugby of Arnold and Temple came nearer to the full breadth of Greek culture than any group since the days of the Greeks themselves (Coulton 1923: 46), and some of the Rugbeians of the 1890s did not fall behind their predecessors. The central issue, however, was not the attainments of the few but the general standard of the many. For them there is the suggestion of a steady mediocrity, competent but uninspired. Two judgements of 1909 and 1913 perhaps reflect an atmosphere when criticism was more common than it had been in 1900. Ian Hay, writing in 1913, thought public school men conscientious, generally efficient, never tyrannical or corrupt, though seldom brilliant and often very dull: 'If this be mediocrity, who would soar?' (quoted in Quigly 1982: 230). Cyril Norwood and A. H. Hope were much more critical:

> They [the schools] generally produce a race of well-bodied, well-mannered, well-meaning boys, keen at games, devoted to their school, ignorant of life, contemptuous of all outside the pale of their own caste, uninterested in work, neither desiring nor revering knowledge.
>
> (Norwood and Hope 1909: 187)

This was an extreme view, but it stated in a positive form the reservations hinted at or half-expressed by many contemporaries.

12 The public schools and society

Some of the elements of the public school image were suggested in the last chapter – the concentration on team games, the stress on chivalry and the knightly life, the ideal of self-sacrifice for the empire and on the field of battle. The positive side of this was a loyalty, hardihood, and common feeling which deeply affected men's work in the world. The negative side was a tendency to press boys into a common mould, the surrender of freedom and spontaneity to a mask of good form, a narrowness of sympathy towards those who did not belong to the elite group. The public school ideal was in many ways totalitarian, yet it maintained its influence in a society which was not at all totalitarian and which was affected by many other currents – liberal, egalitarian, socialist – of many different kinds. It says something for public school training that its products were sufficiently adaptable to preserve their influence in a rapidly changing world.

To many boys, masters, and public figures the magic began to work on the games field. Boys had always played games, though up to the middle of the nineteenth century they often did so in the face of opposition rather than support from their schoolmasters. It has been argued that the organization of games and their assumption of a definite place within the general school curriculum dates from the 1850s (*HSE*: 267). However, games did not become generally compulsory until the later part of the century, and there were differences in practices and priorities between different schools.

The majority of the public schools were boarding schools, and in such schools there had always been problems in keeping boys occupied when they were not in the classroom. The primary reason for promoting school games was disciplinary. They kept boys occupied and they prevented poaching on the land of local farmers. Since they made boys physically tired and filled up their time, they were a useful prophylactic against masturbation and homosexuality, evils of which contemporaries were very conscious, but about which they were unwilling to express themselves publicly. Clement Dukes, the Rugby doctor who was the chief authority on health at school, argued that boys should join in well-organized games. These should be compulsory, though time should be allowed for other leisure activities. 'The whole time', he wrote, 'during which a boy is not at work, asleep or feeding, should be spent in recreation of some kind, both for the purposes of health and the expenditure of superfluous force' (Dukes 1894: 287). This fear of freedom reinforced the attention given to games. There was a great contrast here between the Rugby of Thomas Arnold, which was in many ways a very free society, and the Rugby of John Percival (1887–95), perhaps the greatest of late Victorian heads. Percival was a man of rather terrifying earnestness who feared what mischief the devil might find for idle hands to do. Boys were to have a detailed time-table and they were to be watched (Hope-Simpson 1967: 120). Not all the watching took place on the games field, but compulsory games made it easier to achieve.

For many, perhaps for most, boys games were not an engine of discipline but a source of pleasure. Schoolmasters therefore used this sense of enjoyment to instil a sense of loyalty and to identify themselves more closely with their pupils. In an age when so many schools were newly established and others had greatly expanded, the games field provided an important focus of loyalty which it might have been difficult to create in other ways. A. G. Butler, the first Master of Haileybury, wrote in his first year there that the games had saved him 'a world of anxiety'. He had been able to develop inter-house feeling and meant to have compulsory football. The boys had no leaders as yet, but that would all come in time (Coulton 1923: 58). The implication is clear that the games field would be a principal source of such leadership.

The motives for promoting school games which have so far been examined are comprehensible enough. What is much more difficult for the modern observer to understand is the moral value which was given to games and the semi-religious status which they assumed in the minds of many extremely intelligent and critical people. The best example here is the Harrow housemaster, Edward Bowen. Bowen was a man of great ability, a former fellow of Trinity College, Cambridge, a skilled and successful teacher with a high reputation both inside and outside the school (see pp. 135, 149). He played games himself up to his death. He believed in them passionately as things good in themselves, promoting such virtues as fairness, endurance and courage, dignity and courtesy. He refused to listen to any arguments that too much attention was given to them because he believed that at their best they embodied the moral qualities which he wished his boys to possess. In 1884 he wrote an essay on games for a schoolmasters' society. Here, he claimed, was boyhood at its best because the most fully devoted to the common good:

And when you have a lot of human beings, in highest social union and perfect organic action, developing the law of their race and falling in unconsciously with its best inherited tradition of brotherhood and of common action, I think you are not far from getting a glimpse of one side of the highest good. There lives more soul in honest play, believe me, than in half the hymn books.

(Bowen 1902: 331)

It is not surprising that, after one keenly contested Eton and Harrow match which had been won in the last few overs, he was so exhausted that he could not recall the run of the play until he had been refreshed with food (ibid.: 150).

Bowen probably carried to extremes sentiments which were expressed by others in a more moderate form. The Cheltenham master, E. Scot Skirving, in an essay on games in education, argued that boys enjoyed them and that parents were interested in them. The cleverest boys were not necessarily fitted to rule others, and the function of games was to give boys an opportunity to exercise their sense of duty and responsibility. Obedience was to be based on trust, not, as in Germany, on organization alone (Morgan 1968: 117–18). E. M. Oakeley of Clifton claimed that compulsory games were especially beneficial to 'the physically indolent and morally soft', for they provided the precocious young brains with sound physical development (*Great Public Schools* n.d.: 211–12).

The games system became fully formed after 1880 (Mangan 1981). A committee of games, in which masters played a large part, was set up to manage the general organization of a system which involved the commitment of much time and financial resources. More and more schoolmasters were athletes, recruited for their football or cricketing skills, who regarded the advancement of games as their chief interest. They had Bowen's passion for games, but neither his intellectual distinction nor his skills as a teacher. In earlier days many schools had their own football codes. As the Rugby and Association rules became formalized, inter-school matches became important landmarks in the school year; cricket followed the same path. Many old boys were keen supporters and parents often regarded athletic success as more important than academic achievement because it was more likely to lead their sons to success in later life. J. E. C. Welldon of Harrow wrote that the great importance placed on games was due, not so much to the tone of the schools as to 'the general tone of society and of the world in Great Britain. It is not the time spent upon games, but the time spent in reading, talking and thinking about them, that is the danger of modern life' (Welldon 1915: 96).

A few examples will further fill out the picture. At Clifton, founded in 1860, games were not very popular at first, but by the late 1870s they had become compulsory (Christie 1935: 73–4). At Cheltenham H. A. James, principal 1889–95, made games compulsory for all boys in 1889 (Morgan 1968: 107–8). At Radley compulsion also dated from the 1880s. Ten years later the tone of the school was described as very philistine and the cult of the 'bloods', the heroes of the field and the river, was in full force (Boyd 1948: 238–9). At Malvern under S. R. James (1897–1914) games were taken with great seriousness. C. S. Lewis, who went there in 1913, wrote later: 'games [and gallantry] were the only subjects, and I cared for neither' (C. S. Lewis 1955: 97). R. St. C. Talboys, who went to teach at Wellington in 1904, wrote:

> School discipline was diverted from the training of scholars to that of sportsmen and athletes; and it was to the latter that the power and the plums of school life were given. Boys of mental ability and secondary physique could rarely hope for admission to the ruling caste and to whatever advantages an experience of responsibility or leadership might give them.
>
> (Talboys 1943: 33)

The prominence of games derived from causes wider than their influence on the internal life of the schools. This was the period when organized games came to play a new and important role in English life. The Football League and the FA Cup were established. England and Australia contended for the Ashes. The Oxford and Cambridge boat race was a major national event. The public school enthusiasm for games mirrored one preoccupation of their society which affected people of all social classes. In addition games were thought to evoke a tough and hardy character which was a national asset when so many young men went abroad to the colonies or were involved in the administration and business life of an expanding empire. Edward Thring believed that, in the previous generation, hundreds of boys had been sent to boarding schools who would not have gone to them in an earlier period. There they had learned responsibility and independence, to bear pain, to abandon luxury, to play games. It was the public schools which had created this manly spirit: 'I think myself that it is this which has made the English such an adventurous race' (Parkin 1898: ii, 195–6). The French critic Hippolyte Taine thought that an English education produced 'moral and physical wrestlers' with both the advantages and the drawbacks of such a regime (Taine 1872: 127–8).

There were other activities outside the classroom, though they take a much more limited place than games in the school histories. Volunteer and cadet corps started in the 1860s – Edmond Warre was commandant of the cadet corps at Eton – but they were not very prominent until the time of the South African War (Best 1975: 133–6). Among cultural interests music was prominent. Thring was a pioneer in appreciating its importance. Uppingham had a fine choir, and a third of the school took lessons in instrumental music. Percival gave great attention to music at Clifton, and H. M. Butler appointed John Farmer organist and instructor in music at Harrow in 1864. Farmer created an active musical tradition there; it was the collaboration between him and Edward Bowen which produced the Harrow school songs. At the end of the century both Rugby and Marlborough had school orchestras. Rugby also had a debating society, and it possessed, like Marlborough, an active Natural History Society and a school museum. A brilliant Rugby generation in the 1890s, which included both R. H. Tawney and William Temple, belonged to 'Eranos', a society which met to hear papers on literary subjects. In the very different surroundings of urban St Paul's, F. W. Walker encouraged G. K. Chesterton and the group which produced the magazine called *The Junior Debater*, though Chesterton was badly behind with his school work. The rule of the philistines did not prevail in all schools (Parkin 1898: i, 305–9; Rouse 1898a: 313–20; Gardiner and Lupton 1911: 132–3; E. Graham 1920: 174–8; Temple 1921: 33; A. G. Bradley and others 1923: 232, 302–13; and Hope-Simpson 1967: 153).

After the triumphs of the cricket pitch and the debating society came the world of active life. Public schoolmasters looked on their pupils far more as future soldiers, pioneers, or administrators than as future industrialists or businessmen. For many of them the complex of games playing, personal hardihood, and imperial service had assumed the status of a substitute religion, far more real to many people than the official creed preached in school pulpits (Vance 1985). The religion of the late nineteenth-century public school was sincere, but in many cases the stream had run very thin, and had sometimes become little more than respect for good form and established order. Edmond Warre, headmaster of Eton 1884–1905, had been a great oarsman and pioneer of the school volunteer corps. He was himself a deeply religious man, but his religion was far more a matter of ethics than of doctrine (Hollis 1960: 288).

Edward Bowen, unlike Warre, was a layman, very reserved in matters of religion and a man on whom Christian dogmas sat lightly. For him true religion meant the desire to do right, and he had little interest in the mystical and doctrinal aspects of Christianity. He once wrote that he had no desire to be more religious than his boys (Bowen 1902: 201). That, taken at its face value, is an extraordinary statement. As head of the modern side Bowen would not have argued that he should accept the knowledge possessed by a 14-year-old as the standard for judging the accuracy of French prose. No doubt he acknowledged that boys' cricket was improved by coaching. He was, as we shall see, no imperialist, no glorifier of empire or war. It may be thought that, since his own religious beliefs had become so attenuated, the games which occupied so much of his thoughts had expanded to fill the gap. If there were no standards other than the purely ethical, the values of the games field provided higher targets than many others which might have been offered.

A similar spirit pervades the verse of the Cliftonian poet, Sir Henry Newbolt (1862–1938), though in his case it was combined with a strong dose of the imperialism which Bowen rejected. Newbolt, the son of a Black Country clergyman, had been a boy under John Percival, who made a deep impression on him (Thorn 1962: 155–67). Much of his verse concentrates on athletic and patriotic themes, interpreted in ethical and moralistic tones. Two of his poems, 'He fell among thieves' and 'Clifton Chapel', appear in the *Oxford Book of English Verse*, and an analysis of them is rewarding. The first tells the story of a man captured by robbers on the Indian frontier and executed by them at dawn. During his last night the scenes of his past life pass before him – his home, the church across the park, his college at university, his school –

> He saw the School Close, sunny and green,
> The runner beside him, the stand by the parapet wall,
> The distant tape, and the crown roaring between,
> His own name over all.

At the end, before he is executed, he prays:

> O glorious life, who dwellest in earth and sun,
> I have lived, I praise and adore Thee.

In 'Clifton Chapel' a father speaks to his son and urges him

> To set the cause above renown
>   To love the game beyond the prize,
> To honour, while you strike him down
>   The foe that comes with fearless eyes;
> To count the life of battle good,
>   And dear the land that gave you birth,
> And dearer yet the brotherhood
>   That binds the brave of all the earth.

What will happen in life, the father says, is uncertain, but the noblest end is death in battle.

> '*Qui procul hinc*,' the legend's writ, –
>   The frontier-grave is far away –
> '*Qui ante diem periit*:
>   *Sed miles, sed pro patria*.'

The two poems bring out certain themes. Life is good, but death in a noble cause is better. Life is painful, but glorious too, and the memories of school, the chapel, and the playing fields help men to bear their burdens and unite them in a fellowship which binds together all the brave, whether friend or foe. The spirit is certainly religious. Courage, nobility, self-sacrifice are exalted as supreme standards of conduct. Yet it might be disputed how far the message is Christian in any orthodox sense. Both Bowen and Newbolt were preaching a new kind of religious faith, whether they appreciated it or not.

To most public school men there was no contradiction between the religion of athleticism and imperial rule and the religion preached Sunday by Sunday in the churches and school chapels of the land. Those chapels held their memorials of Empire, their commemorative tablets, their Sir Galahads in statuary or stained glass (Girouard 1981: ch. 11). In the old chapel at Cheltenham in the 1890s there were memorial tablets on either side of the altar to the seventy or so Cheltonians who had fallen in the campaigns of the preceding fifty years, beginning with the Crimea and including the name of Lieutenant Melvill of the 24th Foot, who saved the colours after the battle of Isandwhlana in the Zulu War of 1879 (*Great Public Schools*: 125–6).

British imperial expansion is far too large a subject to tackle in any detail here, though it would be impossible to ignore it in any discussion of the later Victorian public school. The memorial tablets at Cheltenham offer a reminder that public school men were closely involved in the long series of colonial wars (Best 1975: 129–46; Mangan 1988). Strongly patriotic sentiments were expressed by many of the leading figures. Thring wrote in 1885 about imperial federation: 'we ought at once to put ourselves at the head of a great empire. We ought to fly our flag on every unoccupied land essential to our great colonies' (Parkin 1898: ii, 243). H. W. Moss of Shrewsbury was a strong Tory and imperialist and supporter of the rifle corps (Oldham 1952: 150). William Johnson (Cory) of Eton was an enthusiastic patriot with a keen interest in the army (Girouard 1981: 174–5).

Yet there is another side to the public school tradition of that day which it is easy to forget. Johnson, if he was a strong patriot, was radical, indeed republican in his politics. Bowen was a Radical who stood for Parliament in 1880 as a Liberal candidate. In home affairs he was an opponent of clerical influence in elementary schools, and in foreign affairs he opposed the South African War (Bowen 1902: 179). Temple was a Liberal, as were Percival and Wilson, the first and second headmasters of Clifton, and many of the Clifton staff (Christie 1935: 355–6). Later, when Percival was at Rugby, he raised a storm by advocating Welsh disestablishment (Temple 1921: 118–23). Most of those who have been mentioned were young men in the 1850s and 1860s when Liberalism was the predominant creed among young men of ability. By the end of the century the position was different, Liberalism weaker and Conservatism much more intellectually respectable. It seems, though it is difficult to be certain, that by 1900 Tory and imperialist views were much more strongly represented among heads and their staffs than they had been thirty years before. If this assessment is correct, it mirrors the general movement of opinion in the country.

The *Public School Magazine* for 1899 picked out the two successive headmasters of Harrow, H. M. Butler and J. E. C. Welldon, as 'the two Public School men who have most clearly and exactly enunciated the Imperialism of the day'. For Welldon, it was said, the two most wonderful things in the world were Christianity and the British Empire (*Public School Magazine* III (1899): 14). In 1898 he had left Harrow to become

Bishop of Calcutta. In an essay written at that time he said that a headmaster will not forget that his pupils are destined to be 'the citizens of the greatest empire under heaven'. He will teach them a high ideal of duty, he will inspire them with a belief in the mission of their country and their race, and in the principles of truth, religion, and duty which they are to carry into the world (Welldon 1899: 284).

There were many strands in the imperialist faith. Welldon was preaching a creed of duty and mission, the knightly task of taking light to dark places. This Christian chivalry was sometimes yoked rather uneasily with the Social Darwinian belief that there was a struggle between nations like the struggle between individuals and species for the survival of the fittest. Those nations would triumph who were the toughest and the most ruthless. The qualities which led a nation to greatness, according to Benjamin Kidd (*Social Evolution*, 1894) were resolution, enterprise, and devotion to duty. The purely rational and intellectual qualities might be harmful rather than valuable in the quest. Kidd's arguments sound like a travesty of the ideas of a certain kind of public school apologist. Great as the national success had been in all the continents of the world, there was always an undercurrent of fear that the British Empire, like the Roman, might decline and fall. This was strikingly expressed in Kipling's poem 'Recessional', written for the Diamond Jubilee of 1897. It became even stronger after the military unpreparedness revealed in the South African War had shaken the confidence of the 1890s (Jenkyns 1980: 334–5; Dunae 1980: 105–21).

The public schools stood at the meeting-point of all these pressures because they produced a large number of the men who had to work the system – the plain men doing their jobs without fear or favour whom Kipling celebrated in his poems and stories. A very large number of old boys made their careers overseas, and J. A. Mangan has shown that accounts of colonial life and imperial service took up considerable space in school magazines (Mangan 1975: 157; 1986a: 58). The South African War seems to modern observers, living in the shadow of 1914–18 and 1939–45, a very minor affair, but it made a great mark in its day, not least in the public schools because so many of their alumni were involved. Table 12.1 gives a list of officers who served in South Africa and who were old boys of the principal schools. The numbers relate in part to school sizes – Eton, for example, was much larger than the other schools – but in general they are much what might have been expected. They illustrate very clearly the commitment of the schools to the armed forces in the first major crisis of British imperialism.

By the time of the South African War the public schools were training what has been called an 'imperial service elite', closely linked with the army and the overseas empire (Stone and Stone 1984: 412). The future Governor-General of Nigeria, Frederick Lugard, when he was a boy at Rossall in the 1870s, debated whether he should go into business or into

Table 12.1 Number of officers from thirty-two public schools who served in the South African War, 1899–1902

Eton	1,326	Dover College	103
Harrow	592	Bradfield	93
Wellington	521	Shrewsbury	91
Cheltenham	438	Repton	90
Marlborough	379	Rossall	78
Charterhouse	367	Elizabeth College, Guernsey	75
Clifton	313	Glenalmond	74
Haileybury	281	Edinburgh Academy	73
Winchester	274	Tonbridge	69
Rugby	236	Sherborne	65
Uppingham	178	Dulwich	65
Bedford Grammar School	144	Stonyhurst	57
Malvern	132	Fettes	53
St Paul's	132	Felsted	52
Westward Ho! (United Services		Westminster	52
College)	116	Portsmouth Grammar School	51
Radley	108		
Total	6,678		

Source: A. H. H. Maclean, *Public Schools and the War in South Africa, 1899–1902. Some facts, figures and comparisons, with a list of specially distinguished officers* (1903: 14–15).

the Indian Civil Service (ICS). The latter, he thought, was 'a thoroughly gentlemanly occupation', which could not be said for 'an Assistant in a Sugar Factory'. 'Of course "a gentleman is a gentleman wherever he is", but still the Lugards have been in the Army and the Church, good servants of *God* or the *Queen*, but few if any have been tradesmen.' In the end he failed the ICS examination and went into the army instead (Wilkinson 1964: 18). Lugard's comments suggest a world of shared values, based on certain levels of social expectation at one end and of career patterns at the other.

As has already been suggested, the public schools had become attractive, not only to the old ruling class but also to the representatives of new money. To work out the social backgrounds of the parents who sent their sons to public schools would be an enormous task and one for which much of the evidence is lacking. The main available source for many schools is the printed admissions register. These registers are often informative about future careers, but many of them give little information about parents beyond mere names and addresses. These are helpful only when the title reveals the profession, as in the case of clergymen and army officers. The most complete information known to me relates to fathers of Wykehamists born between 1820 and 1922, calculated for ten-year periods. For the four birth-decades 1850–1890 information is available for about 70 per cent of the total number of boys. Of the major groups the percentage totals were as follows. The clergy fell sharply from

37.4 (1850–9) to 16.8 (1880–9). HM Forces varied from 10.8 to 16.5. Lawyers rose from 12.2 to 17.9. Businessmen, using that term in a very broad sense to cover manufacture, commerce and the City, rose sharply from 7.2 in 1850–9 to 11.4 in 1860–9 and then levelled off at around the latter figure. Gentlemen of leisure were steady at around 16. Winchester was quite a fashionable school, and that percentage would probably have been lower at Cheltenham or Uppingham (Bishop and Wilkinson 1967: 104–7).

Information for other schools is much more impressionistic. At Marlborough there seem to have been considerable social changes after the scarlet fever epidemics of the early 1870s (*Great Public Schools*: 273). Uppingham, under Thring, recruited heavily in Lancashire and Yorkshire. In two of the school's great crises, the struggle with the Endowed Schools Commission and the migration to Borth (see pp. 122, 146), it was northerners led by W. T. Jacob of Liverpool, who was a cotton merchant, and T. H. Birley of Manchester, who was an industrialist, who fought hard to save the school. J. H. Skrine, who had been both boy and master at Uppingham, under Thring, wrote after the latter's death:

> It was not from the likeliest quarters that his new friends had sprung up. They were chiefly north country business men, who had placed sons under his care, but who were not otherwise called upon by their circumstances to be enthusiastic in educational causes. But they understood, I think, what good work is; they knew a man when they saw him, and they held the robust view that good work and good men should be helped, wherever you find them.
>
> (Skrine 1889: 106, 180–1)

No doubt many boys from such backgrounds were not very polished, and they must have raised the occasional eyebrow among their more snobbish fellows and schoolmasters, but they brought new strengths to the schools which they entered. Moreover their presence at Uppingham or Rugby can be related to important social changes in the communities from which they came. In Lancashire, for example, the Industrial Revolution had created great wealth, but at mid-century the employers had been sharply divided between churchmen and dissenters, Tories and reformers. By 1900 these barriers were breaking down as men of means came to share the same leisure pursuits, the same rural interests, the same boarding school education (Walton 1987: 221–38).

Examples are not difficult to find. Among steel manufacturers there was a growing tendency among men who themselves came from business backgrounds to send their sons to public schools. In the period 1905–25 31 per cent of steel manufacturers had themselves attended public schools as against 16 per cent for the 1875–95 and 10 per cent for the 1865 samples (Erickson 1959: 32–8). In an earlier generation the great Bradford industrialist Titus Salt (1803–76) had sent his sons to Huddersfield College, a local proprietary school, and to Mill Hill, a school for the sons of Dissenters. For Salt's generation this was a typical pattern of education. His friend and contemporary, the dyer Henry William Ripley, who also made a large fortune, had attended a commercial school in Bradford. Yet he sent his eldest son to Rugby and Oxford (Reynolds 1983: 68–9, 82). Across the Pennines, George Kemp was managing director of the Rochdale textile firm of Kelsall and Kemp in 1903. Rochdale-born, he had been educated at Shrewsbury and Trinity College, Cambridge. He was an officer in the yeomanry, an MP, he played cricket for Cambridge and for Lancashire, and he married a peer's daughter. He was eventually made a peer himself (Walton 1987: 224). Assimilation between new wealth and old traditions could go no further.

T. W. Bamford found from a study of the school registers that, of the boys who entered Harrow and Rugby between 1830 and 1880, a large number went into the armed forces and the legal profession. Numbers of those entering the Church declined and of those going overseas increased. Few boys took up science, engineering, or medicine. At both schools there was a sharp increase in the 1860s in numbers going into business. Patterns for Cheltenham, Clifton, Durham, and Sedbergh were not very different (Bamford 1967: 209–22). At Harrow the careers have been traced of the twenty-two boys who formed the school debating society in 1866 and who were the leading lights of what was the *annus mirabilis* of H. M. Butler's headmastership. Nine of them became lawyers; one of these was a Scottish judge, and another was described as 'philanthropist', which suggests that his legal work was not his chief concern. Four became university teachers, three clerics (one of them, R. T. Davidson, a future Archbishop of Canterbury), and two joined the ICS. Of the remainder, one was a banker, one a surgeon, one agent to the family estates, and one had no recorded career (E. Graham 1920: 150–1). Apart from the banker there was no link with business, but boys intended for business careers probably left lower down the school. At another Clarendon school, Winchester, there was a sharp fall, among boys born between 1850 and 1890, in the numbers entering the Church and an increase in the numbers entering HM Forces. The percentage entering business had risen sharply in the 1840s to 12 per cent. Thereafter it increased, but steadily rather than rapidly; it was 17 per cent for the birth-decade 1880–9 (Bishop and Wilkinson 1967: 65–7).

The careers of old boys from three schools, Charterhouse, Haileybury, and Uppingham, for the decade 1880–9 are shown in Table 12.2. That decade falls in the middle of the period covered by this book. By 1880 all three schools were prosperous and well established, while the picture is not distorted, as it would have been for later decades by the effects of the First World War. Of three schools, Charterhouse was chosen to represent the Clarendon seven. Haileybury was a Victorian foundation

Table 12.2 Careers of old boys of three schools, 1880–89

	Charterhouse	Haileybury	Uppingham	Totals
No details	199	229	371	799
Went to other schools/died young	60	75	38	173
Church	81	113	37	231
Colonies: overseas	133	142	70	345
Army	227	192	63	482
Landed proprietor; farmer	24	17	11	52
Law (barrister/solicitor)	178	116	82	376
Business; Stock Exchange; manufacture	222	110	145	477
Teaching (school/university)	49	35	11	95
Medicine	67	68	34	169
Government service – home/overseas	64	51	22	137
Engineer	61	51	32	144
Architect	12	16	8	36
The arts (painter, musician, etc.)	11	7	6	24
Author; journalist	17	12	6	35
Land agent; surveyor	21	20	11	52
Other careers	26	8	5	39
Grand total	1,452	1,262	952	3,666

Sources: F. K. W. Girdlestone, E. T. Hardman, A. H. Tod, *Charterhouse Register 1872–1910*, vol. I, *1872–1891* (2nd edn, 1911); L. S. Milford, *Haileybury Register 1862–1910* (4th ed, 1910); [J. P. Graham], *Uppingham School Roll 1880–1921* (5th issue 1922).

and Uppingham an endowed grammar school with a strong entry from Yorkshire and Lancashire. There are differences between the three. Uppingham, for example, sent fewer boys into the Church and the army, and Haileybury sent a smaller contingent into business, but the broad patterns do not vary very much.

Of the total entries for the three schools for the decade (3,666) no career details are available for 799 (21.8 per cent), while another 173 (4.7 per cent) went on to other schools or died young before they had established themselves. Of those whose careers can be traced, much the largest group went into the army (482 or 13.1 per cent) or into business (477 or 13 per cent). The later term is used, as before, in a very broad sense to cover all kinds of commerce and manufacture. Professional soldiers alone, so far as it was possible to determine this, are included; no account has been taken of the considerable number of men who volunteered to serve during the South African War. After the army and business the next largest groups were the lawyers (376 or 10.2 per cent), a majority of them solicitors, and those working overseas (345 or 9.4 per cent), a total which covers businessmen, ranchers, and planters. The Church still attracted a considerable number (231, or 6.3 per cent).

Since it is often said that few public schoolboys became engineers or doctors, the total percentages for those professions are surprisingly large. Engineers (144, or 3.9 per cent) and doctors (169, or 4.6 per cent) are both more numerous than government servants (137, or 3.7 per cent). Most of the officials entered the Indian Civil Service or other Indian services like the forests, some went to the colonies, very few were employed in the Civil Service at home. Comparatively few (95, or 2.6 per cent) went into teaching of all kinds, and many of these were preparatory schoolmasters. Very few were involved with the land (52 proprietors and farmers and probably most of the 52 land agents and surveyors – 1.4 per cent in each case). Possibly some of those for whom no profession was recorded were landowners of independent means. The numbers earning their livings in the arts or as journalists or authors were small (59, or 1.6 per cent in both categories). With them might be grouped the 36 architects (1.0 per cent). The 39 (1.1 per cent) 'other careers' included a few analytical/industrial chemists, officials in the Chinese Imperial Services, dental surgeons, and lay workers in religious and charitable fields. Apart from the engineers the involvement with science or technology was small indeed. Of the three schools Charterhouse seems to have had the most aristocratic entry, but all of them were largely patronized by families whose sons had their livings to earn. A small study of this kind is revealing, but it cannot be conclusive, and it could be extended on similar lines to cover more schools.

13 The public school community

Not much can be said here about the histories of individual schools. On the whole, once they had established themselves, they experienced fewer vicissitudes of fortune than had been common in the eighteenth and early nineteenth centuries. Much always depended on the skill – and the good luck – of individual heads, and there were some serious casualties like W. S. Grignon of Felsted, one of the original members of the Headmasters' Conference, who quarrelled with one of his assistants and was eventually dismissed by the trustees, despite support given him by other headmasters (1875–6) (Craze 1955: 180–91). Another victim of a quarrel with an assistant master, leading to a lawsuit and to bitter wrangles in the school community, was E. M. Young of Sherborne, who finally resigned in 1892 (Gourlay 1951: 162–70; Honey 1977: 334–5).

The most notorious of such cases was that of Temple's successor at Rugby, Henry Hayman, a story that illustrates the readiness of the Victorians to enter into public controversy and to fight with few holds barred (Hope-Simpson 1967: 66–100; Honey 1977: 227–32). Temple was a great headmaster, but he had aroused opposition by his Liberal views and his involvement in the controversial Broad Church *Essays and Reviews*, published in 1860. When he was appointed Bishop of Exeter in 1869, the Rugby trustees chose as his successor, in preference to other strong candidates, the headmaster of Bradfield, Henry Hayman, who was a high churchman and a Conservative. Hayman had no easy start. There was controversy about the validity of the testimonials which he had used when he applied for the post, there was criticism of his qualifications (he had only a second class degree), and all the school staff, with one exception, petitioned against his appointment. Even more important was the fact that Temple did nothing to conceal his hostility. Within a couple of years he had become a member of the new governing body set up under the Public Schools Act, and was in a strong position to express his opposition. It seems extraordinary that he was prepared to behave in such a way towards his successor.

Hayman himself seems to have been tactless and good at making enemies, and he lacked some of the qualifications for the post; for

example, he was a poor preacher. It was more serious that, when controversial matters were under discussion, he sometimes showed a strange
inability to tell the whole truth. The difficulties between Hayman and
his colleagues – in particular over the position of one master, E. A.
Scott – dragged on for several years with several appeals to the trustees,
who were fairly evenly divided between the pro- and anti-Hayman forces.
The disputes were not confined to the school; they were frequently aired
in both the local and the national press. By 1873 Hayman's position had
become impossible. Numbers had fallen seriously and as a result some
members of the staff had to be dismissed. These dismissals led to further
problems, as a result of which the governing body first asked Hayman
to resign and then, when he refused to do so, dismissed him from April
1874. Hayman then appealed to the Court of Chancery, which refused
to hear the case, though the judge was very critical of the governing
body, and in particular of Temple and of G. G. Bradley, a former Master
of Marlborough and member of the Rugby staff. The story reflects very
little credit on any of those concerned in it. Any school less well established than Rugby would have been ruined by the open dissension and
adverse publicity. As it was, the situation was quickly restored under T.
W. Jex-Blake (1874–87).

One of the most prominent among the heads of the other Clarendon
schools was George Ridding of Winchester (1866–84), who raised the
numbers to an agreed maximum of 420, acquired new playing fields,
improved the boarding houses, and widened the curriculum. Many of
the reforms which he achieved were financed out of his own pocket. The
historian A. F. Leach, who was one of his pupils, wrote that what
impressed the older boys about Ridding 'was the sense of a great reserve
of power, of strength without narrowness. Breadth was his distinguishing
characteristic' (Leach 1899: 524; Ridding 1908).

At Eton, Edmond Warre had a long reign, from 1884 to 1905. He
was a reformer in some ways but stood strongly for tradition in others.
He had been a keen rowing coach and an enthusiast for the volunteer
corps. He was a convinced Christian and a strong supporter of the college
mission in Hackney Wick, but his Christianity was almost entirely a
matter of ethics. In a fashion very characteristic of his period he wanted
his Etonians to be honest and brave and to serve their country without
hesitation (C. R. L. Fletcher 1922; Mack 1941: 130; Hollis 1960: 286–9).
H. M. Butler (Harrow, 1860–85) was a more considerable figure than
Warre, and under him Harrow prospered greatly. He was early in seeing
the importance of science and he encouraged the development of a
modern side, which aimed to achieve equal status with the classics. In
the traditional way he looked upon himself as a teacher rather than as
an organizer because it was in the classroom that he could influence the
ablest boys. Butler seems to have been able to bring out the best in his
colleagues, a great and rare gift. Edward Bowen wrote to him on one

occasion: 'to be able to pick out and recognize merits in colleagues, when they either exist or seem to exist, has been not the least of the virtues of your administration' (Graham 1920: 293).

Among other boarding school heads four have been selected for further notice – Frederick Temple, E. W. Benson, John Percival, and Edward Thring – though any such choice must be very arbitrary. Something will be said later about the heads of day schools, a group who are often forgotten. Temple (Rugby 1858–69) and Benson (Wellington 1859–73) were both to become Archbishops of Canterbury. They had completed their main scholastic work by 1870, when our period begins. Temple, 'granite on fire' as he was described, had made a very deep impression upon both masters and boys. He had played a major part in the work of the Schools Inquiry Commission. His Rugby pupils and colleagues helped to develop many other schools. Perhaps his Rugby years mark a period of happy equilibrium, a point at which the system had developed stability and coherence while it had not yet fallen into the regimentation of the later Victorian period.

It was Temple who suggested E. W. Benson for the mastership of the new foundation of Wellington College, established in memory of the great duke, in which the Prince Consort took a great interest. The original objective had been to educate the orphan sons of army officers. The Prince, who had little regard for the English public school system, wanted to create a new kind of education for practical life in which history, political science, and the natural sciences would all be important (N. Ball 1980: 18–24). Whether such a scheme was or was not practicable at that time, the Prince was not likely to get it from Benson. They got on well personally, but the new master, who had been eighth classic and first Chancellor's medallist at Cambridge, stood firmly in the old classical tradition, and he set himself to create a public school on traditional lines. After the Prince's death in 1861 he had a much freer hand. He set up a classical side and he took boys other than the sons of army officers. He encouraged boys to stay on at school, he tried to raise the intellectual standard, and to create links with the universities. He was a man of passionate temper and sharp swings of mood, but he was creative and forceful as well. He worked tirelessly and was concerned with every detail. When he left in 1873, he had made Wellington, in the face of many difficulties, into a great school (Talboys 1943: 16, 19; Newsome 1959).

Though E. W. Benson and John Percival were very different people, Clifton owed as much to the latter as Wellington did to the former. Percival was the son of a Westmorland farmer who went from Appleby Grammar School to Queen's College, Oxford. After a short period of teaching at Rugby he was recommended by Temple for the headship of the new school at Bristol, Clifton College, which opened in September 1862 (Temple 1921; Scott 1962: 1–19). He reached his twenty-eighth birthday just after the school opened. He remained at Clifton until 1879 and, after a period as president of Trinity College, Oxford, he was headmaster of Rugby from 1887 to 1895. At Clifton he created one of the most distinguished of Victorian schools. He gathered a staff of remarkable and diverse talents. His pupils won success both at the universities and in the army. He made the teaching of science an important part of the curriculum. He was keenly interested in outside issues like women's education and social conditions in the city of Bristol. In politics he was a strong and uncompromising Liberal, ready to fight hard for what he believed in, even though both he and the school might suffer as a result.

His personality was reserved and he found it difficult to show feeling, though beneath the reserve lay a strong fire and passion of spirit. He could be kind and he understood boys very well, but he was a Puritan who drove himself, his colleagues, and his boys very hard. These aspects of his character seem to have been even more prominent at Rugby than they had been at Clifton. Perhaps he felt that he had limited time to reform a school which had become rather slack in his predecessor's later years. Though many people did not like him and many others feared him, there was a general consensus among those who worked with him that he was a great man. G. F. Bradby, a Rugby colleague, wrote of him:

> He had infinite patience with anybody who tried, and infinite sympathy with people who had no chances; but *no* sympathy with people who had the chances but wouldn't take them. . . . It was as a spiritual influence that he counted most.
>
> (Hope-Simpson 1967: 130–1; see also F. Fletcher 1937: 75;
> Simpson 1954: 55)

His puritanism could be slightly absurd, as in the orders at Rugby that boys should wear football shorts reaching below the knees and that elastic should be worn to hold them there. Underneath the surface lay a fear of ostentation, a demand for unselfishness and self-surrender which offered a striking corrective to the greed and materialism of later Victorian society. In his sermon at the Clifton College jubilee in 1912, Percival spoke of the need for men of pure tastes and public spirit both earnest of purpose and tolerant of mind, 'true Christian citizens – strong, faithful and not afraid'. He called them 'social missionaries of a new type' (Temple 1921: 60–1). His successor at Clifton, J. M. Wilson, speaking at the same celebrations, claimed that Percival had a vision of a new kind of public school, . . . 'a nursery or seed-plot for high-minded men . . . a new Christian chivalry of patriotic service' (J. M. Wilson 1932: 113). It was an ideal that represented the best side of the later Victorian public school. Percival made a strong appeal to those with whom he worked because he had a clear idea where he was going.

Percival, like Temple and Benson, was a highly successful head who went on to a distinguished career in the Church. The fourth member of the group, Edward Thring of Uppingham (1853–87), received no public recognition of his work. By 1870 he had been at Uppingham for seventeen years and so the essential character of his system had been worked out before this study begins (*HSE*: 249–50; Leinster-Mackay 1987). Thring believed that every boy must be given individual attention and that no one, however hopeless he seemed, must be given up. To accomplish these ends he laid great emphasis on proper buildings and facilities – on what he called 'the almighty wall'. He did not believe that these objectives could be achieved in a very large school. Total numbers were to be limited to 300, boarding houses to 30, classes to 20–5.

By 1870 his school had become very successful. The story of his share in the creation of the Headmasters' Conference has already been told (see pp. 122–3). After a hard fight with the Endowed Schools Commissioners he seemed to have achieved success when the school was again imperilled by a serious outbreak of typhoid fever in the town of Uppingham. The epidemic led him to remove the school to Borth, on the mid-Wales coast, until the sanitation of the town had been improved. Thring and his colleagues seem to have regarded the migration to Borth as a purification which had brought the school through the fire back to higher ideals (Tozer 1985: 39–44; Skrine 1889: 215). The last ten years – Thring died in office in October 1887 – were generally a quieter, mellower period. His character showed a strange blend of optimism and pessimism, and in some moods he felt that he had failed. J. H. Skrine recorded a conversation with him about a common friend who had left a certain post and whose work there was not likely to survive him:

> 'Well', said Thring, 'his work is in the hearts he has won. The visible work probably won't go on. *This* is not going to go on.' Then in reply to a remonstrance, 'Ah! you think not; but I am old; I *know*. This will not go on.'
>
> (Skrine 1889: 242)

Though he had created a successful school, it was hardly the school of his vision, and under his successor Uppingham lost its distinctive qualities.

Though Thring held a considerable place in the educational world, it was rather different in kind from that of the other leading heads. He did not always work smoothly with his colleagues, and he himself thought that he had failed in leading them (Skrine 1889: 142–3; Parkin 1898: i, 325). On the other hand, he influenced the work of many other teachers through his writings. His *Theory and Practice of Teaching*, originally published in 1883, went into several editions, and was widely read both in England and in America. He was very interested in women's education, and in 1887 he invited the Association of Headmistresses to hold their annual meeting at Uppingham. G. R. Parkin, whom Thring asked to be his biographer, was a Canadian whom he had first met at the Headmasters' Conference at Winchester in December 1873. When Parkin was writing his book, he found people in many countries of the world who treasured Thring's letters and had been affected by his ideas (Willison 1929: 32–4; Rigby 1968: 366).

Thring's real achievement lay less in creating a successful public school than in appealing to teachers and educators in many countries who knew little about the English public school system. He was a visionary who was also a practical man. The words that occur over and over again in his sermons are 'life' and 'true life'. In the preface to the first edition of *Theory and Practice* (1889) he wrote:

> Perhaps a strong belief that anything, which has a touch of true life in it, will live somewhere or other is at the bottom of it all, however overlaid by chiller wisdom. So this bit of life goes forth.

He was a pioneer of school missions in the cities (see p. 150), and after returning from a visit to North Woolwich, he wrote in his diary that he had less and less hope for the future in Uppingham:

> but in the life I trust I do feel an intense faith – in the seed growing somewhere, and this North Woolwich meeting was a kind of visible embodiment of that invisible somewhere, a sort of making known of the life that has gone out.
>
> (Norwood 1929: 116)

This sense of life endlessly welling up in new forms helps to explain his dislike of examination and inspection and of all bureaucratic interference with the freedom of the teacher. He feared convention and routine. He was little concerned with success because he knew that true life would triumph even through failure. His approach was intuitive, even emotional, rather than purely rational, and his ideas sometimes sound vague and formless. But he appealed to many teachers because of his concern for ultimate principles, quite apart from the particular circumstances in which the individual had to work. No other nineteenth-century English headmaster had such a message to proclaim.

Everything so far written in this chapter has related to the great boarding schools. The major day schools must not be forgotten because they had their own tradition. Their atmosphere was more open; they were less concerned with social distinctions. They had high academic standards and they were comparatively cheap so that they gave opportunities to boys from modest backgrounds. Some of their heads were very able men, and three have been chosen as examples: E. A. Abbott of City of London (1865–89), A. H. Gilkes of Dulwich (1885–1914), and F. W. Walker of Manchester (1859–76) and St Paul's (1877–1905) (Leake and others n.d.; McDonnell 1909; Gardiner and Lupton 1911; Douglas-

Smith 1937; Graham and Pythian 1965; Cannell 1981: 245–62; Hodges 1981). Abbott was a classical scholar who promoted both the teaching of science and of English literature. Gilkes had been a Shrewsbury master who preferred day schools to boarding schools. He was himself a good athlete, but he abhorred the competitiveness and publicity-seeking to which he believed athleticism gave rise. The school under his rule had a good record of university successes, but he put character far above academic achievement. Like Thring and Percival his influence was spiritual and moral.

F. W. Walker had the unique record of remaking two great schools. At Manchester he became high master after the school had suffered a difficult period in the 1840s and 1850s. He extended the buildings and widened the curriculum, and he was particularly skilled in picking out able boys and, if they were poor, finding means of keeping them at school. Unlike most of the heads of the day he did little formal teaching, seeing himself rather as the activator of the whole school machine. At St Paul's with wider opportunities he proceeded on much the same lines. In 1884 the school moved from the City to West Kensington. Academically his rule was highly successful, but during the 1890s he had to fight a sharp battle with the Charity Commissioners to maintain St Paul's as a first-grade school and to prevent changes which, in the name of widening the scope of the foundation, would in his view and in the view of Old Paulines, have reduced the school's status and lowered the level of its work. In the end he was successful and what he had fought for was safeguarded in the scheme of 1900. Like Gilkes he believed in day schools and in the influence of home. He expressed his ideal for St Paul's very clearly at his last Apposition (speech day) in 1905. The school, he said, could not rival or give the polish of the great boarding schools:

> We strive, not without success, to make our boys intellectually strong, industrious, loyal, and as far as man can do, morally upright. The rest we are forced to leave, and I do not regret it, to fathers and mothers and the influences of home.

> (Picciotto 1939: 96)

There were other major day schools, well known in their own areas, like Bedford or Bradford or Nottingham, which might with justice have made similar claims. They represent a strand in the public school tradition to which proper tribute has never been paid.

Both Gilkes and Walker were laymen, and until 1900 it was only in the day schools that laymen had the chance of winning headships. When Frank Fletcher was appointed to Marlborough in 1903, *The Times* described him as 'one lay apple in the clerical dumpling' (F. Fletcher 1937: 108). This clerical monopoly of the major schools meant that by the latter part of the century, heads were being picked from a small pool of candidates because by that time assistant masters were predominantly laymen. Lay appointments to masterships had become common after the 1850s (Bamford 1967: 54–5; Honey 1977: 308). The fact that some later Victorian heads seem to have been men of lesser calibre than their predecessors may be connected with the fact that the pool of clerical candidates was small.

In the 1850s and 1860s the major schools had attracted to their staffs some very able men, both clerical and lay. One who would stand very high on any list was Edward Bowen of Harrow, whose work as house-master and games enthusiast has already been discussed. He was the first head of the modern side and a brilliant teacher. He wrote the school songs, most of them set to music by John Farmer, the most famous of which, 'Forty Years On', was taken by many other schools. At Clifton Percival gathered a very able staff. One of his early appointments was the Manx poet, T. E. Brown, who became a school institution. Henry Newbolt wrote that he had never been taught by Brown, and he had little contact with him outside the classroom, but 'he ranked among the powers who created and directed our daily life: he was one of our household gods' (*Brown, Thomas Edward*, 1930: 168). Probably the greatest pure scholar was T. E. Page, who was sixth-form master at Charterhouse 1873–1910. Frank Fletcher called him 'the most dis-tinguished man whom I have known if distinction be measured not by worldly success or prominence but by intellectual powers and personality' (F. Fletcher 1937: 244).

Men like Bowen, Brown, and Page were not replaced in the ensuing generation by men of equal calibre. By the end of the century there were better opportunities for able graduates than there had been in 1860. India and the colonies offered a variety of careers. Once fellows of Oxford and Cambridge colleges were allowed to marry, there was new incentive to stay on in university work, while other men were attracted to the new universities and university colleges. It is possible too that, once the public schools, which in their hey-day of expansion had been exciting places to work in, had settled into a routine of games and good form, they became less attractive to able young men. By 1914 the leading figures in the schools were no longer the outstanding individuals, but the good team players, strong on character and games and not very interested in the things of the mind. That, on the whole, was what the parents wanted.

If it is true that there was more competition for able graduates in 1900 than there had been in 1860, the public schools must have suffered in the struggle from the fact that assistant masters were poorly paid. A few men, who became housemasters in the major schools, did well. The situation of the remainder is suggested by figures given in a book pub-lished in 1909 (Norwood and Hope 1909: 227–41). In three or four of the oldest schools a master began at £300 non-resident. The majority of the Victorian foundations started at about £125 resident, going up to

£200 after four years with a few men rising to £250 after ten years. There was normally no automatic increase if a master wished to marry. In day schools the position was generally worse; at Bedford Grammar School, for instance, many form masters were paid £100–50 non-resident. There was no salary scale, 'each man fights for what he can get'. There was a tremendous contrast too between the salaries of the head and of his assistants, the former usually receiving ten times as much as the latter. At Tonbridge the assistants had less than £200, the headmaster £5,000 and upwards. Such figures suggest that much of the success of the schools was based on the exploitation of their staff. Moreover, since most assistant masters were laymen, they had no expectation of a living to provide a change of occupation or an effective pension for their later years.

Religious and moral training and discipline, health and sanitary problems, and the shape of the curriculum were major issues which affected all the schools. It has already been argued that moral precept and gentlemanly behaviour loomed much larger in public school religion than any distinctively Christian doctrine. One movement characteristic of the period was the creation of school missions and clubs in the poor districts of great cities. The supporters thought that the missions would bring Christian teaching, linked with welfare agencies like boys' clubs, to the slums. Public schoolboys would, through such contacts, learn something about the working and living conditions of the poor and thus some social barriers would be broken down. The missions would offer work to old boys, both clergy and laymen, and so the links with the schools would be further strengthened.

Thring – not surprisingly – was the pioneer. Uppingham adopted the idea of a mission in East London in 1869, first in North Woolwich and then in Poplar (Tozer 1989: 323–32; Parkin 1898: i, 312–13). Winchester followed in 1876, first in East London and then in Landport, Portsmouth (Ridding 1908: 144–7). At Clifton both Percival and J. M. Wilson took a keen interest in the poor districts of Bristol and in the mission of St Agnes (J. M. Wilson 1932: 138–41). Similar ventures were started by many other schools. The club and mission movement, though it elicited much generosity and hard work from many people, achieved far less than the pioneers had hoped. The problems of the late Victorian city were too grave for much to be accomplished by such methods. On the schools themselves the missions made no great impact. The gap between the two sides was too wide to be bridged, and many boys and assistant masters were not very interested (C. R. L. Fletcher 1922: 137–9). At Cheltenham the missioner's annual reports regularly complained that few boys or old boys visited the mission at Nunhead in south London (Morgan 1968: 135). At Clifton many parents thought that Wilson devoted to the mission energies which ought to have been used for the school (Christie 1935: 128). For individuals, of course, the contacts could be important. It was the Haileybury Club in Stepney in East London which brought C. R. Attlee (Haileybury 1896–1901) to Socialism and to a political career which ended in the prime ministership.

The missions and clubs formed a major link with the outside world. Internally, discipline was maintained on traditional lines by corporal punishment and by the authority of the older over the younger boys. The Clarendon Commission thought that the brutality and tyranny which had earlier been common had largely disappeared. In general they supported the monitorial system and the institution of fagging as likely to produce men of manly and independent character (*HSE*: 235–6, 262–3). Hippolyte Taine pointed out that flogging was not unpopular and was not regarded as humiliating. He thought that fagging was brutal and that the system encouraged the dominance of the strong over the weak (Taine 1872: 129–32). Heads probably varied a good deal in their disciplinary styles. Thring had a reputation for inspiring fear, and others, like John Mitchinson of Canterbury, gave severe punishments (Skrine 1889: 38; Woodruff and Cope 1908: 227–8). Probably, extreme severity was less common at the end of the nineteenth century than at the beginning.

Abuses of power were less likely to arise from the actions of a headmaster than from the authority of the prefects and the possibility of its misuse. One case that aroused considerable notoriety was that of 'tunded Macpherson' at Winchester (1872). Tunding – flogging with a ground ash – was a common punishment in the school. On this occasion the senior commoner prefect gave a boy of 17 who had refused to be examined in 'notions' (the traditional school language) thirty strokes. In the course of the affair five ground ashes were broken. The case became public knowledge, there was considerable correspondence in *The Times* to which Ridding, the headmaster, made an unwise contribution, and the governors held an inquiry. They condemned the severity of the punishment, but supported the power of the prefects to punish, and expressed their confidence in the headmaster. The existence of divided opinions is suggested by the fact that both the chairman and another governor resigned (Ridding 1908: 98–101; Dilke 1965: 82–91). Tunding was not ended, though there were no later scandals. Towards the end of the century discipline may still have been severe; but it was certainly more discreet.

The control of infectious disease and the management of public health were major problems in late Victorian England, and the public schools shared the same difficulties as everyone else. It is noteworthy how much attention is given to infectious diseases, especially scarlet fever, in Dr Clement Dukes' book on health at school (Dukes 1894). The removal of Uppingham to Borth has already been mentioned (see p. 146). Wellington had difficulties during the 1880s with its water supply and drainage, and after an outbreak of diphtheria the school was evacuated to Malvern in 1892 (Newsome 1959: 208–20). Similar problems beset a number of other schools, and the constant danger of epidemic disease was a major threat.

The Clarendon Commission had argued that the curriculum of the public schools should remain primarily classical, though they were anxious to give a definite place to science, mathematics, and modern languages (*HSE*: 240). During the 1860s there was strong pressure towards a broader curriculum, particularly towards teaching more natural science. This was exemplified in *Essays on a Liberal Education* (1868), edited by F. W. Farrar, which contained an essay by J. M. Wilson, then an assistant master at Rugby, on science teaching in schools. Himself a Cambridge mathematician and senior wrangler, Wilson had been encouraged by Temple to develop science teaching at Rugby, which was one of the first public schools in which this was done. During the same period Wilson was also one of the founders of the Mathematical Association. His claims for natural science were very moderate. Two hours a week with the same time for preparation out of school was what was allowed at Rugby, and was as much as he would wish to see at the start. Later this might rise in the upper school to three or four hours a week (F. W. Farrar 1868: 261; J. M. Wilson 1932: 59–69).

The spread of natural science teaching in the public schools was slow (Meadows and Brock 1975: 95–114). Most heads had been trained in the classical tradition, and able boys took classics almost as a matter of course. There were a large number of classical entrance scholarships at Oxford and Cambridge colleges, and both Greek and Latin were essential for entry to both universities. Some schools, however, took science seriously. There was a long tradition of science teaching at City of London (Douglas-Smith 1937: 104–5, 189). Percival encouraged it from the start at Clifton, and opened a laboratory in 1867 (Temple 1921: 32). Part of F. W. Walker's reforms at Manchester involved the teaching of both science and modern languages (Mumford 1919: 327–9, 337). Tonbridge opened a science building in 1887 and extended it in 1894; the subject quickly proved that it could hold its own (Rivington 1910: 283–5, 295). Applied science made its appearance when F. W. Sanderson was made head of a new engineering side at Dulwich in 1887 and an experimental steam engine was acquired for the new department. After Sanderson became head of Oundle in 1892, he was to develop a new concept of public school education based on the scientific method and on co-operation rather than competition. But that story belongs to the twentieth century rather than to the nineteenth (Leake and others n.d.: 7, 47–9; *Sanderson of Oundle* 1923).

Science was only one of the newer subjects. Mathematics had a much longer academic pedigree, particularly at Cambridge, and made its way more easily. Modern languages proved rather a Cinderella. It was difficult to get good teachers, and the French and Germans who were employed were sometimes figures of fun. In many schools all this work was organized into modern sides, with the needs of army candidates particularly in mind. At Cheltenham, a school with strong service connections, there were 218 boys in the modern department as against 300 in the classical in the late 1860s. The modern side curriculum included mathematics, Latin, English, history, geography, French, German, Hindustani, natural sciences, design, drawing plans and fortifications. The distribution of time in the higher classes was as follows: mathematics 8–10 hours; modern languages 5–7 hours; design 4–5 hours; English literature 4–5 hours; natural sciences 3 hours (Demogeot and Montucci 1868: 329, 332). Later in the century Cheltenham had a fine record of success in the Woolwich examinations (Morgan 1968: 70–1).

At the turn of the century G. G. Coulton, who had taught in several public schools, wrote very critically about modern language teaching (Coulton 1901). He thought that public schoolmasters lacked professional training and skill. Modern sides generally attracted both inferior masters and inferior pupils, and the masters had poor promotion prospects. Headmasters were often 'only eminent amateurs'. The organization of army examinations actually increased the likelihood of cramming and the educational system trained future officers to lack reasoning power and to neglect books. Coulton's criticisms were directed at one particular part of the structure, but what he said had a wider application. The small minority of boys who rose to the top of the better schools received a good, though narrow, education. For the great mass of their schoolfellows a stodgy diet of fact and rote learning was provided, which stimulated them very little. The great difficulty was that the public schools had never regarded the provision of a well-thought-out curriculum for the average boy as one of their primary objectives. Learning was something to be endured; it was not to be enjoyed or made use of in after life. The heart of the schools lay rather on the playing field and in the chapel than in the schoolroom.

It is not easy to form a balanced judgement of the late nineteenth-century public school. Many of its failings have been suggested. By the end of the century the schools had hardened into a deadening conformity. When men like Edward Bowen and John Percival were beginning their careers, public schools were often exciting places staffed by able men keen to promote new ideas. In a sense the schools became the victims of their own success. They had preached a creed of loyalty to school, regiment, and country which often choked initiative and branded originality as deviance. As school life became more highly structured, every moment of the day was filled so that boys had little opportunity to pursue their own interests. For all this a price had to be paid. The atmosphere at the end of our period is skilfully suggested in *The Lanchester Tradition*, a novel by the Rugby master, G. F. Bradby, published in 1914. Everything at Chiltern School is dominated by the tradition supposedly created by Abraham Lanchester, headmaster at the end of the eighteenth century. Yet Lanchester had in reality been a radical. His name was being used to consecrate a philistine games-oriented culture resistant to any change.

Though many public school men came from families that had made their money in business and industry, the ethos of the schools tended to lead them away from such occupations towards public service, the army, and the empire. The schools had few links with science and technology, and it has been argued that the anti-business culture which they propagated was positively harmful to a country that depended on trade and industry for its prosperity and that faced increasingly keen competition from Germany and the United States. Martin J. Wiener has argued persuasively that the public schools formed part of a social structure which lured rich men away from business and industry towards the leisured life of the landed gentry and so weakened the thrust to increase commercial and industrial wealth (Wiener 1985; Mathieson and Bernbaum 1988: 126–74).

The reasons for Britain's comparative decline are very complex, and it would be difficult to establish in detail how far and in what ways the movement of businessmen into the landed classes harmed the standards of British economic management. It is a subject on which generalization is much easier than detailed research. The power of commercial and industrial wealth in late nineteenth-century England was very great. If there is truth in the argument that the schools helped to turn Englishmen away from business, there is also truth in the counter-argument that the schools set up an ideal of service and self-sacrifice which was of value in a society in which materialistic forces were very strong. The hey-day of the public schools was the hey-day of imperialism, and an attempt has been made to draw out the links between them. The virtues of the subaltern on the Indian frontier or the pioneer in the Australian bush may not always be those that appeal to late twentieth-century Englishmen, but they dealt – not unsuccessfully – with the situations which late nineteenth-century Englishmen had to face. Up to the First World War, at least, the public schools provided a leadership which was effective and popular in the country. When the schools are criticized, their positive achievements should not be forgotten.

Part IV

Private and private foundation schools

14 Private schools: strengths and weaknesses

As the public schools grew in prestige and importance after 1850, the private schools, which had reached their hey-day in the first half of the century, had declined. One clear sign of change was the tendency of men who had been pupils at private schools of one kind or another to send their sons to public schools and then to Oxford and Cambridge. The Worcestershire ironmaster Alfred Baldwin had left the Wesleyan Collegiate Institution at Taunton at the age of 16 to go into the family firm. His son Stanley, the future prime minister, born in 1867, was sent to an exclusive preparatory school, Hawtrey's, then to Harrow and to Trinity College, Cambridge (R. Jenkins 1987: 34; see also pp. 138–9). The decline of the private schools can be exaggerated. They remained important up to the end of the century, particularly in educating girls, because in many parts of the country there were few high schools of the new type and many parents did not favour them even when they were available. However, after 1870, private schoolmasters and mistresses felt themselves increasingly a beleaguered race, confronted by ever keener competition with, as they saw it, the dice loaded against them in favour of endowed and state-aided schools.

The private schools were of many different sizes and of several different types. The commonest type, both for boys and girls, was that owned by an individual or by two or three partners and conducted for private profit. It was a scholastic business which had no cushion against failure other than the success of the owner in paying his or her own way. Other schools were at once semi-private and semi-public. They were public because they were owned and managed by groups of people sharing common and enduring interests. They were private because they lacked either the charters or the endowments of the old grammar schools and, like the schools owned by individuals, they had to pay their way in order to survive. For all the varied schools of this class 'private foundation school' is a convenient general title (*HSE*: 6–7). One substantial subgroup in this class consisted of the proprietary schools, established by proprietors or shareholders, generally on the lines of the old classical grammar schools. These had been a major development of the 1820s and

1830s. After 1860 boys' schools of this kind declined in importance, but bodies of shareholders like the Girls' Public Day School Company and the Church Schools Company played a crucial role in the expansion of girls' secondary education. The other major sub-group was the schools of religious foundation, where all the major churches played a part. Among the Anglican founders Nathaniel Woodard and J. L. Brereton were outstanding. Both Methodists and Quakers were active. The Roman Catholics ran both boarding schools, which in the twentieth century were to establish themselves as leading public schools, and a growing number of day grammar schools for both boys and girls.

These private foundation schools of various kinds will be examined in more detail later. For the present attention will be concentrated on the schools owned by individuals or partnerships – the private schools in the strictest sense. Since the eighteenth century schools of this kind had catered for both boys and girls, and indeed until the creation of the new girls' public secondary schools, they were, with insignificant exceptions, the only places of secondary education for girls which existed. The continuing importance of girls' private schools right up to the end of the century is shown by statistics given in the Bryce Commission Report (1895) of the number of scholars in private schools in six counties (Bedfordshire, Devonshire, Lancashire, Norfolk, Surrey, the West Riding of Yorkshire). These show totals of 4,764 boys in 107 schools and 8,274 girls in 220 schools (*BC* I, Appendices, 434–5).

These private schools had enjoyed their hey-day during the first half of the century when few boys were sent to public schools and many of the grammar schools were in a poor state. The report of the Schools Inquiry Commission provides a balanced judgement of the position of the private schools at that time (SIC I: 283–322). They suffered, it was said, from certain major weaknesses. There were no means of distinguishing good schools from bad, and success was often obtained by managing and manipulating parents. The schools had no recognized position and superior men were often unwilling to accept situations in them. The assistant commissioners had found that schools varied from good to very bad; indeed all observers throughout the period made the point that it was very difficult to generalize. Many heads, the report said, were men of ability; others were described as 'pretenders'. Generally, the assistants, who were poorly paid, were unsatisfactory. One special difficulty was the existence of strong class feeling which meant that parents were unwilling to send their children to schools with those whom they regarded as their social inferiors. 'In fact the inferior private schools owe their very existence to the unwillingness of many of the tradesmen and others just above the manual labourers to send their sons to the National or the British School' (SIC I: 297). It was indeed these third-grade schools, with teaching levels not much above the elementary, which were regarded as particularly bad. One criticism, voiced by the assistant commissioners, was that the schools were too small to be efficient. James Bryce in Lancashire thought that 'the present system, with its crowd of schools each too small and too poor to be good, each keeping the others down by competition, is the most wasteful that can be thought of' (SIC IX: 581).

The judgement of the commission was, however, by no means entirely unfavourable. The private schools lacked tradition and permanence, but on the other hand, they accepted innovation more easily than the grammar schools. Parental pressure had its bad side, but it did keep the masters up to a minimum level of efficiency if they were to attract any pupils at all. The curricula were generally 'modern' in type with particular attention to arithmetic, English, and French. There was little Greek and many boys did not take Latin. The curricula lacked depth, but they often provided a quick and efficient basis for commercial pursuits. The schools had sent in candidates for the University Local and the College of Preceptors examinations. They claimed to give individual attention, and they were often successful with backward boys, two characteristics which may have been linked with the small size of school which had been criticized as a defect. The verdict, like that of many critics, was mixed. The commissioners touched on the central issue when they argued that in education the commercial principle could not operate effectively on its own. The truth or falsity of that statement was at the core of the debate.

In the period between the reports of the Taunton (1868) and the Bryce (1895) Commissions the private schools were exposed to much keener competition than they had had to face in the first half of the century. The public schools took pupils from the more expensive boarding schools. The town day schools, where fees were lowest and profit margins narrowest, suffered from the steady improvement of the endowed grammar schools. The cheapest private schools, as much elementary as secondary in their curriculum, suffered in many towns from the competition of the higher elementary schools which could offer a better education at a lower fee or even at no fee at all. There was an overall decline, but it affected boys' schools much more than girls', and it varied very much from area to area.

A. P. Laurie, the Bryce assistant commissioner who looked at boys' schools in the West Riding, had been given the names of thirty-three schools of which thirteen made returns. J. G. Fitch, who had inspected the same area for Taunton, had cited 147 boys' schools of which seventy-four made returns. The boys' schools, Laurie thought, were 'already of small importance in the educational scheme of the county' (*BC* VII: 257). In Leeds there were no secondary schools of this type for boys in the city, though there were two in the suburbs, with 40 and 41 boys, respectively (*BC* VII: 163). In Sheffield J. F. Moss, the clerk to the school board, thought the private schools 'neither numerous nor important' (*BC* III: 94: 7017).

But the picture at the end of the century was not uniform. H. Llewellyn Smith pointed out that boys' private schools in London had been affected both by the expansion of the board schools and the revival of the endowed schools. 'Thirty years ago, when St Olave's Grammar School (Southwark) was at a low point, there were nine flourishing private schools in the parish; now St Olave's educates several hundreds of boys, all the private schools have disappeared' (Acland and Llewellyn Smith 1892: 165). In suburban Middlesex, on the other hand, Margaret Bryant considered that most girls continued to be educated in private schools and that it is difficult to establish how far these schools had been affected by the newer type of high school (*VCH Middlesex* I: 267). The northern parts of Cheshire resembled Middlesex in being deeply affected by neighbouring urban growth. The commercial academies seem to have declined more slowly than the classical type, which felt the competition of the public schools. In Stockport English and commercial schools seem to have reached their peak in about 1880, when at least forty-three were recorded. Thereafter numbers fell, but there were still about twenty-two in 1900. In Chester and in north-east Cheshire and the Wirral, where the expansion of Liverpool and Manchester was strongly felt, there was so much demand for middle-class education that little decline was felt at all (Wardle, *VCH Cheshire* III (1980): 221–2).

In many rural counties private schools remained very important. In Wiltshire, for example, they provided most of the available secondary education for both boys and girls, and in some places public secondary schools were later established partly on foundations which they had laid (Butcher, *VCH Wiltshire* V (1957): 349).

Some figures for secondary schools of all types in Norfolk are given in Table 14.1. Though in Norfolk there were considerably more boys in endowed schools than in private schools, the total in the latter class is

Table 14.1 Pupils at Norfolk secondary schools, *c.* 1894

		Boys	Girls	Totals
Endowed schools: County boroughs		500	–	
Administrative county		400	52	
	Total	900	52	952
Proprietary schools: County boroughs		–	260	
Administrative county		–	114	
	Total		374	374
Private schools: County boroughs		180	600	
Administrative county		320	400	
	Totals	500	1,000	1,500

Source: Bryce Commission Evidence VI, *PP* 1895 XLVIII: 392.

considerable. For girls the numbers in private and proprietary schools are overwhelming – 1,374 against 52 in endowed schools.

Though in the 1890s many private schools continued to operate successfully, principals felt themselves under increasing pressure. The only statistical survey carried out during the period was the return of pupils in public and private secondary schools of 1897 which will be discussed later (see pp. 171–2). The return is prefixed by two letters. The first was from a master 68 years of age and head of a school established over seventy years. In 1865 he had a school of fifty-four boarders; at the time of writing he had six boarders and eleven day pupils, and was just about to give up the school. The second was from the mistress of a school set up in 1852 and carried on from that date by members of the same family. During the previous ten years the number of pupils had steadily declined as the result of the competition of schools supported by rates and taxes which, the principal pointed out, she had to pay herself. Her school was, she admitted, old-fashioned: 'Scholarships and certificates were things undreamed of in a woman's career in my youth and *sans* certificates in a teacher of to-day means "*sans* everything" ' (*PP* 1897 LXX: 566). The problem of the private school head whose school had faded away as he or she had grown older was no new one, but these writers were victims of a changing situation where new kinds of education were being demanded which the old-fashioned private school was not well equipped to provide.

The most trenchant critic of the middle-class private school had been Matthew Arnold, who argued that a good secondary education could not be based on the principles of supply and demand and who satirized the advertisements for an 'educational home' where 'discipline is based on moral influence and emulation, and every effort is made to combine home comforts with school-training' (Smith and Summerfield 1969: 100 – from *A French Eton* (1863–4)). Private school heads were often ridiculed as men with few qualifications or none at all, who prospered by catching the latest winds of fashion. Arnold created Archimedes Silverpump, PhD, of Lycurgus House Academy – 'none of your antiquated rubbish – all practical work – latest discoveries in science – mind constantly kept excited – lots of interesting experiments – lights of all colours – fizz! fizz! bang! bang!' (Arnold 1871: 53).

Certainly some school principals accumulated worthless certificates and degrees in order to impress parents who, from their side, sometimes drove hard bargains in return for sending a second or third son or daughter to follow the first. Sometimes education was traded for food and groceries. A. H. D. Acland, in a parliamentary debate, quoted a newspaper advertisement: 'To Butchers and Grocers – Education. A young lady can be received in a first class and old established school on the sea coast on reciprocal terms' (*Hansard* 325: 814, 27 April 1888). The assistant teachers who were poorly paid and held a low status were even more severely criticized than their principals. Michael Sadler, who was a friendly critic, said of some of the private schools of Liverpool that 'the really weak spot . . . is the lack of qualified assistants. When they charge a low fee, private schools cannot afford to pay such salaries as will secure a fully qualified staff' (Sadler 1904a: 26).

The verdict of an administrator of the new age like H. Macan, organizing secretary of the Surrey Technical Education Committee, was distinctly unfavourable. He told the Bryce Commission that some of the more expensive private schools in the county did excellent work in providing special coaching, looking after backward boys and preparing for the public schools, though he thought that, if inspection of buildings and registration of teachers were introduced, most of the cheaper schools, professing to give a secondary education for £4 or £5 a year, would close:

> There are private schools all over the country, which are simply carried on in small private houses; the school is conducted in the dining room or the drawing room, and in some cases there is a shed built out at the back.
>
> (*BC* II: 442: 4693–7)

The case made out by critics like Macan or Matthew Arnold is a strong one and has been largely accepted by historians. In reality the situation was more complex than that, one example being that of the qualifications of private school teachers. The return of 1897 shows that about half the full-time men teachers in boys' schools were graduates, though 20 per cent of boys' schools had no graduates on their staffs at all. The percentage of women graduates was naturally much lower since comparatively few women had enjoyed the opportunity to graduate. Certainly the qualifications of private school teachers left much to be desired, but the critics always concentrate on those who lacked graduate qualifications and ignore the considerable numbers who possessed them (*PP* 1897 LXX: 569–75).

This question of qualifications brings out from one particular angle the point stressed in the Taunton Report – that there were great variations in efficiency between different schools. Private schools were often criticized as ephemeral growths, here today and gone tomorrow. Sometimes this was true, but some of them endured for a long time, which suggests that they met a continuing demand from their clientele which would not have been satisfied by flashy brilliance of the Archimedes Silverpump variety (Leinster-Mackay 1978: 1–7). A survey of boys' and girls' schools in Doncaster shows that several of them lasted over many decades (J. A. Harrison 1961: 70–8). In the Teeside village of Gainford Bowman's Academy, founded in 1818, was conducted by members of the same family until competition from the new North Eastern Counties School at Barnard Castle forced it to close in 1899, and even after that date F. E.

Bowman ran a boarding tutorial establishment in the same village (*Gainford in the 1880s*: 54–8). Of the two heads cited in the return of 1897, one was head of a school established over seventy years, the other of a school started in 1852 – hardly mushroom growths.

A strong case was made throughout the period by defenders of the private schools (Leinster-Mackay 1983: 1–6), though their arguments are very largely forgotten, while Matthew Arnold's strictures are well remembered. The most prominent of the defenders was the Liberal economist Robert Lowe, author of the Revised Code, Chancellor of the Exchequer in Gladstone's 1868 government. Lowe was highly suspicious of educational endowments, believing that they led to inefficiency and stagnation. In his view they bribed parents to accept inferior teaching at a cheaper rate. Parents were best qualified to choose what they wanted, and, since the private schoolmaster had to attract their custom in order to succeed, it was in his interest to provide an attractive programme. Normally the master's views would be a little ahead of the parents, though they were ready to accept new and improved ideas. Consequently there was a built-in tendency towards innovation, and no limit could be set to the improvement of the private schools. Lowe saw the contest between them and the endowed schools as a fight between immobility and progress (Lowe 1868).

The case made by Lowe was developed in pamphlets published some ten to fifteen years later and in the propaganda of the Private Schools Association, which grew out of meetings held by principals in 1878–9 and which gave evidence to the Bryce Commission (Knightley 1876; A. Wilson 1877; Hiley 1884; G. Robinson 1966 and 1971). It was claimed that competition was a spur to efficiency. Great play was made with the argument that private schools were more flexible and more ready to innovate than the public and endowed schools. Standards in general had risen and examination results were good. Private school teachers organized their work better, and they were often men of much greater professional experience than their public school colleagues who were equally dependent on the profit motive, for example, through their boarding houses. The private schools did not use harsh punishments, and they had much smaller classes, so that they could give careful attention to boys of all levels of ability.

One great weakness in putting across the case for the defence was that it was very difficult to get private school principals to co-operate. They tended to work in isolation and to be jealous of those whom they regarded as their rivals, a situation which considerably hampered the work of the Private Schools Association (*Secondary Education* V (1900): 130; VII (1901): 194). Its representatives, Mr W. Brown and Miss S. Allen Olney, told the Bryce Commission that 584 school principals were members – a good number but only a portion of those who might have joined (*BC* III: 279: 9258). Most of their evidence relates to the problems of reorganizing secondary education in the 1890s, but the information which they provided about themselves throws interesting light on the achievements of two people who had built up successful schools in a difficult period.*

Both their schools were in north London, Brown in Finsbury Park, Miss Olney in Hampstead. Brown had trained as an elementary teacher, had spent six or seven years training teachers in Ireland, and had taken a London degree. He bought Tollington Park School in 1879 and had built it up to 400 pupils. His average fee was £11 5s 0d a year, and the boys came between the ages of 7 and 16:

> We have organized it as a science school. We have a chemical labora-tory; we have 16 boys, 10 taking the first year course, and six the second year course. We take the subjects of electricity and magnetism in the same way; we take natural history; we take high mathematics; we take French and German, and, for those who are willing, Spanish.
> (*BC* III: 298: 9433)

Subsequently, Brown also opened a school at Muswell Hill which grew to 225 boys (Bryant, *VCH Middlesex* I (1969): 274).

Miss Olney had studied abroad, and when she returned had passed 'various examinations connected with the Higher Local and the St And-rew's'. She had taught privately and had been for eight years head-mistress of one of the schools of the Girls Public Day School Company. In 1886 she and her sister had built their own private school, which numbered over 100 pupils:

> We prepare our pupils for the Cambridge Locals and send them up to the London Matriculation and for various other examinations. We prepare them for a great many examinations, though I must say that we have quite the wealthy class, and that they are much averse to allowing their daughters to work for examinations.
> (*BC* III: 298: 9436)

Miss Olney's day school fee at 15 guineas was rather more expensive than Brown's. She also took boarders.

Both Brown and Miss Olney were working in north London suburbs where there was a large demand from middle-class parents for good secondary education. Some of the reasons for their success stand out clearly. They both had good qualifications and professional experience. Neither school was cheap and both were large – Brown's very large – so that the income from fees was considerable. Clearly they had both measured their market. Miss Olney emphasized her examination suc-cesses and her wealthy clientele. Brown stressed science, mathematics, and modern languages. They had both set out stalls from which people were anxious to buy. Their success helps to redress the balance against the general picture of shabbiness and inefficiency which is all too easily painted for all the private schools.

The more successful private schools benefited from the popularity of private enterprise and the fear of state interference which was still felt by many parents. It has recently been argued that the same kind of voluntaryism ensured the long continuance of many working-class private elementary schools (P. Gardner 1984). The defenders of the private schools had a reasonable case, but, even at that time, it was never fully accepted and there was always nagging doubt about what should be done. The dilemma can be seen in the discussions of the Social Science Association in the 1870s and early 1880s. Some speakers thought that there was no way of distinguishing between good and bad schools, and that private schools were likely to decrease in number and to become less effective (*TSSA* 1872: 57–8 (G. W. Hastings); 1879: 63 (Lyulph Stanley); 1883: 49 (F. S. Powell)). Others considered that secondary education must always be based on voluntary activity, or feared the way in which government control checked the development of private enterprise (*TSSA* 1880: 497 (J. H. Rigg): 1883: 338 (Rowland Hamilton)). The feelings of this group were probably strengthened by dislike of the centralized management of elementary schools under the Revised Code. Though the Bryce Commission supported a wide increase in state activity, they were anxious that private schools, provided that guarantees could be taken for their efficiency, should continue to play an important role (*BC* I: 292–5). Michael Sadler said much the same in his local surveys. The private schools had certainly lost ground in the last third of the nineteenth century, but in 1900 there was still a chance that they might have an important part to play. Their demise was the result of events in the twentieth century rather than because of what happened in the late Victorian age.

15 Private schools: policies and practices

Though the defenders of the private school praised their readiness to take up new ideas, they showed, in fact, much less keenness to innovate in the final third of the nineteenth century than in earlier decades. The only real exception to that statement is the small group of progressive schools, beginning with Cecil Reddie's foundation of Abbotsholme in 1889 (see pp. 189–90). Where new ideas like the kindergarten method or the Swedish 'slöjd' method of manual training came in, they influenced the work of younger rather than of older children. As the endowed schools were gradually reformed, they took up the subjects like mathematics and modern languages which had earlier been left to the private schools, and all the secondary schools approximated more and more closely to a single model. This was an important process because it was only in this way that a common secondary school curriculum, which hardly existed in 1850, could come into existence. However, as it developed, the former distinctiveness of the private schools was reduced.

One major force for change was the public examinations, which dated from the 1850s. The College of Preceptors were the pioneers, followed quickly by the Local Examinations of the universities of Oxford and Cambridge, and later by the Oxford and Cambridge Joint Board. At the same time it became common to use the matriculation examination of London University as a leaving examination for abler pupils. The numbers who took it were small, but it was the most formidable hurdle which a boy or girl of the period had to face. Finally the growing popularity of science led to many pupils being entered for the examinations of the Department of Science and Art (Roach 1971).

The private schools entered pupils for the new examinations from the beginning, and girls participated as well as boys from an early date. At the Cambridge Locals centre at Wolverhampton in 1866, for example, there were sixty-nine successful candidates. It is difficult to be certain about the types of school from which they came, but the most likely division is forty-two from grammar schools and twenty-seven from private and proprietary schools and from private tuition (Cambridge University Library, Univ. Papers 1820–67 (Archives UP 5)). Table 15.1 gives an analysis of the candidates for the Cambridge examination of December 1893, provided by J. N. Keynes, secretary of the local examinations syndicate. If the tiny figure for higher elementary schools is excluded, Keynes' figures give a total of 5,100 boy and 3,357 girl candidates. The percentages of the total figure provided by the three main groups were as follows:

	Boys	Girls
Endowed	46	19.6
Other public	23.8	24.5
Private	30.1	55.8

If it is assumed, as is probably the case, that 'other public' is another way of describing what are called here 'private foundation' schools, the private and 'other public' schools represent 54 per cent of the total boys' entry and 80.4 per cent of the total girls' entry.

Table 15.1 Candidates for Cambridge Local Examinations, December 1893

No. of schools		*Boys* No. of junior candidates	No. of senior candidates	Total
205	Endowed schools	2,117	233	2,350
61	Other public schools[a]	1,125	89	1,214
9	Higher grade elementary schools	45	0	45
338	Private schools	1,414	122	1,536
		Girls		
54	Endowed schools	472	187	659
100	Other public schools[a]	507	317	824
8	Higher grade elementary schools	42	3	45
720	Private schools	1,185	689	1,874

Source: Bryce Commission Evidence V, *PP* 1895 XLVII: 274–5.
[a] Schools administered by a governing body of a representative or public character, but not endowed.

In those terms the private and 'other public' groups showed up well, but it must be noted that the average entry per school was very low.

	Boys	Girls
Endowed	11.5	12.2
Other public	19.9	8.2
Private	4.5	2.6

When every allowance has been made for the fact that many schools were small, that they sometimes entered pupils for different examinations, and that averages are misleading anyway because schools differed so much between themselves, it is clear that many schools had very few examination candidates. The point was picked up by F. E. Kitchener who surveyed the industrial district of south Lancashire (the hundreds of Salford and West Derby) for the Bryce Commission. He produced figures for 1893–4 for boys and girls taking the Oxford and Cambridge Locals, the Preceptors and Joint Board examinations in 70 boys' schools and 109 girls' schools of all the types described:

> Of these, only 28 boys' schools and 28 girls' schools have passed five candidates and upwards, and in all 728 boys and 455 girls passed . . . even if allowance is made for failures, the number of boys entered is probably under 1,100 and the girls under 700, a small outcome for the enormous population of the two hundreds.
>
> (*BC* VI; 239 and Appendix C: 192–205)

Though the number of candidates in any school was often small, the public examinations and their requirements had a major influence on the curriculum of all types of secondary school. It is significant that the Locals and the Preceptors examinations were prominently featured in school advertisements. The quest for competitive success may have cut back some freedom and spontaneity, though it probably raised overall standards – at least in the better schools. The point to be noted is that the process affected endowed and private schools alike. All were seeking the same kind of achievement, all had their eyes on future career prospects. In the process both kinds of school lost many of the characteristics which had distinguished them in the earlier part of the century as a common pattern of secondary education developed.

Another change, which linked many boys' private schools closely with the public schools, was the growth of the preparatory school for boys of 7–8 to 13–14 years (BOE Special Reports, *Preparatory Schools for Boys* (1900); Leinster-Mackay 1984). In the earlier part of the nineteenth century public schools had taken some boys at primary age. Others had gone first to private schools or had moved on from the local grammar school. After about 1870 the pattern of a move from preparatory to public school at 13–14 became general, and many private school heads found it advantageous to concentrate on the younger boys. The career of J. V. Milne, father of the author, A. A. Milne, is interesting from this point of view. The elder Milne had been a clerk, an engineer, an usher in various schools, and had taken his London BA degree by evening study. He ran an all-age private school of the traditional kind at Kilburn in north London for several years until he became convinced that the area was going down socially and further that there was no future for his type of school. 'The only private school which could now succeed was the preparatory school for boys under fourteen.' With the proceeds of a legacy Milne rented a house at Westgate-on-Sea in the

Isle of Thanet where he built up a successful preparatory school (Milne 1939: 15–18, 84–5, 154). A number of other private school principals probably took a similar course.

The private schools were affected by the same pressures as the public schools. Team games became increasingly popular. Before 1850 private schools often limited themselves to games in the playground, but later cricket and football became common. Since these schools were usually small, these games were not easy to organize and grounds were sometimes difficult to acquire. Yet sporting facilities were often mentioned in advertisements, and old boys wrote in their reminiscences about them. Epidemic disease was a constant problem for all boarding schools, public or private (see p. 151). In 1880–1 *The Lancet* carried out an enquiry into school management and hygiene, which covered thirty-nine boarding schools, varying in size from over 100 to fewer than 20 boys (*The Lancet* 1880, I: 689–90; 1881, II: 21–7, 94–7, 506–8, 715–17). The schools are not identified, but it is fairly safe to assume that most of the smaller ones will have been private schools.

Questions were asked about premises, about diet, about the time devoted to work and play, and about illness and sanitary arrangements generally. In most schools the day-closets and urinals were outside the house in a courtyard or playground. Generally schools made a favourable report on their drainage, but it was thought that, if more examples had been available, the situation would have seemed less good. More attention was paid than had been the case in earlier years to washing and bathing arrangements. Contagious diseases had broken out in a number of schools, though they had often been quickly isolated. In a few schools there had been serious outbreaks. In one school in Kent of eighty-five boarders aged from 12 to 19, for example, there had been thirty cases of mumps and two cases of congestion of the lungs in March/April 1879 and ten cases of measles in February 1880.

Though there were variations in school programmes, a typical school day began at 6.30 a.m. and ended at 9 p.m. This allowed 7½ hours for school work, 5 hours for recreation and about 9½ hours sleep. However, among the twenty-two schools which gave information, the hours of school work varied from 5½ to 8½. On some days no school work was done in the afternoons. Generally, the amount of food provided was satisfactory, and the main meal of the day was a liberal one.

The report commented on the wide variation between schools in the number of cubic feet of space allowed in the dormitories and the classrooms. Generally, the allowance was less than it should have been, particularly in the dormitories where boys spent a long continuous period of time. Stress was laid on two particular requirements. Care must be taken to see that classrooms were well lit, and that no sewer gas or air from privies and urinals gained access to the dormitories. The drainage system of schools should be separated as far as possible from that of the town, and where this could not be done, care must be taken to provide traps in the drains and ventilation shafts so as to isolate the school from the town system. In general, the intercourse of boys with the townspeople should be limited as far as possible. Throughout the report there is a strong emphasis on the contemporary belief that sewer gas and fumes emanating from neglected piles of rubbish caused a major danger to health.

All these pressures – to win examination successes, to provide better games facilities, to create higher standards of health and hygiene – cost money which could be found only from school fees. The principals were operating in a market in which competition to survive was becoming ever keener (Bryant 1986: 164–5). What might be called the limits of viability were much higher in 1890 than they had been fifty years earlier. The problem was felt most severely by the cheaper day schools where fees were too low to provide an efficient education. Though the cause of private enterprise still attracted many defenders, there was a growing fear that the state would take a hand.

Many of the leading figures in the private school world appreciated that measures had to be taken to differentiate between good schools and bad. The chief measures suggested were the inspection of schools and the registration of teachers. It was hoped that county council scholarships, which had become so important in the 1890s, might be held in recognized private schools (see pp. 111–12; *BC* IV: 217–18: 14559). Such arrangements would, it was argued, both help local authorities in areas where no endowed schools existed and provide efficient private schools with more pupils. The Technical Instruction Act 1889 and the Local Taxation (Customs and Excise) Act 1890 had prohibited a local authority from making any payments from the local rate for instruction in a school conducted for private profit. However, this was not held to apply if the dividend did not exceed 5 per cent and if the capital had been actually expended on buildings or maintenance. In 1900 fourteen county councils offered scholarships tenable in proprietary schools, especially in those of the Girls' Public Day School Company (*Record* IX (1900): 76–8), but such concessions were not extended to the privately-owned schools.

Bodies like the College of Preceptors as well as individuals campaigned for better training and higher qualifications for teachers. In 1890 two teacher registration Bills were presented to Parliament, one of which did and the other of which did not recommend professional training as a prerequisite of registration. In 1891 a select committee, after hearing evidence from a number of witnesses, made no definite recommendations, though approving in general of both training and registration. There, for the time, the matter rested. In 1902 a Teachers' Registration Council was set up, but registration was not made compulsory (Rich 1933/1972: 267–8, 273). Among individuals who worked hard to raise professional standards were Joseph Payne and C. H. Lake. Payne had a school first in south London and then, for about eighteen years, at the Mansion House, Leatherhead, which was described as 'one of the very first private schools in this country' (Payne 1883 I (obituary notice and introduction)). He became a strong advocate of the scientific study of education, a subject to which he devoted himself after he retired from his school in 1863. The College of Preceptors appointed him first lecturer and then professor of the science and art of education (1873), the first person to hold that title in England, though the course was suspended after the second year (Rich, 1933/1972: 255–7). Payne died in 1876; a volume of his lectures was published in 1880. His friend, C. H. Lake, was head of Oxford House School, Chelsea, a school of 120 boys and 10 masters. He took the College of Preceptors diploma and later a London degree, and like Payne he was keenly interested in educational ideas and in professional training. He became one of the founders of the Teachers' Guild (1884), which was concerned both with educational studies and with matters like employment, pensions, and materials and equipment (Bryant, *VCH Middlesex* I (1969): 279).

The careers of men like Payne and Lake do something to remove the Archimedes Silverpump image of the private school principal, but there were not enough of them to make a major impact on national policy making. During the 1890s the Private Schools Association was active in making the case for the schools on the lines already suggested. Their representatives told the Bryce Commission that parents were able to pay for secondary education which should be entirely self-supporting. Middle-class parents should not be required to pay an education rate in addition to what they already paid for elementary education. There was a danger, they claimed, in over-educating children who would not be able to find work in a market where competition for non-manual jobs was already intense (*BC* III: 300: 9452; 302: 9491; 312–13: 9637). The Education Act of 1902 did require the new LEAs, in exercising their powers in higher (i.e. secondary) education, to 'have regard to any existing supply of efficient schools or colleges', a requirement that the private schools regarded as a major victory for them. Yet only a year later the new president of the association complained that their claims were being ignored by the local authorities and by the Board of Education (*Secondary Education* VII (1902): 201; VIII (1903): 231).

Though there is useful statistical material in the Bryce Commission papers, the only authoritative statement is the Return of 1897 of pupils in public and private secondary and other schools (*PP* 1897 LXX: 557–665). The Education Department sent out some 10–11,000 letters and 6,209 schools replied. These contained 291,544 children (158,502 boys and 133,042 girls). Many of these, of course, were in endowed schools. The figures for the schools considered in this section are shown in Table 15.2.

Of the grand total of 291,544 children 65.3 per cent (190,330) were in

Table 15.2 Pupils in private secondary and other schools, 1897

| | Boys | | Girls | | Mixed | |
	Schools	Pupils	Schools	Pupils	Schools	Pupils
Private enterprise	1,311	46,617	2,886	80,286	970	26,027
Subscribers	70	8,719	99	6,321	28	3,626
Companies	48	5,188	99	13,238	3	308
Totals	1,429	60,524	3,084	99,845	1,001	29,961

Source: Return of Pupils in Public and Private Secondary Schools in England, *PP* 1897 LXX: 557–665.

these three classes of school. Of the 190,330, 152,930 pupils or 80.3 per cent were in private enterprise schools. In those schools 39 per cent of the boys and 19.3 per cent of the girls were boarders; in mixed schools the percentages were much lower.

Many of the private enterprise schools were small and the pupils very young. Forty-eight per cent of boys in boys' schools were under the age of 12. Both these points are illustrated in Table 15.3. It is clear that many schools in the return could hardly claim to rank as secondary schools at all. The London Technical Education Board's figures for private and semi-private schools entering candidates for the major public examinations repeat the same story. They recorded 126 schools which had replied out of a total of about 360. Of the pupils in them 2,279 out of 3,466 boys (65.75 per cent) and 2,080 out of 3,641 girls (57.1 per cent) were under 13. The percentage of younger pupils was much higher in these schools than in eighty-four public endowed and public proprietary schools where the comparable percentages were 37.3 per cent for boys and 40.7 per cent for girls (*BC* IX Appendix. Statistical Tables D: 430, 437).

Most nineteenth-century private schools are shadowy institutions which

Table 15.3 Private schools: age of pupils and size of schools, 1897

	Total number of schools	Schools with no pupils over 14
Boys	1,311	309 (23.6%)
Girls	2,886	491 (17%)
Mixed	970	601 (62%)

Over half these schools had fewer than 31 pupils and over three-quarters less than 50:

| | | Schools | |
	Total number	Under 31	Under 50
Boys	1,311	732 (55.8%)	1,039 (79.2%)
Girls	2,886	1,598 (55.4%)	2,460 (85.2%)
Mixed	970	692 (71.3%)	880 (90.7%)

Source: Return of pupils in Public and Private Secondary Schools in England, *PP* 1897 LXX: 557–665.

survive only through their advertisement in the press or in scholastic directories. However, directories do provide a good deal of information, and I have selected two of them for closer analysis. The first, F. S. de Cartaret-Bisson's *Our Schools and Colleges* (4th edn, 1879) is national in scope. The second, *Our Yorkshire Schools* (1873), produced by a Leeds printer, covers only schools in a wide area around Leeds. From the total number of entries in *Our Schools and Colleges* I have excluded endowed schools and others which appeared to be either preparatory or small coaching/cramming establishments; proprietary and private foundation schools are included. This produced a total of 958 boys' schools in England, which does not include names on a secondary list where the author says that he has been unable to obtain detailed information. Some schools on this secondary list can be traced in other sources, and so it is reasonable to regard the total size of the group covered by *Our Schools and Colleges* as above 1,000 schools, which relates fairly closely to the number of boys' schools listed in the 1897 return. Too much stress should not be laid on the resemblance between the two sets of figures, but it does suggest that de Cartaret-Bisson's directory had a wide national coverage.

Table 15.4 gives a breakdown of the 958 boys' schools on a county basis. As might have been expected, the distribution of schools over the country was very uneven. London and Middlesex together count 197 schools, and there were concentrations of boarding schools in the seaside towns of Sussex and Kent. Of the 72 Lancashire entries 8 were in

Table 15.4 Private schools, county by county, 1879 (boys' schools)

Bedfordshire	7	Leicestershire/Rutland	6
Berkshire	12	Lincolnshire	13
Buckinghamshire	9	Middlesex	27
Cambridgeshire	7	Norfolk	20
Cheshire	33	Northumberland	4
Cornwall	18	Northamptonshire	5
Cumberland/Westmorland	8	Nottinghamshire	12
Derbyshire	12	Oxfordshire	15
Devon	37	Shropshire	6
Dorset	12	Somerset	44
Co. Durham	14	Staffordshire	19
Essex	28	Suffolk	13
Gloucestershire	19	Surrey	35
Hampshire	37	Sussex	53
Herefordshire	5	Warwickshire	18
Hertfordshire	16	Wiltshire	8
Huntingdonshire	2	Worcestershire	7
Kent	67	Yorkshire	66
Lancashire	72	London (Postal district)	172

Source: Compiled from the entries in de Cartaret-Bisson, *Our Schools and Colleges* (4th edn 1879).

Southport, 15 in Liverpool, and 18 in Manchester. The 33 Cheshire schools suggest the high demand for schooling from the middle class of South Lancashire. Of Yorkshire's 66 entries, on the other hand, Leeds, Bradford, and Sheffield accounted for only 3 each. In addition to the main list there is a list of 36 Roman Catholic schools, the great numbers being in Lancashire (6) and in London and the home counties (13).

Much information is also provided about curricula and examinations, Many schools advertised their successes in the Oxford and Cambridge Locals, and there are many references to the Preceptors' examinations, to London Matriculation, and to the examinations for the Civil Service and for the legal and medical professions. All this material reinforces the point already made about the strong influence of the public examinations on private schools. The subjects mentioned fall into the standard pattern – the English subjects, Latin and Greek, modern languages, mathematics. Once again it seems likely that the curriculum had become much more standardized than it had been in the earlier part of the century. Some schools claimed to give special attention to modern languages or to science and engineering, and sometimes the more 'practical' subjects like book-keeping, land surveying, and mensuration are mentioned. In more general terms schools often claimed to give a good English education, a sound middle-class education, or a preparation for commercial, mercantile, or professional life. The fees charged varied enormously. A day boy could find a place at £4–5 per annum and a boarder for £25–30, but fees of £15 for day pupils and £70–80 for boarders were quite common.

Our Yorkshire Schools, since it is purely regional, provides a smaller sample. The information naturally runs on much the same lines as *Our Schools and Colleges*, and the two books are close in date. There is a similar stress on examinations. Ilkley College, a 'select' school for forty boarders, claimed to have a higher percentage of success in the Locals than any other college or boarding school in Yorkshire. The Collegiate and Commercial School, De Mowbray Villa, Sand Hutton, Thirsk, claimed to have gained 106 certificates in competitive examinations in the preceding six years. There are also references to the Department of Science and Art and to science teaching generally. One school, Wharfedale College, Boston Spa, claimed that science was 'taught experimentally'.

Fees were generally moderate, not above £40 for boarders; it is possible that the more expensive Yorkshire schools did not advertise in this directory. In many cases the basic fee did not cover subjects like modern languages, drawing, and music, which were charged as extras. Many schools were in fact considerably more expensive to parents than the basic fee would suggest. Several of the schools clearly took boys only up to about 14 years of age – not, I think, because they were preparatory schools but because they were third-grade schools for lower middle-class boys who left school early. One school announced that 'corporal punishment is carefully avoided'. There are references to playgrounds, cricket fields, gymnasia. Pannal House, Harrogate, had a cricket field of 8 acres. Nether Hall Collegiate School, Doncaster, had nearly 11 acres of grounds for recreation. It is perhaps surprising, since games and physical exercise had become so popular by the 1870s, that there were not more references of this kind. Such facilities were probably difficult for the cheaper schools to provide. Dissent was strong in Yorkshire, and there are several Nonconformist schools on the list like the Moravian school for 80 boys and 60 girls at Fulneck, between Leeds and Bradford, and the Primitive Methodist school at Elmfield, York. At Turton Hall, Gildersome, near Leeds, the Rev. John Haslam was supported by a group of Baptist referees. He had one visiting master and five residents. He charged £22–30 per annum, though classics, modern languages, drawing, and music were all extras. There were no day boys. A gymnasium and cricket field were provided.

16 Some individual schools

Though some information about individual schools can be gleaned from the directories, there are not many institutions about which enough is known to provide a more detailed picture. One of the most interesting experiments of the day was the International College at Spring Grove, Isleworth, opened in 1866–7 under the headmastership of Dr Leonard Schmitz, who had been tutor in Edinburgh to the Prince of Wales. The college formed part of an international education movement which planned to establish schools in several countries as a means of increasing the understanding between nations (Bibby 1956–7: 25–36; Stewart and McCann 1967: 317–26; *VCH Middlesex* I (1969): 256–7). Among the promoters of the English college were Richard Cobden, who died before it opened, the philanthropist William Ellis, who advanced a large part of the money for the site and buildings, and the scientists John Tyndall and T. H. Huxley (*HSE* 203–4; P. N. Farrar 1987: 498–515).

The college prospectus linked its aims with those of the associated institutions at Godesberg near Bonn and Chatou near Paris (West Sussex Record Office CP 477). They planned 'to afford an education of the highest order, harmonizing with the wants and spirit of the age'. In order to achieve this, special attention was to be given to modern languages and to the natural sciences. Languages were to be taught so that pupils might speak and write them fluently. In the sciences pupils were to be brought 'into direct contact with the facts furnished by observation and experiment'. Latin and Greek were to be learnt at a later age than usual, and, like all linguistic studies, were to be preceded by a study of the grammar of the mother tongue. Boys were to be admitted from 10 years and upwards, and the curriculum was to cover a period of seven to eight years. The school was quite expensive – 80 guineas for boarders, 24 guineas for day boys, though there were very few extras.

In 1867 there were 10 day scholars and 58 boarders. Huxley himself drew up a scheme for the teaching of science, though Tyndall criticized this as too ambitious, and a modern writer considers that the work in science was not particularly successful (Bibby 1956–7: 33). In 1880 all the pupils learned mathematics, science, Latin, French, and German, and those on the classical side learned Greek. There were two science laboratories. Many of the pupils came from overseas, and, perhaps for that reason, there were difficulties in maintaining discipline. The German observer, Ludwig Wiese, who went to Spring Grove in the early 1870s, spoke of a 'motley assemblage' and of the 'extraordinary difficulties with which the instruction in the institution had to contend' (Wiese 1877: 85–6). Nevertheless, there were 100 pupils during the 1880s. For reasons that are not clear, the college closed in 1889, and the buildings were bought by Borough Road Training College. The International College never fulfilled the high ideals of its founders, but it was fairly successful for twenty years or more, and it was the most original development of a period when little new thinking was coming out of the private school world.

The Bowman family's academy at Gainford in Co. Durham has already been cited as an example of longevity (see pp. 162–3: *Gainford in the 1880s*: 54–8, 91). An advertisement of 1883 listed five classrooms, a cricket pitch, five tennis courts, a chemistry laboratory, engineering and surveying classes, and a preparatory division for boys aged 8 to 11. The 1881 census named seven masters and forty boarders, and there were probably day boys as well. The principal, William Bowman, then aged 63, was entered as schoolmaster, minister of the Gainford Independent chapel, and farmer of 52 acres. The boarders ranged in age from 10 years to two young men of 20, with the largest group aged between 13 and 15. Perhaps the two young men were foreigners who had come to learn English because it is known that such people attended the school in later years. The school took the usual examinations; Cartaret-Bisson's directory records that forty-six certificates had been gained in the Cambridge Locals (*Our Schools and Colleges*: 624). Football, cricket, and tennis matches were played against teams from the area, and each Whitsuntide the academy ran a bazaar for which special trains were put on from Darlington.

Private school principals appreciated the value of the publicity offered by such events. At Doncaster W. T. Jackson, who ran a school in Hall Gate until he retired in 1921, hired the Guild Hall for his open day in 1896. The Vicar of Doncaster distributed the prizes and certificates, after which the guests watched 'a performance of "Columbus", an historical comic opera, the characters including King Tapioca, a savage monarch, Banana Bill, his prime minister, and Mademoiselle Sago Palm, a Caribbee prima donna'. In the 1880s and 1890s there was a school magazine, an essay and debating society, a museum, and a winter programme of lectures and debates. The school had a playing-field, a partly covered playground, and a workshop under the supervision of a skilled cabinet-maker. On the other side of the street from Jackson was Miss Teasdale's Merton School for girls. In 1892 she hired Brown's Rooms for her prize distribution and exhibition of the children's work. After the prize giving there was an entertainment with recitations and singing by two choirs of pupils. The evening ended with a dance and refreshments (J. A. Harrison, Pt 4 1962: 108–9).

Few original records of private schools have survived which makes the admissions register and other papers (1869–91) of St Andrew's Middle-class School, Litchurch, Derby, of considerable interest. Established in 1869 by J. Erskine Clarke, vicar of St Michael's, Derby, the bishop of the diocese was the visitor. Another clergyman who was closely involved was M. H. Scott, vicar of St Andrew's, who, like Clarke, had a strong interest in providing better welfare and recreational facilities for Derby working people (Crane 1981). The headmaster throughout the period was George Sutherland; when he married in 1871, the school gave him 'a handsome silver gilt letter balance' (*DM*, 27 December 1871). The fees were low – £4–5 a year in 1879 (*Our Schools and Colleges*: 592) – and the curriculum fairly limited. In 1871 it included Scripture, reading and recitation, mathematics, writing and printing, Latin and English grammar, history, geography and mapping, and drawing (*DM*, 12 July 1871).

St Andrew's seems to have been a third-grade school, designed to give a higher elementary/junior secondary course to boys who would leave at about 14. Parents of this class, it was said, valued their independence. In 1872 M. H. Scott spelt out what he saw as the school's main characteristics:

> its freedom from all taint of charity and from all Government control, the varied syllabus which it afforded for study, and the good education which parents in the district were enabled to give their children at a comparatively small cost.
>
> (*DM* 17 July 1872)

The most important of the surviving records is the admission register (1869–90 with some entries for 1891), a total of 1,000 in all. There is also a daybook for the years 1887–97 which appears to show a boy's expenditure on books when he entered the school, and a 'List of bad deeds', kept by Mr Sutherland, which catalogues a typical list of delinquencies – insolence to masters, copying, fighting, truancy. The admissions book gives the age at entry and the fathers' occupations, though not the length of school life. For the years up to 1876 there is some information about pupils' occupations after they left school. In the first year (1869) 71 boys entered and in 1871, 58. After that the entry in most years was about 40, running slightly lower in the 1880s than in the 1870s. If the book-bills for 1887–97 can be taken as recording the entries in those years, the average for that decade was slightly over 23 a year with numbers falling off very much in the years 1895–7.

The 1,000 boys who entered between 1869 and 1891 joined the school at very different ages, as Table 16.1 shows. Since in most years the total entry was some 35–40 boys, each new group embraced small numbers

Table 16.1 Ages of admission to St Andrew's Middle-class School, Litchurch, Derby, 1869–91

Age not given	Under 6	6–7	7–8	8–9	9–10	10–11	11–12	12–13	13–14	14–15	Over 15	Total
18	9	37	65	88	111	126	146	178	133	63	26	1,000

Source: Compiled from the admissions register of the school.

of children at widely differing ages. The biggest concentration was in the 11–13 age-group, but some children came at 7 or younger, and a considerable number at 14 or older. Some came from other private schools, some from National, British, or Board schools, but the available information here suggests no special pattern. Perhaps, as in many such schools, the older boys came for a year or so to 'finish' before they went to work. With so many small age-groups it must have been very difficult to plan a coherent curriculum.

The occupations of parents are also recorded, and these are given in Table 16.2, arranged into ten groups. A summary of this kind can never be more than approximately correct because it is difficult to know where to put certain occupations. I have included 'engineers' in group 6, though this title is very difficult to interpret. Similarly it is difficult to draw the line between groups 7 and 8, and probably a number of the men in group 8 were railway workers (group 9). But with such reservations the list is probably accurate enough. Its one distinguishing feature – the considerable number of parents in group 9 – reflects the fact that Derby was an important railway centre. Of those listed, 32 parents were engine drivers, 17 inspectors, and 8 guards. Others include the chef at the Midland Hotel and a Pullman car superintendent.

Table 16.2 Occupations of parents, St Andrew's Middle-class School, Litchurch, Derby, 1869–91

1	No father	71
2	Occupation not given or unknown	19
3	Clerks	109
4	Publicans	47
5	Farmers	52
6	Professional	46
7	Managers, business, tradesmen	316
8	Skilled and semi-skilled workers	238
9	Railway	88
10	Unskilled workers	14
	Total	1,000

Source: Compiled from the admissions register of the school.

The dominant groups are 7 and 8. In the former there were 37 commercial travellers, 17 managers, 26 builders, 26 coal merchants, and 14 grocers. In the latter there were 17 foremen, 16 fitters, 9 each of plumbers and boilermakers, and 18 joiners, with a wide variety of other trades. There were also 109 clerks (group 3). Of the small professional group 6, eleven were engineers, and I have already expressed some uncertainty about their status. Of the 14 parents in group 10, 7 were labourers. A school like St Andrew's existed for the children of the lower middle class and skilled artisans. The comparatively small amount of information that survives about the careers of old pupils suggests that they took up jobs very similar to their fathers', though several became pupil-teachers.

Something has survived of private schools of different types in reminiscence and autobiography. H. G. Wells, who was born in 1866, attended Mr Thomas Morley's commercial academy at Bromley, Kent, from 1874 to 1880. Morley's school was probably a smaller version of St Andrew's, Litchurch. It consisted of one room built out over a scullery, and Morley ran it himself with a little help from his wife. He had 25–35 boys, half of them boarders. Wells thought that the teaching was better than in the National School, and that Morley did his best for his pupils, one of his goals being 'the production of good clerks (with special certificates for book-keeping)' (Wells 1934, I: 90–1). At the age of 13 Wells had learned to use English well and had a good foundation in mathematics. Later he himself taught in several schools. Of one in north Wales he had a very low opinion. He also spent a year (1889–90) at J. V. Milne's school, Henley House, which has already been mentioned (see p. 168). Wells admired Milne, and they continued to be friends after he had left the school. Wells thought Milne an excellent teacher in whom the boys had confidence, though the school was not very successful financially. One of Milne's successes was to encourage a boy named Alfred Harmsworth, who was making little progress with his school work, to produce a school newspaper. That boy, who always recognized what he owed to Milne, was to become the great newspaper proprietor Lord Northcliffe (Wells 1934, I: 317–33).

The experience of Robert Somervell, son of a Kendal leather merchant, was at a rather higher academic level. He was sent at the age of 11 to a Quaker private school in Kendal as a boarder, and he remained there for three years. He was well taught in classics, German, Euclid, and algebra, and had pleasant memories of playing cricket and fives. After Kendal he had four terms at the Rev. Nathaniel Jennings' school in St John's Wood, north London. Mr Jennings had 20–24 boys, and the curriculum was much the same as at Kendal, including both French and German. The boys played games such as prisoners' base in the playground, and in the summer they played cricket twice a week. There was no football in winter, and they walked in the afternoons to Hampstead Heath and back. Mr Jennings was anxious that Somervell should stay another year to take the London Matriculation examination, but his father took him away from school at 15 (December 1866) in order that he might make a start in the business. His son wrote later:

> On the whole it would appear that my father was as well taught in these obscure Dissenters' academies as he would have been in most of the schools with famous names at that period. He was given a grounding in two classical and two modern languages.
>
> (Somervell 1935: 26)

One headmaster who drew boys from business families rather like the Somervells was Richard W. Hiley of the Grange, Thorparch, near Tadcaster in the West Riding (Hiley 1899: 241–99). His father, who started teaching at 17, had, after many years of struggle, bought the site and built the school which the younger Hiley purchased in 1861. He retired at Christmas 1889. He started with 38 boys and built up to 80, many of them over 17 years old. Like many heads he was nearly ruined by a serious scarlet fever attack in 1870 in which one boy and two of his own children died, though he was able to reopen the school quite quickly. Initially, most of his pupils were sons of businessmen who wanted their boys well taught in French and German. Later he attracted more professional people and was able to send some boys to university, though he was often disappointed in not being able to persuade parents to do this. Most of the boys were, however, destined for commerce and did not reach a high standard academically; some of them were delicate or of limited intellect. The school became well known for its cricket, which probably attracted some pupils, though Hiley was anxious lest too much time and attention should be given to games. Like many private school heads he was not optimistic about the future. After he retired the school was not successful, and it was bought by the Leeds School Board for an industrial school. The board bought for £3,500 an estate which had cost Hiley £15,000.

The education of girls was much more radically transformed in the second half of the nineteenth century than the education of boys. As a result the attention of historians has been largely concentrated on the new girls' high schools, and the older type of private school which preceded them has been dismissed as of little value. Like the boys' schools the girls' private schools varied greatly in cost, in equipment, and in effectiveness. The German observer, Ludwig Wiese, thought that some of the more fashionable boarding schools concentrated on accomplishments and mere superficialities, while others gave a thoroughly good education. He welcomed the growth of the new high schools, though he feared the dangers of overstrain and of what he called 'the loss of the genuine female character' (Wiese 1877: 238–44).

Information about girls' private schools over the whole country can be gathered from sources such as volume II (Girls) (1884) of de Cartaret-Bisson's *Our Schools and Colleges* and C. E. Pascoe's *Schools for Girls and Colleges for Women* (1879). Cartaret-Bisson gives details about slightly more than 400 schools (after endowed schools have been excluded). Almost all the 400 were private schools, though there are a few religious foundations like St Mary's and St Anne's, Abbots Bromley. Many more schools were listed, but since in this second group only names and addresses were given, not much information is really provided about them. These 400 schools form only a small proportion of the total listed in the return of 1897 (see pp. 171–2); a large proportion of those described were in London. Where numbers were quoted, the schools were generally small. A few had only 4–6 girls, but a common total would be 30–60. Many schools took boarders only, but the mixture between boarders and day pupils was common. The largest school in Cartaret-Bisson's list was the French Protestant College at Bedford with 45 boarders and 100 day girls, but such figures were quite exceptional. Sometimes 'limited numbers' were mentioned, probably with the implication that such small numbers meant that the school was socially select or that the girls were especially well looked after. A few of the entries advertise 'the comforts of a refined home' or some similar phrase. Fees varied widely. The cheapest boarding schools charged £25–30 per annum; £40–60 was common and a few went as high as £120–50. Many day girls paid from £6 to £10, though some schools charged as much as £30. Extras were often mentioned, and probably the total cost was a good deal higher than the quoted basic sum. C. E. Pascoe, on the basis of fees charged by a group of ten schools in different parts of the country, estimated that the average charge for board and tuition (including music, a modern language, and callisthenics) was about 60 guineas per annum.

The entries in Cartaret-Bisson's directory pick out some special features. A few schools specialized in taking delicate or backward children, and a number made special arrangements for those whose parents were abroad or in India. Some of the descriptions were quite general like 'a liberal education' or an education 'on the modern system', but others pick out special advantages or attractions. Modern languages were frequently mentioned. There were references to science, to Greek, and to training for cookery or household management. There were a few offers of training for future governesses or for civil service appointments. A number of schools were said to be managed 'on high school principles' or on lines 'similar to the public schools'. Clearly the girls' schools were affected by the growing vogue for games and exercise. There were a number of references to a gymnasium, a playground, a field for tennis and cricket, a croquet and tennis lawn. A very large number of schools mention public examinations – the Locals, the Preceptors, the examinations of the music colleges. The DSA examinations and the Higher Locals were mentioned occasionally. Pascoe, in his book of 1879, lists the private schools which had been successful in the Local examinations of Oxford, Cambridge, Durham, Glasgow, and Edinburgh, and in the Preceptors' examinations. Of these schools 409 were in England and Wales, and 48 in Scotland. The French Protestant College at Bedford, which was an exceptionally large school, advertised in the same book that since 1877 1 pupil had passed the Cambridge Higher Local, 6 the Oxford and Cambridge Senior Locals, 8 the Junior Cambridge, and 10 the examinations of Trinity College of Music.

The advertisements in *Our Yorkshire Schools* (1873) outline something of what was available in one area – west and north Yorkshire. The fees varied widely. The cheapest boarding fee was around £20–5. Several schools charged between £30 and £50, and one, Denmark House at Scarborough, charged 80–100 guineas. Day pupils paid £4–8. As in the case of boys' schools subjects like languages, music, and drawing were often charged as extras. Not all schools gave their fees, and some gave no details at all other than the title and the principal's name. In the case of schools drawing pupils from a small area, such information would have gone around easily among neighbours by word of mouth.

A few entries go into much more detail. The Misses Greenwood at Upper Winter Edge, Hipperholme near Halifax, charged their boarders £30 (day pupils £6), and taught 'English Language, History, Geography, Reading, Writing, Arithmetic, Plain & Fancy Needlework etc. & Callisthenics' (ibid.: 7). Mrs and the Misses Kettlewell, St James's Villas, New Leeds, Leeds, offered 'the English Language, Literature &c; the French and German languages; Music, Vocal and Instrumental; Drawing and Painting; Natural Science (including Chemistry); and Callisthenics' (ibid.: 37). They did not mention their fee. At East Hardwick near Pontefract a man, who was probably the principal's husband, taught mathematics, writing, and book-keeping (ibid.: 41). Several schools spoke more generally of a sound English education or a high middle-class education. Resident French and German governesses were often mentioned, and sometimes the principal claimed to have taught abroad. Only one school, Prospect House at Malton, mentioned the Cambridge Locals, a striking contrast to the Cartaret-Bisson lists already cited. Miss Hargrave's school at Ilkley, obviously anxious to avoid the charges of espionage and petty tyranny which were often made, stated: 'full liberty of correspondence with Friends allowed without inspection' (*Our Yorkshire Schools*: 43).

What that comment means is explained in Winifred Peck's account of the very old-fashioned school at Eastbourne which she attended as a day girl. The principal, Miss Quill, was a strong Evangelical who followed 'the already old-world methods of perpetual watchfulness, espionage, draconic codes and regulations' (Peck 1952: 63). The staff were poorly qualified, and the teaching, with the exception of that of one French mistress, left no impression. There were endless rules and a weekly ceremony at which girls who had earned punishment marks were fined. There were no organized games, and the only exercise was walking in crocodile. Finally, Winifred was taken away by her father after a disciplinary upset which he did not view as severely as Miss Quill had done. Later she was sent to a high school and then to Wycombe Abbey, one of the new type of girls' boarding schools founded on public school lines (ibid.: 111; see p. 224).

There were happier and better old-fashioned schools than Miss Quill's, like the school at Lewes, kept by three Quaker ladies, of which an account, dating from a period about 10 or 15 years earlier than Winifred Peck's, has survived (M. Robinson 1935: 622–6). There were twenty-five boarders, almost all of them Quakers, drawn from all parts of the country, plus half a dozen day girls. Some of the teaching sounds old-fashioned; for example, they still used Lindley Murray's English grammar, first published in 1795. They did a lot of needlework and learned a great deal of poetry by heart. Visiting masters taught French and drawing, and one of the mistresses taught the German Bible to those who wished to learn it. Other visiting staff gave lectures on light, heat, and electricity, and there was a drilling master. There were no examinations and – surprisingly – only one-third of the pupils learned music. The girls played at 'jumping the long rope', they jumped against one another in two teams, three or four on either side of an oaken plank, they had a swing. There were no general games, but they sometimes played cricket, and they took walks over the downs. There was plenty of sociability because they were frequently invited to houses in the town. Clearly the author of this account enjoyed her schooldays. It all sounds a little unexciting, somewhat conventional, but genuine within its own range.

Quakers like the Lewes ladies had a good reputation as school-keepers. One Quaker private school with a long history was Polam Hall at Darlington, which was taken over in 1888 by Hannah and Rachel Lockwood, who had given up their school in Kendal because of serious health problems (Davies 1981: 36–78; *HSE*: 156). In 1894 Rachel Lockwood was joined by Hannah Bayes, who had been both pupil and teacher in leading Quaker schools, and who was a games enthusiast and an admirer of the public schools. The numbers grew rapidly – by 1905 there were about 200 girls – and, though Polam was still privately owned, it developed very much on the lines of the new high schools, with girls working for London Matriculation and the Joint Board examinations, and with a general requirement to take part in games.

Another prominent school with a Nonconformist background – this time Methodist – was Hannah Pipe's 'Laleham' at Clapham Park in south London. Miss Pipe came to London from Manchester in 1856 and she ran the school until 1890 (Stoddart 1908; Pritchard 1949: 276–81, 285–8; *HSE* 154–5). Most of the girls were daughters of well-to-do Wesleyan families in Lancashire and Yorkshire, and Miss Pipe's objective was rather to train them for their future place in home and in society than for a career. She was at first rather critical of the new examinations for women, but in her later years many of her girls went to university, and one of them, Alice Gardner, was placed in the first class of the historical tripos at Cambridge in 1879. The school was small, numbering about twenty-five girls, and was rather like a large and cultured family. Many of the girls came very badly prepared, and Miss Pipe tried to provide an appropriate curriculum. She employed an able staff, including the poet and novelist George MacDonald and the historian S. R. Gardiner. She was also very interested in philanthropy and was anxious that her girls should help in the orphanage she had founded. Miss Pipe created a school with good teaching and a liberal atmosphere. She is one of the most attractive figures among private school heads. She had a genius for friendship and several of her staff went on to found other schools on lines similar to 'Laleham'.

Another good school of about the same size was the Misses Robinsons' school, Alston Court, Cheltenham, which E. E. Constance Jones, later mistress of Girton, attended for a year as a boarder in 1866 (E. E. C. Jones 1922: 35–44). Most of the older girls, she noted, had been there for several years. She found it 'a delightful school'. The house was well furnished and there was no tyranny or spying. She learned Latin, a little Greek and some Euclid, French and Italian music, dancing, and drawing. The only outdoor game was croquet, plus the usual unpopular walks. The girls were taken to concerts and readings. She heard the famous tenor Sims Reeves and Dickens reading the trial scene from *Pickwick* and a 'most pathetic piece' from *The Old Curiosity Shop*. In her judgement the school and the principals combined both goodness and intellectual gifts: 'all that was best in the old order which was beginning to pass and the new order which was beginning to come in'. A similar verdict might be passed on 'Laleham' and Hannah Pipe.

A balanced judgement of the girls' private school, because it must take account of both Miss Pipe and Miss Quill, is not easy to make. The bad side is shown by the account given by the Bryce assistant commissioner of a school in a small country town in Devonshire. There she found the headmistress and one assistant

> teaching over 30 girls in two wretched little garrets over an outhouse, the roof of which I could almost touch with my hand, approached by a dangerous staircase. The prospectus for this school comprised almost every subject ever taught in schools, and the fees for day pupils for the ordinary course, along with drawing, painting, and German, amounted to 141. 14s. per annum, only 6s. less than is paid in most of the best high schools in the country.
>
> (*BC* VI: 96)

On the other hand, the assistant commissioners reported that the principals were in many cases doing their best and were often held back by the prejudice and ignorance of parents and the local community (*BC* VI: 297–300; VII: 300).

About ten years after the Bryce inquiry Michael Sadler carried out surveys for nine of the new authorities set up under the 1902 Act – Birkenhead, Derbyshire, Essex, Exeter, Hampshire, Huddersfield, Liverpool, Newcastle-upon-Tyne, and Sheffield. What he said about private schools, both for boys and for girls, is very similar in tone to the Bryce report. He was anxious that the schools should be inspected and that those that were declared efficient should receive certain advantages. They might have the right to enter pupils for county scholarships and such scholarships might be held at private schools. They might also be helped by loans, materials, and educational apparatus. Sadler found private schools deserving of praise in many places, selecting in particular several schools in Essex (Sadler 1906). Once again there was the same range from very good to very poor. What he wrote about the private schools of Newcastle will serve as a general judgement on what he found. They are, he wrote, 'of various types and of very different grades of efficiency. Some are of high excellence, several do meritorious work, others again are an element of considerable weakness in the educational life of the City' (Sadler 1905b: 52). When Sadler selected schools for praise, they tended to be girls' schools, which is not surprising because by 1900 they were more numerous and more important than boys' schools. He does not, however, differentiate between schools for the two sexes in his remarks. It is not surprising that he and the Bryce assistant commissioners found bad private schools. What must be stressed is that they also found good ones. The blend of Dotheboys Hall and Matthew Arnold's 'educational homes', which has dominated historical writing for so long, is only part of the story.

17 Semi-public and private foundation schools

This last chapter of Part IV will be devoted to the few private schools that achieved semi-public status and to the private foundation schools (see p. 157). In the first group Hely Hutchinson Almond and Loretto stand alone, for 'Lorettonianism' was a unique product (Mackenzie 1906; Tristram 1911; Darwin 1931: 144–56). Almond was born in Glasgow in 1832, the son of a clergyman. He went very young to Glasgow University and then to Balliol. He did well academically, but made no particular mark at Oxford and rather drifted into teaching. After being second master at Merchiston, in 1862 he bought Loretto School at Musselburgh near Edinburgh, which was then chiefly a preparatory school. He began with twelve boys and two new boys joined him. He remained there until he died in 1903. After his death the school was turned into a company in which money raised by a memorial appeal was used to buy shares. In his early days Almond had a sharp financial struggle and almost went bankrupt. His school was never large. By 1882 it had grown to 120, at which size it remained. A large part of his strong personal influence over the boys was due to the fact that he was able to know them all personally.

Loretto became well known largely through Almond's strong interest in physical fitness. The boys took a great deal of exercise in all weathers. They wore flannel shirts and left their coats off if the weather was warm, a style of dressing that their headmaster shared. They went on long walks and stayed out under canvas. For a small school Loretto enjoyed phenomenal athletic success at Oxford and Cambridge. In 1884 seven old boys played rugby football for Oxford in the varsity match. Almond enjoyed games and was a strong believer in physical fitness, but he did not see games as an end in themselves, but rather as part of a spiritual ideal. There should, he believed, be a close alliance between the athlete and the Christian. Both were enemies of indolence, intemperance, and cynicism. Both devoted themselves to the common good, to an unselfish quest for the ideal. Religion must find its place among the rough work of ordinary life. Physical prowess must promote temperance, courage and *esprit de corps* – what his biographer called the 'Sparto-Christian ideal' (Mackenzie 1906: 247). This quest for courage and devotion to duty also involved the rejection of the commonplace and the conventional. It was the essence of 'Lorettonianism' to think for oneself, to get to the root of things. He wrote in a letter of 1877: 'isn't training a lot of fellows up not to go on like sheep, but to get into the habit of asking the why and wherefore of everything you do, worth more than numbers plus conformity?'(ibid.: 194).

For all his genuine belief in independent thought the boys generally believed what he said. The key to Almond's power in the school was his influence over them. He always tried to carry them along with him when he wanted to make a change rather than imposing it by command, he had no sense of false dignity, he was always ready to listen to what a boy had to say. The academic side of the school was the part that interested him least. Though himself a man of good intellectual capacity, he was more concerned with action than with thought. He was hostile to scholarships, to competition, and to examinations, and he was always ready to upset the school routine if he wanted the boys to do something else.

Well as he understood the boys, he often worked badly with the masters, whom he considered to be less sympathetic with his plans and more unwilling to have their routine disturbed. Probably adults were less susceptible than boys to his kind of personal influence; from the point of view of his staff he must often have been maddening to work with. When he died after forty years at Loretto he had created a school of marked individuality and had disseminated to many other schools a new concept of the importance of physical fitness. Yet his broader aims had little influence on education in general. The crusade for independence of mind and rational living often appeared to be little more than a preference for open-necked flannel shirts and cold dormitories.

Cecil Reddie of Abbotsholme, who resembled Almond in some ways, had a career of mixed successes and failures. Yet unlike Almond, who stood alone, Reddie created the progressive movement which had considerable influence both in this country and abroad and was to remain a force in the twentieth century (Reddie 1900; Ward 1934; Stewart 1968; Searby 1989: 1–21). He lost his parents in boyhood and, after an education at Fettes College and Edinburgh University, he took a PhD in chemistry at Göttingen. The influence of Germany on him was profound. He admired what he saw as the intellectual force and ordered method of German life as compared with the disorder and sectarianism of England, and he took his own task as training boys of the directing class to give order and structure to a divided society. He taught for brief periods at his old school and at Clifton, and he admired the public schools, though he criticized both their concentration on examinations and on team games. He was strongly influenced in his earlier years by the social planner Patrick Geddes and the utopian socialist Edward Carpenter.

In October 1889 he opened his new school, Abbotsholme in

Derbyshire, in co-operation with two partners, though the partnership soon broke up and after a few months he was left in sole control. He planned that the new school should become an 'educational laboratory' in which all the powers of boys' mind and nature might be developed, a community in which they might achieve fulfilment both as men and as citizens. How he planned to achieve these goals was explained in an article published some months before Abbotsholme opened. The new school was to offer an education based on four constituents. The first, physical and manual, included manual labour, athletic exercise, agriculture, gardening, and the care of farm animals. The artistic and imaginative side covered poetry, art, and handicrafts. The literary and intellectual was to begin with English. Another modern language, Latin and Greek were to be taught, history and geography were to be closely interrelated, and close links were to be made between practice and theory, particularly in mathematics and the natural sciences. All boys were to learn music. In the moral and religious sphere there was to be frankness and trust between masters and boys. Religious teaching was to be unsectarian, and based on the precept of Jesus that by love man is redeemed from his baser self. Boys were not to be crammed for prizes and scholarships, and Reddie was hostile to specialization, though in practice this had to be allowed to some extent for older boys.

To these ideas, sketched before the school opened, Reddie remained faithful. What this meant in practical terms was explained by a foreign observer after the school had been open for several years. In the 24-hour day, 5 hours were given to intellectual work, 4½ to physical exercise and manual work, 2½ to artistic work and indoor recreation, 9 to sleep, and 3 to meals and spare time (Demolins 1898a: 60). Reddie denied that the triple division of the day – mornings for class work, afternoons for physical and manual work, evenings for music and social recreation – meant that a boy's life was split into separate parts. Rather the parts were interlocked, and the links between them exercised a strong influence on the developing personality (Reddie 1900: 145). An important part of Reddie's view of moral education was that boys should be given systematic sex instruction, and Abbotsholme was the first English school in which this was done. Since he regarded this as so crucial, he was anxious that boys should come to the school at 10 or 11 since the usual transfer age of 13–14 came in the middle of the major period of physical development. Though an advocate of sex instruction Reddie was a strong opponent of co-education, believing that after the age of 11 boys should be taught by men.

His first decade at Abbotsholme was his most successful. The school was small. He aimed at 100 boys, and by 1899 he had 60. In 1894 he was able to buy the estate and buildings and in 1899 a new building was opened. His ideas, as we shall see later, attracted interest in France and Germany. Yet there were difficulties. His personality was erratic and his relationships with his colleagues difficult. An early recruit to the staff had been J. H. Badley from Rugby and Trinity College, Cambridge. In later years Badley paid tribute to the power of Reddie's personality, and recognized how much he himself had learned from his headmaster. Yet Badley felt that Reddie's influence over boys was too dominant and his leadership too authoritarian. When Badley wished to marry, he left Abbotsholme in 1892, believing that Reddie was unwilling to give a proper place to women's influence in the school (Ward 1934: 72–4; Badley 1955: 104–20).

After 1900 Abbotsholme faced many problems. Reddie had a serious breakdown in health, and on more than one occasion there was serious trouble with the staff. In the years immediately before 1914 things improved, but the First World War was a serious blow and when Reddie retired in 1927, there were only two boys left. Yet the power of his work is shown by the fact that the school was rescued and put on its feet by its old boys. Reddie is unusual among English educators in that his impact was stronger abroad than at home. Through contacts with Wilhelm Rein at the university of Jena, Reddie met Hermann Lietz who spent a year teaching at Abbotsholme, and later founded on similar lines the *Landerziehungsheime* schools in Germany, the first of which opened in 1898. In France the social theorist Edmond Demolins promoted the ideas both of Reddie and of Badley, who had opened his own school, Bedales, in 1893. Demolins believed that in the struggle for international power the English were defeating the French because of their superior education which trained young men to be independent and to conquer difficulties (Stewart 1968: 72; Anderson 1973: 168–9; Demolins 1898a). Reddie's system, he thought, trained energy and willpower and formed practical men, fit for the rough and tumble of the world. Demolins sent his own son to Bedales as a pupil, and later founded his own school, L'Ecole des Roches in Normandy, in 1899, on the lines of the English schools which he admired.

In a second book Demolins gave an account of life at Bedales over a complete year (Demolins 1898b: 176–238). The daily routine was similar to that of Abbotsholme, with an emphasis on manual work, farming and gardening, and on music and cultural activities. The boys made cycle trips on Sunday afternoons to visit local churches, there were longer trips to London, and a camping holiday on the Sussex coast. In his account Demolins stressed the freedom given to the boys and the responsibilities placed upon them. The school, which began in Sussex, moved to its permanent home near Petersfield in Hampshire in 1900. Reddie and Badley were very different people. Badley had a very secure home and family life, considerable private means, and a background of Rugby and Cambridge, though he did not wish to teach in a school like his own. He had a restrained and stable temperament. He did not see his school as a one-man band, and he had an excellent capacity to work with his staff and to retain them for long periods (Stewart 1968: 13–17, 268–81). Bedales rapidly became much better known than Abbotsholme, and in its sixth year it became co-educational, a change in which Mrs Badley had considerable influence. By about 1914 there were about 200 pupils, 100 boys and 60 girls in the main school and 40 of both sexes in the junior house (Badley 1955: 149).

There is no space here for more than a brief mention of other new schools of the day like Alexander Devine's Clayesmore and King Alfred School, Hampstead (Stewart 1968: 17–33). Of the two major figures Badley is a more sympathetic personality than Reddie and a far more successful schoolmaster. Yet it was Reddie who gave Badley the lead he needed when he knew what he disliked in education, but not what he wished to do. Badley's statement in his old age of the aims of the new school movement would have been acceptable to both of them:

> first, a school-life in all respects as healthful as a carefully chosen environment and carefully planned conditions could ensure; the second, as wide a range as possible of school work, not only of the more formal kind but also in the arts and in manual training, in order to discover and ensure the development of individual ability; and the third, a community organised on the lines of a family, in which willing co-operation for common ends should be the main motive and mode of activity rather than competition and regimentation.
>
> (Badley 1955: 163)

The private foundation schools form the last group to be considered. Proprietary schools for boys, most of them established in the 1830s and 1840s, had declined in importance after 1860. Many of them had been established to meet the demands of middle-class families in London. In 1892 there were still ten of them, educating 1,800 boys (Acland and Llewellyn Smith 1892: 148), but they gradually closed. King's College School survived only by moving from the college buildings in the Strand to Wimbledon (1897) (Bryant 1986: 210–12). One of the best known, Blackheath in south-east London, closed in December 1907. It had been faced by keen competition from the new secondary schools and from schools like Tonbridge and St Dunstan's. The setting had ceased to be rural and the buildings were poor. Numbers fell as the result of a severe outbreak of scarlet fever. The school committee was unwilling to take LCC scholars (Kirby 1933; Ord 1936: 93–4). Though each school had its own particular problems, Blackheath's were typical. In many cases locations, which had been pleasant residential areas in the earlier part of the century, did not attract middle-class parents by the end of it.

Events in other cities followed a similar course. In Huddersfield as in several towns two proprietary schools had been founded, one Anglican, the other non-sectarian. Both schools experienced difficulties after 1870. They were united in 1887, but the united school soon ran into trouble, and the company was wound up in 1893. The buildings were purchased by the school board and re-opened as a higher grade school (Brook 1968: 199–202, 208).

Some schools were successful for a time, but proved unable to sustain themselves for a long period. Hull was a large provincial town in which secondary education was very defective. The standard of the grammar school was low, and earlier efforts to set up proprietary schools had collapsed (*HSE*: 186). In the mid-1860s a group of local businessmen planned a new proprietary school, the Hull and East Riding College, which opened in 1867. Plans to incorporate the old grammar school endowment into the new foundation were unsuccessful, the shares were never fully subscribed, and the financial position was always uncertain. The new college had serious ups and downs, but in the 1880s it was flourishing with good examination results, both in the Locals and in university scholarships, and active games and music. However success was to be short-lived. In 1893 Hymers College, one of the very few new endowed schools of the late nineteenth century, opened, and the proprietary school directors decided to close in order to avoid competition between the two schools (Lawson 1958: 27–49; 1963: 248–9; Lawson, *VCH Yorkshire, East Riding* I (1969): 352–3).

The most successful private foundation schools were those where the dominant impulse was religious. The leading figures among Anglican school founders were Nathaniel Woodard and J. L. Brereton, both of whom had worked out their basic ideas well before 1870, though they continued to be active in the later part of the century (*HSE*: 167–71; Honey 1977: 47–103). Woodard died in 1891. By that date his schools had expanded from their original Sussex base with the foundation of Denstone in Staffordshire (1868) and Ellesmere in Shropshire (1884) and the acquisition of King's College, Taunton (1880). Several girls' schools were also associated with the Woodard corporation (see pp. 225–6). Brereton, who lived until 1901, was far less successful than Woodard. His financial management was poor and he fell badly into debt. His schools, which were meant to appeal particularly to farmers, ran into a difficult period with the onset of agricultural depression. Cavendish College at Cambridge, founded in 1873 for students younger than the normal undergraduate age, closed in 1892 and the Norfolk County School finally went into liquidation in 1893. The Graduated County Schools Association for the education of girls had collapsed some years earlier.

Woodard was an Anglo-Catholic, Brereton a Broad Churchman. A distinctively Evangelical viewpoint was affirmed in the foundation of several schools, independent of one another, but broadly similar in their aims. The first of them was Trent College (1866), followed by Weymouth College and St Lawrence College, Ramsgate (1879). St Lawrence was founded by a clerical and lay association, and a similar body created Dean Close School, Cheltenham (1886), founded on 'sound scriptural

Evangelical and Protestant principles'. Dean Close appealed to parents of moderate means; by 1890 the tuition fee was £15 and the boarding costs £30 a year (R. J. W. Evans 1986). In 1885 the various clerical and lay associations had founded a central union in London, one of whose objects was 'education in Evangelical principles'. In later years Trent, Weymouth, and Monkton Combe, which had started in 1868 as a private school (Lace 1968), were all taken over by bodies linked with the union, though neither that body nor its rather shadowy successors created the kind of central force represented by the Woodard Corporation.

Among Nonconformist schools some were denominational, some rested on a broader foundation. Of the latter type the most prominent was Mill Hill, founded in 1807 (Brett-James n.d.; Bryant 1986: 215–16). It closed briefly in the later 1860s, but reopened in 1869 and had a prosperous period under R. F. Weymouth. After another time of decline it fully established its reputation under J. D. McClure, who was headmaster from 1891 to 1922. Among the denominations the most active were the Methodists and the Quakers. Something will be said here about their boys' schools, leaving the girls' schools for Part V. Two of the Wesleyan Methodist schools, Kingswood and Woodhouse Grove, had been founded solely for the education of ministers' sons. Boys had stayed only up to the age of 15, and in 1875 the system was reorganized. Woodhouse Grove took the younger boys and Kingswood the older; some of the latter were able to go to university. E. E. Kellett, writing of the period around 1880, commented on the high level of ability among the Kingswood boys, many of whom became fellows of colleges, professors in universities, or distinguished figures in other professions (Kellett 1936: 263). The system of junior and senior schools lasted only until 1883. Thereafter Kingswood remained a school for ministers' sons. Woodhouse Grove under a new foundation became an ordinary boys' secondary school (Ives 1970; Pritchard 1978).

By 1900 there were about thirty secondary schools for boys and girls which were in some way linked to the various Methodist churches, most of them proprietary schools. After 1902 the Wesleyans made arrangements to bring many of their schools under the management of the connection as a whole (Pritchard 1949: 264–5, 303–4, 334–5). The most interesting development of the period was the creation of The Leys School, Cambridge, opened in February 1875. For some years previously pressure had been building up among Wesleyan Methodists for the provision of secondary education of a public school type. As the community became richer, its need for this kind of schooling grew, while the fear was frequently expressed that children from Methodist homes were being lost to the Church of England because they did not attend Methodist schools. The abolition in 1871 of the university tests concentrated attention on Oxford and Cambridge. There the required kind of school might most appropriately be founded; there lay a pastoral task in caring for

Methodist undergraduates whose numbers might be expected to grow. Originally Oxford rather than Cambridge was favoured as the location of the new school, but a convenient site was acquired in Cambridge, and Cambridge Methodists were active in getting the scheme launched (Baker 1975).

The Wesleyan Conference appointed W. F. Moulton as first head of the new school. Educated at Wesley College, Sheffield, he had been ordained and was at that time tutor at the theological college at Richmond. A distinguished biblical scholar and one of the company of biblical revisers, he was able to combine the roles, hitherto separated in Methodist institutions, of clerical governor and headmaster, and he was one of the few ministers able to do this. He remained headmaster of The Leys until he died in 1898. His character and methods were highly individual, and the school under his rule must have had its own distinctive character. It was small, but an unusually large number of subjects was taught, and Moulton went to a good deal of trouble to arrange special teaching for individuals. But financially The Leys was not a success, the wealthy men of Methodism did not support it to any considerable extent, and when Moulton died, there was a debt of £60,000. During his headship a third of the money spent by the governing body represented interest payments. Under his successors the school was more orthodox, more conventional – and more successful. In 1912, when efforts were being made to negotiate a royal visit, it was described as 'the Eton of Nonconformity' (Baker 1975: 240). By that time The Leys had established its claim to rank as a public school, but it had done so at the cost of some of the creative and original ideas which had marked the Moulton generation. But creativity and originality did not rank very high among the requirements of the average Edwardian public school parent.

The incorporation of The Leys into the general public school world was part of that acculturation of Nonconformity into conventional social patterns which was very marked in the years around 1900. The Quaker schools experienced the same pressures, though in their case the results were rather different. The oldest of their schools was Ackworth, a dual school, that is a school where boys and girls were both admitted but taught separately, founded in 1779. Among the ten or so 'Meeting' schools which existed in 1900, two of the most prominent were Bootham (boys) and The Mount (girls) at York, both founded about fifty years later than Ackworth and aiming at a higher social class and a more advanced intellectual level (*HSE*: 174–6). As in the case of the Wesleyans there was strong pressure among Quakers to establish a school for boys taking them up to university entrance standard. In 1890 'The Friends' Public School Company' opened Leighton Park School, Reading, to meet this need (Stewart 1953: 81–2; Bryant 1986: 221–2). Many, though not all, the 'Meeting' schools were co-educational, and in the twentieth century they developed on lines very similar to the progressive schools like

Bedales (Stewart 1968: 44–6). They too had moved out of their older isolation into one major stream of educational development, though not into that of the traditional public schools. In either case the older Nonconformist styles of education were very much changed.

The Roman Catholic schools faced similar problems in both preserving their traditions and relating themselves to a wider society (Barnes 1926; Evennett 1944; Battersby 1950a: 322–36; Norman 1984: 178–83). In the early part of the nineteenth century the Roman Catholic community consisted of a small group of old families at one end of the social scale and a large number of poor people, mostly Irish, at the other. There was only a very small middle class. At secondary level the work of teaching lay largely in the hands of the religious orders. The work of the women's congregations will be discussed in Part V as part of the wider story of girls' education. The boys' schools were divided into two groups. Many of the boarding schools which educated the upper class were run by the Jesuits and the Benedictines. As the middle classes grew in numbers in the later part of the century, the number of day secondary schools increased. The Jesuits were also active in this field, as were congregations like the De la Salle brothers, the Xavierians, the Marists, and the Salesians.

Among the boarding schools Stonyhurst, the senior Jesuit foundation, shared the predominance with Oscott near Birmingham, though the latter became exclusively a seminary for training priests after 1889. Another school which attracted boys of good family was the Oratory School, Birmingham, founded in 1859. In the 1870s Stonyhurst was criticized for the severity of its discipline. Many Catholics of good family wanted an environment for their sons rather like that of the Protestant public schools where boys were allowed to grow up with a good deal of personal freedom (McClelland 1972: 257–77). It was not until the end of the century that the boarding schools began to move out of what had become a rather isolated existence. When after 1895 Roman Catholics were allowed by their own authorities to study at Oxford and Cambridge, there was an increasing demand for the type of education which would lead on naturally to the life of the older universities. At the Benedictine schools changes were brought about by new headmasters, at Downside by Dom Leander Ramsay (1902–18) and at Ampleforth by Dom Edmund Matthews (1903–24). As a result of these reforms the major Roman Catholic boarding schools took their place among the public schools and formed an important and distinctive sector of that whole group.

Schools like Stonyhurst and Ampleforth catered for only a very small part of the whole number of Roman Catholic boys who wanted a secondary education. Between 1840 and the end of the century secondary schools were founded in most of the major towns as well as in London, where H. E. Manning, who became Archbishop of Westminster in 1865, was active in promoting middle-class education for both boys and girls.

His own particular contribution was the establishment of St Charles' College, Kensington, with a good building and excellent facilities. It continued as a school until 1905, when it became a training college for women teachers. When Manning died in 1892 there were over twelve middle-class schools in London. However, his ambitious plans for a university college were not successful, and that institution survived for only four years (1874–8) (McClelland 1962: 87–128).

Two boys' schools, one in the north and one in the south, will be taken as examples of the whole group of Roman Catholic grammar schools. The northern school, St Francis Xavier's College, Liverpool, was another Jesuit foundation, opened in 1842 as a 'preparatory classical and commercial day school' (Whitehead 1984). In the 1870s the school grew steadily. In 1877 a new building was opened, and there were about 300 boys. In 1875 the teaching of chemistry began, and at about the same time boys began to take the Oxford Locals and London Matriculation. Under Fr. Terence Donnelly, who was prefect of studies 1888–98, the school qualified for a technical instruction grant, boys were entered for DSA examinations, and in 1899–1900 a school of science was set up (Whitehead 1986a: 353–68). After 1898 inter-school football matches were introduced, and the school became well known for its games. As in so many schools boys left very early; in 1891–2 the average leaving age was 14.3 years. Yet Donnelly boasted in 1896 that the pupils were given such an education 'as would fit them to go forth on terms of equality with their non-Catholic fellow countrymen', and Sadler spoke well of the school in his Liverpool report (Sadler 1904a: 24–5).

The selected school in the south is St Joseph's College, Clapham in south London, founded by the De la Salle brothers in 1855, which has been called 'perhaps one of the most significant middle-class schools of Victorian London' (Bryant 1986: 227). In 1870 Brother Potamian, Irish by birth but brought up in the United States and Canada, had joined the staff and stayed for twenty years, much of that time as headmaster (Battersby 1953). This was a successful period for the school. Potamian himself was a physicist of some distinction who took the London degree of DSc in 1883. He was a fine teacher of physics and he encouraged science generally. The school did well in external examinations, and the brothers attracted favourable attention as the result of their contributions to the education section of the International Health Exhibition of 1884. In 1888 the school moved to a new building in Tooting, though this proved too expensive to maintain, and it had to be sold in 1895. However the school survived and gradually built up its numbers again (Bryant 1986: 231–2).

In 1896 an important step was taken when the Conference of Catholic Colleges was set up. In the twentieth century the Catholic schools found their place in the wider world of English education. Though they retained many of their own characteristics, they were moulded by the same pressures which affected their non-Catholic compeers – the public school ethos, state funding and scholarships systems, external examinations, and organized games. The Methodist and Quaker schools depended on a fairly small, middle-class, fee-paying community. The Roman Catholics covered a far wider social range, from the old families who patronized the Oratory or Ampleforth to the lower middle class and the scholarship boys of the towns. It was no mean achievement to have created such a wide range of institutions; without the devoted work of the religious orders it could not have been done.

Part V
The education of girls

18 Endowed schools – 1

The Schools Inquiry Commission had investigated the girls' private schools and had examined witnesses like Miss Davies, Miss Buss, and Miss Beale. In their general report the commissioners wrote that the existing girls' schools were unsatisfactory and generally weaker than the boys' (SIC I: 546–70). One particular obstacle to improvement was the failure of middle-class parents to take any trouble over the education of their daughters. Among the subjects taught, arithmetic and mathematics were especially weak. Greek was very little taught and though Latin was suitable for girls, it was often taught badly. French was better and girls were said to achieve more in it than boys. Too much time was given to learning instrumental music and too little to any form of exercise. Girls' schools were generally smaller than boys', and this often made them less efficient, though there were strong arguments in favour of small schools for girls. The question was also asked: had girls similar capacity for intellectual attainment to boys? A good deal of reliance was placed upon American examples, and in general the answer was yes, though there were differences between the sexes and no complete assimilation should be attempted. The experiment of opening the Cambridge Local examinations to girls, which had recently been made, had been successful, and it was not true, in the view of the commissioners, that women were likely to suffer in health from greater intellectual effort.

Obtaining good teachers was a very serious difficulty. The report was in favour of setting up a higher college or colleges for women, though it was difficult to see how much demand there would be for such courses. It was unjust that women had hardly any share of existing endowments, though it was not likely for all sorts of reasons that girls would acquire a share of them equal to that enjoyed by boys. There was much more opposition in girls' than in boys' schools to the admixture of social classes. Some of the Taunton assistant commissioners commented on the problems of women's education, prominent among them James Bryce in Lancashire. He argued that in every town there ought to be a publicly managed high school for girls 'where a plain, sound education should be offered at the lowest prices (from 5 l. per annum upwards) compatible with the provision of good salaries for teachers, and which should be regularly examined by competent persons thereto appointed' (SIC VII: 836).

Bryce's aspirations for such a network of public high schools were not fulfilled until the twentieth century. At a time when state support was not available, there were two ways by which the crying need for more and better girls' schools could be met. One was through the foundation of schools by shareholders on lines similar to the boys' proprietary schools of the 1830s and 1840s. The second, which attracted much attention from the reformers of the 1870s, was the diversion to girls' schools of some of the endowments hitherto devoted entirely to boys. Conditions in different places varied; in some places one solution was favoured, and in others the other. In both cases men as well as women were leaders in the new projects, and under conditions in which women had no experience of public life, much less would have been done without the activity of the men sympathizers who campaigned to reform old endowments and who staffed governing bodies.

The progress made in establishing girls' high schools of the new type was steady rather than spectacular. The Bryce Commission report said that in 1864 there had been 12 endowed schools for girls, a total which by the mid-1890s had increased to about 80. In addition there had been a substantial growth of proprietary schools. The report recorded 36 schools of the Girls Public Day School Company (GPDSC) with 7,111 pupils and 27 schools of the Church Schools Company (CSC) with 2,166 pupils (*BC* I: 15, 76). CSC, unlike GPDSC, had also attempted to found boys' schools, but almost all its pupils were girls. Despite the growth of the high schools, Alice Zimmern estimated that 70 per cent of the girls receiving secondary education were in private schools, though she gave no source for her figures (Zimmern 1898: 167).

A speaker at the Social Science Association congress in 1875, only a few years after the redistribution of endowments had begun, estimated that the annual value of the whole was about £280,000 per annum. The work of the Endowed Schools Commissioners had ensured that girls received about 10 per cent of this sum (Merrifield, *TSSA* 1875: 435–45). It has already been made clear, however, that the commissioners' efforts had had very mixed success. At Bedford and at Birmingham the governors themselves had suggested the foundation of girls' high schools. At Bristol the commissioners failed to get the first-class girls' school which they had originally planned. They did graft a plan for a girls' school onto the Colston's Hospital foundation, but the school was not opened until 1891. At Leeds, where the commissioners encountered long years of bitter and entrenched opposition, the claims of girls' education to a share of the endowment was not settled until the end of the century (see pp. 204, 206). When endowment money was made available, it was not always sufficient for what was needed. At Bradford, for example, it had originally been suggested that three-eighths of the endowment, or about £300 a year, should be set aside for a girls' school. In the final scheme this had been reduced to £200, plus another £50 at the determination of certain pensions. A capital sum of £5,000 was raised in addition by a committee of ladies to launch the school (PRO, Ed. 27: 5721; Zimmern 1898: 88–9).

C. S. Bremner considered that the commissioners had been steady friends to the education of girls, though it had not been possible to achieve anything like equality. Where endowments had been shared, the most common arrangement had been two-thirds for boys to one-third for girls (Bremner 1897: 87, 90). Though there was strong opposition in many places to spending money on girls' schools, the real difficulty was that there was never enough endowment money for all the claims made upon it. In the view of one modern study the Endowed Schools Commission was much more active than the Charity Commission, and the movement to find money for girls' education gradually slowed down, since there was widespread reluctance to divert money from educating boys. The Charity Commissioners took a more legalistic view, and saw themselves much less as policy-makers than their predecessors had done. Moreover their task was made more difficult by the rising pressures to spend money on the poor which has already been studied in the cases of Scarning and West Lavington (S. Fletcher 1980; see pp. 60–8).

The Bryce Commission provided information about the position in the 1890s. In the seven counties studied in detail there were only a few girls' high schools, whether endowed or proprietary, and in many areas there were none at all. In Surrey, for example, there was a particular shortage of schools charging lower fees and only one school in the county at which girls could hold elementary school scholarships (*BC* VII: 28). In Warwickshire the high school at Warwick was the only endowed secondary school for girls in the county, outside Birmingham (*BC* VII: 110).

Of the schools in the major West Riding towns special praise was given to Sheffield High School, a GPDSC school founded in 1878. There were 340 girls plus a large kindergarten class. The art and music were of good standard, and 7–8 girls went every year to Oxford and Cambridge (*BC* VII: 167–8). Leeds, under a local high school company, was much smaller – about 150 girls. They came at any age between 8 and 16 and some stayed until they were 19 or 20. There was no desire to attract scholarship pupils because of the strength of class feeling (ibid.: 153–4). The girls' grammar school at Bradford was much bigger than the high school at Leeds – 335 girls, 70 of whom had attended elementary schools (ibid.: 181). Two entrance scholarships were offered each year, and most of the candidates came from elementary schools. Scholarships were also offered for further education, though the number of candidates was reduced by the difficulties in paying for maintenance and clothing during the years at school (REC West Riding *PP* 1897 LXVII, Pt 5: 140, 142).

The Bryce information about West Riding schools can be supplemented from the Returns on Endowed Charities of a slightly later date. There were successful high schools at Keighley and at Wakefield. At Keighley the school, established by the scheme of 1871, had 160 pupils by 1893, about one-third of them being the children of artisans, and the girls took the junior and senior Cambridge examinations (*PP* 1897 LXVII, Pt 5: 470–1). At Wakefield a girls' school had been set up by the scheme of 1875. In the early years there was some opposition to it because no technical school had been founded, and it was felt that the money for this had been devoted to the girls' school. However, the girls' school steadily made its way and in 1897 there were 180 girls, many of them receiving free tuition. There were ten girls in the sixth form, though most of the girls in the school were aged between 10 and 16 (*PP* 1899 LXXIII: 642–4; Hardcastle n.d.). At Dewsbury there had been local opposition to a scheme put forward by the Charity Commissioners for the Wheelwright charity, which was not approved until 1888. About ten years later the girls' school had 83 pupils, the boys' school 122 (*PP* 1899 LXXI: 181–2).

In all these cases new schemes had got under way and had been reasonably successful. In a few places – Fartown and Longwood near Huddersfield and at Knaresborough – mixed schools had been set up (*PP* 1899 LXXI: 674–6, 692–6; *PP* 1899 LXXII: 266–70). In some places the girls had got little or nothing. At Batley a girls' school had been closed in 1870, and although various proposals had been made to revive it, nothing had been done, though there was an effective boys' school (*PP* 1899 LXXI: 97–9). At Rishworth the trustees of the wealthy Wheelwright charities had opposed the commissioners' plans. The girls' school educated and boarded thirteen children; they were not allowed to stay beyond the age of 14, and the average age was 12 (*PP* 1899 LXXI: 308). At Elland in the same area there were two boys' grammar schools, one of which the commissioners had wished to reconstitute as a girls' school, but the governors had refused to consent. There was no provision in the town for girls' secondary education, and a widespread feeling existed that something should be done to remedy the situation (ibid.: 308).

The plans of the commissioners had been opposed with particular obstinacy at Leeds. Their struggles with the grammar school trustees have already been examined (see pp. 28–30), but there was also a long battle over the education of girls. The Endowed Schools Commissioners had raised the subject of provision for them in the first negotiations of 1870, though at that time the governors stated that they did not think it possible to make any such provision (Ed. 27: 5976). These first negotiations achieved no result, and in 1876 a local company set up a girls' high school (Procter 1926; Jewell 1976). In 1878 the trustees of the Poor's Estate made £700 a year from their charitable funds available for scholarships at the grammar school. The women's group were not informed in time about what was going on and failed to obtain any of the transferred money for girls, though it seems likely that there had been some discussion that this might be done. In 1886 Nathan Boddington, principal of the Yorkshire College, told the commissioners:

> that when Scheme for Poors Este was made it was felt that girls had as good a claim as boys, & there was a tacit understanding that at the earliest opportunity girls should also be benefited out of the endowment.
>
> (Ed. 27: 5981, 29 June 1886; see also S. Fletcher 1980: 185–7)

The earliest opportunity was a long time in coming. In 1884 the commissioners took up the affairs of the Leeds endowment again, and when assistant commissioner Stanton met the trustees, they expressed considerable resistance to the suggestion that money might be applied for a girls' school. In the view of the vicar of Leeds, Dr Gott, girls' education did not need help. It was already sufficiently provided for by the girls' high school and by the Church and Mechanics' Institute middle-class schools, none of which was full (Ed. 27: 5981, 14 March 1884). The governors were prepared to discuss the possibility of making additional funds available for exhibitions for both boys and girls, but only on condition that the constitution of the governing body remained unaltered. This point has already been examined; it was a condition which the commissioners could not accept.

Sir George Young, the commissioner who was dealing with the matter, was strongly in favour of appropriating money for the girls, and when a draft scheme was published in August 1885, it contained a clause that £500 per annum should be applied for that purpose from the grammar school revenues. The governors' reactions were as hostile as might have been expected. Their funds were, they claimed, insufficient to meet all the demands made upon them, including the education of girls (Ed. 27: 5981, 2 December 1885). To put the matter in proportion £500 represented about one-ninth of an annual endowment income, including the scholarship and exhibition funds, of about £4,500. Stanton observed rather wryly, in reply to a suggestion that the provision for girls might be made conditional on the availability of funds: 'I fear there is not much doubt that the time at which the Foundn could, in the opin. of Govs, afford to pay the £500 would be a very distant one' (7 December 1885). The governors subsequently repeated their claim that the money should be granted 'as far as the funds will allow'. In the view of the commissioners this was unacceptable because of the directions given by section 12 of the Act of 1869.

In June 1887 the scheme was sent by the commissioners to the Education Department. They were prepared to reduce the £500 to not less than £400 in any one year if special circumstances could be established but beyond this they would not go. The governors claimed that they could not even find £400 and suggested reducing this figure to £250 to be spent on scholarships at the high school or at other schools. Moreover they suggested that this sum might be found by reducing the scholarships for boys, so that such benefits as the girls received would be paid for by depriving boys of scholarship opportunities. Such an adjustment was unacceptable to the commissioners. They totally opposed altering the Poor's Estate settlement of 1878 for scholarships for boys. It must have seemed to them as if the trustees were trying to rob Peter to pay Paul. And there for that time the matter rested.

Negotiations were resumed in 1894, and a new scheme for the grammar school was finally made in 1898. In the final negotiations the allocation of money for the girls was a major issue. The official line was to maintain the claim for £500 a year. Vice-President Dyke Acland minuted in 1895: 'I should give £500 to girls with share in increase and not in decrease' (Ed. 27: 5982, 12 June 1895). The governors still wished to reduce the sum. Finally, in 1897 they changed their policy, suggesting a capital payment of £12,000, a proposal which the commissioners accepted. It was agreed that this sum should be set aside from the date of the establishment of the new scheme, while the exhibition and scholarship funds were to remain as before. Negotiations then began for the purchase of the existing high school, since there was strong opposition to the establishment of a new school (Ed. 27: 5984, 5978). In December 1898 the governors resolved that they were prepared to take over the girls' school as an integral part of their foundation and, in addition to the capital payment, to set aside at least £250 a year for it. There was to be a separate governing body on which they would be represented, and four of its members were to be women. No wonder the secretary of the girls' high school company wrote to assistant commissioner A. F. Leach: 'I must say I think the progress that the two resolutions show is quite wonderful' (Ed. 27: 5978, 15 February 1899). Even after that there was a last effort at further delay, but agreement was finally made to rebuild the girls' high school and the scheme was finally approved in May 1901.

Thus the Leeds Girls' High School was accepted into the grammar school foundation and the long wrangle brought to an end, though the terms were not generous in relation to the total endowment income. The story deserves detailed attention because it illustrates the strength of the opposition against which the advocates of better schooling for girls had sometimes to contend. It is unique because of the length of time for which the struggle continued. The difficulties, seen in their most extreme form in this case, help to explain why the transfer of endowments was likely to offer only a partial answer to the demands for new girls' schools.

19 Endowed schools – 2

The Leeds case was exceptional; there were many success stories as new endowed schools were set up and old schools reformed. There were cases too where private/proprietary schools received help from old endowments, two outstanding examples being Miss Buss's schools – the North London and the Camden – and Manchester High School. In 1870 Miss Buss's highly successful private school had been in existence for twenty years. From the mid–1860s she had considered putting the school, which was her personal property, into the hands of trustees. This was done in July 1870 and in the following year the Camden School was set up with much lower fees to provide education for girls of lower middle-class families up to the age of 16. There were in addition some scholarships to carry promising pupils from the Camden to the North London. The immediate problem was to acquire an endowment, particularly for the Camden with its low fees. Miss Buss tried very hard to raise money and found it extremely difficult. An especially galling blow was the discovery that £5,000 which had been raised for a girls' school in the City of London had instead been added on to £60,000 already raised for boys' education (A. E. Ridley 1895: 93, 127–9).

It was fortunate for Miss Buss and her supporters that the Endowed Schools Commissioners were very sympathetic to their efforts, and that means were found to tap the Platt endowments, derived from the St Pancras area, which were controlled by the Brewers Company. The Platt money had been spent on maintaining Aldenham School in Hertfordshire, but there was sufficient surplus available for the commissioners to suggest that some of it should be spent on schools at Watford and some of it on girls' education in St Pancras. The Brewers Company proved to be sympathetic – indeed the files suggest that some of the initiatives came from their side. There was a good deal of opposition from the parishioners of Aldenham who wanted more money for their elementary schools, but the scheme of 1875 transferred £20,000 to the North London schools, together with a further claim on the endowment income (PRO Ed 27: 1637, 1639 (Aldenham); Ed. 27: 3191).

Later, further help came from another Brewers' charity, Dame Alice

Owen's foundation at Islington. Once again there were local rumblings about spending money on the education of girls. However, a new Owen's girls' school was set up and the Brewers suggested a capital grant of £2,000 to the North London building fund, together with a loan of £6,000 to be repaid, capital and interest, over fifteen years. The scheme was approved on 14 August 1878 (Ed. 27: 3117, 3119). In the same year another scheme (26 March 1878) provided that loan funds controlled by the Clothworkers Company might be spent on building a large hall at the North London school (Ed. 27: 3195).

The generosity and readiness to help shown by the Brewers and Clothworkers form a major contrast to the niggardliness and obstructiveness of other corporate bodies. Another privately founded school which benefited from endowment money was Manchester High School for Girls, opened by a group of local activists in 1874. The school began in two rented houses, but in 1881 occupied a substantial new building. Numbers had grown rapidly, but the financial position was difficult because there was a rent charge on the new site and a mortgage of £10,000 on the building. As early as 1875 a memorial had been sent to the Charity Commissioners, asking for aid from charitable funds, and in particular from the Hulme charity. The income from the Hulme estates was considerable – £8,036 in 1881 – and when a scheme was made for the charity in 1881, it was provided that a boys' grammar school should be set up, and that an annual sum of not less than £500 and not more than £1,000 should be paid to the girls' high school trustees. If such a scheme were not made within three years, a separate girls' school was to be founded (Ed. 27: 2171; Burstall 1911). In fact the girls' school did rather better than the original arrangements had suggested. Finally it was agreed that the Hulme governors should set aside £15,000 to redeem the rent charge and the mortgage on the high school property, and should in addition pay £1,000 annually (scheme approved, 2 February 1884). Generosity of course is a comparative term. There were those who argued that the girls had received an insufficient share of the considerable wealth of the Hulme estates (S. Fletcher 1980: 189–90).

Only a few examples can be given of the many endowed schools newly established or reformed by the commissioners. At Birmingham the girls' high school of King Edward's foundation opened in 1883. Under the long rule of Edith Creak, which lasted until 1910, the school was very successful. Academic standards were high and the school was a pioneer in science teaching. The new building, opened in 1896, contained good science laboratories. Both domestic subjects and hygiene were taught, and Miss Creak was an early advocate of the plan that girls should not take external examinations until they reached the age of 16 (Vardy [Mrs E. W. Candler] 1928).

The pattern of development at King Edward's is similar to that of other successful schools. At Bedford the scheme of 1873 had provided both a girls' high school and a modern school, in parallel with the grammar and modern schools for boys. In apportioning the endowment three boys were to receive the same as five girls. In the modern schools pupils were not to remain over the age of 17. The high school fees were to range from £6 to £20, the modern school fees from £1 10s to £4 (Ed. 27: 9). The girls' schools did not open until 1882, though governors for the new schools had been appointed in January 1874. Much of the delay was due to financial difficulty. Initially it had been planned to build the Modern School first since there was no provision for girls at that level, while there were several superior private schools. However in November 1878 a group of parents and residents pressed for the prompt establishment of the High School, and the two schools opened at the same time in 1882, sharing different parts of the same building. In 1892 the Modern School moved to an independent site, and the High School took over the whole of the original structure (Westaway 1932; Godber and Hutchins 1982; Broadway and Buss 1982; Hunt 1984).

In early years the High School was much the more successful of the two schools. In 1894 it had 553 girls while there were only 146 at the Modern School. The first head of that school, Mary Porter, experienced serious financial problems, while the High School had higher fees and greater social prestige. Its first head Mrs McDowall (Ada Benson), who had been head of two GPDSC schools, died after a few months in office. Her two successors, Marian Belcher (1883–98) and Susan Collie (1898–1920), were both very able women who had taught under Miss Beale at Cheltenham and brought something of the Cheltenham atmosphere with them. Academic standards were good and a number of girls went to the university. At the turn of the century girls stayed on at school to study for the London external BA Degree and many took the London Intermediate. The science facilities were poor and, though there was a gymnasium from the start, there was little provision for games until a playing field was opened in 1900. The Modern School began to make its way under Edith Dolby (1894–1925), who succeeded Miss Porter. The curriculum was extended and girls began to stay on longer. By 1908 the numbers had reached 312. At the Modern School the parents of girls entering in 1892–3 included a colonel, a mathematics master at the boys' modern school, farmers, an engineer, and a Baptist minister, together with a large number of tradesmen (Broadway and Buss 1982: 22). At the High School ten years earlier there were a large number of professional men – clergymen, lawyers, doctors, army officers – together with men in a large way of business, farmers, millers and brewers (Godber and Hutchins 1982: 368–9).

Unlike the girls' schools at Birmingham and Bedford, which were new grafts onto old foundations for boys, the Godolphin School at Salisbury was an old foundation for girls, established in 1708 to provide a liberal education in the principles of the Church of England to twelve orphan gentlewomen between the ages of 12 and 19. Some fee payers were received in addition (Ed. 27: 5283, 5284; Douglas and Ash 1928). The foundation was exclusive in both social and religious terms. When it came under the consideration of the Charity Commissioners in 1884 there were 16 girls – 6 foundationers, 6 boarders, and 4 day girls, all the daughters of gentlefolk, 'according to the best of the Trustees' belief – a term which they held to exclude any tradesmen. . . . The Trees [Trustees] are careful to satisfy themselves as to gentility and orthodoxy of the nominees' parents.' There was considerable pressure in Salisbury to open up the school more widely because it was feared that, unless this was done, a new middle-class school for girls would be opened. The headmistress favoured the admission of tradesmen's daughters and complained about the inadequacy of the entrance examination. Clearly the governors were anxious to press ahead with changes. A new scheme was made in 1886 under which six scholarships for orphan gentlewomen, born of Church of England parents, were maintained, though scholars had to pay part of the cost of their education.

In November 1889 Mary Alice Dougles, who had been a colleague of Alice Ottley at Worcester (see p. 222), became headmistress and the school made real strides under her leadership. An assistant commissioner reported in 1897 that the school impressed him very favourably. 'The Head Mistress seemed to be happy and successful in her work & on excellent terms with staff and pupils.' There were 98 girls – 20 of them boarders and 20 living in authorized houses, though very few girls came from the neighbourhood of the school. A list of parental occupations is appended to the 1897 report. There were a good many clergymen's daughters and many from trade and business backgrounds, so the gentility barrier seems to have been safely broken. None, it was observed, had come from public elementary schools (Ed. 27: 5283, 18 August 1897).

Almost all the endowed schools so far described were high schools, keeping some pupils up to the age of 18 or 19 and aiming to send some to university. Camden and the Girls' Modern at Bedford, on the other hand, are examples of 'middle' or 'modern' schools, for different terms were used. They were second-grade and designed for girls who would leave between 15 and 17. There were a number of such schools in London. Among the largest of them in 1890 were Camden (427 pupils), Roan's, Greenwich (350), Grey Coat, Westminster (336), and James Allen's, Dulwich (296). The annual fees varied from £3 15s to £8 (Acland and Llewellyn Smith 1892 (Clara E. Collet); Bremner 1897: 119–21).

Historically, the roots of these London schools varied. Some were old charity schools, some were old elementary schools re-founded at secondary level, some represented a conversion to educational purposes of old endowments of a different kind. Among charity schools was the Burlington School in the parish of St James, Piccadilly, reorganized in 1876. The syllabus included French, natural science, and bodily exercises (Burgess n.d.). James Allen's at Dulwich, founded as a reading school for boys and girls in the eighteenth century, was reconstituted in 1882 as a school for 300 girls and financed by a capital sum and an annual payment from the Alleyn's endowment. By the end of the century the curriculum had developed a strong scientific bent with a strong interest in botany (Bryant 1979: 101; 1986: 339). The Grey Coat was one of the Westminster hospital schools which had been involved in the bitter early battles of the Endowed Schools Commission (see pp. 9–10). It had opened as a day school in 1874 and had quickly grown in numbers. By the end of the century some girls were working for London Intermediate Arts and for Oxford scholarships (Day 1902).

It is a general rule of educational history that successful schools raise their objectives. Many of the girls' schools which had been designed for pupils of 16 or younger were soon anxious to prepare students for university, and others moved from third- to second-grade status. Two examples of reconstructed elementary endowments where such changes occurred are Dame Alice Owen's at Islington and the Roan Schools at Greenwich. The Owen's girls' school opened in 1886 with eighty-three scholars. By 1900 there were 300. A report of 1899 commented that the work was high second-grade. Natural science was taught throughout the school and considerable attention was given to music. The development of the Roan Schools under a scheme of 1873 was similar. According to a report of 1894 the girls' school had better buildings than the boys'. Girls had done well in the Cambridge Locals though the headmistress told the Bryce Commission that it was difficult for them to get as much benefit from secondary education as their brothers because of the many home duties which lower middle-class girls were required to perform. At that time there were 338 girls in the school with a wide mixture of classes. A large proportion had attended elementary schools because pupils from these schools came in at half fees. The Roan Schools were doing excellent work and were popular in the area. With the aid of a proposed LCC technical education grant their work should be raised to a very high level. Each school possessed a leaving exhibition and in the ten years before 1894 girls who had won it had attended University College, Cardiff, University College, London, and Somerville (Ed. 27: 3120; Dare 1963 (Owen's); Ed. 27: 3026; *BC* II: 345–57; REC London *PP* 1899 LXIX: 284–91 (Roan Schools)).

Other schools were created out of endowments which had become obsolete. Two examples are the Mary Datchelor School in London and the girls' high school at Skipton in the West Riding. The Mary Datchelor was financed from a charity in the parish of St Andrew Undershaft in the City of London originally given for the maintenance of a family tomb. In 1871 a board of trustees was set up and given £20,000 to found a girls' school. Property was bought in 1876 at Camberwell, and in 1877 the school opened with thirty girls. By 1900 there were over 400. The

most distinctive feature of the school was its involvement with the training of student teachers. A training college was organized with two departments; in one students worked for the Cambridge Higher Locals and
later for the London BA, and in the other for the Cambridge or the
London teaching diploma. Mary Datchelor was one of a number of girls'
secondary schools which ran school-based teacher training of this kind.
It was a development unique to them; there was no boys' equivalent
(*VCH Surrey* II (1905): 220; *Mary Datchelor School, The Story of* 1957;
Bryant 1986: 337–8).

Sylvester Petyt's charity at Skipton had an income of £840 in 1867
which was paid out in doles. In 1875 the Charity Commissioners began
an inquiry, and the suggestion was made in the town that some of the
Petyt money might be spent on a middle school for girls (see Ed. 27:
6171). A Chancery scheme of 1879 for Petyt's charity provided that some
of the income should be spent on exhibitions for boys and that the
residue should be applied to establishing a middle school for girls. In
addition there was the possibility of some help from Giggleswick School
some 15 miles away, where the scheme provided for the expenditure of
£100 a year on girls' education (see p. 41).

In November 1882 assistant commissioner Durnford held an inquiry
and negotiations began which concluded with the scheme of 1886. There
was an active local pressure group in the town which was prepared to
raise money and which started a school while the discussions were in
progress. They favoured a school with fees lower than the commissioners
wanted. On the other hand, the Giggleswick governors, who were not
unsympathetic, wanted a school on more expensive lines and were anxious that their money should be spent on boarding accommodation. This
indeed was not unreasonable in a thinly populated district where pupils
would need to be drawn from a large area. As in many other places
there were protests by the poorer townsmen against what they saw as
the alienation of money in the interests of a wealthier class. There
was a sharp disagreement between the commissioners, who wanted the
curriculum to include Latin, and C. S. Roundell, MP, and the Petyt
trustees, who thought it an unsuitable subject for a school of this kind.
The scheme of 1886 set up a day and boarding school with tuition fees
of £4 to £12 according to age. Pupils were to be admitted between 7 and
17, and Latin was included in the subjects to be taught. There were to
be scholarships from elementary schools in the ancient parish of Skipton.
The school was to receive the residue of the Petyt income and £100 a
year from Giggleswick. New buildings for 100 scholars and 20 boarders
were completed in 1890, and at the end of the decade were filled to
capacity. Indeed, if the money could have been found for more building,
the number of boarders could have been increased. About 40 girls came
into Skipton daily by train (REC West Riding *PP* 1897 LXVII, Pt 5:
771–4).

The subject of scholarships has already been discussed (see pp. 75–83, 111–12). According to the Charity Commissioners' figures for 1882, there were 219 secondary schools in which scholarships were held. Most of these will have been boys' schools, but even so the number of awards held by girls was small – 296 against 2,365 held by boys. Most of the awards were held in second- and third-grade schools. The returns of 1884 and 1886 fill out the picture. The 'Fortescue' return of 1884, listing schools under schemes made up to 31 December 1880, includes 3 first-grade, 9 second-grade and 14 third-grade girls' schools. In almost all cases the totals of scholarship holders were in single figures. Among schools already mentioned, Roan's had 9 scholarships of £15 for three years, all held by girls from elementary schools. The Burlington School had 2. Among second-grade schools Mary Datchelor had 7 (6 of £10 and 1 of £15), plus education free for two years. Wakefield, classed as first-grade, had 10 girls from public elementary schools and 6 others at half fees. In the case of the ten elementary scholars a governor paid the half fee; children would not attend if only half the fees were remitted.

The return of 1886, which aimed to discover how many scholarship holders were the children of parents employed in manual labour, was much more selective, covering only thirteen girls' schools, though it does give valuable detail about the (unnamed) schools which it recorded. Manual workers were well represented among parents in second- and third-grade schools; no first-grade school reported. A fairly typical return is that of a second-grade school in a large manufacturing town in the West Midlands. Eleven out of the seventeen parents were manual workers: forgeman, monthly nurse, brush-maker, china-maker, joiner, mechanic, cabinet-maker, warehouseman, potter's foreman, porter. In one case the occupation was not known. The other parents were two schoolmasters, two publicans, and a butcher. The analysis of parents of scholarship-holders in girls' middle schools in London (Table 19.1) presents a similar mix of occupations.

Table 19.1 Occupations of fathers of girls admitted to London middle schools with scholarships, *c.* 1890

Railway guard	Oilskin dresser	Jeweller (2)
Ship carpenter (3 children held scholarships)	Waterproofer	Coachman
	Board schoolmaster (3)	Clerk (5)
Joiner	Master blacksmith	Foreman
Gatekeeper	Printer (2)	Sorter PO
Caretaker	Commercial traveller (3)	Joiner
Wheelwright	Builder	Manufacturer
Ironplate worker	Tax collector	Engineer
Cheesemonger		Tailor

Source: Coliet, in Acland and Llewellyn Smith, *Studies in Secondary Education* (1892: 210).

The average leaving age of eighty-nine free scholars from elementary schools in this London sample was 13.96 and their average stay at school 1.65 years. In London, it was claimed, the scholarship system benefited middle-class much more than working-class girls. What the latter needed, much more than scholarships, were continuation classes in practical subjects.

The schools who responded to the 1886 return commented that, although scholarship pupils often took some time to settle to secondary work and to become accepted by the other girls, they had in the end achieved both objectives. Where their future occupations can be traced, they became teachers, worked in the Post Office and insurance offices, took up dressmaking, became clerks and shop assistants (*PP* 1886 IX: 539–76; Acland and Llewellyn Smith 1892: 218–19). They passed in fact into that lower middle-class world to which most of the other girls who attended the same secondary schools belonged. There is little sign of girl scholarship-holders going on to higher education or more advanced careers, though Elizabeth Day of Manchester High School told the Bryce Commission that she had had a few scholarship girls who had won awards at Girton and Newnham. However, the view of the Headmistresses' Association as expressed by Miss Day herself and by Harriet Morant Jones of Notting Hill High School, was that too many awards were made to girls of only average ability and that it would be desirable to limit the numbers given (*BC* IV: 21–43).

In fact the number of scholarship awards to children of both sexes increased greatly in the 1890s as a result of the work of the technical instruction committees (see pp. 111–12; Zimmern 1898: 193). Another very experienced headmistress, Sara Burstall, took a much more optimistic view than Miss Day and Miss Morant Jones had done. The results of the scholarship system over the previous thirty years had, she thought, been remarkable, especially in London. Able girls, some from elementary schools, some from the 'poorer professional classes' had been able to qualify themselves for higher professional posts (Burstall 1907: 188, 192–3). Though she did not say so, Miss Burstall herself, who had gone with a scholarship from the Camden to the North London and then to Girton, was an example of that process. Perhaps there had been a major change over the turn of the century, but the evidence remains inconclusive. The growth of the scholarships system should be noted, but too much must not be claimed for it as an agent of social and educational change.

20 Proprietary and other schools – 1

The two most distinguished headmistresses of the later nineteenth century, Frances Mary Buss and Dorothea Beale, had established their reputations well before 1870. Miss Buss died in office at Christmas 1894 after a headship of forty-four years, and in that role she was one of the central figures in the history of nineteenth-century English education (Ridley 1895; Burstall 1938; Kamm 1958).

In her own school she worked tirelessly to train and to encourage pupils and colleagues. In a period when class consciousness offered a serious obstacle to the free development of new girls' schools she cared nothing for such things. As an old pupil wrote, 'no one asked where you lived, how much pocket-money you had, or what your father was – he might be a bishop or a rat-catcher' (Hughes 1946: 184). Her interests extended far beyond her own school and she worked indefatigably for women's education in general; she was one of the founders of the Headmistresses' Association, of the Cambridge Training College for Women, and of the Teachers' Guild. She was actively interested in the College of Preceptors. She was without self-importance or desire to arrogate praise to herself. She was ready to listen to others and to accept advice from people she trusted. There were less attractive aspects to her system. The problems that she had to face were immense, and she tended to solve them by creating an endless mass of rules. Much time was spent on the collection and recording of marks. The staff had a heavy burden of work to get through and the girls were subject to considerable strain. Yet she was far from being a cold and remote pedant. She could be hot-tempered and sometimes even unjust, but she was also warm-hearted, hospitable, and anxious to give young people a good time.

One of her great successes was to find and train her successor, Sophie Bryant. Widowed in early life, Mrs Bryant joined the North London staff to teach mathematics. She became Miss Buss's right hand and eventually followed her as headmistress. A woman of great intellectual ability, she was the first woman to be awarded the London DSc degree. Keenly concerned to promote the development of the individual student, she was also, like Miss Buss, active in affairs outside the school. She was a member of the London University Convocation and Senate and of the Technical Education Board. She was a keen supporter of Irish Home Rule and of women's suffrage. Like Miss Buss she was much concerned about the professional development of her own staff. Sara Burstall, who served as her second mistress, wrote that she had often gone to her after hours of wrestling with some problem of the time-table. 'She would shake the thing a little and it would come out right' (Burstall 1933: 128). One of her pupils thought that she was by no means a clear teacher, 'but [she] had the rare quality of inspiring us to work and think things out for ourselves' (Hughes 1946: 202; Scrimgeour 1950: 78–87; Milburn 1969: 29–30).

Frances Mary Buss and Dorothea Beale worked well together pro-fessionally – they were, for example, joint-founders of the Head-mistresses' Association – but as people they were very different. Miss Beale was the daughter of a London medical man. After studying at Queen's College, Harley Street, and a period of teaching there, she was for a brief and unhappy period headmistress of the clergy daughters' school at Casterton in Westmorland. She became principal of the Ladies' College at Cheltenham, a proprietary school for girls established a few years previously, in 1858, and she remained in charge until her death in 1906 (Raikes 1908; Steadman 1931; Clarke 1953; Kamm 1958; *HSE*: 296–7). The first years at Cheltenham were very difficult, but success came gradually and, after the opening of a new building in 1873, the college progressed steadily to become rather a complex of educational institutions than a mere secondary school.

Miss Buss was a sincere Christian, but religion was not the driving force in her plans. Miss Beale possessed great practical gifts, but they were united with a deep and rather mystical spirituality which was the driving force in all she did. She had a special devotion to the memory of the Saxon abbess, St Hilda of Whitby, and she hoped to set up a religious order, but, although this never proved possible, her work was directed by a spirit of devotion, service, and self-abnegation similar to that of a professed religious. If this deep spirituality could rise to great heights, it could also sink to great depths. In the years around 1880 Miss Beale suffered a long crisis of faith which led her to draft a letter of resignation, though it was never sent. After a time the crisis passed and she was able to return to many more years of productive work.

In its early years the college took largely day pupils, but it gradually became almost entirely a boarding school. The changes did not happen without creating problems over the position of the housemistresses and the financial arrangements for their houses. Some Cheltenham people had opposed the changes and there were tensions about the extent of the principal's authority. These problems were overcome by a reform of the constitution of the college council in 1875, and in 1880 the share-holders renounced all financial interest in their shares and the college was incorporated. The North London and the high schools which followed its example pursued a policy of admitting girls from a wide range of social backgrounds. The Ladies' College, like the boys' Cheltenham College, restricted entry to the daughters of professional men and those of comparable social standing. Parents had to give references and introductions were required (*BC* III: 167: 7965; 170: 8003).

By the 1890s the Ladies' College had become a very large institution. Miss Beale told the Bryce Commission that in all departments there were nearly 900 girls, many of them from overseas. Boarding and tuition fees for older girls ranged from £100 to £120 per year. Miss Beale, like Miss Buss, was very interested in teacher training for the highly practical reason that the new girls' schools had experienced serious difficulties in recruiting good teachers. Miss Buss favoured training in separate institutions. Miss Beale favoured close involvement between training and the secondary school. She had prepared future teachers in the college for a number of years, and in 1885 she opened St Hilda's College, Cheltenham, as a residential college for teachers in secondary schools. In 1893 she opened the associated St Hilda's Hall in Oxford, which was eventually to become a full college of Oxford University. Training was also provided for future teachers in kindergartens and elementary schools. In addition to all this professional work, the Ladies' College had a strong course for London degrees. Miss Beale refused to see all these activities in isolation. To her they all formed part of a common whole, and she was the driving force behind the whole enterprise.

The two women also differed in their attitudes to competition and examinations. Miss Buss was not worried about the dangers which they presented. Miss Beale allowed girls to take examinations, but put little emphasis on them and did not encourage intensive preparation for them. She disliked competitive entrance scholarships, though she had discretion to admit girls at lower fees and did this to a considerable extent. She took little interest in games, though she accepted the increased prominence which they enjoyed in her later years. She feared that they would damage the gentleness and courtesy which she valued in girls' nature, and she refused to allow competitive matches with other schools. Though she had serious outside interests, for example, in the work of the Froebel Society and of the Parents' National Education Union, the college was her central concern. She was deeply absorbed in it and appeared to need little relaxation from it. It was typical of her approach to life that the members of the old girls' guild had to undertake a commitment to self-education and to service to the community. Let the final word be left with her successor, Lilian Faithfull, who wrote that one of Miss Beale's greatest conquests had been the conquest of her successor. Miss Faithfull, when she first came to Cheltenham, had quickly recognized that behind the everyday practices of the school 'lay the mind of a very thoughtful, wise and independent woman' (Faithfull 1924: 129, 131).

Miss Buss and Miss Beale stand out as independent personalities to a much greater extent than the other headmistresses of the new girls' schools. They held office for long periods of time and for a whole generation they were closely identified in the public mind with the cause of girls' education. After 1870–80 the pattern changes. The individual leader becomes less important and events are dominated by groups or networks of like-minded people, who bring to the work the strength of numbers and of organization. Collective replaces individual leadership.

Some of these networks were purely local and their work was limited to the creation of a single school. Others were regional or national in importance, and exercised an influence on the growth of women's education as great or greater than that of the endowed schools. One of the first of these groups was the London Association of Schoolmistresses, founded in 1866 which, until it was wound up in 1887–8, provided a useful means of exchanging professional information and promoting professional skills. Emily Davies was its secretary for most of its life and Frances Buss was a prominent member (Bryant 1979: 97; 1986: 326–8). The most important groups consisted rather of laymen and women than of schoolmistresses themselves. One major regional association was the Yorkshire Ladies' Council of Education, first created in 1871 as an offshoot of the Yorkshire Board of Education which had been set up to organize examinations and scientific instruction. The Ladies' Council became an independent body in 1875 (I. Jenkins 1979: 27–71). It depended on a group of ladies experienced in committee work, who created a network of committees throughout the area. They helped to provide a library for women who were taking the Cambridge Higher Locals. They tried to set up courses for governesses to improve their qualifications. They helped to found the Leeds Girls' High School in 1876, and they pressed the women's claims in the long struggle over the Leeds endowments which has already been described. They had close relationships with the Yorkshire College of Science which was to grow into the University of Leeds. One of their major achievements was to create a school of cookery which began in Leeds in 1874.

The most important of these networks were the two limited companies which founded schools all over the country. The smaller group, the Church Schools Company, will be discussed later as part of the story of denominational education (see p. 225). The larger group, the Girls' Public Day School Company (later Trust), has been a major force in girls' secondary education since its creation in 1872. The founders were the two Shirreff sisters, Maria (the widowed Mrs W. G. Grey) and Emily. Among their close women associates were the Dowager Lady Stanley of Alderley and Mary Gurney, and they attracted support from men like Lord Lyttelton, Bishop Temple, Sir James Kay-Shuttleworth, J. G. Fitch and the philanthropist Samuel Morley. They gained the patronage of Princess Louise, one of the Queen's daughters, and so their work enjoyed the kind of social and intellectual support which went a long way towards ensuring success in mid-Victorian England.

The Shirreff sisters had been concerned with the problems of women's education for twenty years before 1870. In their joint book, *Thoughts on Self-culture Addressed to Women* (1850), they had examined the means by which self-improvement might be achieved. They did not dispute that women's status was subordinate to men's, but they were anxious that women should gain a general development of the mind – what they called 'that well-grounded and equable discipline of all the faculties' (ibid.: 27).

By the early 1870s the Shirreff sisters and their friends had become active propagandists in the women's cause. In 1871 Mrs Grey, in a lecture to the Society of Arts, reviewed the criticisms made by the Taunton Commission. What was needed, she argued, was a general organization, 'an educational league embracing all those who are actively interested in the cause', and prepared to implement three essential points: the equal right of women to the best education, the right to a share in the educational endowments, and the training and registration of teachers (Grey 1871: 555–61). The group found a ready hearing at the meetings of the Social Science Association. Mary Gurney spoke in 1871, Emily Shirreff in 1872 and 1875. Mrs Grey, in 1871, had made much the same points to that body as in her address to the Society of Arts. She denied that more advanced education would damage women's feminine characteristics. Two years later she rejected any claim that women would usurp the place of men, but she claimed for them the right of full development – not least in the interests of those who needed to earn their own livings (*TSSA* 1871: 366–8, 371; 1873: 361–2, 369 (Mrs Grey); 1872: 271–2; 1875: 445–8 (Emily Shirreff); 1871: 366–8 (Mary Gurney)). The arguments of the reformers were always, as we shall see later, rather uneasily balanced between the personal development approach which applied to all women and the financial independence approach which applied only to some.

The sisters were no mere theorists and the 'educational league' soon came into existence. In 1871 the National Union for the Education of Girls of all Classes above the elementary (Women's Education Union for short) was created. It was dissolved in 1882, but its purposes survived in two continuing bodies, GPDSC launched in 1872, and the Teachers Training and Registration Society, founded in 1875, which created what was to become the Maria Grey training college. GPDSC aimed at raising a capital sum of £12,000 in 2,400 shares of £5, the capital to be used for the purchase and furnishing of school buildings. Any profit was to be applied to the payment to the shareholders of a 5 per cent dividend. Eight hundred shares were taken up at once, and the first school, at Chelsea in south-west London, was opened in January 1873 (L. Magnus 1923; Kamm 1971).

The Company established a school only where there was strong evidence of local support, and during the ensuing thirty years their success was remarkable. The chairman, W. H. Stone, and Mary Gurney told the Bryce Commission that there were thirty-six schools with upwards of 7,000 pupils. The maximum salary for a headmistress was £700 a year, and assistants were paid from £70 to £200. The average fee for a pupil was £14–15 a year. Some schools had boarding houses, though the Company did not manage them. £250,000 had been raised for buildings, and the shareholders received a 5 per cent dividend. However, the dividend represented only about 4 per cent of the gross receipts, and, if it were reduced or given up, there would be little difference in the sum available for the schools. Nearly all the schools took the Oxford and Cambridge Joint Board examinations, and many girls had gone to college. The witnesses claimed that the Company had begun the work when no one else was prepared to do it. They had had many imitators, and they had created an atmosphere something like that of the major boys' public schools, with which they claimed to rank (*BC* II: 168–77, 240–54).

The Company's claims for itself are supported by independent evidence. Another of the Bryce witnesses, R. W. M. Pope, an Oxford don who had for many years examined the schools for the Joint Board, testified to the high standard of the work. The teaching was thorough and accurate, the preparation for university work excellent. The schools and some others working on similar lines had 'brought about a new era in female education' (*BC* V: 206–7). Lilian Faithfull, who had in her early days taught at the GPDSC Oxford High School, said much the same (Faithfull 1924: 75).

Happily the Shirreff sisters lived to enjoy the success of their enterprise. Emily died in 1897, Maria in 1906 at the age of 90. Like the North London, the GPDSC schools set up no social distinctions. 'All our High Schools', wrote one headmistress, 'receive, and rejoice to receive, girls of all classes' (R. D. Roberts 1901: 82 (Florence Gadesden)). They gave non-denominational religious instruction as well as operating a conscience clause. Some of their heads, like Harriet Morant Jones of Notting Hill (1873–1900) and Florence Gadesden of Blackheath (1886–1919), were very able women. An old girl thought that the teaching and equipment at Notting Hill were poor, but the head was 'keenly ambitious for her pupils and we caught fire from her. She had an exalted idea of school honour and of public spirit in the world outside' (Swanwick 1935: 75). Miss Gadesden was remembered for her strong character and powers of leadership – 'rather like a bird, perhaps a robin . . . firm, abrupt, even combative on her own ground' (Kamm 1971: 102). Among the leading heads of the provincial schools was Mrs Woodhouse of Sheffield (1878–98), who took a strong interest in physical education. Later she moved to Clapham in south London (1898–1912) (Paul n.d. Education Department; *Special Reports on Educational Subjects* 2 (1898): 133–44).

The picture of the schools can be filled out a little from the examiners' comments and headmistresses' reports preserved in the GPDST archives (GPDST, *Minutes of Council and Committees* 1879–90). Some examiners were critical. There were complaints of languor and lack of animation, although it was more common to praise the briskness and intelligence of the girls, their eagerness to answer, and their general enthusiasm. In 1879 the examiner reported an interesting contrast between the work at Sheffield and at Gateshead. At the former the girls were bright and lively; at the latter they seemed jaded. There was no reason to believe that more work was demanded at one school than at the other. 'But at Sheffield the work done seems to be selected with reference to the capacities of the taught – at Gateshead with reference to the capacities of the teacher.' On another occasion the kindergarten and science work at Sheffield was warmly praised. At Oxford it was thought that the policy of not beginning Latin before the age of 15 had excellent results. Blackheath in Miss Gadesden's early days was thought to have grown too quickly and the forms were over-large, though good progress had been made in Latin. Notting Hill was praised by several examiners. One commented on the ease and confidence of the older girls; another thought that in all the work 'a higher and more equal level than in any school I examined' was maintained.

Not all the schools were as successful and several heads reported problems. It was too much to hope, wrote the headmistress at York, that the school would be profitable because there was no public institution in the city which was not in debt. On another occasion she complained about the heavy pressure which examinations put on her older girls. At Clapton and Hackney the standard was low because many girls did not enter until they were 12 or 13 years old after attending such inferior schools that the staff had to start from the very beginning. At Portsmouth the head had to face the unwillingness of parents to spend money on the education of their daughters. Numbers had fallen as the result of a letter in a local paper about the girls' manners: 'The prejudice against a Public School for girls is still so strong in this place that it is far more easily confirmed than dispelled.' The reports also give a few more informal glimpses of school life. Several heads commented on the keen interest taken in games, though facilities were often very limited. The head at Kensington reported that her younger girls had bought a rocking horse for the crèche in the poor parish of All Hallows, Southwark:

I am afraid the recipients at first regarded it as a monster of unknown species, and were more alarmed than gratified when hastily and uncomfortably mounted on it by the eager donors; but I have since heard that it has quite won its way into their affections, and was much appreciated at the Christmas treats, to which a good many of our children persuaded their parents to take them.

21 Proprietary and other schools – 2

In 1906 the Girls' Public Day School Company (GPDSC), which had experienced problems about its status as a commercial company paying dividends, was converted into a trust (L. Magnus 1923: 28–30; Kamm 1971: 110). By that time a number of other high schools, established on similar lines by local groups, had been flourishing for a generation. A few examples will illustrate different aspects of the movement. Worcester High School opened in 1883 as the result of the efforts of W. J. Butler, a canon of the cathedral and earlier founder of the sisterhood of St Mary's, Wantage, who had been impressed by the success of the GPDSC Oxford High School. The Worcester school had a religious basis with definite church teaching, and it developed successfully under an outstanding head, Alice Ottley (1883–1912), who resembled Miss Beale in her mixture of deep, rather mystical religious feeling and strong practical talent (James 1914; Noake 1952).

Bristol was a city where the commissioners had failed to set up a first-grade school for girls, and Clifton High School was founded in 1877 to fill the gap. There was a strong link in the early days with the GPDSC group. Mrs Grey's National Union had a branch there, and the first head, Miss M. A. Woods, had been head of the company's Chelsea High School. The new school also had a close link with Clifton College, the headmaster of which, John Percival, had been one of the major promoters, and it enjoyed a solid constituency in the middle-class families of Clifton with their strong intellectual and philanthropic interests. The liberal outlook of the head, Miss Woods, is embodied in her three principles: that the school should be open to girls of good character without social discrimination, that both staff and pupils should enjoy religious freedom, that the school should be non-competitive without prizes, marks, or place-taking (Glenday and Price 1977).

Manchester High School was one of the most successful of these schools set up by civic groups. Among its founders were both Jews and Unitarians and when the scheme incorporating an endowment from the Hulme estates was being made (see p. 208), fears were expressed that insufficient protection was being given for the religious freedom which was a basic feature of the high school. The advocates of this view wished to add a clause that 'the foundation shall be absolutely free from any condition of creed or religious persuasion' (PRO Ed. 27: 2171, 6 February 1883), but the commissioners thought that this would unduly fetter the discretion of the governors and were not ready to accept it. As a result, a leading governor resigned. The dispute is worth noting because it shows the power of religious issues to cause difficulties. On one side were those like Canon Butler of Worcester who wanted a school with a definite credal basis; on the other side were the Manchester Jews and Unitarians, two large communities both of which were prominent in Manchester, who feared the reimposition of religious shackles from which they had only recently escaped.

The Manchester school had two extremely able heads in Elizabeth Day (1874–98) and her successor Sara Burstall (Burstall 1911 and 1933; *BC* VI: 125, 372). The reminiscences of old girls of that time convey a sense of excitement and achievement in their school lives, and numbers rose to 550. Later they fell away as more and more people moved out of the centre of the city into the suburbs, though attempts were made to meet this trend by establishing Pendleton and North Manchester High Schools. There is no means of knowing whether the religious problems already mentioned had anything to do with the decline. When Miss Burstall became head in 1898, there were only 330 girls and a sixth form of half a dozen. One major difficulty was the tendency of many girls to leave early, and Miss Burstall tried to deal with this by setting up parallel courses which did not require Latin and by creating housewifery and secretarial courses. By 1902–3 the numbers had risen to well over the 400 necessary for financial stability, and a new cookery school and biology laboratory were being built. Relationships with the local university were strengthened when in 1899 the inspection and examination of the school was undertaken by the Victoria University instead of by Cambridge as had been the case earlier.

One Scottish school, founded by another local group, was to become the first of a new type of girls' boarding school working on lines similar to the boys' public school with a strong emphasis on organized games and on personal responsibility and independence. This was St Leonard's at St Andrews, founded by a group with strong connections with the university. The first head, Louisa Innes Lumsden (1877–82), was one of the first students at Miss Davies' college at Hitchin. Her successor, Jane Frances Dove (1882–95), who had been an original member of the St Leonard's staff, had also been one of the very early Hitchin/Girton students and one of the first women to take the Natural Sciences Tripos at Cambridge (Grant, McCutcheon, and Sanders n.d.; Lumsden 1933; Bowerman n.d.).

Both Miss Lumsden and Miss Dove had taught at Cheltenham under Miss Beale. Under their able leadership St Leonard's developed rapidly.

It was the first girls' school to have boarding houses as an integral part of its system, and the housemistresses were full members of the teaching staff. Classics and mathematics were prominent in the curriculum, and science was taught from the beginning. All the main team games except football were played, and they were valued not only for the exercise that they provided, but because they were believed to instil valuable qualities of self-control, good temper, and co-operation, and to help to create a strong corporate spirit. In 1895 Miss Dove resigned in order to start a similar school in England, and Wycombe Abbey opened the following year in Buckinghamshire. Miss Dove was headmistress of Wycombe Abbey for fifteen years. One of her old girls, Winifred Knox (Winifred Peck), spoke in later years of her 'intense vitality, fierce driving power, originality, indomitable will and courage: she would obviously charm and bully by turns' (Peck 1952: 112). Winifred had herself been very happy at school, though some of her contemporaries had found it less appealing. She herself thought the routine over-full and considered that the girls, when they left school, were apt to seem too unsophisticated for adult life.

Quite independent in its origins but working on rather similar lines to St Leonard's and Wycombe Abbey was Roedean School in Sussex, the creation of the three Lawrence sisters, Penelope, Dorothy, and Millicent. The sisters were members of a large and supportive family of fourteen children, several of whom were also concerned with the running of the school. In 1885 Dorothy and Millicent persuaded Penelope, who had been a student at Newnham, to join them in opening a school at Brighton. This was very successful, and in 1899 it moved to new buildings at Roedean outside the town (de Zouche 1955). From the time of their first prospectus the sisters put a strong emphasis on team games as part of a system of physical training, believing that this aspect of girls' education had been hitherto neglected. Like the St Leonard's founders, they stressed the self-control and discipline which games helped to produce. It was an exaggeration to claim that games led to neglect of school work; as a rule the two reacted well together (Lawrence, Education Department, *Special Reports* 2 (1898): 145–58). The three sisters maintained their joint management until they retired in 1924. Four years earlier a new Roedean School Company had been set up and Roedean ceased to be a private school. Such a joint headship for almost forty years in what is normally a highly individualistic craft must be unique. It was certainly very successful. By 1914 there were 361 girls (including those in the junior house).

The great majority of the girls' high schools were non-sectarian or interdenominational by deliberate policy. There were, however, a number of denominational foundations, sponsored by members of all the major churches, who were anxious to imbue the new girls' education with a distinctively religious atmosphere. Pioneers among the Anglicans were the Rev. and Mrs Francis Holland. He was minister of Quebec Street Chapel (later the Church of the Annunciation, Marble Arch) and subsequently canon of Canterbury. She became interested in girls' education when considering the needs of his parish. They both admired the work of the non-denominational high schools, but were anxious to provide an education with more specific religious teaching and greater emphasis on worship. In 1877 the Church of England High School for Girls Ltd was formed, and in 1878 a school opened with fifteen pupils in Upper Baker Street, Marylebone. In 1881 a second school was opened in Belgravia, which soon found a permanent home in Graham Street. The two schools flourished, though Holland was no businessman and the administration was organized by Moberly Bell, business manager of *The Times* and father of five pupils. Yet Holland's influence (he died in 1907) permeated the schools. He remained in close touch from his Canterbury canonry and came up to London to teach scripture. 'He desired only', wrote one of the headmistresses of Graham Street, 'that the School should stand for religious education, and help the spiritual life of those who came to it, many or few' (Dunning 1931: 46 (Mary Wolseley-Lewis); Bryant *VCH Middlesex* I (1969): 266; Bryant 1986: 334). It was natural, therefore, that many of the early Graham Street girls went to work in the mission field.

Francis Holland was a member of the committee set up in 1883 by the Central Committee of Diocesan Conferences to consider the foundation of schools for middle-class boys and girls to be conducted on Church of England principles. There were initial difficulties about a conscience clause; the Archbishop of Canterbury decided that this should be included, which lost some support. An appeal for £100,000 was made, and the Church Schools Company (CSC) founded (Bell 1958). Though there were difficulties between the central council and local committees, and very little success in setting up schools for boys, the initiative clearly met a need. By 1897 there were 28 schools in existence with a roll of 2,445 children. Most of the schools were small, but the external examiners' reports were favourable and a small but regular dividend had been paid. The kind of local situation that produced the demand for a school can be illustrated from the example of Hull. CSC opened Hull High School for girls in 1890 after the failure of an attempt to get part of the Hymers' endowment for girls had drawn attention to the need (*VCH Yorks. East Riding* I (1969): 355; see also p. 193).

Nathaniel Woodard, the most active and successful of the Anglican founders of boys' schools, did not wish to extend his work to girls, though he had controlled a girls' school – St Michael's, Bognor – since 1864 (Heeney 1969: 35). The pioneer of girls' education within the Woodard corporation was E. C. Lowe, formerly headmaster of Hurstpierpoint, who became provost of the society of St Mary and St John of Lichfield in 1872. Denstone College for boys was opened in 1873 and

Lowe had ambitious plans for seven girls' schools in the Midlands. In 1874 he opened St Anne's in the Staffordshire village of Abbot's Bromley as a middle-class boarding school for girls with fees of 30–40 guineas per annum. In 1882 St Anne's was followed by St Mary's in the same village, a lower middle-class boarding school with a fee of £21, aiming to give girls a plain education to fit them for home life or to enable them to take posts as 'teachers, needlewomen, nurses, shorthand clerks or the like' (Rice 1947: 110). In both cases the availability of accommodation put limits on numbers. In 1905 there were 120 girls at St Anne's and in 1911 there were 89 at St Mary's (Macpherson 1924: 72; Rice 1947: 229). The two schools were united in 1921. After Woodard's death in 1894 a new constitution of the corporation specifically permitted the divisions to open and to own girls' schools, and their number was considerably increased in the twentieth century (Kirk 1937: 148).

Among the Nonconformist bodies the Quakers had a strong interest in education, and some of their schools like Ackworth had always taught both boys and girls. Their leading girls' school, The Mount at York, was praised in the 1860s by J. G. Fitch, who emphasized the amount of time devoted to intellectual culture as opposed to accomplishments. In the 1890s there were about sixty girls, nearly one-third of them in the training department. The various school societies were active, increased attention was being given to games, and in 1891 a gymnasium fully equipped with Swedish apparatus was opened. By that time it had become possible to appoint only women with university qualifications to the staff (Sturge and Clark 1931).

The Wesleyan Methodists had a school for ministers' daughters at Trinity Hall, Southport, and several girls' schools such as Queenswood in Hertfordshire, Penrhos College in North Wales, and Edgehill College, Bideford, had been opened by the various Methodist bodies. Many of these schools admitted both boarders and day girls (Pritchard 1949: 283, 289–92). The leading Congregationalist institution was Milton Mount College near Gravesend, started in 1871 to educate ministers' daughters and to train teachers. It was well equipped with a laboratory, gymnasium, and domestic science and handwork departments. Nearby there grew up a high school, a middle-class school, and a technical school for girls. In 1893 the high school was given up, and gradually more day pupils were admitted. After 1902 any number of them were allowed so long as they did not hinder the admission of ministerial pupils (Harwood 1959).

The secondary education of Roman Catholic girls was very largely in the hands of the religious orders, which had their own traditions and went their independent ways without much concern for the non-Catholic world around them. By 1850 there were over twenty orders of nuns engaged in educational work at every level (Battersby 1950b: 340), and their numbers grew at the end of the century as many religious sought refuge in England from anti-clerical legislation in France. Many of the

most active orders were French or Belgian, and French traditions persisted strongly in their schools, for example, the prominence given to
the French language and the idea of a curriculum centred on moral
philosophy (Percival 1939: 241).

Volume 2 (Girls) of de Cartaret-Bisson's directory, *Our Schools and
Colleges* (1884), lists eighty Roman Catholic schools and convents,
twenty-four of them in London. Only four of these appear to have been
conducted by secular teachers, and in only four entries were public
examinations such as the Locals or the Preceptors referred to. The eighty
entries in fact represent a rather larger total of schools because in some
cases convents maintained a middle-class day school in addition to the
more socially exclusive school, which sometimes took only boarders and
sometimes day pupils as well. In some places the sisters also ran an
elementary school for poor children. The prospectus of the boarding
school of the Notre Dame sisters at Blackburn, dating from the 1860s,
probably gives a fairly typical picture of the scholastic programme:
'Religious Instruction, the English and French Languages, Sacred and
Profane History, Geography, the use of the Globes, Arithmetic, Book-
keeping, Epistolary Correspondence, Natural Philosophy, Botany, Plain
& Ornamental Needlework.' The fees were 28 guineas a year. Music,
German, Italian, and drawing and painting were extras, as was laundry
(Linscott 1966: 146).

The nuns tended to be conservative in their educational philosophy,
but the teaching they gave was thorough, and they were certainly neither
inefficient nor reactionary. Two of the leading figures in England were
both converts. The American Mother Cornelia Connelly (1809–79), founder of the Society of the Holy Child Jesus, produced a systematic and
forward-looking book of studies for her Order in 1863 (Marmion 1984;
HSE: 181). In 1911 Mother Janet Erskine Stuart published *The Education
of Catholic Girls*. Janet Stuart had been brought up in an East Midland
rectory, and had as a girl been influenced by Edward Thring. In 1879
she became a Roman Catholic. Three years later she joined the Society
of the Sacred Heart and was principal of their house at Roehampton
from 1894 to 1911 (Monahan 1922).

The Education of Catholic Girls lays heavy stress on religion and on
purity of character. In the curriculum little emphasis is given to mathematics and experimental natural science, though children are said to
learn much from nature study. Languages, both native and foreign, make
a major contribution towards training for life. Art demands a spirit of
renunciation, and the love of beauty must be used in the service of faith.
High standards of manners and behaviour must be demanded because
they are linked with the self-sacrifice and devotion expressed in religion.
Mother Stuart voiced her doubts about what had been achieved by the
higher education of women. The students should have aimed at self-
restraint, but many of them were seeking emancipation from control.

Quietness, self-discipline, and subordination were appropriate for women. They were not created to innovate.

Mother Stuart's ideas were very different from those of the more radical women educators. Her ideal is basically aristocratic. Little is said about examinations or careers, and where such topics are mentioned, it is with distrust and dislike. The discussion of higher education for women poses an ideal quite different from that thought appropriate for men. Nothing is said about the girl who needs to use her education to earn her own living. Everything said seems to relate to the girl of good family who is being prepared for home and family duties. The emphasis is very much on discipline, self-control, submission, and what reads like a fear of independence and self-expression, which are expected to lead to the breakdown of moral and spiritual order. The general objectives of the women educators of the time have still to be discussed. There was in fact a surprising amount of common ground between Mother Stuart and the more conservative, spiritually-oriented heads like Dorothea Beale and Alice Ottley. Their objectives too were traditional in many ways.

One of Mother Stuart's points – her emphasis on high standards of manners and behaviour – was a characteristic of all the convent schools, and one that appealed strongly to parents, Roman Catholic and non-Roman Catholic alike. When HM inspectors began to visit these schools in the early twentieth century, they commented very favourably on the refinement and good taste which they found in them (Summerfield 1987: 162). M. E. Sadler's comments in his surveys were similar. At Liverpool, for example, he was greatly impressed by the range of institutions managed by the Notre Dame sisters, including the first Roman Catholic women's training college, established in 1855. The lasting impression, he wrote, was not of size or numbers: 'It is rather the sense of quiet, cheerful, untiring labour and care for each individual that lingers in his mind, and comes back vividly to his thoughts as he recalls what he heard and saw' (Sadler 1904a: 25–6).

22 The girls' schools and their objectives

After considering the development of the schools, it is time to examine the objectives of those who founded them. In one sense the founders of the women's movement were revolutionaries because they were fighting to secure new opportunities for women, and that has been the generally accepted historical interpretation of the movement. Since the late 1970s many women scholars have urged that this view exaggerates the extent of the changes that took place (Burstyn 1977: 11–19). Their general argument runs like this. Though the traditional roles of women were modified by the changes, they were not abandoned. Women continued to live their lives in a family structure that was still dominated by men. Men were the leaders of opinion, the breadwinners of the upper- or middle-class family, and women had to work within the narrow limits laid down by these social and sexual relationships. Women, once they had become better educated, certainly found it easier to earn a living and in some cases to follow a professional career. Yet, as a general rule, they were trained, not to function as independent persons, but to become intelligent wives and mothers, more equal companions for their husbands and sons, better equipped to engage in social or voluntary work outside the home. On this line of argument the changes look much less like a revolution, much more like a reform within structures that remained largely unchanged and that still left women in a distinctly inferior position.

The advocates of the new high schools and colleges had gained much support, but as we have seen had also attracted much resistance. Sometimes the diehard view comes out most clearly in some local debate, remote from London and the centres of power. For example, the select committee of 1886 heard evidence about a plan to turn an old boys' grammar school endowment into a new girls' high school at Blandford in Dorset. The plan was stoutly opposed by the rector, the Rev. C. H. Fynes Clinton (*PP* 1886 IX: 331–4: 5,020–112). He claimed that a GPDSC school which had been set up at Weymouth had been a failure. 'They have a B.A. or M.A. or whatever it is from Girton or elsewhere as head mistress; it has the whole high pressure system.' Mr Clinton and those who thought like him complained that this 'high pressure system' made women unfeminine. It was not appropriate that they should undertake careers, and if they did so, they would reduce opportunities for men and thus harm the interests of families who depended on a male breadwinner. Physiological arguments were brought forward too. Over-education would produce overstrain and this physical sterility. Women's minds were not creative or original and their brains were less developed in size and structure than men's (Burstyn 1980).

Statements of this kind were strongly rebutted by the headmistresses nd those who supported the new schools, but they set up a constant barrage of criticism and created a situation in which the heads had to be hyper-cautious to avoid giving hostages of fortune to their enemies. Many people, for instance, were unwilling to accept that high schools should admit girls from a wide range of social backgrounds (see p. 220). Such social prejudices reinforced the arguments of the opposition and they help to explain the existence of two rules which helped to cut down the amount of social mixing between pupils. Many schools had a silence rule – that conversation was not allowed at all on school premises, except during morning break. Also quite common was the walking rule – that girls might walk to and from school together only with the approval of their parents, certified to the school authorities (Godber and Hutchins 1982: 370, 376). The dilemmas confronting headmistresses are apparent in a report from the head of the Perse School for Girls in Cambridge to her governors (March 1887), in which Miss Street commented that it was undesirable to send to parents a copy of the school list:

> This seems to me so very unwise in a place like Cambridge. I fear it will do a great deal of harm, considering the strong social feelings of Town and Gown. This is equally strong on both sides, and the Public School system, which must ignore such prejudices, is not yet so fully established in Cambridge that we can afford to draw attention too plainly to the mixture of classes.
>
> (M. A. Scott 1981: 29–30)

The women's problem has been called that of 'double conformity' (Delamont and Duffin 1978: 140). On the one hand, educated women had to conform fully to the conventional standards of ladylike behaviour. On the other hand, they were required to take the same academic courses as men and to achieve good results on the same tests. The issues are clearly set out in the conflicting policies of the two Cambridge women's colleges. Miss Davies at Girton insisted that women should omit nothing from the university requirements laid down for men. Miss Clough and the Newnham group were prepared to sit more lightly to the regulations and to accept concessions on a path which was difficult enough for the women pioneers in any case. The rigorist line at least met the argument that 'separate but equal' facilities may be separate, but are never equal, and that those who accept concessions are always accused of taking the soft option.

When the student at high school or college had negotiated all the hazards the question remained of the uses to which her hard-won education was to be put. The women's movement in education has often been interpreted as a means of enabling women to qualify for careers, particularly since, because there were more women than men in the population, many of them would not be able to marry. Certainly better training for careers had been one objective of the movement (*HSE*: 296). Miss Buss once wrote of the misery of women of her own class for want of a good elementary training and of her determination to alleviate the situation of those 'brought up "to be married and taken care of", and left alone in the world destitute' (Ridley 1895: 93).

Career opportunities were important for some women, but they were not the principal objective of the reformers. Of course, the position varied from school to school and from family to family. The movement for better secondary education affected principally upper- and middle-class girls whose families did not expect their daughters to work in gainful occupations. In middle/second-grade schools girls took up clerical work, work in the Post Office, and teaching. The great majority – the girls in the elementary schools – were unaffected by secondary education until the twentieth century.

When headmistresses wrote about their objectives for their pupils, they often did so either in terms of personal development or of the contribution which they would make to family life. Miss Beale herself forms an interesting example. Both she and her school were rather set apart from pressures for monetary reward. She was a woman of some means, and most of the Cheltenham girls were not likely to need to earn their own livings (Faithfull 1924: 159). In an article of 1866, Miss Beale had answered the question: 'What is the use of a girl learning this or that?' by saying that the development of all the human powers was a good in itself (Beale 1866: 509–24). Thirty years later she said that pupils must be taught to know the truth, to feel nobly, and to act rightly. She justified women pursuing the study of natural science to an advanced stage on the ground that it would enable them to become the companions of able men, the friends of their brothers, the first teachers of their sons (Beale, Soulsby, and Dove 1898: 202, 256–7). Self-development is understood in a rather abstract sense, and certainly not within the context of professional life and work. Secondly, in the example given, what has been learnt is not so much a personal possession but rather something that is fulfilled in relation to husbands, brothers, children – the family environment broadened and put to new uses but not radically changed.

It has been said that the headmistresses aimed to train an 'educated, thinking and socially useful woman' (Hunt 1984: 130), and in most cases they envisaged that these qualities would be exercised within the life of the family. Some quite casual comments of the day pick up the point. The headmaster of Bromsgrove told the girls of Worcester High School at their speech day in 1895: 'it is the cultivation of home life which is the duty of girls. To train themselves to be daughters, sisters, and possibly someday wives and mothers, is the highest aim of all' (Noake 1952: 47). The examiner at Notting Hill High School, commenting on the high intellectual standards of the senior girls, added:

> It is difficult to overrate the effect on English social life from this stream of brilliant girls poured annually into our drawing rooms, if only they keep up after leaving school the intellectual habits and temperament with which it has endowed them.
>
> (*GPDSC Minutes and Examiners Reports* 1884: 31)

It may be thought that men, like the Bromsgrove head and the GPDSC examiner, might be expected to argue like this. Yet some at least of the headmistresses expressed similar views. Alice Ottley of Worcester who, like Dorothea Beale, was on the conservative wing (Pedersen 1981: 463–88), said that home was the first place in which our vocation to be saints was to be fulfilled. Home life demanded self-sacrifice and deference to the wills of those in authority. Older girls who were going home to look after younger brothers and sisters would find more happiness in those duties than in seeking their own pleasure (James 1914: 47–8). The tone is very similar to that of Janet Stuart's *Education of Catholic Girls*. And Elizabeth Hughes, first head of the Cambridge Training College, who was a much more secular-minded figure than either Miss Ottley or Mother Stuart, argued for increased expenditure on girls' education because it would provide homes with better educated wives and mothers (Bremner 1897: viii).

Some families offered much support to their ambitious daughters, but there were many clashes between the claims of home and the aspirations for work in the outside world which could not always be settled by the regime of self-sacrifice and submission advised by Miss Ottley. Grace Hadow (1875–1940), a parson's daughter, later head of the Oxford Society of Home Students and a pioneer in social work, is an interesting example. At the age of 16 she was sent to Truro High School, whose head, Miss Arnold, asked her in 1893 to stay on for a further year or more as a pupil-teacher. Grace was anxious to accept, but she knew that her mother was anxious to have her at home to help with the parish and the private pupils studying at the vicarage. The situation was saved by her mother giving up the private pupils and her eldest brother promising to make up the loss of family income. Grace was able to have another year at school, though she did not go up to Somerville until some years later (*DNB* 1931–40; Deneke 1946: 18–21).

Grace Hadow's story must have been fairly typical, at least for those who were able to achieve their ambitions, but it does bring out the tensions which many educated women experienced. The concept that their daughters should be employed and earn a salary was something which many families found very difficult to accept. Mary Alice Douglas, daughter of a Worcestershire clergyman, who had taught under Miss Ottley at Worcester, was appointed head of the Godolphin School, Salisbury, in October 1889. One of her early pupils, the daughter of another clergyman in the same county, wrote later that her father admired Miss Douglas and thought the school very lucky to secure her, but he was not at all anxious that his own daughter should follow the same career:

> To-day, when it is taken for granted that girls as well as boys should be prepared for a career of independence, the home claims are naturally and easily put aside even if they are admitted to exist. It was not so forty years ago. I can remember how some of the parents of my friends and contemporaries were puzzled and even shocked and fearful of the future for me when I did take up teaching.
>
> (Douglas and Ash 1928: 73–4)

As the idea gradually became accepted that women should be trained for careers, a choice was established between the professions and the home (Delamont and Duffin 1978: 164–87 (Sara Delamont)). Career women remained celibate. Married women were involved with their families or with voluntary social work, which in an age of little state activity in such matters offered them much wider opportunities than would be available to similar people today (Godber and Hutchins (1982: 474). The deeply religious motivation of many of the early leaders meant that self-sacrifice and humility were highly esteemed qualities. In the case of career women another set of tensions sometimes developed between these ideals, which were considered especially womanly, and their professional obligations and ambitions (Burstyn 1980: 147; Dyhouse 1981: 30, 74–5, 144). Many professional women retained close ties with their own families and gained much support from them. For others the new institutions, like boarding schools, colleges, and hospitals, created a substitute family environment in which intense personal relationships sometimes grew up (Vicinus 1985).

A picture can be built up from school records of the careers followed by their old girls. The magazines of Edgbaston High School, Birmingham, recorded in about 1890 that two old girls had pictures in the Royal Academy. One had been decorated by the Sultan of Turkey for her work as head of the English Girls' High School in Constantinople, and another was in charge of the Clapham Maternity Hospital. One old girl had published a volume of Latin dialogues, and others recorded included an historian, a chicken farmer, and a professional singer. A few years later a group of old girls was running a kindergarten for poor children in the Warwick Road (Whitcut 1976: 51). At the turn of the century the GPDSC Paddington and Maida Vale High School had old pupils at

Newnham, Westfield, and Somerville Colleges. One was a clerk in the Bank of England, one had begun training as a rent-collector, one had entered the Domestic Economy Training School at Battersea Polytechnic, there were clerks in the Prudential Assurance Company, and another old girl had passed the highly competitive examination for the Post Office Telephone service (Bryant, *VCH Middlesex* I (1969): 269).

Two old girls of another GPDSC school, Norwich, provide examples of the wider opportunities opening to women of ability. Ethel Nucella Williams (1879–82) was one of the first women doctors to practise in Newcastle. She was a pioneer in the women's suffrage movement, she worked in the two world wars for refugees, and she was active in the League of Nations Union and the National Council of Women. Lily Roberts was one of the first students at the school (1875–8), one of the first students at Somerville, and an original member of the staff of Bedford High School. Later she was headmistress for thirty-three years at Bradford Girls' Grammar School, and she served on educational delegations to the USA and to India (*Norwich High School 1875–1950* n.d.: 112–13).

Not many girls had such good careers and many of those who started on professional work gave it up when they married. At a lower level many women found work as clerks, telegraphists, and telephonists, and such posts were very attractive to candidates from lower middle-class/artisan families, who generally left school at 14 or 15. Table 22.1 shows the occupations of pupils from two London middle schools who had formerly attended elementary schools. Those in List 1 had been free scholars; those in List 2 had been fee-payers.

Table 22.1 Occupations of former pupils (girls) from two London middle schools, *c.* 1890

List 1		List 2	
Elementary teachers	21	At home	9
Post Office and telegraph clerks and sorters	18	Book-keepers and clerks	8
		Elementary teachers	7
At home	10	Post Office and telegraph clerks	6
Milliners	5		
Dressmakers	6	Shop assistants	5
Clerks	4	Dressmakers	4
Shop assistants	4	Kindergarten teachers	1
Private school teachers	3	Teaching brother and sisters	1
Typewriters	2		
Total	73	Total	41

Source: Collet, in Acland and Llewellyn Smith (eds), *Studies in Secondary Education* (1892: 218–19).

Table 22.1 gives some idea of the opportunities available in London to those who had gone through the lower ranges of secondary schooling.

As might be expected, there were a large number of teachers of various kinds, though it was said that secondary school girls were unwilling to become teachers in elementary schools. In addition to clerks and post office workers, there is a sizeable group of milliners, dressmakers, and shop assistants. In these lists not many girls are 'at home'. At that social level most of them needed to earn their own livings. Of the high school population in general, recruited at a higher social level than this, it is not possible to estimate what proportion went back into the family circle and what proportion into higher training and paid work. It would be a reasonable guess that in 1900 the first group would have been much larger than the second (Bowerman n.d.: 57; Stack 1963: 9). Though the search for better career opportunities was certainly one objective of the women's education movement, its importance can be exaggerated.

Among the professional groups which women entered the teachers were of special importance, both because they were the most numerous and because without their skill and devotion the new girls' education would never have been able to develop as it did. The crucial role of the headmistresses has already been emphasized. Many of the early heads were young women, not highly qualified because few opportunities were open to them. They were captains on a voyage of great adventure. They had everything to discover on the way, something that helps to explain the great sense of excitement which pervaded both the school staffs and their pupils in the early days. Excitement would not last for ever; it was reinforced by the creation of a body of trained teachers. As we have seen, teacher training had been one of the major interests of the Shirreff sisters. Miss Beale had established the two St Hilda's Colleges, at Oxford and at Cheltenham. Schools like the Mary Datchelor at Camberwell had set up school-based training programmes. Miss Buss had played a large part in setting up the Cambridge Training College for Women (1885). For teachers of young children the Froebel Education Institute opened in 1894, and Charlotte Mason started the House of Education at Ambleside for training home governesses in 1892 (Cholmondeley 1960: 37). Teaching also attracted many of the students at the women's colleges. Fifty-two per cent of the students who left Newnham between October 1871 and June 1893 were engaged as teachers (*BC* I: 238).

One professional achievement exclusive to women was the formation of a corps of specialist physical training teachers. Men did not enter this field until the 1940s, so the women physical educators were able to set their own standards of excellence. The pioneer was the Swede, Martina Bergman-Österberg, who introduced the system of Swedish gymnastics, first into the schools of the London School Board and later in her own training college, opened at Hampstead in 1885 and moved to Dartford in Kent in 1895. Mme Österberg was followed by other women who set up colleges – Dorette Wilke (Chelsea), Rhoda Anstey (at Erdington, near Birmingham), Irene Marsh (Liverpool), and Margaret Stansfeld

(Bedford). At a time when games and physical exercise were being taken much more seriously in girls' schools and when there was a great deal of concern about health, the physical training mistress became an essential member of staff in girls' secondary schools and a valued inspector/adviser in local authorities. She organized both games and gymnastics, her subject had a clear link with discipline and character formation, she often became a central figure in her school. The physical training colleges and their students made a distinctive contribution to girls' secondary education in the first half of the twentieth century (S. Fletcher 1984; McCrone 1988: 101–19; May 1969).

23 The internal life of girls' schools

The internal life of the girls' schools can conveniently be considered under three headings: curriculum; games and social life; health. The curriculum followed much the same lines as that of the boys' schools, though there was a better balance between the different subjects. There was nothing in the high schools like the traditional emphasis in boys' schools on the classics. Since girls soon began to take the same public examinations, they necessarily followed the same curriculum. They have often been criticized for doing so, yet it was very important in the early days that they should be seen to succeed in the same tests and at the same standards as the boys. There is a rather touching story about an excited Miss Buss announcing to the school that a woman, Philippa Garrett Fawcett, had been placed above the senior wrangler in the Mathematical Tripos of 1890. Miss Buss told the school how, when she had been examined by the Schools Inquiry Commission, she had been asked whether she thought that girls would be able to learn mathematics. She had replied that they could, and would do so. 'Then, she almost shouted, "Today these gentlemen have their answer", and more quietly, "I wonder how many of them are remembering, as I am remembering, their question to me twenty-five years ago, and my answer?" ' (Scrimgeour 1950: 64).

Sara Burstall recalled that she had been well taught mathematics at the North London in the mid–1870s by Mrs Bryant, and the school retained a good reputation for teaching the subject (Burstall 1933: 54–5). The classical scholar, W. H. D. Rouse, wrote in 1898 that it was not to be expected that classics should receive the same amount of attention as they did in boys' schools. The staples of girls' education, he thought, had always been music, drawing, and modern languages (Beale, Soulsby and Dove 1898: 67). Science teaching came in rather slowly. Some schools had good facilities, but in general laboratory accommodation was poor. Miss Gadesden's picture in 1901 was not very favourable. Some progress was being made, but little time was allowed and much of the teaching was still on 'the old didactic lines', though many schools used heuristic or experimental methods (R. D. Roberts 1901: 100). Even at

Cheltenham around 1890 science was still taught by demonstration. The teacher did the experiment before the class, and the girls wrote down in their notebooks what they had seen (Steadman 1931: 44). At the turn of the century some schools introduced commercial courses, but the heads tended to approach these much more as a means of instilling accuracy and neatness than as a means of acquiring technical skills (Milburn 1969: 254; Bryant 1986: 346–7).

Mrs Bryant wrote an outline of the curriculum in 1898, which is very similar to the GPDSC prospectuses for the same period (Education Department, *Special Reports* 2 (1898): 99–123; Zimmern 1898: 66–7). Girls and boys should, Mrs Bryant argued, be treated on the same broad lines, though what the girls did was affected by the special function of women in 'the making of the home and the preservation of the social side of society'. The complete course for girls should consist of the humanities, science (including mathematics), art, religion, and morality. French and German were important, though only two languages should be studied at a time. In a first-grade school there should be Latin and some Greek, though this did not mean that girls should spend as much time on them as boys did. Moreover they should be started later in the course than modern languages. Physical science should begin at 11 or 12 years old with a course of elementary physics followed by chemistry. The foundations of biology should be laid early, and as a subject it was especially useful for the backward and for the very young. Art, music, and gymnastics should be included, as well as hygiene and domestic economy. No problems in teaching religious knowledge had occurred in the secondary schools. Biblical literature and history should be taught, together with the basic Christian truths and everyday morality.

Mrs Bryant's programme is a good deal better balanced than that offered in most of the boys' schools of the day. The main difference in organization – as opposed to curriculum in the strict sense – was the general prevalence in girls' schools of the long four-hour morning session with the afternoons free for art and music, for games, for preparation, and in day schools for home and family life. This plan had been introduced by Miss Beale at Cheltenham in 1864. Initially, she met with strong resistance, but this soon died away. The plan was adopted by Miss Buss in 1865 and the GPDSC used it generally in their time-tables (Raikes 1908: 121–3). Miss Burstall described it as the normal practice in the high schools, and, though it was sometimes said that the long morning of study put strains upon the girls, the free afternoon did provide considerable flexibility (Burstall 1907: 52–3).

Games played an increasingly important part in girls' activities by 1900, and the attention given to them was closely related to the general debate about health and fitness, which will be discussed later. The advocates of games generally defended them on two grounds – that exercise was an aid to concentration and intellectual work, and that games promoted qualities of co-operation, unselfishness, judgement, and self-reliance, which were invaluable morally. The second argument is particularly identified with the leaders of the boarding school group like Louisa Lumsden, Jane Frances Dove, and Penelope Lawrence (Lawrence, Education Department *Special Reports* 2 (1898): 145–58; Beale, Soulsby, and Dove 1898: 396–423 (J. F. Dove); Delamont and Duffin 1978: 92–133 (Paul Atkinson)). However, advocacy of games and physical exercise was not confined to them. Sheffield High School (GPDSC) was one of the first in the country to have a gymnasium (1884), and the head, Mrs Woodhouse, described the school programme of physical tests. Games were voluntary, but two hours daily exercise was considered necessary, and enquiries were made to ensure that this was taken (Mrs Woodhouse *Special Reports* 2 (1898): 133–44; Kamm 1971: 75).

Games were never as important in girls' schools as in boys'. Yet they played a large part in the life of the Oxford and Cambridge women's colleges, and the old students took their enthusiasm with them when they went to teach in the high schools (McCrone 1988: 53). Miss Buss was interested in gymnastics, swimming, netball, and athletic sports. Mrs Bryant introduced hockey, and a sports ground was acquired in 1909. Miss Beale, though she made concessions in her later years, was always hesitant. To the end of her life she would allow no outside matches; there was some coaching but not much (Steadman 1931: 84, 155). Some parents thought games unladylike, or feared that their daughters would catch colds and chills, like the Oxford High School mother who insisted that her daughter played hockey 'in a long green pelisse with a tippet edged with black lambswool and a green matching cap with a feather'! (Stack 1963: 61–2).

The absurdity of such garments on the hockey field led to the spread of freer and less constricting games clothes and to the beginnings of dress reform for women (Grant, McCutcheon, and Sanders n.d.: 102). In general the games movement marks an important stage in their emancipation. It gave them a new sense of personal freedom, a new command over their bodies, and a stake in areas of social life which had been entirely male-dominated. Games elicited both new skills and new confidence. Nor must the impact of the safety bicycle be forgotten, since it increased mobility and personal freedom for women even more than for men.

The health of girls and young women was a constant subject of debate at the end of the nineteenth century. Many people believed that more intensive education led to overstrain and to harmful physical effects as the human frame became overstretched. The issues were not entirely limited to girls' education; there was, for example, a controversy in the 1880s about over-pressure in the elementary schools, in which some medical men expressed serious concern (Robertson 1972: 315–23). However much of the criticism was concentrated on the girls' schools. Dr

Alexander Keiller told the Social Science Association in 1880 that children developed at very different rates and could not all be treated alike. Much damage was done by brain fatigue and excess of mental work: 'The present system of educating young females is utterly imprudent and wrong' (*TSSA* 1880: 430; 1883: 354–94).

The critics never had it all their own way. Headmistresses were able to show that great care had been taken to see that girls worked under healthy conditions. Miss Buss, for example, began a system of regular medical inspections in 1882 (Delamont and Duffin 1978: 110; *BC* V: 375–9 (Dr Julia Cock)). Miss Burstall claimed that the pioneers took great care to see that the girls were strong and healthy (Burstall 1907: 91). Many headmistresses thought that girls' health was damaged much less by school and college study than by idleness and the want of any real objectives in life.

The critics maintained their attack, which was a two-fold one. Immediately there was the danger of mental overstrain resulting from long hours of homework, testing competitive examinations, and the general pressure to do well. But the second attack was the more profound: that these mental problems had physical consequences. Girls had only a limited amount of physical energy. If they misused it, that would lead to serious physiological consequences, to sterility, to the inability to bring up children, and to a general weakening of the reproductive processes (Social Science Association *Sessional Proceedings* (1879–80): 130 (Dr Andrew Clark)). Once again the women fought back. Emily Pfeiffer and Mrs Sidgwick of Newnham both published surveys in the 1880s which failed to find any evidence that higher education involved danger to women's health or to their reproductive capacities (Dyhouse 1981: 157–8). There was also a good deal of debate about the effects of games and physical exercise. The arguments of the supporters have already been examined. The critics used the overstrain argument once again, claiming that games made excessive demands on women's physical capacities at an age when energies needed to be reserved for marriage and motherhood.

At the end of the century the debate about health and overstrain was caught up into the wider arguments about Social Darwinism – that there was an active competition between the different races for success and dominance in the world. The Social Darwinists attempted to apply the ideas of biological evolution to politics. Stress was laid on the differences between men and women since it was believed that in higher evolutionary stages there was greater differentiation between the sexes. There was a fear of racial degeneration, and women were seen primarily as homemakers and guardians of the future of the race. According to this line of thought the pioneer women educators had gone too far in assimilating women's education to that of men. What was needed for girls was more emphasis on domestic subjects and on a distinctively feminine curriculum.

This school of thought was only beginning to be prominent at the time of the Education Act of 1902, but it was influential in the new century when much stress was laid on the concept of national efficiency in all sectors of life (Dyhouse 1976: 41–58; and 1977: 21–35).

Though the development of women's education had never been free from controversy, the leaders of the movement could, in the early years of the twentieth century, look back with much satisfaction on what had been achieved. Women had not obtained their fair share of the old educational endowments, nor had they freed themselves from many of the shackles laid on them by society. The headmistresses had been forced to tread a very narrow path with the demands of innovation on one side and the canons of social responsibility on the other. Working-class girls were really untouched by the changes, but for their middle- and upper-class sisters much had been done. It had been proved that, intellectually, women could compete on equal terms with men. Women had become teachers and doctors and, at a lower level, were filling more and more clerical posts. The many educated women who remained at home had widened their interests in social work and community life. Games had brought to many women a new sense of achievement and of independence. Through all these activities women had enlarged their potentialities and widened their friendships. Any study of the changes must fail unless it conveys something of the sense of excitement felt by that first generation of teachers and students. They had embarked on uncharted seas, and they needed all their courage and wisdom to make a safe landfall. It is remarkable, when the perils of navigation are remembered, that so many of the voyages were a success.

Conclusion

Matthew Arnold, writing in the 1860s, had drawn a sharp contrast between the disorder of English secondary education and the effective state organization, which had been developed in France, Germany, and Switzerland. The results for the English middle classes were very harmful because in many parts of the country there were no good secondary schools at all. His criticisms remained valid until the end of the century. The state had, as we have seen, taken an active part in policy-making in many instances. The problem was that, since there was no coherent plan, the energies exhibited by a body like the Department of Science and Art were apt to add to the confusion. It has recently been argued that in Western Europe generally the more academic and less applied forms of learning enjoyed more prestige than more practical studies, and were the preserve of the higher social classes (Müller, Ringer, and Simon 1987). In Prussia the Gymnasium became more exclusive at the end of the nineteenth century in order to defend the interests of its upper-class clientele against the dangers of excessive social mobility. In France a second-grade modern curriculum and a third-grade higher primary school developed alongside the lycée with its strong, upper middle-class connections. In England the three grades of the Taunton Report reflect a similar pattern. The highest social and academic standing was enjoyed by the public schools which, unlike the lycée or the Gymnasium, were private foundations over which the state exercised no control after the passing of the Public Schools Act of 1868. Matthew Arnold had acknowledged that the best of the public schools were excellent. Their very prestige made it seem less important that the state should create a general system of secondary education for the whole country.

By 1870 the public schools had become the models which less prestigious institutions attempted to emulate. From the nine schools of the Clarendon Inquiry they had expanded to form, by 1900, a community of about 100 schools, though these varied greatly in rank and prestige among themselves. It has already been suggested that the role of the late nineteenth- early twentieth-century public school was social rather than intellectual. In their social role they were highly successful because they gave English society a leadership which was popular and generally acceptable. They had a major influence on other schools, particularly through masters who had been boys or members of staff, and who carried the ideal to schools all over the country which sprouted caps and colours, games and prefects of the approved type. Intellectually the public schools had been less successful. The more important of them educated many able boys, but the general academic level was not high, and far more attention was given to the successes of the playing-field than to those of the classroom. The prestige of the athlete reached its height at the turn of the century. In so far as intellectual activity was valued, it was the classics which ranked the highest and scientific and technological subjects the lowest. The public school ethos was not likely to promote the economic interests of a country becoming very conscious that it was falling behind in the international economic race.

If the public schools did little for the country's economic future, and if they perpetuated an anti-intellectual cast of thought among their old boys, what values did they promote? The answer has been suggested in the analysis of Henry Newbolt's two poems in Chapter 12. Pre-eminent was the concept of gentlemanly behaviour, the good fighter, the brave loser, the team player loyal to his friends. The outward trappings were Christian; what lay behind them was a secularized creed of courage and good form. Such an ethos looked to the public service, the army and navy, and especially the Empire and Britain overseas. At home the schools promoted the concept of an exclusive social group. Though in a country where great fortunes had been made and lost, there was in fact much social mobility, public school men saw themselves as part of a leadership circle which demanded complete assimilation from those it deigned to admit and set up strict barriers against those who were outside. In H. A. Vachell's novel about Harrow, *The Hill* (1905), Scaife, the son of a parvenu who has made a large fortune, is sent to Harrow to achieve the social acceptance which could not be gained entirely by his father's money. The author makes it very clear that, wealth or no, Scaife is not quite a gentleman. It is difficult to avoid the conclusion that by 1900 the atmosphere of the public schools, however great their prestige, had become more narrow, more internalized upon their own concerns, more remote from the true needs and interests of the country. One sign of the change, which has already been mentioned, was the weakening in creative leadership. The system had become the victim of its own success, imprisoned in a straitjacket of ideas which had once been new and challenging.

In Part I the fortunes of the endowed grammar schools were studied in detail. The hope that the reform of the old endowments would lay the foundation of a national system of secondary schools had never been fulfilled. Though the Endowed Schools and Charity Commissioners had certainly achieved important reforms and in consequence the number of pupils in the schools had greatly increased, the improvements gained seem hardly proportionate to the effort expended. As we have seen, the fate of individual schools had varied greatly, and the implementation of new schemes implied no guarantee of success. As one of the speakers at the Oxford Conference of 1893 remarked about one rural district: 'You may give an endowed school an admirable governing body, an admirable body of statutes and a good Headmaster, but you cannot by any legislation give him pupils' (Oxford Conference 1893: 207). In some cases the grammar schools were squeezed between their competitors. At one end the popularity of the public boarding schools drew some boys away. At the other, in towns where school boards had created higher grade schools, boys whose parents wanted a 'modern' type of education and an early leaving age, went to those schools and not to the local grammar school.

The last decade of the nineteenth century was a difficult time for the grammar schools. For many of them the situation began to change when the grants of the technical education committees made it possible to employ more staff and to provide buildings and equipment for science teaching. After 1902 most of the grammar schools were financed and controlled by the local authorities. It was the injection of public funds which transformed the situation. The opinion expressed by G. W. Hastings at the Social Science Association meeting in 1872 remained true thirty years later: 'Nothing less than the collective action of the nation can give us the supply of secondary schools which we require, and place our middle classes on an educational equality with other countries' (*TSSA* 1872: 59).

It is very difficult to assess how great was the demand for secondary education in this period. In general it remained a middle-class preserve, though scholarships had been established to provide openings for poor but able pupils. The parentage and future careers of boys in grammar and higher grade schools, both fee-payers and scholarship holders, have been reviewed in Chapters 7 and 10, and the comparatively small amount of information available about girls in Chapter 19. Though there was general agreement that poor but able children should be given the chance of a better education, it was thought that the numbers would be quite small, and there was always anxiety about producing too many well-educated people who would not be able to find suitable work. The material collected by the Bryce Commission suggests that class barriers were getting lower, though such changes affected boys more than girls. As general living standards rose, more people wanted and could pay for better education for their children, though it was difficult to run efficient schools at a fee that was both economic and yet within the means of lower middle-class or skilled artisan parents.

Part of the demand had been met, particularly in the industrial towns of the north, through the creation of the higher grade schools. Many of the larger school boards had started these schools because they met a need for more advanced levels of work after the basic demands for elementary education had been met. The growth of these schools, of the Science and Art Department, and of the technical education committees has been examined in Part II. By the mid–1890s all these bodies were supporting what was in effect a publicly financed system of secondary education, though their activity was uncoordinated and the very success of the different agencies produced major problems of structure and planning. Moreover this 'new secondary education' with its scientific/technological emphasis aroused the fears and jealousies of the supporters of the traditional grammar schools.

Most of what has been said so far in this chapter relates primarily to the education of boys. One of the major achievements of the period had been the creation of a network of schools, some endowed, some proprietary, for the secondary education of girls, with which must be linked the development of women's higher education in colleges and universities. At the time of the Taunton Commission the only schools available to girls were private schools, many of them of a poor standard. Within a generation girls had been given opportunities for secondary and higher education as good as those available to boys. The new movement was led by a number of very able women, and it soon became clear that girls could compete with boys on equal terms. The changes were not all plain sailing, and the difficulties experienced by the pioneers have been dealt with in Part V. At the end of the nineteenth century there was a reaction in some quarters which suggested that the assimilation between boys' and girls' studies had gone too far. However, by that time, the solid achievements of the women's movement in education were there for all to see, and the clock was not likely to be turned back. In the new century the issue of women's claim to equal educational opportunities was to merge into the wider question of women's political rights.

Between 1870 and 1900 the public schools had expanded, the grammar schools had been reformed, the girls' high schools had been created, and in some areas higher-grade schools had been established. All of these were institutions which were publicly managed or owned, commonly by boards of trustees or proprietors who either stood to make no personal profit or, like the GPDSC, offered a strictly limited dividend to their shareholders. Public management, as thus defined, preceded public ownership in many cases. Those who suffered from the change were the private school masters and mistresses, who in the first half of the nineteenth century had controlled much of the secondary education of boys and almost all that of girls. The speed of the decline of the private schools can, as has been shown in Part IV, be exaggerated, and in 1900 they were still important, particularly for girls. The Bryce Commission gave them a good deal of attention, and anxiety was expressed that efficient private schools should be guaranteed a place within a future public system. The reasons why this did not happen are a matter of twentieth- rather than of nineteenth-century history. One of the weaknesses of the private schools was the fact that their heads did not combine effectively to promote their cause. Most of them were individualists who wanted only to be left alone and who did not aspire to influence public policies. The Private Schools Association was a much less powerful pressure group than the Incorporated Association of Headmasters, the organization of the secondary heads.

By the date of the Bryce Report there were two crucial questions in educational planning: what part was the state to play in it, and in what ways was public control to be organized at national and local levels? A national ministry of education was soon to be created by the Board of Education Act of 1899. At local level the choice lay between an *ad hoc* education authority, perhaps some kind of development from the school boards, or putting the necessary powers into the hands of the all-purpose county and county borough councils set up in 1888, or in some kind of compromise between the two principles. The Bryce Report recommended the establishment of a central authority under a minister who should also have charge of elementary education. The central office should take over the work of the Charity Commissioners in controlling educational endowments, and it should absorb the Department of Science and Art. Local administration of secondary education should be based on the counties and county boroughs. The county authority should have a majority of its members appointed by the county council, with some co-opted and some nominated by the minister. In county boroughs the authority should be chosen partly by the council, partly by the school board, with some co-opted members. These authorities should also have charge of the higher-grade schools, of organized science schools, and of evening schools and technical institutes.

These proposals, which strongly favoured the county solution, may have been influenced by what had been done in Wales under the Welsh Intermediate Education Act of 1889, which the Bryce Report praised for its success in concentrating and co-ordinating the various local forces (*BC* I: 13). Wales was poorly provided with educational endowments, and in 1881 the Aberdare committee on higher and intermediate education had recommended that a parliamentary grant should be given for the creation of university colleges, that secondary schools should be financed by a grant and/or a local rate, and that machinery should be set up for the inspection and examination of schools.

Legislation did not follow until 1889 (G. E. Jones 1982: 1–41). By the Act of that year a joint committee was to be set up in each county to make enquiries and to draw up schemes for submission to the Charity Commissioners. Power was given to raise a rate not exceeding ½d in the £, and the amount so raised was to be matched by a parliamentary grant. The old endowments were to be added to the available funds.

County and district governing bodies were to be set up to manage the new schools. The minimum age of entry to them was normally ten years, and most of the schools were second grade. Places were to be provided in the ratio of three girls to five boys, and most of the schools were 'dual', that is with separate departments for boys and girls, but with a common staff of teachers and a single head. The new developments were greatly reinforced by the payment of the 'whisky money' to the county councils; in 1890 £34,000 became available in this way. In addition private individuals subscribed generously for the new schools. In 1896 the Central Welsh Board for inspection and examination of schools was established. By 1897–8 there were 88 schools in existence with 6,877 scholars (3,679 boys and 3,198 girls). Some of these schools were old foundations, but most were newly established. Though there were problems, for example, the familiar difficulty that many pupils stayed at school for too short a time, this was a remarkable achievement in less than ten years.

The Welsh developments attracted a good deal of attention in England. Sir George Young, one of the charity commissioners, gave evidence about them to the Bryce Commission, and they are, as we have seen, mentioned in its report. They were discussed in books of the day like the Acland and Llewellyn Smith, *Studies in Secondary Education* (1892), and they were treated in an Education Department publication (*Special Reports* II (1898): 1–58). Yet it would be difficult to argue that they directly influenced what was happening in England where the problems were very different. Certainly what was happening in Wales was well known, and it may be that the use in Wales of the county/county borough as the administrative unit may have influenced what was happening in England.

The issue of secondary school organization in England was finally settled for political rather than educational reasons. The Education Act of 1870, though the work of a Liberal government, had not been keenly contested on party lines. By the mid–1890s, however, educational policy had become a keenly political question. The Bryce Commission had been appointed by a Liberal government. In 1895 the Conservatives came to power and held office for ten years. Not only had the Liberals to face a long period in opposition, but their effectiveness was limited by their deep divisions over the South African War of 1899–1902. The Liberal Party, much of whose support was Nonconformist, favoured the school boards and were hostile to the voluntary church schools. The Conservatives, pre-eminently the Church of England party, supported the voluntary schools and were hostile to the school boards, whose policies they regarded as aggressive and inimical to church interests. Among all boards the London School Board had excited particular dislike and, in considering the policies of Conservative politicians like Sir John Gorst, who became vice-president of the committee of council on education in 1895, the dislike, even fear, of the major boards which they felt must always be remembered. In consequence they favoured the counties/county boroughs as the local authorities in a reformed education system because they were thought to be more sympathetic to the voluntary schools and to Conservative policies generally.

The clash between board and voluntary schools did not directly affect secondary education but, because of the deep religious and political passions involved, it was bound to influence profoundly the shape of any future legislation. The boards had thus made themselves unpopular with powerful interests in the Church, with Conservative politicians, with some civil servants, and with the supporters of the grammar schools for two major reasons. The first, the rivalry with the voluntary schools, has already been mentioned. The second was their penetration into secondary education through the work of the higher-grade schools, financed through the grants of the Science and Art Department (Marsden 1987: 108–33). These schools offered a curriculum very different from that of the traditional grammar school, and they provided a broad road of advancement from the elementary schools to those who wished to take it. The Bryce Commission had regarded technical education as one form or type of secondary education in general. The grammar schools and their supporters wanted to separate the two. In addition, the secondary schools were to be sharply divided from the elementary. Room might be found in the higher school for a few able boys and girls, but there was to be no question of a general breakdown of the lines between the two sectors. If, in the view of the traditionalists, that were to happen, standards would fall and the essence of true secondary education be lost. The higher-grade schools had to be curbed and elementary education confined to its proper sphere.

The major issues were clear enough. Was the system to be administered by *ad hoc* bodies or through the all-purpose machinery of local government? What attitudes would the politicians and the Churches take up? What kind of schools were the secondary schools of the future to be and how were they to be related to the elementary schools? In 1896 Gorst introduced an Education Bill which proposed to make counties and county boroughs authorities for secondary education, to increase the grant to voluntary schools, and to permit denominational teaching in board schools. The Bill was keenly contested, but it passed its second reading, only to be abandoned in committee over difficulties about the powers to be given to non-county boroughs (Kazamias 1966: 86–90; Daglish 1987a: 91–104). This Bill had made no provision for a central authority. The Duke of Devonshire, the Lord President, advised that priority should be given to this matter, and in 1899 the Board of Education was founded. It took over the powers of the Education Department, of the Science and Art Department, and of the Charity Commissioners in respect of educational endowments, though it was not likely to be very effective until a unified system of local authorities had been created.

In 1897 the government set up two committees on educational matters. One of these, consisting of representatives of the grammar and higher grade schools, reached an amicable agreement about their respective spheres of activity. The other committee produced a new Department of Science and Art Directory. Clause VII of this permitted the counties and county boroughs, through their technical instruction committees, to become the responsible authorities for DSA instruction in their areas. In consequence of this the school boards complained that new authorities for secondary education were being set up surreptitiously. This opposition by the boards to the new clause VII reached its climax when the London Technical Education Board decided in November 1898 to apply for clause VII powers. In fact, the London County Council, the parent body, applied for recognition in its own name, and this was granted, though not until Cabinet approval had been given (Eaglesham 1956: 108, 114; Lilley 1982: 99–111).

By 1897–8 a struggle was clearly developing, and the centre of this lay in London, though there were also clashes with some of the major provincial boards. The London School Board had wide ambitions to extend its work, and had long been condemned for extravagance by ratepayers and local politicians. The legal position under which the boards had founded higher-grade schools and set up evening classes of an advanced standard was not very clear, though the provisions of the Education Act of 1870 and supplementary Acts, which were the basis of the school boards' powers, had been stretched a good deal. The London board received warnings about exceeding their powers, though the control through the auditor of the Local Government Board, who had the power to disallow expenditure, had become more lax during the 1890s, and the impression had gained ground that the Education Department was more influenced by the expediency of a course of action than by its strict legality (Eaglesham 1956: 86–7).

In 1899, through the instrumentality of William Garnett, secretary of the Technical Education Board, complaint was made to the auditor, T. Barclay Cockerton, about London School Board expenditure on Science and Art schools and classes. Cockerton found against the board and surcharged the members with the disallowed expenditure. The issues, in the words of E. J. R. Eaglesham, were twofold:

(1) Could school boards lawfully use the rates in conducting schools or classes, whether by day or evening, under the rules of the Science and Art Department?
(2) Could school boards educate adults out of the rates?
                    (Eaglesham 1956: 113–33; Taylor 1982: 329–48)

The case then went to the Court of Queen's Bench and to the Court of

Appeal, both of which upheld Cockerton's decision. After such a blow at the work done by the major boards legislation could not be further delayed.

The practical experience of administration in London also contributed to the debate through the work of Sidney Webb and the Fabians. Webb was the first chairman of the technical education board, whose great achievements were evidence of what a county authority could accomplish. He had not originally been hostile to the school boards, but he gradually became convinced, as he experienced the overlapping and confusion of the various bodies, that there must be a concentration of power in the hands of the county councils (Cole 1949/1974: 75–97 (A. M. McBriar); Judges 1961: 33–48; McBriar 1962: ch. viii; Brennan 1972: 174–99; and 1975). In his influential Fabian tract, *The Education Muddle and the Way out* (1901) (Brennan 1975: 85–104), Webb suggested the creation of a single education authority in each district, which should be the county or county borough council. The school boards were unsuitable because they were too unpopular, they did not cover the whole country, and many of them were too small. If a new type of *ad hoc* authority were set up, it would be hampered by religious animosities among its members. However, in the tract as eventually published, Webb suggested that the boards would survive to control elementary education in the majority of the county boroughs. The powers of the Board of Education should be strengthened, and it should be able, through its grants, to secure a 'national minimum' of education. What was needed, Webb claimed, was to extend popular control, 'to link together the municipal life of our local authorities with the intellectual life of the schools by the concentration of all local services under one local body'.

Webb's ideas reinforced, from a very different political quarter, the policies which the Conservative government were already pursuing. After the 'Cockerton judgment' temporary legislation had to be passed to authorize the work that had been declared illegal, and Acts of Parliament were passed in 1901 and 1902 to do this. Requests to carry on these schools and classes had to be approved by county and county borough councils. Before the Cockerton case had finally run its course, the government had acted to cut back the development of the higher grade schools. The Higher Elementary Schools Minute of 1900 had provided that these schools should give a four-year course and that pupils were not to remain after the end of the school year in which they reached the age of 15. The higher elementary schools never prospered. The official policy was to confine them to a narrow range of subjects and to ensure that they did not compete with the secondary schools (Eaglesham 1956: 50–2; Daglish 1987b: 36–50).

The policy of concentration of power in the hands of a single authority, towards which Conservative policy had been steadily moving, was finally carried into effect by the Education Act of 1902. Steered through the

House of Commons by A. J. Balfour, who became prime minister in July 1902, with the help behind the scenes of Robert Morant, the Bill was keenly fought over the issues of denominational education and the voluntary schools, where the Nonconformists were bitterly hostile to what was proposed. The Education Act became law in December 1902. The school boards were abolished and the new education authorities, the counties and county boroughs, were given the power to supply or to aid 'the supply of education other than elementary' and to raise for that purpose a rate not exceeding 2d in the £, unless special permission were given by the Local Government Board.

The Act of 1902 settled the major questions which had been debated during the previous decade. For the first time the state had committed itself to provide secondary education, which was to be controlled by an all-purpose authority as part of the ordinary machinery of local government. In 1902 only the principles had been established; the task of setting up the new order was to be the work of the Board of Education under Robert Morant, who became permanent secretary in April 1903. Most of the existing grammar and girls' high schools were incorporated within the new system. The private schools gradually withered away. The public schools and a few of the major grammar schools remained outside, and the state system suffered because it never incorporated these prestigious schools. There remained the question of what the new secondary schools were to teach and who was to enter them. Here the abolition of the school boards and the restrictive provisions of the Higher Elementary Schools Minute of 1900 severely limited the development of new forms of curricula which had been going on in the higher-grade schools. Moreover secondary and elementary education were to be sharply divided with a scholarship bridge taking some able boys and girls from one sector to the other. Secondary education after 1902, under the guidance of the Board of Education, was to be firmly rooted in the grammar school tradition.

Bibliography

(All books are published in London, unless another place of publication is cited.)

MANUSCRIPT SOURCES, PRIVATE AND LOCAL COLLECTIONS

Public Record Office, Kew

Ed. 27 Secondary education: endowment files 1850–1945

Aldenham, Grammar School: 1637, 1639
Bedford charity: 8A, 8B, 9
Birmingham, Schools of King Edward VI: 4891, 4893, 4894, 4899, 4910
Bradford, Grammar School: 5721, 5722, 5723
Brentwood, Sir Anthony Browne's School and Almshouse Foundation: 1060, 1061, 1062, 1063
Bristol, Free Grammar School (including Queen Elizabeth's Hospital and Red Maids' School): 1289, 1291, 1293, 1312, 1313
Bristol, Colston's Hospital (including sub-file on the Diocesan Trade School): 1274
Chepping Wycombe (High Wycombe), Royal Grammar School: 130
Coventry, Grammar School: 5009, 5010
Exeter, St John's Hospital Charity: 695, 697
Greenwich, Roan Schools: 3023, 3025, 3026
Islington and Clerkenwell, Dame Alice Owen's Foundation: 3117, 3119, 3120
Leeds, Grammar School: 5976, 5981, 5982, 5983, 5984, 5978
Leicester, Wyggeston Grammar School Foundation: 2419, 2420
Macclesfield, Foundation of King Edward VI: 266, 269, 270
Manchester High School for Girls: 2171, 2172
Middlesbrough High School: 5586, 5587, 5588
Newbury, St Bartholomew's Grammar School: 70, 71, 73
St Pancras, North London Collegiate and Camden School for Girls: 3191, 3195
Salisbury, The Godolphin School: 5283, 5284
Sherborne, Foster and Digby Foundation: 886
Sherborne, King's School: 906, 907
Skipton, The Girls' High School: 6171
Warrington, Grammar School: 2304
West Lavington, Dauntsey School Foundation: 5291, 5292, 5293, 5294, 5295, 5296, 5297, 5298

Westminster, United Westminster Schools Foundation (Emanuel Hospital): 3363, 3364, 3365, 3369, 3371

Ed. 21   Elementary education: public elementary school files

Scarning Free School 1871–1911: 12996

Ed. 49   Elementary education: endowment files

Scarning Endowed School 1856–1935: 5526

OTHER COLLECTIONS

Bradford	Libraries and Information Service:
	School Board, *Triennial Reports 1876–1903; Return relating to Higher Grade Schools with special reference to the payment of a fee* (March 1894)
Cambridge	University Library, University Archives:
	University Papers 1820–67 (UP5)
Derby	St Andrew's School, Litchurch:
	Admission Register 1869–91; Day Book 1887–97; 'List of Bad Deeds' (in my own possession)
London	Girls' Public Day School Trust:
	Minutes of Council and Committees, Headmistresses' Reports, c. 1879–90
Manchester	City Archives:
	Cheetham Higher Grade School, Log-book 1894–1924 (M66/34/1/1)
	Public Libraries. Local History Library:
	School Board, *General Reports 1871–1900*
Sheffield	Local Studies Library:
	School Board, *Minutes and Committee Reports* 1879–81, 1887–1902 *Annual Reports* 1873–1902
	Sheffield Grammar School, Minute Books 1863–90, 1890–1904
West Sussex	Record Office:
	International College, Spring Grove, *Prospectus* (?1867) (CP477)

OFFICIAL PUBLICATIONS

Public General Statutes

32 & 33 Vict. 1869: 197–208. Cap. 56, Endowed Schools Act 1869
36 & 37 Vict. 1873: 315–20. Cap. 87, Endowed Schools Act 1873
37 & 38 Vict. 1874: 288–90. Cap. 87 An Act to amend the Endowed Schools Acts

Parliamentary Papers

1864 XX 1   Report of HM Commissioners on Revenues and Management of certain Colleges and Schools . . . (Clarendon Commission) vol. I, Report

1867–8 XXVIII   Report of Commissioners on Education in Schools in England, not comprised within Her Majesty's two recent Commissions on Popular Education and Public Schools (Schools Inquiry or Taunton Commission)
vol. I   Report of Commissioners: Part I, 1
vol. VII Minutes of Evidence – Southern Counties: Part VI, 1
vol. IX Minutes of Evidence – Northern Counties: Part VIII, 1

1872 XXIV, 1, ⎱
1875 XXVIII 1 ⎰   Report of Endowed Schools Commissioners to Committee of Council on Education
Report of Commissioners on Scientific Instruction (Devonshire Commission):

1872 XXV 1   Second Report
1875 XXVIII   Sixth Report
1873 VIII 299   Report of Select Committee on operation of Endowed Schools Act 1869

1874 II: 79–86   Bill to amend the Endowed Schools Acts, 2 July 1874
1881 XXXIII 1   Report of Committee on the condition of Intermediate and Higher Education (Wales and Monmouth) (Aberdare Committee)

1884 XXIX, ⎱
1884 XXXI ⎰   Royal Commissioners on Technical Instruction (Samuelson Commission). Second Report
1884   House of Lords paper, no. 29. Return of Schemes etc. to an order of the House of Lords dated 31 July 1883 (Fortescue return)

1884 IX 1   Report of Select Committee on Charitable Trusts Acts
1886 IX 1, ⎱
1887 IX 235 ⎰   Reports of Select Committee on Endowed Schools Acts
Reports of Royal Commission on Elementary Education Acts (England and Wales) (Cross Commission):

1887 XXIX 1   Second Report
1888 XXXV 1, ⎱
1888 XXXVII 1 ⎰   Final Report
1892 LX: 151–241   Endowed Schools Acts foundations (England) . . . Return of foundations . . . the endowments of which are . . . recorded in the books of the Charity Commissioners . . . as subject to the . . . Endowed Schools Acts . . . for 1890

1894 XI 1   Report of Select Committee on Charity Commission
1895 XLIII 1, 1895 XLIV 1 ⎱
1895 XLV 1, 1895 XLVI 1 ⎰ Royal Commission on Secondary Education. Report and Evidence (Bryce Commission) 9 vols:
1895 XLVII 1, 1895 XLVIII, 1, 439
1895 XLIX 1, 213

1897 XXXIII 421   Report of Committee on Distribution of Science and Art Grants
1897 LXX: 557–665   Education Department. Return of Pupils in Public and Private Secondary Schools in England . . . and of Teaching Staff in such schools on 1st June 1897
Returns comprising Reports made to Charity Commissioners in result of Inquiry . . . into Endowments subject to Charitable Trusts Acts . . . (Returns on Endowed Charities):

1897 LXVI Part II 1 ⎱
1899 LXIX 1 ⎰   London

1897 LXVII Parts V & VI ⎫
1899 LXXI 1   ⎪
1899 LXXII 1   ⎬ Yorkshire, West Riding
1899 LXXIII 1   ⎭
1908 LXXX 67   Wiltshire, Northern Division
1909 LXV 507   County Borough of Exeter
1900 LXIII 59–224   Return showing the occupation of the parents of the win-
                     ners of County Council Scholarships during the past three
                     years (1896–9)
1902 LXXX 863   Return of the Statistics of Schools of Science conducted
                     under the Regulations of the Board of Education

Charity Commissioners, annual reports

20 1873 XXI 13	29 1882 XX 23	38 1890–1 XXVI 15
21 1874 XV 13	30 1883 XXI 337	39 1892 XXVII 15
22 1875 XX 13	31 1884 XXII 333	40 1893–4 XXV 15
23 1876 XX 19	32 1884–5 XXI 499	41 1894 XXVIII 15
24 1877 XXVI 13	33 1886 XX 15	42 1895 XXVI 17
25 1878 XXIV 13	34 1887 XXVII 15	43 1896 XXV 15
26 1878–9 XX 15	35 1888 XXXIV 19	44 1897 XXIV 17
27 1880 XVIII 89	36 1889 XXVIII 19	45 1898 XXI 17
28 1881 XXVIII 13	37 1890 XXVI 19	46 1899 XIX 17

Department of Science and Art, annual reports

1 1854 XXVII 269	16 1868–9 XXIII 131	32 1884–5 XXVIII 1
2 1854–5 XXVII 215	17 1870 XXVI 409	33 1886 XXIX 1
3 1856 XXIV 1	18 1871 XXIV 81	34 1887 XXXIV 1
4 1857 (Sess. 2) XX 1	19 1872 XXIV 239	35 1888 XLII 1
5 1857–8 XXIV 219	20 1873 XXVIII 25	36 1889 XXXIII 1
6 1859 (Sess. 1) XXI	21 1874 XXI 105	37 1890 XXXII 1
Part II 433	22 1875 XXVII 121	38 1890–1 XXXI 1
7 1860 XXIV 77	23 1876 XXVI 99	39 1892 XXXII 1
8 1861 XXXII 1	24 1877 XXXIII 1	40 1893–4 XXIX 1
9 1862 XXI 321	25 1878 XXXVI 1	41 1894 XXXII 1
10 1863 XVI 21	26 1878–9 XXVI 1	42 1895 XXXI 1
11 1864 XIX Part I 1	27 1880 XXV 1	43 1896 XXX 1
12 1865 XVI 301	28 1881 XXXVII 1	44 1897 XXX, XXXI
13 1866 XXV 337	29 1882 XXVI 1	45 1898 XXIX, 243 and
14 1867 XXIII 1	30 1883 XXVII 1	XXX, 1
15 1867–8 XXVII 419	31 1884 XXVIII 1	46 1899 XXVII, 245 and
		XXVIII, 1

Special reports on educational subjects (Education Department/Board of Education)

2 (1898):   1–58 (Charity Commissioners) 'Welsh Intermediate Education
                                          Act 1889; its origin and working'
         : 99–123 Mrs Bryant   'The Curriculum of a Girls'
                                          School'

: 133–44 Mrs Woodhouse   'Physical Education at the Sheffield High School for Girls'
: 145–58 Penelope Lawrence   'Games and Athletics in Secondary Schools for Girls'
6 (1900)   'Preparatory Schools for Boys, their place in English secondary education, considered in various aspects'

BOOKS, THESES, ARTICLES

(Where abbreviations are used, see List of Abbreviations, p. xiii)

Acland, A. H. D. and Llewellyn Smith, H. (eds) (1892) *Studies in Secondary Education*, Percival.

Adamson, J. W. (1930/1964) *English Education 1760–1902*, Cambridge, Cambridge University Press.

Allen, B. M. (1933) *William Garnett: A Memoir*, Cambridge, Heffer.

Allsobrook, D. I. (1973) 'The reform of the endowed schools: the work of the Northamptonshire Educational Society, 1854–1874', *HE* 2, 1, 35–55.

—— (1985) 'An episode in the reform of Gloucestershire endowed schools', *Transactions of the Bristol and Gloucestershire Archaeological Society* 103, 201–6.

—— (1986) *Schools for the Shires: The Reform of Middle-class Education in Mid-Victorian England*, Manchester, Manchester University Press.

Anderson, R. D. (1973) 'French views of the English public schools: some nineteenth-century episodes', *HE* 2, 2, 159–72.

—— (1983) *Education and Opportunity in Victorian Scotland: Schools and Universities*, Oxford, Clarendon Press.

—— (1985) 'Secondary schools and Scottish society in the nineteenth century', *Past and Present* 109, 176–203.

'Anstey, F.' (T. A. Guthrie) (1936) *A Long Retrospect*, Oxford, Oxford University Press.

Argles, M. (1964) *South Kensington to Robbins: An Account of English Technical and Scientific Education since 1851*, Longman.

Armytage, W. H. G. (1957) *Sir Richard Gregory: His Life and Work*, Macmillan.

Arnold, M. (1863–4) *A French Eton or Middle-class Education and the State*; see P. Smith and G. Summerfield (1969), *Matthew Arnold and the Education of the New Order*, Cambridge, Cambridge University Press, 76–156.

—— (1871) *Friendship's Garland: being the Conversations, Letters and Opinions of the late Arminius, Baron von Thunder-Ten-Tronckh*, Smith, Elder.

Atkinson, P. (1978) 'Fitness, feminism and schooling', in S. Delamont and N. Duffin (eds), *The Nineteenth-century Woman: Her Cultural and Physical World*, Croom Helm, 92–133.

Badley, J. H. (1955) *Memories and Reflections*, George Allen & Unwin.

Baker, D. (1975) *Partnership in Excellence: A late Victorian Educational Venture: The Leys School, Cambridge, 1875–1975*, Governors of the Leys School.

Balfour, G. (1898) *The Educational Systems of Great Britain and Ireland*, Oxford, Clarendon Press.

Ball, F. (1979) 'The Taunton Commission and the maintenance of the classical curriculum in the grammar schools', *JEAH* XI, 2, 8–12.

Ball, N. (1980) 'Education for life: plans for Wellington College', *JEAH* XII, 1, 18–24.

Balls, F. E. (1968) 'The Endowed Schools Act 1869 and the development of the

English grammar schools in the nineteenth century – II. The operation of the act', *Durham Research Review* V, 20, 219–29.

Bamford, T. W. (1967) *The Rise of the Public Schools: A Study of boys' Public Boarding Schools in England and Wales from 1837 to the Present Day*, Nelson.

Banks, J. A. (1954) *Prosperity and Parenthood: A Study of Family Planning among the Victorian Middle Classes*, Routledge & Kegan Paul.

Barker, Sir E. (1953) *Age and Youth: Memories of three Universities and Father of the Man*, Oxford University Press.

Barnes, A. S. (1926) *The Catholic Schools of England*, Williams & Norgate.

Baron, G. (1954–5) 'The origins and early history of the Headmasters' Conference 1869–1914', *Educational Review* 7, 223–34.

Barr, B. (1984) *History of Girls' Schools and Related Biographical Material, a Union List of Books*, Leicester, Librarians of Institutes and Schools of Education.

Battersby, W. J. (1950a) 'Secondary education for boys', in G. A. Beck (ed.), *The English Catholics 1850–1950*, Burns Oates, 322–36.

— (1950b) 'Educational work of the religious orders of women', in G. A. Beck (ed.) *The English Catholics 1850–1950*, Burns Oates, 337–64.

— (1953) *Brother Potamian: Educator and Scientist*, Burns Oates.

Beale, D. (ed.) (n.d.) *Reports Issued by the Schools Inquiry Commission on the Education of Girls. Reprinted with the sanction of her majesty's commissioners*, David Nutt.

— (1866) 'On the education of girls. By a utopian', *Fraser's Magazine* LXXIV, 509–24.

Beale, D., Soulsby, L. M. H., and Dove, J. F. (eds) (1898) *Work and Play in Girls' Schools*, Longmans Green.

Beck, G. A. (ed.) (1950) *The English Catholics 1850–1950: Essays to commemorate the Centenary of the Restoration of the Hierarchy of England and Wales*, Burns Oates.

Bell, E. M. (1953) *Storming the Citadel. The Rise of the Woman Doctor*, Constable.

— (1958) *A History of the Church Schools Company 1883–1958*, SPCK.

Best, G. F. A. (1975) 'Militarism and the Victorian public school', in B. Simon and I. Bradley, *The Victorian Public School*, Gill & Macmillan, 129–46.

Bibby, C. (1956–7) 'A Victorian experiment in international education: the college at Spring Grove', *BJES* V, 1, 25–36.

Binfield, C. (1981) *Belmont's Portias: Victorian Nonconformists and Middle-class Education for Girls*, Dr Williams's Trust.

Bingham, J. H. (1949) *The Period of the Sheffield School Board 1870–1903*, Sheffield, J. W. Northend.

Bishop, A. S. (1971) *The Rise of a Central Authority for English Education*, Cambridge, Cambridge University Press.

Bishop, T. J. H. and Wilkinson, R. (1967) *Winchester and the Public School Élite: A Statistical Analysis*, Faber.

Blumenau, R. (1965) *A History of Malvern College 1865–1965*, Macmillan.

Board, M. J. (1959) 'A history of the private adventure school in Sheffield', unpublished MA thesis, University of Sheffield.

Bowen, W. E. (1902) *Edward Bowen: A Memoir*, Longmans Green.

Bowerman, E. (n.d.) *Stands there a School: Memories of Dame Frances Dove, D.B.E. Founder of Wycombe Abbey School*, Wycombe Abbey School Seniors.

Boyd, A. K. (1948) *The History of Radley College 1847–1947*, Oxford, Basil Blackwell.

Boyden, B. (ed.) (1975) *'Call Back Yesterday': A Collection of Reminiscences to mark the Centenary of the Nottingham High School for Girls G.P.D.S.T.*, Nottingham High School for Girls.

Bradby, G. F. (1914) *The Lanchester Tradition*, Smith, Elder.

Bradford, Education in . . . since 1870 (1970), Bradford Corporation.

Bradley, A. G. and others (1923) *A History of Marlborough College*, John Murray.

Bremner, C. S. (1897) *Education of Girls and Women in Great Britain*, Swan Sonnenschein.

Brennan, E. J. T. (1959–61) 'Sidney Webb and the London Technical Education Board', *Vocational Aspect of Secondary and Further Education*, 3 parts: XI, 23, 85–96; XII, 24, 27–43; XIII, 27, 146–71.

—— (1972) 'Educational engineering with the Webbs', *HE* 1, 2, 174–99.

—— (ed.) (1975) *Education for National Efficiency: The Contribution of Sidney and Beatrice Webb*, Athlone Press.

Brett-James, N. G. (n.d.) *The History of Mill Hill School 1807–1923*, Reigate, Thomas Malcomson.

Broadway, C. M. and Buss, E. I. (1982) *The History of the School. 1882 B.G.M.S.–D.A.H.S. 1982*, Luton, White Crescent Press.

Brook, R. (1968) *The Story of Huddersfield*, Macgibbon & Kee.

Brown, Thomas Edward: A Memorial Volume 1830–1930 (1930) Cambridge, Cambridge University Press.

Bryant, M. E. (1979) *The Unexpected Revolution: A Study in the History of the Education of Women and Girls in the Nineteenth Century*, University of London Institute of Education.

—— (1986) *The London Experience of Secondary Education*, Athlone Press.

Bryce, J. (1903) *Studies in Contemporary Biography*, Macmillan.

Burgess, M. A. (n.d.) *A History of Burlington School* (no publisher).

Burstall, S. A. (1907) *English High Schools for Girls: Their Aims, Organisation, and Management*, Longmans Green.

—— (1911) *The Story of the Manchester High School for Girls 1871–1911*, Manchester, Manchester University Press.

—— (1933) *Retrospect and Prospect: Sixty years of Women's Education*, Longmans Green.

—— (1938) *Frances Mary Buss: An Educational Pioneer*, SPCK.

Burstyn, J. N. (1977) 'Women's education in England during the nineteenth century: a review of the literature 1970–1976', *HE* 6, 1, 11–19.

—— (1980) *Victorian Education and the Ideal of Womanhood*, Croom Helm.

Butterworth, H. (1960) 'The development of technical education in Middlesbrough 1844–1903', *Durham Research Review* III, 11, 27–34.

—— (1968) 'The Science and Art Department 1853–1900', unpublished Ph.D. thesis, University of Sheffield.

—— (1970) 'The Department of Science and Art (1853–1900) and the development of secondary education', *History of Education Society Bulletin* 6, 34–45.

—— (1971) 'South Kensington and Whitehall: a conflict of educational purpose', *JEAH* IV, 1, 9–19.

Candler, Mrs E. W. See Vardy, W. I.

Cannell, G. (1981) 'Resistance to the Charity Commissioners: the case of St Paul's Schools 1860–1904', *HE* 10, 4, 245–62.

Carleton, J. D. (1965) *Westminster School: A History*, Rupert Hart-Davis.

Cartaret-Bisson, F. S. de (1879) *Our Schools and Colleges: Being a complete compendium of practical information upon all subjects connected with Education and Examination recognized in the United Kingdom at the present day: collated from original sources*, 4th edn, Simpkin, Marshall.

—— (1884) *Our Schools and Colleges*, Vol. II, *for Girls*, Simpkin, Marshall.

Cholmondeley, E. (1960) *The Story of Charlotte Mason 1842–1923*, Charlotte Mason Foundation, J. M. Dent.

Christie, O. F. (1935) *A History of Clifton College 1860–1934*, Bristol, J. W. Arrowsmith.

Clarke, A. K. (1953) *A History of the Cheltenham Ladies' College 1853–1953*, Faber & Faber.

Cole, M. (ed.) (1949/1974) *The Webbs and their Work*, Brighton, Harvester Press.

Cole, S. (1882) *Sheffield School Board. Statement on the work of the Board*, Sheffield, Pawson & Brailsford.

Collet, C. E. (1892) 'Secondary education in London (girls)', in A. H. D. Acland and H. Llewellyn Smith (eds) *Studies in Secondary Education*, Percival, 200–21.

Collings, J. and Green, J. L. (1920) *Life of the Right Hon. Jesse Collings*, Longmans Green.

Cookson, C. (ed.) (1898) *Essays on Secondary Education* (by various contributors), Oxford, Clarendon Press.

Coulton, G. G. (1901) *Public Schools and the Public Needs: Suggestions for the Reform of our Teaching Methods in the Light of Modern Requirements*, Simpkin, Marshall, Hamilton, Kent.

—— (1923) *A Victorian Schoolmaster: Henry Hart of Sedbergh*, G. Bell.

Cowan, I. R. (1971) 'Higher elementary, secondary and pupil-teachers' education in Salford, 1870–1903', Pt I, *Vocational Aspect* XXIII, 56, 163–72.

Cowie, E. E. (1982) 'Stephen Hawtrey and a working-class Eton', *HE* 11, 2, 71–86.

Crane, M. A. (1981) 'Education and improvement in nineteenth-century Derby', unpublished MA thesis, University of Sheffield.

Craze, M. (1955) *A History of Felsted School 1564–1947*, Ipswich, Cowell.

Cross, M. C. (1953) *The Free Grammar School of Leicester*, University College of Leicester Department of English Local History. Occasional Papers no. 4.

Cunningham, P. (1976) *Local History of Education in England and Wales: A Bibliography*, Museum of the History of Education, University of Leeds.

Daglish, N. D. (1987a) 'Planning the Education Bill of 1896', *HE* 16, 2, 91–104.

—— (1987b) 'The politics of educational change: the case of the English higher grade schools', *JEAH* XIX, 2, 36–50.

Dare, R. A. (1963) *A History of Owen's School*, Wallington, Carwal.

Darwin, B. (1931) *The English Public School*, Longmans Green.

Davies, K. (1981) *Polam Hall. The story of a school*, Darlington, G. Prudhoe.

Day, E. S. (1902) *An Old Westminster Endowment. Being a History of the Grey Coat Hospital as recorded in the Minute Books*, Hugh Rees.

Delamont, S. and Duffin, L. (eds) (1978) *The Nineteenth-century Woman: Her Cultural and Physical World*, Croom Helm.

Demogeot, J. and Montucci, H. (1868) *De l'Enseignement secondaire en Angleterre et en Ecosse. Rapport adressé à son Exc. M. le Ministre de l'Instruction Publique*, Paris, Imprimerie Impériale.

Demolins, E. (1898a) *Anglo-Saxon Superiority: To What it is Due*, English trans. from 10th French edn, Leadenhall Press.

—— (1898b) *L'Education nouvelle: L'École des Roches*, Paris, Firmin-Didot.

Deneke, H. C. (1946) *Grace Hadow*, Oxford, Oxford University Press.

Derby Mercury (1870–3).

Dilke, C. (1965) *Dr Moberly's Mint-Mark: A Study of Winchester College*, Heinemann.

Douglas, M. A. and Ash, C. R. (eds) (1928) *The Godolphin School 1726–1926*, Longmans Green.

Douglas-Smith, A. E. (1937) *The City of London School*, Oxford, Basil Blackwell.

Dove, J. F. (1898) 'Cultivation of the body', in D. Beale, L. M. H. Soulsby and J. F. Dove (eds) *Work and Play in Girls' Schools*, Longmans Green, 396–423.

Draper, F. W. M. (1962) *Four Centuries of Merchant Taylors' School 1561–1961*, Oxford, Oxford University Press.

Duffy, J. B. (1983) 'The growth of popular education in the colliery districts of Northumberland and Durham c. 1800 to 1902', unpublished Ph.D. thesis, University of Manchester.

Dukes, C. (1894) *Health at School Considered in its Mental, Moral, and Physical Aspects* 3rd edn, Rivington, Percival.

Dunae, P. A. (1980) 'Boys' literature and the idea of empire', *Victorian Studies* 24, 1, 105–21.

Dunning, B. (ed.) (1931) *Francis Holland Church of England School for Girls: Graham Street Memories*, Hazell Watson & Viney.

Dyhouse, C. (1976) 'Social Darwinistic ideas and the development of women's education', *HE* 5. 1. 41–58.

—— (1977) 'Good wives and little mothers: social anxieties and the schoolgirls' curriculum 1890–1920', *Oxford Review of Education*, 3, 1, 21–35.

—— (1981) *Girls Growing Up in late Victorian and Edwardian England*, Routledge & Kegan Paul.

Eaglesham, E. (1956) *From School Board to Local Authority*, Routledge & Kegan Paul.

Easton, A. P. (1900–1) 'Wesley College Sheffield' (Sheffield Local Studies Library).

Edwards, D. L. (1957) *A History of King's School Canterbury*, Faber & Faber.

Elliott, A. (1981) 'The Bradford School Board and the Department of Education 1870–1902: areas of conflict', *JEAH*, XIII, 2, 18–23.

Ellis, A. B. (1965) 'Higher grade schools in Bradford before the 1902 Education Act', unpublished M.Ed. thesis, University of Durham.

Erickson, C. (1959) *British Industrialists. Steel and Hosiery*, Cambridge, Cambridge University Press.

Evans, A. J. (1947) 'A history of education in Bradford during the period of the Bradford School Board (1870–1904)', unpublished MA thesis, University of Leeds.

Evans, R. J. W. (1986) 'Town, gown and cloth: an essay on the foundation of the School', in M. A. Girling and L. Hooper (eds) *Dean Close School: The First Hundred Years*, Cheltenham, 1–39.

Evennett, H. O. (1944) *The Catholic Schools of England and Wales*, Cambridge, Cambridge University Press.

Faithfull, L. M. (1924) *In the House of my Pilgrimage*, Chatto & Windus.

Farrar, F. W. (ed.) (1868) *Essays on a Liberal Education*, 2nd edn, Macmillan.

Farrar, P. N. (1987) 'Richard Cobden, educationist, economist and statesman', unpublished Ph.D. thesis, University of Sheffield.

[Fleming Report] (1944) *The Public Schools and the General Educational System*, HMSO.

Fletcher, C. R. L. (1922) *Edmond Warre . . . sometime Headmaster and Provost of Eton College*, John Murray.

Fletcher, F. (1937) *After Many Days: A Schoolmaster's Memories*, Robert Hale.

Fletcher, S. (1980) *Feminists and Bureaucrats: A Study in the Development of Girls' Education in the Nineteenth Century*, Cambridge, Cambridge University Press.

—— (1982) 'Co-education and the Victorian grammar school', *HE* 11, 2, 87–98.

—— (1984) *Women First. The Female Tradition in English Physical Education 1880–1980*, Athlone Press.

Foden, F. (1970) *Philip Magnus. Victorian educational pioneer*, Vallentine, Mitchell.

Gadesden, F. (1901) 'Secondary education of girls and the development of girls' high schools', in R. D. Roberts (ed.), *Education in the Nineteenth Century*, Cambridge, Cambridge University Press, 82–105.

Gainford in the 1880's (n.d.) Department of Adult and Continuing Education, Durham University.

Gardiner, R. B. and Lupton, J. (eds) (1911) *Res Paulinae: The Eighth Half-century of St Paul's School*, St Paul's School.

Gardner, B. (1973) *The Public Schools: An Historical Survey*, Hamilton.

Gardner, P. (1984) *The Lost Elementary Schools of Victorian England. The People's Education*, Croom Helm.

Girdlestone, F. K. W., Hardman, E. T., and Tod, A. H. (1911) *Charterhouse Register 1872–1910* vol. I, *1872–1891*, 2nd edn, Chiswick Press.

Girouard, M. (1981) *The Return to Camelot: Chivalry and the English Gentleman*, New Haven and London, Yale University Press.

Glenday, N. and Price, M. (1974) *Reluctant Revolutionaries: A Century of Head Mistresses 1874–1974*, Pitman.

—— (1977) *Clifton High School 1877–1977*, Clifton High School.

Godber, J. (1973) *The Harpur Trust 1552–1973*, Bedford, The Harpur Trust.

Godber, J. and Hutchins, I. (eds) (1982) *A Century of Challenge: Bedford High School 1882 to 1982*, Biggleswade, Charles Elphick.

Gomez, F. G. (1974) 'The Endowed Schools Act 1869 – a middle-class conspiracy? The south west Lancashire evidence', *JEAH* VI, 1, 9–18.

Gordon, P. (1966) 'Some sources for the history of the Endowed Schools Commission 1869–1900', *BJES* XIV, 3, 59–73.

—— (1980) *Selection for Secondary Education*, Woburn Press.

Gosden, P. (1970) 'Technical Instruction Committees', in History of Education Society, *Studies in the Government and Control of Education since 1860*, Methuen, 27–41.

Gosden, P. H. J. H. and Sharp, P. R. (1978) *The Development of an Education Service. The West Riding 1889–1974*, Oxford, Martin Robertson.

Gourlay, A. B. (1951) *A History of Sherborne School*, Winchester, Warren.

Gowing, M. (1978) 'Science technology and education: England in 1870', *Oxford Review of Education* 4, 1, 3–17.

Graham, E. (1920) *The Harrow Life of Henry Montagu Butler, D.D.*, Longmans Green.

Graham, J. A. and Pythian, B. A. (eds) (1965) *The Manchester Grammar School 1515–1965*, Manchester, Manchester University Press.

[Graham, J. P.] (1922) *Uppingham School Roll 1880–1921*, 5th issue, Edward Stanford.

Grant, J. M., McCutcheon, K. H. and Sanders, E. F. (eds) (n.d.) *St Leonard's School 1877–1927*, Oxford University Press.

Great Public Schools (n.d.) various authors, Edward Arnold.

Grey, Mrs W. G. (Maria) (1871) 'On the education of women', *Journal of the Society of Arts* 967, XIX, 555–61.

Grey, Maria (Mrs W. G.) and Shirreff, E. (1854) *Thoughts on Self-culture Addressed to Women*, 2nd edn, Hope.

Guthrie, T. A. See Anstey, F.

Haig Brown, H. E. (ed.) (1908) *William Haig Brown of Charterhouse: A Short Biographical Memoir*, Macmillan.

Hall, M. E. and Macpherson, V. M. (1961) *Marcia Alice Rice. The Story of a Great Headmistress*, Shrewsbury, Wilding.

Hammond, N. G. L. (ed.) (1962) *Centenary Essays on Clifton College*, Bristol, J. W. Arrowsmith, for the Council of the College.

Handford, B. W. T. (1933) *Lancing. A History of SS. Mary and Nicolas College, Lancing 1848–1930*, Oxford, Basil Blackwell.

Hansard Parliamentary Debates 3rd series.

Hardcastle, M. (n.d.) *Wakefield Girls' High School 1878–1978* (no publisher).

Harrison, J. A. (1961–9) *Private Schools in Doncaster in the Nineteenth Century*, Parts III-VI, Doncaster Museum Publications.

Harrison, J. E. (1925) *Reminiscences of a Student's Life*, Hogarth Press.

Harwood, H. (1959) *The History of Milton Mount College*, Independent Press.

Heeney, B. (1969) *Mission to the Middle Classes. The Woodard Schools 1848–1891*, SPCK.

Hewitt, W. (1927) *The Technical Instruction Committee and its Work 1890–1903: a Chapter in the History of Education in Liverpool*, Liverpool, Liverpool University Press/London, Hodder & Stoughton.

Higginson, J. H. (1972) 'Evolution of "secondary education" ', *BJES* XX, 2, 165–77.

Hiley, R. W. (1884) *Sundry Attacks on Private Schools and Strictures Thereon*, Longmans Green.

—— (1899) *Memories of Half a Century*, Longmans Green.

Hill, C. P. (1951) *The History of Bristol Grammar School*, Pitman.

Hobhouse, A. (1880) *The Dead Hand: Addresses on the Subject of Endowments and Settlements of Property*, Chatto & Windus.

Hobhouse, L. T. and Hammond, J. L. (1905) *Lord Hobhouse: A Memoir*, Arnold.

Hodges, S. (1981) *God's Gift: A Living History of Dulwich College*, Heinemann.

Hollis, C. (1960) *Eton: A History*, Hollis & Carter.

Holmes, G. M. (1964) 'The parliamentary and ministerial career of A. H. D. Acland 1886–97', *Durham Research Review* IV, 15, 128–39.

Honey, J. R. de S. (1977) *Tom Brown's Universe. The Development of the Victorian Public School*, Millington.

Hope-Simpson, J. B. (1967) *Rugby since Arnold: A History of Rugby School from 1842*, Macmillan.

Horn, P. (1989) 'The Victorian governess', *HE* 18, 4, 333–44.

How, F. D. (1904) *Six Great Schoolmasters*, Methuen.

Howarth, J. (1985) 'Public schools, safety nets and educational ladders: the classification of girls' secondary schools', *Oxford Review of Education* 11, 1, 59–71.

Hoyland, G. (1946) *The Man who Made a School: Thring of Uppingham*, SCM Press.

Hughes, M. V. (1946) *A London Family 1870–1900: A Trilogy*, Oxford, Oxford University Press.

Hunt, M. F. (1984) 'Secondary education for the middle-class girl: a study of ideology and educational practice 1870 to 1940, with special reference to the Harpur Trust girls' schools, Bedford', unpublished Ph.D. thesis, University of Cambridge.

—— (ed.) (1987) *Lessons for Life: The Schooling of Girls and Women 1850–1950*, Oxford, Basil Blackwell.

Hutton, T. W. (1952) *King Edward's School Birmingham 1552–1952*, Oxford, Basil Blackwell.

Ives, A. G. (1970) *Kingswood School in Wesley's Day and Since*, Epworth Press.

Jackson, A. H. (1932) *A Victorian Childhood*, Methuen.

James, M. E. (1914) *Alice Ottley. First Head-mistress of the Worcester High School for Girls 1883–1912*, Longmans Green.

Jenkins, I. (1979) 'The Yorkshire Ladies' Council of Education 1871–91', *Thoresby Society Miscellany* 17, Part I, 27–71.

Jenkins, R. (1987) *Baldwin*, Collins.

Jenkyns, R. (1980) *The Victorians and Ancient Greece*, Oxford, Basil Blackwell.

Jewell, H. M. (1976) *A School of Unusual Excellence: Leeds Girls' High School 1876–1976*, Leeds Girls' High School.

Jewels, E. N. (1963) *A History of Archbishop Holgate's Grammar School York 1546–1946*, Foundation Governors of the School.

Jones, E. E. C. (1922) *As I Remember: An Autobiographical Ramble*, A. & C. Black.

Jones, G. E. (1982) *Controls and Conflicts in Welsh Secondary Education 1889–1944*, Cardiff, University of Wales Press.

Judges, A. V. (1961) 'The educational influence of the Webbs', *BJES* X, 1, 33–48.

Kamm, J. (1958) *How Different from Us: A Biography of Miss Buss and Miss Beale*, Bodley Head.

—— (1965) *Hope Deferred. Girls Education in English History*, Methuen.

—— (1971) *Indicative Past. A Hundred Years of the Girls' Public Day School Trust*, Allen & Unwin.

Kazamias, A. M. (1966) *Politics, Society and Secondary Education in England*, Philadelphia, University of Pennsylvania Press.

Kellett, E. E. (1936) *As I Remember*, Gollancz.

Kipling, R. (1913) *Stalky and Co.*, Macmillan.

Kirby, J. W. (1929) *History of the Roan School (The Greycoat School) and its Founder*, Blackheath Press.

—— (1933) *The History of the Blackheath Proprietary School*, Blackheath Press.

Kirk, K. E. (1937) *The Story of the Woodard Schools*, Hodder & Stoughton.

Kitson Clark, G. (1974) 'The Leeds elite', *University of Leeds Review* 17, 2, 232–58.

Knightley, W. P. (1876) *A Plea for Private Schools*, Brighton, H. & C. Treacher/ London, Hamilton Adams.

Lace, A. F. (1968) *A Goodly Heritage: A History of Monkton Combe School 1868 to 1967*, Bath, Sir Isaac Pitman, for the School.

Lancet, The (1880 i and ii).

Lawson, J. (1958) 'Middle-class education in later Victorian Hull: the problem of secondary education 1865–1895', *Studies in Education* (University of Hull) III, 1, 27–49.

—— (1963) *A Town Grammar School through Six Centuries: A History of Hull Grammar School against its Local Background*, Oxford University Press, for the University of Hull.

Leach, A. F. (1899) *A History of Winchester College*, Duckworth.

Leake, W. R. M. and others (n.d.) *Gilkes and Dulwich 1885–1914: A Study of a Great Headmaster*, Alleyn Club.

Leclerc, M. (1894a) *L'Education des classes moyennes et dirigeantes en Angleterre*, Paris, Armond Colin.

—— (1894b) *Les Professions et la société en Angleterre*, Paris, Armand Colin.

Leinster-Mackay, D. (1974–5) 'Private schools of nineteenth-century Warwickshire', *Warwickshire History* II, 5, 3–23; II, 6, 3–19.

—— (1978) 'A question of ephemerality: indices for longevity of 19th century private schools', *JEAH* X, 2, 1–7.

—— (1981) 'Victorian quasi-public schools: a question of appearance and reality or an application of the principle of the survival of the fittest', *BJES* XXIX, 1, 54–68.

—— (1983) 'Private or public schools: the educational debate in *laissez-faire* England', *JEAH* XV, 2, 1–6.

—— (1984) *The Rise of the English Prep School*, Brighton, Falmer Press.

—— (1987) *The Educational World of Edward Thring: A Centenary Study*, Brighton, Falmer Press.

Lester, L. V. (1896) *A Memoir of Hugo Daniel Harper, D.D.*, Longmans.

Lewis, C. S. (1955) *Surprised by Joy: The Shape of my Early Life*, Geoffrey Bles.

Lewis, R. R. (1981) *The History of Brentwood School*, published by the governors.

Lilley, R. C. (1982) 'Attempts to implement the Bryce Commission's recommendations – and the consequences', *HE* 11, 2, 99–111.

Linscott, (Sister) M. (1966) *Quiet Revolution. The Educational Experience of Blessed Julie Billiart and the Sisters of Notre Dame de Namur*, Glasgow, Burns.

Lowe, R. (1868) *Middle-Class Education: Endowment or Free Trade*, R. J. Bush.

Lumsden, L. I. (1933) *Yellow Leaves: Memories of a Long Life*, Edinburgh and London, Blackwood.

McBriar, A. M. (1949/1974) 'Sidney Webb and the LCC', in M. Cole (ed.), *The Webbs and their Work*, Brighton, Harvester Press, 75–97.

—— (1962) *Fabian Socialism and English Politics 1884–1918*, Cambridge, Cambridge University Press.

McClelland, V. A. (1962) *Cardinal Manning: His Public Life and Influence 1865–1892*, Oxford, Oxford University Press.

—— (1972) ' "The liberal training of England's Catholic youth": William Joseph Petre (1847–93) and educational reform', *Victorian Studies* XV, 3, 257–77.

McCrone, K. E. (1988) *Sport and the Physical Emancipation of English Women 1870–1914*, Routledge.

Macdonald, K. I. (1974) 'The public elementary school pupil within the secondary-school system of the 1890s', *JEAH* VI, 1, 19–26.

McDonnell, M. F. J. (1909) *A History of St Paul's School*, Chapman and Hall.

MacInnes, C. M. and Whittard, W. F. (1955) *Bristol and its Adjoining Counties*, Bristol, for the British Association.

Mack, E. C. (1941) *Public Schools and British Opinion since 1860: The Relationship between Contemporary Ideas and the Evolution of an English Institution*, New York, Columbia University Press.

McKay, S. G. (1975) *Foster's: The Story of a Dorset School*, Dorchester, Friary Press.

Mackenzie, R. J. (1906) *Almond of Loretto, Being the Life and a Selection from the Letters of Hely Hutchinson Almond*, Constable.

Maclean, A. H. H. (1903) *Public Schools and the War in South Africa 1899–1902: Some facts, figures and comparisons, with a list of specially distinguished officers*, Edward Stanford.

MacLeod, R. (ed.) (1982) *Days of Judgement: Science, Examinations and the Organization of Knowledge in late Victorian England*, Driffield, Nafferton Books.

Maclure, S. (1970) *One Hundred Years of London Education*, Allen Lane.

Macpherson, V. M. (1924) *The Story of St Anne's, Abbot's Bromley 1874–1924*, Shrewsbury, Wilding.

Magnus, L. (1923) *The Jubilee Book of the Girls' Public Day School Trust 1873–1923*, Cambridge, Cambridge University Press.

Magnus, Sir P. (1888) *Industrial Education*, Kegan Paul & Trench.

—— (1910) *Educational Aims and Efforts 1880–1910*, Longmans Green.

Mangan, J. A. (1975) 'Athleticism: a case study of the evolution of an educational ideology', in B. Simon and I. Bradley, *The Victorian Public School*, Gill & Macmillan, 147–67.

— (1980) 'Images of Empire in the late Victorian public school', *JEAH* XII, 1, 31–9.

— (1981) *Athleticism in the Victorian and Edwardian Public School: The Emergence and Consolidation of an Educational Ideology*, Cambridge, Cambridge University Press.

— (1986a) *The Games Ethic and Imperialism: Aspects of the Diffusion of an Ideal*, Harmondsworth, Viking Press.

— (1986b) ' "The grit of our forefathers": invented traditions, propaganda and Imperialism', in J. M. Mackenzie (ed.), *Imperialism and Popular Culture*, Manchester, Manchester University Press, 113–39.

— (ed.) (1988) *'Benefits bestowed'? Education and British Imperialism*, Manchester, Manchester University Press.

Marmion, J. P. (1984) 'Cornelia Connelly's work in education 1848–79', unpublished Ph.D. thesis, University of Manchester.

Marsden, W. E. (1987) *Unequal Educational Provision in England and Wales: The Nineteenth-century Roots*, Woburn Press.

Mary Datchelor School, The Story of . . . 1877–1957 (1957) Hodder & Stoughton.

Mathieson, M. and Bernbaum, G. (1988) 'The British disease: a British tradition', *BJES* XXXVI, 2, 126–74.

May, J. (1969) *Madame Bergman-Österberg: Pioneer of Physical Education and Games for Girls and Women*, University of London Institute of Education/ George G. Harrap.

Meadows, A. J. and Brock, W. H. (1975) 'Topics fit for gentlemen: the problem of science in the public school curriculum', in B. Simon and I. Bradley (eds), *The Victorian Public School*, Gill & Macmillan, 95–114.

Milburn, J. (1969) 'The secondary schoolmistress: a study of her professional views and their significance in the educational developments of the period 1895–1914', unpublished Ph.D. thesis, University of London.

Milford, L. S. (1910) *Haileybury Register 1862–1910* 4th edn, Richard Clay.

Milne, A. A. (1939) *It's too late now: The Autobiography of a Writer*, Methuen.

Monahan, M. (1922) *Life and Letters of Janet Erskine Stuart, Superior General of the Society of the Sacred Heart 1857 to 1914*, Longmans Green.

Morgan, M. C. (1968) *Cheltenham College: The First Hundred Years*, Chalfont St Giles, Richard Sadler, for the Cheltonian Society.

Müller, D. K., Ringer, F., and Simon, B. (eds) (1987) *The Rise of the Modern Educational System: Structural Change and Social Reproduction 1870–1920*, Cambridge, Cambridge University Press/Paris, Editions de la Maison des Sciences de l'Homme.

Mumford, A. A. (1919) *The Manchester Grammar School 1515–1915*, Longmans Green.

Murphy, R. J. (1985) 'Higher grade board schools 1870–1902: problems of definition', *Durham and Newcastle Research Review* X, 54, 210–12.

Musgrave, P. W. (1964) 'The definition of technical education 1860–1910', *Vocational Aspect* XVI, 34, 105–11.

— (1985) *From Brown to Bunter: The Life and Death of the School Story*, Routledge & Kegan Paul.

Newsome, D. (1959) *A History of Wellington College 1859–1959*, John Murray.

— (1961) *Godliness and Good Learning: Four studies on a Victorian Ideal*, John Murray.

Newton, R. (1968) *Victorian Exeter 1837–1914*, Leicester, Leicester University Press.

Noake, V. (1952) *History of the Alice Ottley School Worcester*, Worcester, Ebenezer Baylis.

Norman, E. (1984) *The English Catholic Church in the Nineteenth Century*, Oxford, Clarendon Press.

Norwich High School 1875–1950 (n.d.) Norwich, Gorse Press.

Norwood, C. (1929) *The English Tradition of Education*, John Murray.

Norwood, C. and Hope, A. H. (1909) *The Higher Education of Boys in England*, John Murray.

Ogilvie, V. (1957) *The English Public School*, B. T. Batsford.

Oldham, J. B. (1952) *A History of Shrewsbury School*, Oxford, Basil Blackwell.

O'Leary, M. (1936) *Education with a Tradition: An Account of the Educational Work of the Society of the Sacred Heart*, University of London Press.

Ord, H. W. (1936) *The Adventures of a Schoolmaster*, Simpkin, Marshall.

Our Yorkshire Schools: an Educational Guide comprising the prospectuses of various public and private educational establishments, with terms and curriculum of studies (1873) Leeds, J. W. Bean and Son.

Owen, D. (1965) *English Philanthropy 1660–1960*, Cambridge, Mass., Harvard University Press.

[Oxford conference] (1893) *Report of a Conference on Secondary Education in England convened by the Vice-Chancellor of the University of Oxford . . . October 10 and 11, 1893*, Oxford, Clarendon Press.

Parkin, G. R. (1898) *Edward Thring Headmaster of Uppingham School: Life, Diary and Letters* 2 vols, Macmillan.

Pascoe, C. E. (1879) *Schools for Girls and Colleges for Women: A Handbook of Female Education*, Hardwicke & Bogue.

Patterson, A. T. (1975) *A History of Southampton 1700–1914*, vol. III, *1868–1914*, Southampton Records Series, vol. XVIII.

Paul, A. S. (n.d.) *Some Memories of Mrs Woodhouse: Sheffield High School 1878–1898, Clapham High School 1898–1912*, Silas Birch.

Payne, J. (1883) *Lectures in the Science and Art of Education* (Works, vol. I), 2nd edn, Longmans Green.

Peck, W. (1952) *A Little Learning or a Victorian Childhood*, Faber & Faber.

Pedersen, J. S. (1975) 'Schoolmistresses and headmistresses: elites and education in nineteenth-century England', *Journal of British Studies* XV, 1, 135–62.

—— (1979) 'The reform of women's secondary and higher education: institutional change and social values in mid- and late Victorian England', *History of Education Quarterly* 19, 1, 61–91.

—— (1981) 'Some Victorian headmistresses: a conservative tradition of social reform', *Victorian Studies* 24, 4, 463–88.

—— (1987) *The Reform of Girls' Secondary and Higher Education in Victorian England: a Study of Elites and Educational Change*, New York, Garland.

Percival, A. C. (1939) *The English Miss to-day and Yesterday: Ideals Methods and Personalities in the Education and Upbringing of Girls during the last Hundred Years*, Harrap.

—— (1969) *The Origins of the Headmasters' Conference*, John Murray.

—— (1973) *Very Superior Men: Some Early Public School Headmasters and their Achievements*, C. Knight.

Peterson, M. J. (1970) 'The Victorian governess: status inconsequence in family and society', *Victorian Studies* XIV, 1, 7–26.

Picciotto, C. (1939) *St Paul's School*, London and Glasgow, Blackie.

Playfair, L. (1889) *Subjects of Social Welfare*, Cassell.

Pollard, F. E. (ed.) (1926) *Bootham School 1823–1923*, J. M. Dent.

Pritchard, F. C. (1949) *Methodist Secondary Education: A History of the Contri-*

bution of Methodism to Secondary Education in the United Kingdom, Epworth Press.
—— (1978) *The Story of Woodhouse Grove School*, Woodhouse Grove School, Bradford.
Procter, K. E. (1926) *A Short History of the Leeds Girls' High School* Part I, 1876–1906, Leeds, Waverley Press.
Public School Magazine (1898–1902) vols 1–9.
Quigly, I. (1982) *The Heirs of Tom Brown: The English School Story*, Chatto & Windus.
Quiller-Couch, Sir A. (1943) *The Oxford Book of English Verse 1250–1918*, new edn, Oxford, Clarendon Press.
Raikes, E. (1908) *Dorothea Beale of Cheltenham*, Constable.
Record of Technical and Secondary Education, The (1891–1903) vols I-XII, National Association for the Promotion of Technical and Secondary Education.
Reddie, C. (1900) *Abbotsholme*, George Allen.
Reid, W. (1899) *Memories and Correspondence of Lyon Playfair, First Lord Playfair of St Andrew's*, Cassell.
Reynolds, J. (1983) *The Great Paternalist: Titus Salt and the Growth of Nineteenth-Century Bradford*, Temple Smith/University of Bradford.
Rice, M. A. (1947) *Story of St Mary's, Abbot's Bromley*, Shrewsbury, Wilding.
Rich, R. W. (1933/1972) *The Training of Teachers in England and Wales during the Nineteenth Century*, Bath, Cedric Chivers.
Ridding, Lady L. (1908) *George Ridding Schoolmaster and Bishop*, Edward Arnold.
Ridler, A. (1967) *Olive Willis and Downe House: An Adventure in Education*, John Murray.
Ridley, A. E. (1895) *Frances Mary Buss and her Work for Education*, Longman.
Rigby, C. (1968) 'The Life and influence of Edward Thring', unpublished D.Phil. thesis, University of Oxford.
Rivington, S. (1910) *The History of Tonbridge School from its Foundation in 1553 to the Present Time*, 3rd edn, Rivington.
Roach, J. (1971) *Public Examinations in England 1850–1900*, Cambridge, Cambridge University Press.
—— (1986) *A History of Secondary Education in England 1800–1870*, Longmans.
Roberts, K. O. (1969) 'The separation of secondary education from technical 1899–1900', *Vocational Aspect* XXI, 49, 101–5.
Roberts, R. D. (ed.) (1901) *Education in the Nineteenth Century*, Cambridge, Cambridge University Press.
Robertson, A. (1971) 'J. G. Fitch and the origins of the liberal movement in education 1863–1870', *JEAH* III, 2, 9–14.
—— (1972) 'Children, teachers and society: the over-pressure controversy 1880–86', *BJES* XX, 3, 315–23.
Robinson, G. (G.B.) (1966) 'A study of the Private Schools Association (latterly Independent Schools) in relation to changing policies in the administration of education by national and local government agencies', unpublished MA thesis, University of London.
—— (1971) *Private Schools and Public Policy*, Loughborough University of Technology.
Robinson, M. (1935) 'School life at Lewes in the 'seventies', *Sussex County Magazine* IX, 10, 622–6.
Roche, J. W. (1972) 'The first half century of the Headmasters' Conference', unpublished Ph.D. thesis, University of Sheffield.
Roscoe, Sir H. E. (1906) *The Life and Experiences of . . . written by himself*, Macmillan.

Rouse, W. H. D. (1898a) *A History of Rugby School*, Duckworth.
— (1898b) 'Classical studies', in D. Beale, L. M. H. Soulsby, and J. F. Dove, *Work and Play in Girls' Schools*, Longmans Green, 67–93.
Rubinstein, D. (1969) *School Attendance in London 1870–1904: A Social History*, University of Hull Publications.
Sadler, M. E. (1903) *City of Sheffield Education Committee: Report on Secondary and Higher Education*, Sheffield, Loxley Bros.
— (1904a) *Report on Secondary Education in Liverpool*, Eyre & Spottiswoode.
— (1904b) *Report on Secondary and Technical Education in Huddersfield*, Eyre & Spottiswoode.
— (1904c) *Report on Secondary Education in Birkenhead*, George Philip.
— (1904d) *Report on Secondary and Higher Education in Hampshire*, Portsmouth, Holbrook.
— (1905a) *Report on Secondary and Higher Education in Derbyshire*, Derby, Bemrose.
— (1905b) *Report on Secondary and Higher Education in Newcastle-upon-Tyne*, Newcastle-upon-Tyne, Co-operative Printing Society.
— (1905c) *Report on Secondary and Higher Education in Exeter*, City and County of Exeter Education Committee.
— (1906) *Report on Secondary and Higher Education in Essex*, Chelmsford, Essex Education Committee.
(Various contributors) *Sanderson of Oundle* (1923) Chatto & Windus.
Sargeaunt, J. (1898) *Annals of Westminster School*, Methuen.
Scott, M. (1962) 'Percival and the foundation', in N. G. L. Hammond (ed.) *Centenary Essays on Clifton College*, Bristol, J. W. Arrowsmith, 1–19.
Scott, M. A. (1981) *The Perse School for Girls, Cambridge: The First Hundred Years 1881–1981*, Cambridge, Governors of the Perse School for Girls.
Scott, P. (1971) 'The private school in the eighteen-sixties, Anstey's *Vice Versa*', *History of Education Society Bulletin* 8, 13–25.
Scott-Giles, C. W. (1935) *The History of Emanuel School, London*, printed for *The Portcullis*.
Scrimgeour, R. M. (ed.) (1950) *The North London Collegiate School 1850–1950: a Hundred Years of Girls' Education. Essays in honour of the centenary of the Frances Mary Buss Foundation*, Oxford, Oxford University Press.
Seaborne, M. (1968) 'Education in the nineties: the work of the Technical Instruction Committees', in B. Simon (ed.) *Education in Leicestershire 1540–1940: A Regional Study*, Leicester, Leicester University Press, 178–94.
Seaborne, M. and Lowe, R. (1977) *The English School, Its Architecture and Organization, 1870–1900*, vol. II, Routledge & Kegan Paul.
Searby, P. (1979) 'Joseph Lloyd Brereton and the education of the Victorian middle class', *JEAH* XI, 1, 4–14.
— (ed.) (1982) *Educating the Victorian Middle Class*, History of Education Society Conference Papers, December 1981.
— (1989) 'The new school and the new life: Cecil Reddie (1858–1932) and the early years of Abbotsholme School', *HE* 18, 1, 1–21.
Secondary Education (1896–1903) vols I-VIII.
Semmel, B. (1960) *Imperialism and Social Reform: English Social-Imperial Thought 1895–1914*, George Allen & Unwin.
Sharp, P. R. (1968) 'The entry of county councils into educational administration, 1889', *JEAH* I, 1, 14–22.
— (1971) ' "Whiskey money" and the development of technical and secondary education in the 1890's', *JEAH* IV, 1, 31–6.
— (1974) 'The origin and early development of local education authority scholarships', *HE* 3, 1, 36–50.

Shirreff, E. (1858) *Intellectual Education, and its Influence on the Character and Happiness of Women*, John W. Parker.
—— (1876–7) 'Trained teachers for secondary schools', Social Science Association, *Sessional Proceedings* X, 291–312.
—— see also Grey, Maria (Mrs W. G.) and E. Shirreff (1854) *Thoughts on Self-Culture*.
Simon, B. (1960) *Studies in the History of Education 1780–1870*, Lawrence & Wishart.
—— (ed.) (1968) *Education in Leicestershire 1540–1940: A Regional Survey*, Leicester, Leicester University Press.
Simon, B. and Bradley, I. (eds) (1975) *The Victorian Public School: Studies in the Development of an Educational Institution*, Gill & Macmillan.
Simpson, J. H. (1954) *Schoolmaster's Harvest: Some findings of Fifty Years 1894–1944*, Faber & Faber.
Skrine, J. H. (1889) *A Memory of Edward Thring*, Macmillan.
—— (1898) 'The romance of school', *Contemporary Review* LXXIII, 430–8.
Smith, D. (1982) *Conflict and Compromise: Class Formation in English Society 1830–1914: A Comparative Study of Birmingham and Sheffield*, Routledge & Kegan Paul.
Smith, P. and Summerfield, G. (1969) *Matthew Arnold and the Education of the New Order*, Cambridge, Cambridge University Press.
Social Science, National Association for the Promotion of, *Transactions* (1869–84); *Sessional Proceedings* (1876–7, 1879–80).
Somervell, R. (1935) *Chapters of Autobiography, edited with additional material by his sons*, Faber & Faber.
Stack, V. E. (ed.) (1963) *Oxford High School Girls' Public Day School Trust 1875–1960*, Abingdon (Berks), Abbey Press.
Stanier, R. S. (1958) *Magdalen School: A History of Magdalen College School Oxford*, Oxford, Basil Blackwell.
Stansky, P. (1973) 'Lyttelton and Thring: a study in nineteenth-century education', in P. Stansky (ed.) *The Victorian Revolution: Government and Society in Victoria's Britain*, New York, Franklin Watts, 231–51.
Staunton, H. (1865) *The Great Schools of England*, Sampson Low.
Steadman, F. C. (1931) *In the Days of Miss Beale: A Study of her Work and Influence*, ed. J. Burrow.
Steedman, H. (1983) 'Parental demand and the curriculum in the late XIXth century: a comparative analysis', in *The Supply of Schooling, Contributions to a Comparative Study of Educational Policies in the XIXth Century*, Paris, Publications de la Sorbonne, Institut national de recherche pédagogique, 165–74.
Stewart, W. A. C. (1953) *Quakers and Education as Seen in their Schools in England*, Epworth Press.
—— (1968) *The Educational Innovators: Progressive Schools 1881–1967*, Vol. II, Macmillan.
Stewart, W. A. C. and McCann, W. P. (1967) *The Educational Innovators 1750–1880*, Macmillan.
Stoddart, A. M. (1908) *Life and Letters of Hannah E. Pipe*, Edinburgh and London, Blackwood.
Stone, L. and Stone, J. C. F. (1984) *An Open Elite? England 1540–1880*, Oxford, Clarendon Press.
Stuart, (Mother) J. E. (1911) *The Education of Catholic Girls*, Longmans Green.
Sturge, H. W. and Clark, T. (1931) *The Mount School York 1785 to 1814, 1831 to 1931*, J. M. Dent.
Summerfield, P. (1987) 'Cultural reproduction in the education of girls: a study

of girls' secondary schooling in two Lancashire towns, 1900–50', in M. F. Hunt (ed.), *Lessons for Life: The Schooling of Girls and Women 1850–1950*, Oxford, Basil Blackwell, 149–70.

Swanwick, H. M. (1935) *I Have Been Young*, Gollancz.

Taine, H. (1872) *Notes on England*, English trans., 2nd edn, Strahan.

Talboys, R. St. C. (1943) *A Victorian School being the Story of Wellington College*, Oxford, Basil Blackwell.

Tanner, J. R. (ed.) (1917) *The Historical Register of the University of Cambridge . . . to the year 1910*, Cambridge, Cambridge University Press.

Taylor, T. (1982) 'The Cockerton Case revised: London politics and education 1898–1901', *BJES* XXX, 3, 329–48.

Temple, W. (1921) *Life of Bishop Percival*, Macmillan.

Thomas, A. W. (1957) *A History of Nottingham High School 1513–1953*, Nottingham, J. & H. Bell.

Thomas, B. (ed.) (1957) *Repton 1557–1957*, Batsford.

Thorn, J. L. (1962) 'Another centenary – Sir Henry Newbolt 1862–1938', in N. G. L. Hammond (ed.), *Centenary Essays on Clifton College*, Bristol, J. W. Arrowsmith, 155–67.

Thring, E. (1889) *Theory and Practice of Teaching*, 3rd edn, Cambridge, Cambridge University Press.

Timmins, G. T. (1981) 'Secondary education in Coventry in the late nineteenth century', *JEAH* XIII, 2, 29–35.

Tozer, M. (1985) 'Thring at Uppingham-by-the-Sea: the lesson of the Borth sermons', *History of Education Society Bulletin* 36, 39–44.

—— (1989) ' "The readiest hand and the most open heart" Uppingham's first missions to the poor', *HE* 18, 4, 323–32.

Tristram, H. B. (1911) *Loretto School Past and Present*, T. Fisher Unwin.

Turner, B. (1974) *Equality for Some: The Story of Girls' Education*, Ward Lock Educational.

Vachell, H. A. (1905) *The Hill: A Romance of Friendship*, John Murray.

Vance, N. (1985) *The Sinews of the Spirit: The Ideal of Christian Manliness in Victorian Literature and Religious Thought*, Cambridge, Cambridge University Press.

Vardy, W. I. (Mrs E. W. Candler) (1928) *King Edward VI High School for Girls Birmingham 1883–1925*, Ernest Benn.

Vicinus, M. (1985) *Independent Women: Work and Community for Single Women 1850–1920*, Virago Press.

Victoria History of the Counties of England:
  Bedfordshire II (1908): 149–85 – A. F. Leach, 'Schools'.
  Cheshire III (1980): 196–222 – David Wardle, 'Education before 1903'.
  Gloucestershire II (1907): 313–448 – A. F. Leach, 'Schools'.
  Lincolnshire II (1906): 421–92 – A. F. Leach, 'Schools'.
  Middlesex I (1969): 241–89 – Margaret E. Bryant, 'Private Education from the sixteenth century'.
  Nottinghamshire II (1910): 179–251 – A. F. Leach, 'Schools'.
  Somerset II (1911): 435–65 – T. Scott Holmes, 'Schools'.
  Staffordshire VI (1979): 149–81 – C. R. J. Currie, D. A. Johnson, and M. W. Greenslade, 'Schools'.
  Suffolk II (1907): 301–55 – A. F. Leach and E. P. Steele Hutton, 'Schools'.
  Surrey II (1905): 155–242 – A. F. Leach, 'History of Schools'.
  Warwickshire II (1908): 297–373 – A. F. Leach, 'Schools'.
  Warwickshire VII (City of Birmingham) (1964): 549–55 – J. C. Tyson, 'King Edward VI Elementary Schools'.
  Wiltshire V (1957): 348–68 – Emily E. Butcher, 'Education'.

Yorkshire East Riding I (City of Kingston-upon-Hull) (1969): 348–70 – J. Lawson, 'Education'.

Vipont, E. (1959) *Ackworth School: From its Foundation in 1779 to the Introduction of Co-education in 1946*, Lutterworth Press.

Vlaeminke, M. (1987) 'The English higher grade schools – a reassessment', unpublished Ph.D. thesis, University of Leicester.

Wallis, I. H. (1924) *Frederick Andrews of Ackworth*, Longmans Green.

Walton, J. K. (1987) *Lancashire A Social History 1558–1939*, Manchester, Manchester University Press.

Ward, B. M. (1934) *Reddie of Abbotsholme*, George Allen & Unwin.

Wardle, D. (1971) *Education and Society in Nineteenth-century Nottingham*, Cambridge, Cambridge University Press.

Webb, S. (1904) *London Education*, Longmans Green.

Welldon, J. E. C. (1899) 'Schoolmasters', in E. H. Pitcairn (ed.), *Unwritten Laws and Ideals of Active Careers*, Smith Elder, 269–85.

—— (1915) *Recollections and Reflections*, Cassell.

Wells, H. G. (1894) 'Science, in school and after school', *Nature* L, 525–6.

—— (n.d.) *Love and Mr. Lewisham*, Nelson.

—— (1934) *Experiment in Autobiography* vol. I, Gollancz/Cresset Press.

Westaway, K. M. (ed.) (1932) *A History of Bedford High School*, Bedford, F. R. Hockliffe.

Whitcut, J. (1976) *Edgbaston High School 1876–1976*, published by the Governing Body.

Whitehead, M. (1984) 'The contribution of the Society of Jesus to education in Liverpool: the history of the development of St Francis Xavier's College *c.* 1840–1902', unpublished Ph.D. thesis, University of Hull.

—— (1986a) 'The Jesuit contribution to science and technical education in late-nineteenth century Liverpool', *Annals of Science* 43, 4, 353–68.

—— (1986b) 'Military, prompt, unstinting': The religious thinking and educational influence of the Reverend James Harris S.J. (1824–83)', *HE* 15, 3, 161–76.

Wiener, M. J. (1985) *English Culture and the Decline of the Industrial Spirit 1850–1980*, Harmondsworth, Penguin Books.

Wiese, L. (1877) *German Letters on English Education: Written during an Educational Tour in 1877*, Wm. Collins.

Wilkinson, R. (1964) *The Prefects: British Leadership and the Public School Tradition: A Comparative Study in the Making of Rulers*, Oxford, Oxford University Press.

Willison, J. (1929) *Sir George Parkin: A Biography*, Macmillan.

Wilson, A. (1877) *Private Schools: A consideration of certain remarks on their educational position, made by the Rev. Mark Pattison* . . . (no publisher).

Wilson, E. (1968) 'The development of secondary education in Bradford from 1895 to 1928', unpublished M.Ed. thesis, University of Leeds.

Wilson, J. M. (1932) *An Autobiography 1836–1931*, Sidgwick & Jackson.

Woodruff, C. E. and Cope, H. J. (1908) *Schola Regia Cantuariensis: A History of Canterbury School commonly called The King's School*, Mitchell Hughes & Clarke.

Zimmern, A. (1898) *The Renaissance of Girls' Education*, A. D. Innes.

Zouche, D. E. de (1955) *Roedean School 1885–1955* (privately printed).

Index

A. General Themes

Acts of Parliament, Parliamentary Bills:
  Endowed Schools Act 1869 5–7
  Education Act 1870 3, 7, 17, 88
  Endowed Schools Act 1873 7
  Endowed Schools Act 1874 7
  City Parochial Charities Act 1883 88
  Technical Instruction Act 1889 107
  Welsh Intermediate Education Act 1889 68, 107, 247–8
  Local Taxation (Customs and Excise) Act 1890 107
  Education Bill 1896 249
  Board of Education Act 1899 247
  Education Act 1902 251–2
agricultural depression, effects of 40, 70–1
almshouses and charitable payments 15–16

Board of Education 97, 101, 249–50
Brewers' Company 18, 207

careers: county council scholarship holders 111–12; elementary school scholarship holders 81–3; public schoolboys 139–41; pupils in girls' schools 214; pupils in higher-grade schools 114–15; women's education and 231, 233–6
Charity Commission 3, 7, 25, 42, 58–60, 68, 203; and religious issues 32
Church Schools Company 158, 202, 225
City and Guilds of London Institute for the advancement of technical education 87

class barriers 21–2, 24, 79, 158, 244; in girls' education 201, 203, 215, 217, 220, 230
'Cockerton judgment' 250–1
College of Preceptors 166, 170, 171, 183
Coventry, opposition to scheme by freemen 31
curriculum: general 33–42, 166, 174; girls' schools 237–8; public schools 152–3; 'specific' subjects 92, 96; see Greek, teaching of; scientific and technical education

denominational schools: Anglican 193–4, 225; Methodist 194–5, 226; Quaker 195–6, 226; Roman Catholic 196–8, 226–8; in Yorkshire 175

elementary schools 7, 14–15, 16–17, 60, 165
Endowed Schools Commission 3, 5, 6, 7–9, 42, 58; difficulties over religion 31–2; and North London Collegiate School 207; and public schools 121–2
exhibitions see scholarships and exhibitions

Fabian Society 251
free education 3, 16–17, 60–1, 80, 100

games: in girls' schools 221, 224, 238–9; at Loretto 188; in private schools 169, 175; in public schools 129–32
girls' education: achievements of 241, 246; at Birmingham 51; at Bristol 45–9; and endowments 202–3; and

B. Persons

C. Schools and Colleges